MW00581605

THE

50 GREATEST PLAYERS

IN

BOSTON CELTICS

HISTORY

**ALSO AVAILABLE IN THE
50 GREATEST PLAYERS SERIES**

The 50 Greatest Players in Boston Celtics History
The 50 Greatest Players in Boston Red Sox History
The 50 Greatest Players in Braves History
The 50 Greatest Players in Buffalo Bills History
The 50 Greatest Players in Chicago Bears History
The 50 Greatest Players in Cleveland Browns History
The 50 Greatest Players in Dallas Cowboys History
The 50 Greatest Players in Denver Broncos History
The 50 Greatest Players in Detroit Tigers History
The 50 Greatest Players in Green Bay Packers History
The 50 Greatest Players in Kansas City Chiefs History
The 50 Greatest Players in Minnesota Vikings History
The 50 Greatest Players in New England Patriots Football History
The 50 Greatest Players in New York Giants History
The 50 Greatest Players in New York Yankees History
The 50 Greatest Players in Philadelphia Eagles History
The 50 Greatest Players in Philadelphia Phillies History
The 50 Greatest Players in Pittsburgh Pirates History
The 50 Greatest Players in Pittsburgh Steelers History
The 50 Greatest Players in San Francisco 49ers History
The 50 Greatest Players in St. Louis Cardinals History

THE

50 GREATEST PLAYERS

IN

BOSTON CELTICS

HISTORY

ROBERT W. COHEN

LYONS
PRESS

ESSEX, CONNECTICUT

An imprint of Globe Pequot, the trade division of
The Rowman & Littlefield Publishing Group, Inc.
4501 Forbes Blvd., Ste. 200
Lanham, MD 20706
www.rowman.com

Distributed by NATIONAL BOOK NETWORK

Copyright © 2017, 2023 by Robert W. Cohen
First edition, The 40 Greatest Players in Boston Celtics History, published in 2017 by
Down East, an imprint of Globe Pequot
First Lyons Press paperback edition 2023

All rights reserved. No part of this book may be reproduced in any form or by any
electronic or mechanical means, including information storage and retrieval systems,
without written permission from the publisher, except by a reviewer who may quote
passages in a review.

British Library Cataloguing in Publication Information Available

Library of Congress Cataloging-in-Publication Data

Names: Cohen, Robert W, author.
Title: The 50 greatest players in Boston Celtics history / Robert W. Cohen.
Other titles: Fifty greatest players in Boston Celtics history
Description: First Lyons Press paperback edition. | Essex, CT : Lyons
    Press, 2023. | Series: 50 greatest players | Includes bibliographical
    references.
Identifiers: LCCN 2023030181 (print) | LCCN 2023030182 (ebook) | ISBN
    9781493076932 (trade paperback) | ISBN 9781493077663 (epub)
Subjects: LCSH: Boston Celtics (Basketball team)--Biography. | Boston
    Celtics (Basketball team)--History. | Basketball players--United
    States--Biography.
Classification: LCC GV885.52.B67 .C643 2023 (print) | LCC GV885.52.B67
    (ebook) | DDC 796.323/640974461--dc23/eng/20230725
LC record available at https://lccn.loc.gov/2023030181
LC ebook record available at https://lccn.loc.gov/202303018

∞™ The paper used in this publication meets the minimum requirements of
American National Standard for Information Sciences—Permanence of Paper for
Printed Library Materials, ANSI/NISO Z39.48-1992.

CONTENTS

ACKNOWLEDGMENTS

I would like to express my gratitude to the grandchildren of Leslie Jones, who, through the Trustees of the Boston Public Library, Print Department, supplied many of the photos included in this book.

I also wish to thank Troy Kinunen of Mearsonlineauctions.com, Aaron Frutman of DGA Productions, Kate of RMYauctions.com, the City of Boston Archives, George Kitrinos, Keith Allison, Robert Kingsbury, Marissa Gawel, Erik Drost, and Chris Springmeyer, each of whom generously contributed to the photographic content of this work.

INTRODUCTION

THE CELTICS LEGACY

The Boston Celtics came into existence on June 6, 1946, when Walter Brown, who ran the Boston Garden, met with 10 other men who owned either professional hockey teams, large arenas in major cities, or both to discuss the formation of a new professional basketball league they named the Basketball Association of America. The Basketball Association of America spent the next three years operating as a separate entity until it eventually merged with the rival National Basketball League at the conclusion of the 1948–49 campaign to form the newly christened National Basketball Association (NBA), which featured a total of 17 teams.

While the new league spent its formative years struggling to survive, the Celtics attempted to gain a foothold in the New England area as they continued to place near the bottom of the Eastern Division rankings each year. Named after the Original Celtics, a barnstorming team that helped increase the popularity of basketball during the 1920s and 1930s, the Celtics compiled an overall record of just 89-147 from 1946 to 1950, as coaching duties passed from John "Honey" Russell to Alvin "Doggie" Julian.

The situation in Boston changed dramatically prior to the start of the 1950–51 campaign, though, after the NBA underwent a reorganization that reduced the league to just 11 teams, with the best players from the six disbanded franchises being distributed among the remaining clubs. Fortunate to have promising young center Ed Macauley fall in their laps after the St. Louis Bombers folded, the Celtics also benefited from the acquisition of rookie guard Bob Cousy via a dispersal draft of the Chicago Stags' players.

The Celtics' good fortune continued when Walter Brown had the foresight to hire Red Auerbach as head coach that same off-season. The 33-year-old Auerbach, who had led the Washington Capitols to the

Red Auerbach, flanked by Bill Russell and Tommy Heinsohn.
Photo courtesy of LegendaryAuctions.com.

Basketball Association of America Finals two years earlier, quickly trans-
formed the Celtics into winners, with the help of Cousy and Macauley.
Making good use of Cousy's ball-handling skills, Auerbach installed an
up-tempo, fast-breaking offense in Boston that made the Celtics the NBA's
highest-scoring team by his second season at the helm. The acquisition of
sharp-shooting guard Bill Sharman in 1951 gave the Celtics additional
firepower, turning them into an offensive juggernaut.

Nevertheless, even though the Celtics made the playoffs six straight times
between 1951 and 1956, they failed to advance beyond the Eastern Division Semifinals due to their defensive shortcomings. Seeking to strengthen
his team on that end of the floor, Auerbach engineered a trade with the St.
Louis Hawks on April 30, 1956, that sent Macauley and the draft rights to
Cliff Hagan to St. Louis for the second overall pick in the 1956 NBA Draft,
which the Hawks used earlier in the day to select Bill Russell.

The arrival of Russell and, to a lesser degree, fellow rookie Tom Heinsohn
in Boston turned the Celtics into an elite team. Heinsohn gave the squad
another offensive weapon, while Russell immediately established himself as
the league's dominant player. A solid scorer, exceptional rebounder, and superb

shot-blocker, Russell ended up serving as the anchor of Red Auerbach's teams for the next 13 years, enabling the Celtics to create the greatest dynasty in the history of professional team sports. Ably assisted at various times by Cousy, Sharman, Heinsohn, and other standout players such as Frank Ramsey, John Havlicek, Sam Jones, and K. C. Jones, Russell led the Celtics to 11 out of a possible 13 NBA championships between 1957 and 1969.

After the Celtics captured their first title by defeating the St. Louis Hawks in seven games in the 1957 NBA Finals, they returned to the championship round the following year, only to lose to the Hawks in six games. Boston then reeled off an unprecedented eight straight titles, sweeping the Lakers in four straight games in the 1959 Finals, getting the best of the Hawks in both 1960 and 1961, recording back-to-back victories over the Lakers in 1962 and 1963, disposing of the San Francisco Warriors in five games in 1964, and defeating the Lakers two more times in 1965 and 1966.

The Celtics' incredible run came to an abrupt end the following year after Red Auerbach relinquished his coaching duties to Bill Russell, who spent his final three seasons serving as the team's player-coach. However, after being eliminated from the 1967 postseason tournament by Wilt Chamberlain and the Philadelphia 76ers, who defeated them in five games in the Eastern Division Finals, the Celtics won their 10th and 11th championships by defeating the Lakers in each of the next two NBA Finals.

The retirement of Russell following the conclusion of the 1968–69 season left the Celtics in a state of disarray, causing them to finish the ensuing campaign with their first losing record in two decades. But, led by new head coach Tom Heinsohn and the stellar play of John Havlicek, hard-working center Dave Cowens, and perennial All-Star guard Jo Jo White, the Celtics soon entered into their next period of dominance, capturing five consecutive Atlantic Division titles from 1972 to 1976, and winning the NBA championship in both 1974 and 1976.

Unfortunately, an early exit from the 1977 playoffs prompted the Celtics to dramatically change the composition of their roster, leading to another brief period of mediocrity. After Heinsohn relinquished his coaching duties midway through the 1977–78 campaign and General Manager Red Auerbach acquired players such as Sidney Wicks and Curtis Rowe who failed to grasp the "team" concept always stressed in Boston, the Celtics posted a combined record of just 61-103 the next two seasons. Help was on the way, though, in the form of Larry Bird, who resurrected the franchise, leading the Celtics to three NBA titles in his first seven years in Boston, en route to establishing himself as one of the finest all-around players in the history of the sport. Bill Fitch served as head coach in Boston when the

Red Auerbach, with Ed Macauley (left) and Bob Cousy.
Photo courtesy of MearsOnlineAuctions.com.

Celtics defeated Houston in six games in the 1981 NBA Finals, while K. C. Jones directed the Celtics from the bench when they edged out the Lakers in seven games in the 1984 Finals and the Rockets in six games in the 1986 Finals. Meanwhile, Bird received a great deal of help on the court from guard Dennis Johnson, forward Kevin McHale, and center Robert Parish, with McHale and Parish combining with "Larry Legend" to form arguably the greatest front court in NBA history.

Bird's retirement at the end of the 1992–93 campaign, along with the departures of McHale and Parish shortly thereafter, subsequently ushered in a dark period in Celtics history that saw them finish with a losing record in each of the next eight seasons, including a franchise-worst mark of 15-67 in 1996–97. Coaches Chris Ford, M. L. Carr, and Rick Pitino all failed to right the ship during that time, even though the team featured talented players such as Antoine Walker, Dee Brown, and Dino Radja, at different times.

Things finally began to look up again in Boston after Jim O'Brien replaced Pitino at the helm midway through the 2000–01 campaign. Led by standout forwards Antoine Walker and Paul Pierce, the Celtics made their first of four straight playoff appearances the following year after compiling a record of 49-33 during the regular season. Numerous changes in the front office soon followed, with owner Paul Gaston selling the team in 2003 to Boston Basketball Partners LLC, a conglomerate headed by H. Irving Grousbeck, Wycliffe Grousbeck, Steve Pagliuca, Robert Epstein, and John Svenson that chose to hire former Celtic Danny Ainge as general manager.

Unfortunately, the Celtics initially took a step backward under Ainge, compiling a losing record in three of his first four years in charge, before eventually righting themselves under Head Coach Doc Rivers. Led by holdover Paul Pierce and newly acquired stars Kevin Garnett and Ray Allen, the Celtics returned to the top of the basketball world by posting an NBA-best 66-16 regular-season record in 2007–08, before going on to defeat the Los Angeles Lakers in six games in the NBA Finals. Boston remained a consistent contender under Rivers the next five seasons, making the playoffs each year, and advancing to the NBA Finals again in 2010, before losing to the Lakers in seven games.

The Celtics subsequently fell on hard times after Brad Stevens replaced Rivers as head coach prior to the start of the 2013–14 campaign, compiling an overall record of just 65-99 over the course of the next two seasons. However, they performed exceptionally well under Stevens the next five seasons, winning at least 48 games each year, en route to winning one division title and making four NBA Eastern Conference Finals appearances. But the Celtics came up short in the playoffs each season, losing once in the opening round to Atlanta, twice to Cleveland in the Conference Finals, and once each to Milwaukee and Miami in the Conference Finals.

Although the Celtics advanced to the playoffs for the seventh straight time in 2020–21, they finished the season just 36-36, after which Danny Ainge announced his retirement. The Celtics subsequently named Brad Stevens their new president of basketball operations. Stevens, in turn, replaced himself as head coach with former San Antonio Spurs, Philadelphia 76ers, and Brooklyn Nets assistant Ime Udoka.

Faring extremely well under Udoka in 2021–22, the Celtics won the Atlantic Division title by compiling a record of 51-31 during the regular season, before laying claim to the Eastern Conference championship by defeating the Brooklyn Nets (4-0), Milwaukee Bucks (4-3), and Miami Heat (4-3) in the playoffs. However, the Celtics once again failed to achieve their ultimate goal, losing to the Golden State Warriors in six games in the NBA Finals.

Despite the success the Celtics experienced under Udoka the previous season, Boston's head coach found himself being suspended for the entire 2022–23 campaign for violating team policy by engaging in an inappropriate relationship with a female member of the organization. Refusing to allow any outside distractions to affect them on the court, Celtics players have performed equally well under former assistant Joe Mazzulla, who took over for Udoka prior to the start of the regular season. Just past the midway point of the campaign, the Celtics have compiled a league-best record of 34-12. And with outstanding young players Jayson Tatum and Jaylen Brown leading the way, the Celtics seem likely to enter the postseason tournament as one of the favorites to win the NBA title, which would be their record 18th. (The Lakers rank second in league history with 16 NBA championships.) Meanwhile, no team can come close to matching the 11 titles the Celtics won over a 13-year period, with the Chicago Bulls' six championships in eight years (1991–98) representing the closest challenge to Boston's eight straight titles from 1959 to 1966. The Celtics have also made 22 NBA Finals appearances, which places them second in league history only to the Lakers, who have appeared in the NBA Finals a total of 31 times.

In addition to the level of success the Celtics have reached as a team over the years, a significant number of players have attained notable individual honors while playing in Boston. The Celtics boast 10 MVP winners, more than any other franchise in league history. Although Boston has never featured a scoring champion, a member of the team has led the league in rebounding five times and assists 10 times. Meanwhile, 33 members of the Basketball Hall of Fame spent at least one full season playing for the Celtics, 23 of whom had many of their finest seasons in Boston.

FACTORS USED TO DETERMINE RANKINGS

It should come as no surprise that ranking the 50 greatest players ever to perform for a team with the rich history of the Boston Celtics proved to be a difficult and daunting task. Certainly, the names of Bill Russell, Bob

Cousy, John Havlicek, Larry Bird, and Paul Pierce would appear at, or near, the top of virtually everyone's list, although the order might vary somewhat from one person to the next. Several other outstanding performers have gained general recognition through the years as being among the greatest players ever to wear a Celtics uniform. Sam Jones, Dave Cowens, Kevin McHale, and Robert Parish head the list of other Celtic icons. But how does one differentiate between the all-around brilliance of Larry Bird and the defensive and rebounding greatness of Bill Russell, or the exceptional play-making ability of Bob Cousy and the scoring proficiency of Paul Pierce? Not only did the aforementioned players possess dissimilar skill sets, but, in most cases, they played different positions and assumed different responsibilities on the court, making it impossible to definitively draw a direct correlation between the statistics they compiled over the course of their respective careers. The idea of using statistics as the primary criteria for comparing players became even less appealing to me when I considered the fact that many of the men I ended up including in my rankings performed in different eras, under different playing conditions.

To illustrate my last point, Bill Sharman discussed some of the playing conditions that prevailed in the NBA for much of the 1950s in Charles Salzberg's *From Set Shot to Slam Dunk*, a 1987 compilation of interviews with former NBA players and officials: "Many arenas were used for hockey, and we would play right over the ice with no insulation except the basketball floor itself. Suffice to say, with cold, stiff hands and fingers, it certainly didn't help the shooting touch and percentages."

Another drawback to relying too heavily on statistics is their limited availability in some instances. The NBA did not keep an official record of rebounds until the 1950–51 season. Meanwhile, the league did not record steals and blocked shots as official statistics prior to the 1973–74 campaign. As a result, although statistics played a significant role during the ranking process, several other factors received just as much weight.

One of the most important things I needed to consider was the level of dominance a player attained during his time in Boston. How often did he rank among the league leaders in those statistical categories most pertinent to his position? How did he fare in the annual MVP voting? Did he ever win the award? How many times did he earn All-NBA honors or make the All-Star team?

I also needed to examine the overall contributions a player made to the success of the team during his time in Boston. Did he help to make the other players around him better? Did he help to improve the fortunes of the ball club? To what degree did he help add to the Celtics' legacy of winning?

In addition, I considered a player's longevity and the legacy he left behind. For how long was he able to maintain a high level of performance during his time in Boston? What is his place in history? How was he viewed by his teammates and opponents, and what did the coaches around the league have to say about him? And where does he rank among the all-time leaders in Celtics history in the various statistical categories?

There are two other things that I should mention. First, I only considered a player's performance while playing for the Celtics when formulating my rankings. That being the case, the names of exceptional players such as Nate Archibald and Bill Walton, both of whom had most of their best years while playing for other teams, may appear lower on this list than one might expect. Additionally, I chose to examine each player within the context of the era in which he played. Some might argue that 1950s and 1960s stars such as Bob Cousy and Bill Russell would not have been able to dominate the game the way they did had they come along two or three decades later. There likely is a certain amount of truth to that contention. Cousy's and Russell's detractors will also claim that they never competed against the bigger, faster, more athletic players that began entering the league long after they retired. That assertion cannot be denied. However, it could also be argued that, for the most part, players from prior generations possessed a greater grasp of the team concept and the fundamentals of the game. Since there is no way to know, with any degree of certainty, how Cousy, Russell, and other outstanding players of their era would have fared against the modern-day player, I thought it only fair to judge them strictly on the basis of their career accomplishments.

Having established the guidelines to be used throughout this book, we are ready to take a look at the 50 greatest players in Celtics history, starting with number one and working our way down to number 50.

1

— BILL RUSSELL —

You got to have the killer instinct. If you do not have it, forget about basketball and go into social psychology or something.

—Bill Russell

In spite of the all-around brilliance of John Havlicek, the choice for the number-one spot in these rankings ended up coming down to either Bill Russell or Larry Bird. A strong case could certainly be made for Bird, whose basketball skills far exceeded those of Russell. An outstanding scorer and phenomenal outside shooter, Bird posted a career scoring average of 24.3 points per game that surpassed Russell's mark of 15.1 points per contest by a considerable margin. Larry Legend also possessed superior passing and ball-handling skills to Russell, averaging 2 more assists per game (6.3 to 4.3) over the course of his career. Furthermore, Bird won three League MVP awards, appeared in 12 All-Star Games, and earned All-NBA honors 10 times, making it onto the First Team on nine separate occasions.

On the other hand, Russell won five MVP awards, also made 12 All-Star appearances, and earned All-NBA honors 11 times, although he made it onto the First Team just three times. In addition, Russell held a significant edge over Bird as a rebounder and defender, averaging more than twice as many boards per contest during his career (22.5 to 10.0), while establishing himself as arguably the greatest defensive player in the history of the game. Although Russell's huge edge over Bird in rebounding may be attributed, at least in part, to the era in which he played, the fact remains that Russell led the NBA in that category on five separate occasions, en route to compiling the second-highest rebounding average in league history.

Thus, it would seem that each man has a legitimate claim to the top spot here. Making this decision even more difficult is the fact that both

Bill Russell, seen here going up against his greatest rival, Wilt Chamberlain.
Photo courtesy of MearsOnlineAuctions.com.

Russell and Bird greatly improved the fortunes of the Celtics during their
time in Boston, making the other players around them much better in the
process. Both men also proved to be consummate team players and exceptional leaders over the course of their respective careers.

However, after taking everything into consideration, I ultimately decided to go with Russell for one simple reason—his greater legacy of winning. Although Bird led the Celtics to three NBA titles during his time in Beantown, Russell served as the driving force behind 11 league championships over a 13-year period. It could be argued that fewer playoff rounds and the tremendous supporting cast Russell had throughout most of his career made his job somewhat easier than that of Bird, who surpassed Russell as an all-around player. Nevertheless, Russell's pivotal role in creating the greatest dynasty in NBA history proved to be too much for Bird to overcome, relegating Larry Legend to second place in these rankings.

The greatest winner in the history of team sports, Bill Russell established a legacy of winning over the course of his playing career that is second to none. After leading the University of San Francisco to 55 consecutive victories, including back-to-back NCAA titles in 1955 and 1956, Russell served as the anchor of a US Men's Basketball Team that captured Gold at the 1956 Olympic Games. He then proceeded to lead the Boston Celtics to 11 NBA championships in his 13 years with the team, attaining in the process a level of success unmatched by any other professional athlete. Along the way, Russell established himself as one of the greatest rebounders in NBA history, trailing only Wilt Chamberlain in total rebounds and career rebounding average.

Russell also helped to revolutionize the game of basketball from a defensive standpoint, turning shot-blocking into an art form, while simultaneously wreaking havoc on the mindsets of opposing players with his ability to turn away their shots. Possessing extraordinary leadership ability and tremendous determination as well, Russell often found a way to will his team to victory, spending his final three seasons in Boston serving as player-coach of an aging Celtics squad that nevertheless managed to win a pair of NBA Championships. Russell's unique skill set and ability to inspire others ended up earning him 11 top-five finishes in the NBA MVP voting, 1968 *Sports Illustrated* Sportsman of the Year honors, recognition from the *Sporting News* as the Athlete of the Decade for the 1960s, a spot on the NBA's 50th Anniversary Team, and an 18th-place ranking on ESPN's list of the 50 Greatest Athletes of the 20th Century.

Born in racially segregated Monroe, Louisiana, on February 12, 1934, William Felton Russell grew up in poverty, spending most of his youth living in a series of public housing projects, while watching his parents constantly struggle against racial bigotry. After moving with his family to Oakland, California, at the age of nine, young William incurred further hardship when he lost his mother three years later. A late bloomer on the basketball court, the tall and gangly Russell (he stood 6-foot-2 and weighed 130 pounds by the time he turned 15) failed to earn a spot on his junior high school team, even though he possessed outstanding athletic ability, excelling as both a runner and a jumper. Russell—a natural right-hander who switched to using his left hand at the urging of an uncle—finally began to blossom into a star on the court while attending Oakland's McClymonds High School, leading his team to back-to-back state championships in his junior and senior years. Developing a reputation for his unusual style of defense, Russell later noted, "To play good defense . . . it was told back then that you had to stay flatfooted at all times to react quickly. When I started to jump to make defensive plays and to block shots, I was initially corrected. But I stuck with it, and it paid off."

Following his graduation from McClymonds, Russell enrolled at the University of San Francisco, where he emerged as college basketball's most dominant player, leading the Dons to an NCAA-record 55 consecutive victories and back-to-back national championships in 1955 and 1956, en route to earning a pair of All-America selections and national Player of the Year honors as a senior. Subsequently selected by the St. Louis Hawks with the second overall pick of the 1956 NBA Draft, Russell soon found himself headed to Boston after the Celtics acquired his rights in exchange for veteran center Ed Macauley and promising young forward Cliff Hagan, who, even though he graduated three years earlier, had yet to appear in an NBA game due to a previous military commitment. However, Russell chose to delay the start of his professional career, electing instead to compete in the 1956 Olympic Games, where he led the United States to a perfect 8-0 record and a gold medal.

Arriving in Boston two months into the 1956–57 campaign, Russell nevertheless ended up making a huge impact as a rookie, posting a league-leading 19.6 rebounding average, while also averaging 14.7 points per game, en route to earning a runner-up finish to teammate Tom Heinsohn in the NBA Rookie of the Year voting. More importantly, Russell turned Boston's previously porous defense into one of the league's stingiest, using his great quickness, exceptional leaping ability, and tremendous anticipation to become the sport's first great shot-blocker.

In discussing the overall impact Russell made in Boston, Ed Macauley stated in *From Set Shot to Slam Dunk*, "Russell was absolutely perfect for that ball club . . . They didn't have a great defensive club, but with Russell back there you didn't need one because no one could get closer than 15 feet. We played them a couple of times when Russell wasn't in the lineup, and they were just an ordinary ball club. With him, they were just superb."

Bill Russell revolutionized the game of basketball with his rebounding and shot-blocking ability.
Photo courtesy of MearsOnlineAuctions.com.

Russell's presence in the Boston lineup enabled the Celtics to capture their first NBA title in 1957, as they went on to defeat the St. Louis Hawks in seven games in the NBA Finals. Although they came up just a bit short the following year, losing to St. Louis in six games in the Finals, Russell improved upon his overall performance, earning league MVP honors, his first of 12 consecutive All-NBA selections, and All-Star honors for the first of 12 straight times by averaging 16.6 points and a league-leading 22.7 rebounds per game.

The following season, Russell and the Celtics began an extraordinary run that saw them win an unprecedented eight consecutive league championships. Here are the numbers Russell posted over the course of those eight seasons, with the figures in bold indicating that he led the league in that category:

SEASON	POINTS PER GAME	REBOUNDS PER GAME	ASSISTS PER GAME
1958–59	16.7	**23.0**	3.2
1959–60	18.2	24.0	3.7
1960–61	16.9	23.9	3.4
1961–62	18.9	23.6	4.5
1962–63	16.8	23.6	4.5
1963–64	15.0	**24.7**	4.7
1964–65	14.1	**24.1**	5.3
1965–66	12.9	22.8	4.8

In addition to leading the league in rebounding in three of those seasons, Russell finished second to Wilt Chamberlain the other five years. He also averaged more than 42 minutes per game all eight seasons, topping 44 minutes per contest on five separate occasions. Furthermore, although the NBA did not keep an official record of blocked shots until the 1970s, former referee Earl Strom estimated that Russell averaged between 8 and 10 blocks per game throughout most of his career. Russell captured league MVP honors three straight times, winning the award in 1960–61, 1961–62, and 1962–63, before being named MVP for the fifth and final time in his career following the conclusion of the 1964–65 campaign. He also finished second in the balloting on two other occasions.

Russell's intimidating defense, superb rebounding, and excellent outlet passing that keyed Boston's legendary fast break made him easily the most significant figure in his team's rise to prominence, with teammates and opponents alike crediting him for most of the success the Celtics experienced throughout the period. In describing what it was like playing with Russell, Bob Cousy said, "He not only controlled the backboard completely, but he revolutionized the defensive game."

Tom Heinsohn spoke of the impact Russell made on defense, commenting: "He had such great quickness and agility that he could play three or four guys on the same trip up the court . . . switch off, go back to his own man, block the shot; so he would disrupt their entire offense."

Discussing the manner in which Russell influenced the outcomes of games in *From Set Shot to Slam Dunk*, forward George Yardley stated, "There's no question that Bill Russell's coming into the league changed the game. You just couldn't take a layup against him. He just took that portion of the game away from you . . . He was certainly the most intimidating, most dominant person that played sports."

Ed Macauley agreed with Yardley's assessment, proclaiming, "Russell was the most dominant player to ever play the game. There have been a lot of ballplayers who are better, individually—better shooters, dribblers, rebounders. But no one individual who could put it all together was as important to a particular team as Bill Russell was."

Russell even made an impression on those players who entered the NBA long after he left the game. Julius Erving, whose professional career began shortly after Russell's ended, spoke of the impact Russell had on him: "Never when I saw him play did I look at him as the most talented player on the court. But he would be the best player because of what he could bring to the table and how he could make everyone better, and how he was in the clutch, and how he was always a step ahead."

Russell's intelligence, leadership, intensity, and psychological approach to his craft all contributed to his greatness. Known to regurgitate in the locker room before every game, Russell approached each contest with a win-at-all-cost mentality. Providing further insight into Russell's persona, former teammate Tom Heinsohn suggested, "I think Russell was the foxiest, smartest, meanest player, psychologically, that ever played the game. Whatever it took to win, Russell would do."

Validating Heinsohn's contention from an opponent's perspective, Chet Walker noted, "The whole game for Bill Russell was a psychological event. He was always testing you."

Russell himself stated on one occasion, "You got to have the killer instinct. If you do not have it, forget about basketball and go into social psychology or something. If you sometimes wonder if you've got it, you ain't got it; no pussycats, please."

Russell's attitude was the thing that, perhaps more than anything else, separated him from his fiercest rival, Wilt Chamberlain. With Russell and Chamberlain spending most of their careers competing against one another, the two men ended up forming what may well have been the greatest individual rivalry in the history of professional team sports. Russell himself acknowledged that fact when he said, "People say it was the greatest individual rivalry they've ever seen. I agree with that."

The Russell vs. Chamberlain rivalry spawned one of the most intense sports debates ever, with fans of the game expressing differing opinions as to which player surpassed the other in terms of overall greatness. Supporters of Russell pointed to his 11 NBA championships and 85 victories against only 57 defeats vs. Chamberlain-led teams. Meanwhile, Chamberlain backers claimed that the overwhelming superiority of his individual statistics served as evidence of his supremacy.

Chamberlain, for one, always scoffed at the notion that a legitimate comparison could be made between the two players, stating on one occasion, "I had to worry about the Celtics. I didn't have to worry about guarding Bill Russell. I had to worry about Cousy, Ramsey, Heinsohn, Sam Jones, K. C. Jones. They had just too many guns."

While there is certainly a great deal of truth to Chamberlain's statement, his critics often expressed the opinion that he tended to prioritize his individual accomplishments over those of the teams for which he played. Meanwhile, Russell was seen as the ultimate team player who cared little about his individual statistics, a belief he helped validate when he suggested, "The most important measure of how good a game I played was how much better I'd made my teammates play."

Although there will always be two ways of looking at the Russell vs. Chamberlain rivalry, the former's teammates stood firmly in his corner, with Don Nelson once telling the *Boston Herald*, "There are two types of superstars. One makes himself look good at the expense of the other guys on the floor. But there's another type who makes the players around him look better than they are, and that's the type Russell was."

John Havlicek also supported his longtime teammate, noting, "It wasn't a matter of Wilt vs. Russell, with Bill. He would let Wilt score 50 if we won. The thing that was most important to him was championships, rings, and winning."

Yet, even though the unselfish nature of Russell's game left an extremely favorable impression on most followers of the sport, he spent much of his time in Boston fighting an uphill battle against racial prejudice. Already extremely sensitive to matters of race when he first arrived in Boston, Russell grew increasingly hostile through the years as he endured one insult after another. After being denied access to white-owned hotels in segregated North Carolina while touring the United States with other NBA All-Stars during the 1958 off-season, Russell later wrote in his memoir, *Go Up for*

Glory, "It stood out, a wall which understanding cannot penetrate. You are a Negro. You are less. It covered every area; a living, smarting, hurting, smelling, greasy substance which covered you; a morass to fight from."

Similarly mistreated within the confines of the city of Boston, Russell frequently found himself being jeered by fans at his own hometown arena, causing him to isolate himself even further from the local media, which subsequently painted him as an "angry black man." Never one to shy away from controversy, Russell took up the cause, continually pushing for racial equality, becoming active in the Black Power movement, and supporting Muhammad Ali's decision not to enter the United States military. In one of his more militant moments, Russell was quoted in a 1963 *Sports Illustrated* interview as saying, "I dislike most white people because they are people . . . I like most blacks because I am black." Later approached by white teammate Frank Ramsey, who asked him if he hated him, Russell claimed to be misquoted, although few believed him.

Becoming increasingly contentious over time, Russell refused to respond to fan acclaim or friendly gestures from his neighbors, believing such overtures lacked sincerity. Further alienating Celtics fans by saying, "You owe the public the same it owes you—nothing! I refuse to smile and be nice to the kiddies," Russell became known in the local media as "the most selfish, surly, and uncooperative athlete." Things went from bad to worse when vandals broke into his home, covered the walls with racist graffiti, damaged his trophies, and defecated in the beds. In response, Russell described Boston as a "flea market of racism," later being quoted by author Aram Goudsouzian in the book, *King of the Court*, as saying, "From my very first year, I thought of myself as playing for the Celtics, not for Boston. The fans could do or think whatever they wanted."

Nevertheless, Russell remained open and amicable with his Celtics teammates, both white and black, considering them to be part of his extended family. Particularly close to Red Auerbach, Russell accepted the position of player-coach when Auerbach stepped down as coach of the team following the conclusion of the 1965–66 campaign to concentrate exclusively on his duties as general manager. Upon becoming the first African-American head coach in NBA history, Russell told the assembled media in his typically curt fashion, "I wasn't offered the job because I am a Negro. I was offered it because Red figured I could do it."

Boston's eight-year run as NBA champions came to an end in Russell's first year as coach, culminating with a five-game loss to Philadelphia in the 1967 Eastern Division Finals. For his part, Russell had a very solid season, averaging 13.3 points, 21 rebounds, and a career-high 5.8 assists per contest, while appearing in every game for the Celtics for the only time in his career. He followed that up by leading the Celtics to the NBA title in each of the next two seasons, averaging 12.5 points and 18.6 rebounds per game in 1967–68, before posting marks of 9.9 points and 19.3 rebounds per contest in 1968–69. After losing to Russell and the Celtics in the 1968 NBA Finals, Lakers guard Jerry West paid tribute to his adversary by stating, "If I had a choice of any basketball player in the league, my number 1 choice has to be Bill Russell. Bill Russell never ceases to amaze me."

Days after the Celtics again defeated Los Angeles in Game 7 of the 1969 NBA Finals, Russell abruptly announced his retirement, leaving the team without a coach and a center, and causing the local fans and journalists to feel betrayed. Choosing to cut all ties to the Celtics, Russell subsequently sold his retirement story to *Sports Illustrated* for $10,000. He ended his career with 14,522 points scored, 21,620 rebounds, 4,100 assists, and a countless number of unrecorded blocked shots. Over the course of 13 NBA seasons, Russell averaged 15.1 points, 22.5 rebounds, 4.3 assists, and 42.3 minutes per game, while shooting 44 percent from the field and just 56.1 percent from the free-throw line. In addition to ranking second all-time to Wilt Chamberlain in total rebounds and rebounding average, Russell trails only his rival in average minutes played per contest. Meanwhile, his career average of 24.9 rebounds per game in playoff competition is the best ever.

Some years after Russell left the game, John Havlicek said of his longtime teammate:

> There was no bigger winner, no better champion in basketball history, than my friend Bill Russell. Russell was the kind of player who never concerned himself with personal goals—he put his team above all else, and, in the process, he made his teammates better players. If you were a scorer, you were six to eight points better because Russell was around. If you were a good defensive player, you became a great defensive player because, with Russell hanging around, you were able to do things that you weren't ordinarily able to do. You could take more chances, apply more pressure, knowing that Russell was back there protecting the basket.

Meanwhile, another legendary Celtics player, Bill Sharman, had this to say about his former teammate: "He's the one player I would pick to be at my side in the seventh game of the NBA Championship Finals."

Following his playing career, Russell spent some time in the TV broadcast booth, doing color commentary on NBA games, before spending four seasons

Russell retired in 1969 having led the Celtics to 11 NBA titles in 13 seasons.
Photo courtesy of LegendaryAuctions.com.

during the mid-1970s serving as coach and general manager of the Seattle SuperSonics. He also briefly coached the Sacramento Kings a decade later.

A man of strong convictions and great integrity, Russell chose not to be in attendance when the Celtics retired his No. 6 jersey on March 12, 1972, demanding that the ceremony be performed in an empty Boston Garden. He also did not appear at the Naismith Memorial Basketball Hall of Fame when it opened its doors to him in 1975.

Yet, Russell softened his stance somewhat over time, allowing something of a reconciliation to take place between himself and the people of Boston. After spending many years shunning the city of his greatest triumphs following his retirement, Russell paid frequent visits to Boston in his later years. Furthermore, Russell gave his approval when the Celtics approached him with the idea of re-retiring his jersey in front of a sellout audience at their new home when they left the Boston Garden and moved into the FleetCenter (now the TD Garden). Wilt Chamberlain, Larry Bird, and Kareem Abdul-Jabbar also attended the ceremony, which took place on May 6, 1999. After being brought to tears by a prolonged standing ovation from the crowd, Russell thanked Chamberlain for taking him to the limit and "making (him) a better player" and the fans for "allowing (him) to be a part of their lives." Nearly a decade later, the city presented Russell with the We Are Boston Leadership Award.

Additional honors were later bestowed upon Russell, with then-NBA Commissioner David Stern announcing on February 14, 2009, that the NBA Finals Most Valuable Player Award would be renamed the "Bill Russell NBA Finals Most Valuable Player Award" in honor of the 11-time NBA champion. The following day, during halftime of the All-Star game, Celtics co-captains Paul Pierce, Kevin Garnett, and Ray Allen surprised Russell by presenting him with a cake to commemorate his 75th birthday. In 2011, Russell received the further distinction of being awarded the Presidential Medal of Freedom. Six years later, Russell became the inaugural recipient of the NBA Lifetime Achievement Award. And in October 2021, Russell was named to the NBA's 75th Anniversary Team.

Unfortunately, less than one year later, on July 31, 2022, Russell died at his Mercer Island, Washington, home at the age of 88. Upon learning of his passing, NBA Commissioner Adam Silver called him "the greatest champion in all of team sports." Shortly thereafter, the league office announced that Russell's No. 6 jersey would be retired throughout the NBA, making him the first player to be so honored.

While speaking at the Bill Russell Adult Fantasy Basketball Camp some 15 years earlier, Hall of Fame guard Sam Jones paid his longtime teammate perhaps his greatest compliment. With a number of basketball legends that included Jerry West, Kareem Abdul-Jabbar, Magic Johnson, and Julius Erving seated alongside him, Jones said, "No one compares to Bill Russell. With all due respect to the gentlemen around me, Bill Russell was the smartest, most driven basketball player the game has ever seen. To this day, he remains the single most influential force in team sports of any kind."

CELTICS CAREER HIGHLIGHTS

Best Season

There are so many great seasons from which to choose, with the six campaigns that fell between 1958 and 1964 heading the list. Although any of those seasons would have made an excellent choice, I ultimately narrowed it down to 1959–60, 1961–62, and 1963–64. It could be argued that Russell turned in his finest performance in 1963–64, when, playing without Bob

Cousy for the first time as a pro, he battled through injuries to average 15 points and a career-high 24.7 rebounds per game, en route to leading the Celtics to their sixth consecutive NBA title. Russell also performed brilliantly in 1959–60, when he earned a runner-up finish in the league MVP voting by averaging 18.2 points and 24 rebounds per contest, while posting career-high marks in field-goal shooting percentage (46.7) and free-throw shooting percentage (61.2). Nevertheless, the feeling here is that Russell played his best ball for the Celtics in 1961–62, when he earned NBA MVP honors by averaging 23.6 rebounds, 4.5 assists, and a career-high 18.9 points per game, while also amazingly averaging 45.2 minutes per contest, which represented the highest mark of his career.

Memorable Moments / Greatest Performances

An exceptional playoff performer over the course of his career, Russell gave an early indication of what lay ahead in his very first postseason contest, scoring 16 points, pulling down 31 rebounds, and blocking 7 shots during a 108–89 win over the Syracuse Nationals in Game 1 of the 1957 Eastern Division Finals.

Russell helped the Celtics get off to a tremendous start the following season, leading them to their 14th consecutive victory without a loss by scoring 30 points during a 120–107 win over the Knicks on November 27, 1957.

Although the Celtics lost to the Philadelphia Warriors by a score of 110–101 on January 31, 1958, Russell topped his earlier performance, scoring a season-high 32 points during the contest. Russell and the Celtics gained a measure of revenge against Philadelphia some three weeks later, with the Boston center pulling down 38 rebounds and scoring 13 points during a 99–97 victory over the Warriors on February 23.

Russell turned in his two most dominant performances of the ensuing campaign exactly one month apart, leading the Celtics to a 129–120 win over the Knicks on December 25, 1958, by scoring a team-high 32 points, before tallying 20 points and collecting 39 rebounds during a 119–118 overtime win over the Detroit Pistons on January 25, 1959.

Russell helped the Celtics begin the following season in fine fashion, scoring 32 points, in leading them to a 129–125 win over the Cincinnati Royals in the regular-season opener on October 17, 1959. Some three weeks later, on November 7, Russell scored 22 points and pulled down 35 rebounds during a 115–106 victory over the Philadelphia Warriors that marked his first meeting with Wilt Chamberlain, who scored 30 points

Bill Russell—the greatest winner in the history of team sports.
Photo courtesy of LegendaryAuctions.com.

during the contest. Russell also turned in a pair of extraordinary efforts against the Knicks in December, scoring 26 points and accumulating 38 rebounds during a 122–107 Boston victory on December 4, before tallying 15 points and collecting 39 rebounds during a 119–116 win over New York on December 19.

Russell subsequently led the Celtics to their second straight NBA title by averaging 18.5 points and 25.8 rebounds per game during the playoffs, with one of his finest performances coming against Philadelphia in Game 3 of the 1960 Eastern Division Finals, when he scored 26 points and amassed 39 rebounds during a 120–90 Boston victory. Although the Celtics went on to defeat St. Louis in seven games in the NBA Finals, they lost Game 2 to the Hawks by a score of 113–103. Nevertheless, Russell performed brilliantly throughout the contest, scoring 21 points and setting an NBA Finals record by recording 40 rebounds.

En route to capturing league MVP honors for the first of three straight times the following season, Russell scored a career-high 37 points during a 146–129 win over the Philadelphia Warriors on March 5, 1961. (Chamberlain scored 47 points in the same game.) Russell eventually equaled that mark nearly seven years later, on December 17, 1967, when he tallied 37 points during a 123–117 victory over the Los Angeles Lakers.

As well as Russell played in the previous year's playoffs, he performed even better during the 1961 postseason, posting averages of 19.1 points and 29.9 points per contest. He turned in one of his finest efforts in Game 3 of the Eastern Division Finals, leading the Celtics to a 133–110 victory over the Syracuse Nationals by scoring 18 points and pulling down 39 rebounds. Russell also performed magnificently in Game 5 of the NBA Finals, leading the Celtics to a series-clinching 121–112 win over the St. Louis Hawks by scoring 30 points and collecting 38 rebounds.

Russell went on the greatest scoring spree of his career during the early stages of the 1961–62 campaign, following up a pair of 28-point outings with a 35-point performance against the St. Louis Hawks on November 14, 1961, that led the Celtics to a 119–117 victory. Russell turned in one of his most dominant performances of the season some five weeks later, on December 21, pulling down 39 rebounds and scoring 16 points during a 122–103 win over the Knicks.

Russell turned in one of his finest all-around performances against Wilt Chamberlain the following season, leading the Celtics to a 135–118 victory over Chamberlain and the San Francisco Warriors on February 21, 1963, by scoring 25 points and amassing 38 rebounds.

Russell subsequently helped the Celtics capture their fifth straight NBA title by averaging 20.3 points and 25.1 rebounds per game during the playoffs, with his most notable performance taking place in Game 2 of the 1963 NBA Finals, when he led Boston to a 113–106 win over the Los Angeles Lakers by pulling down 38 rebounds and scoring 16 points.

Russell turned in another heroic effort in Game 5 of the 1964 Eastern Division Finals, leading the Celtics to a series-clinching 109–95 victory over the Cincinnati Royals by scoring 20 points and collecting 35 rebounds.

Russell continued his practice of excelling in Game 5 of the Eastern Division Finals the following year, leading the Celtics to a 114–108 win over the Philadelphia 76ers by recording 28 rebounds, 10 blocked shots, 7 assists, and 6 steals.

The holder of every Celtics rebounding record, Russell surpassed 40 rebounds in one game a total of eight times in regular-season play over the course of his career, accomplishing the feat for the first time on November 16, 1957, when he pulled down 49 rebounds and scored 30 points during a 111–89 victory over the Philadelphia Warriors. His total of 32 rebounds in one half of that contest remains an NBA record.

Later that same season, on February 12, 1958, Russell collected 41 rebounds and scored 18 points, in leading the Celtics to a 119–101 win over the Syracuse Nationals. Russell topped 40 boards again exactly 10 months later, recording 40 rebounds and 20 points during a 125–115 overtime win over the Cincinnati Royals on December 12, 1958.

On February 5, 1960, Russell recorded a franchise-record 51 rebounds and scored 23 points during a 124–100 win over the Syracuse Nationals, with his 51 boards remaining the second-highest single-game total in NBA history, trailing only the mark of 55 rebounds that Wilt Chamberlain posted for the Warriors against the Celtics on November 24, 1960.

Russell surpassed 40 rebounds for the fifth time in his career a little over one year later, on February 12, 1961, when he pulled down 40 rebounds and scored 19 points, in leading the Celtics to a 136–125 victory over Wilt Chamberlain's Philadelphia Warriors.

Russell again topped 40 boards on January 20, 1963, turning in one of his most dominant all-around performances by amassing 43 rebounds and scoring 29 points during a 133–121 win over the Lakers.

Russell accomplished the feat for the final two times in his career just three days apart in March of 1965, recording 49 rebounds and 27 points during a 112–100 victory over the Detroit Pistons on March 11, before pulling down 41 rebounds and scoring 20 points, in leading the Celtics to a 106–98 win over the San Francisco Warriors on March 14.

Possessing an extraordinary amount of inner drive and determination, Russell tended to perform at his very best in those games that mattered most. Appearing in a total of 11 decisive playoff games over the course of his career, Russell never lost one, posting a 29.5 rebounding average in those 11 contests. Among his most memorable performances, Russell scored 19 points and pulled down 32 rebounds in leading the Celtics to a 125–123 double-overtime win over the St. Louis Hawks in Game 7 of the 1957 NBA Finals. In another Game 7 against the Hawks three years later, Russell helped the Celtics capture their third league championship by recording 22 points and 35 rebounds during a 122–103 victory over St. Louis in the decisive game of the 1960 NBA Finals.

Russell also scored 30 points and pulled down 40 rebounds, in leading the Celtics to a 110–107 overtime win over the Los Angeles Lakers in Game 7 of the 1962 NBA Finals. In addition to tying his own NBA Finals record that he set two years earlier by collecting 40 rebounds, Russell set an all-time NBA record (playoffs or regular season) by accumulating 19 boards in one quarter.

Facing the Lakers again in Game 7 of the 1966 NBA Finals, Russell scored 25 points and amassed 32 rebounds, in leading the Celtics to a 95–93 victory that gave them the last of their record eight straight league championships.

Those were the sort of efforts that made Russell the most respected man in the game, and that prompted the Professional Basketball Writers Association of America to name him The Greatest Player in the History of the NBA in 1980.

NOTABLE ACHIEVEMENTS

- Averaged more than 20 rebounds per game 10 times, topping 23 boards per contest seven times and 24 rebounds per game on three occasions.
- Averaged more than 18 points per game twice.
- Averaged more than 5 assists per game twice.
- Averaged more than 40 minutes per game 10 times.
- Led NBA in rebounding five times; games played once; and minutes played twice.
- Finished second in NBA in rebounding five times, placing third on three other occasions.
- Led Celtics in rebounding 13 times and assists once.
- Surpassed 40 rebounds in one game eight times, topping 50 rebounds once (51 on 2/5/60).
- Holds Celtics records for most rebounds in a season (1,930 in 1963–64); game (51 on 2/5/60); half (32 on 11/16/57); and quarter (17 on 11/16/57 and 12/12/58).
- Holds Celtics career records for most rebounds (21,620) and highest rebounding average (22.5).

Russell going up for a rebound.
Photo courtesy of LegendaryAuctions.com.

- Ranks among Celtics career leaders in points scored (8th); assists (6th); field-goal attempts (7th); field goals made (8th); free-throw attempts (4th); free throws made (7th); games played (5th); and minutes played (2nd).
- Holds NBA record for highest postseason rebounding average (24.9).
- Ranks second in NBA history in total rebounds (21,620); rebounding average (22.5); and minutes per game (42.3).
- 1962–63 NBA All-Star Game MVP.
- Five-time NBA MVP (1957–58, 1960–61, 1961–62, 1962–63, and 1964–65).
- Finished in top five in NBA MVP voting six other times, placing second on two occasions.

- 1968 *Sports Illustrated* Sportsman of the Year.
- Three-time All-NBA First-Team selection (1958–59, 1962–63, and 1964–65).
- Eight-time All-NBA Second-Team selection (1957–58, 1959–60, 1960–61, 1961–62, 1963–64, 1965–66, 1966–67, and 1967–68).
- 1968–69 NBA All-Defensive First-Team selection.
- 12-time NBA All-Star (1958–69).
- 12-time Eastern Division champion (1957–1966, 1968, and 1969).
- 11-time NBA champion (1957, 1959, 1960, 1961, 1962, 1963, 1964, 1965, 1966, 1968, and 1969).
- Number 6 retired by Celtics.
- Member of NBA's 25th Anniversary Team.
- Member of NBA's 35th Anniversary Team.
- Member of NBA's 50th Anniversary Team.
- Member of NBA's 75th Anniversary Team.
- *Sporting News* Athlete of the Decade for the 1960s.
- Ranked #3 on *SLAM* magazine's Top 50 NBA Players of All-Time list in 2009.
- Ranked #4 on ESPN's Top 75 NBA Players of All-Time list in 2020.
- Ranked #18 on ESPN's 50 Greatest Athletes of the 20th Century list in 1999.
- Named the Greatest Player in NBA History by the Professional Basketball Writers Association of America in 1980.
- Inducted into Naismith Memorial Basketball Hall of Fame in 1975.

2

LARRY BIRD

Larry Bird helped define the way a generation of basketball fans has come to view and appreciate the NBA.

—NBA commissioner David Stern

Blessed with an innate ability to make everyone around him better and an incredible "feel" for the game accorded to only a select few, Larry Bird helped to restore a faltering Celtics franchise to prominence during the 1980s. Upon his arrival in Boston in 1979, Bird turned a team that had compiled a total of only 61 victories over the course of the two previous campaigns into instant contenders, leading the Celtics to an NBA-best 61-21 regular-season record his first year in the league. Employing his exceptional leadership skills and selfless approach to the game, Bird helped to reestablish Celtic pride and tradition, establishing himself in the process as one of the most impactful players in NBA history.

A superbly gifted player as well, Bird excelled in all phases of the game, possessing superior scoring, passing, ball-handling, and rebounding skills, while also doing an outstanding job on the defensive end of the court. Bird's stellar all-around play earned him league MVP honors three straight times, NBA Finals MVP honors twice, a total of 10 All-NBA nominations, and 12 All-Star selections over the course of his career, which he spent entirely in Boston. Along the way, Bird helped the Celtics capture 10 Atlantic Division titles and three league championships, prompting many NBA notables to sing his praises, with former Indiana Pacers coach George Irvine once stating, "As an all-around player, there's never been anyone better."

Born in West Baden, Indiana, on December 7, 1956, Larry Joe Bird grew up in nearby French Lick—a tiny town situated in the middle of Indiana's corn country. After first becoming involved in organized basketball

Larry Bird is considered by some to be as fine an all-around player as anyone who ever lived.
Photo courtesy of MearsOnlineAuctions.com.

at the age of 10, Bird played the game incessantly as a teenager prior to becoming the star attraction at local Springs Valley High School, where he ended up scoring more points than anyone else in school history. Subsequently offered a scholarship to attend Indiana University, Bird spent just one month in Bloomington before returning home and enrolling at Northwood Institute, the local junior college that seemed far less intimidating to him. Bird left Northwood just a few weeks later, though, before he finally decided to give college one more try following the suicide of his father and a marriage that lasted only a brief period of time. After spending the previous few months driving a garbage truck and doing maintenance work for local parks and roadways, Bird enrolled at Indiana State in 1975. He spent the next three years starring for the Sycamores on the court, leading them to an overall record of 81-13 and one NCAA Championship Game appearance during that time, en route to earning College Player of the Year honors as a senior in 1978–79.

With Red Auerbach having the foresight to select Bird with the sixth overall pick of the 1978 NBA Draft, even though he knew the forward might return to college for his senior year, Bird arrived in Boston one year later, joining a team that had finished the previous season with a regular-season record of just 29-53. Viewed with skepticism by some of the Celtics' veteran black players (most notably, Sidney Wicks and Curtis Rowe), who considered him to be just another "great white hope," Bird spent much of his first training camp disproving that misguided notion. While Wicks and Rowe did not make it past the first day of practice under ex-Marine drill sergeant Bill Fitch, Bird quickly earned the respect of Cedric Maxwell, who later admitted that he, too, initially had his doubts about his new team-mate, recalling years later, "I saw Larry and it was like, 'Eh, he looks like just another white guy.'" But, after Bird hit three consecutive long-range jumpers over him, each from farther out, Maxwell started to believe the hype, revealing, "I was like, 'Damn, okay, this white boy can play.'"

Bird ended up taking the league by storm, earning 1979–80 NBA Rookie of the Year and All-NBA First-Team honors for the first of nine straight times by averaging 21.3 points, 10.4 rebounds, 4.5 assists, and 1.7 steals per game. The first-year forward's brilliant all-around play sparked one of the greatest single-season turnarounds in NBA history—a 32-game improvement that saw the Celtics post a league-best record of 61-21 during the regular season. Although they subsequently came up short in the playoffs, losing to the Philadelphia 76ers in five games in the Eastern Conference Finals after earlier sweeping the Houston Rockets in four straight games in the Semifinal round, Bird played well in his first postseason, posting marks nearly identical to the ones he compiled during the regular season: 21.3 points per game (ppg), 11.2 rebounds per game (rpg), 4.7 assists per game (apg), and 1.6 steals per game (spg).

After acquiring Kevin McHale and Robert Parish during the subsequent off-season, the Celtics took another step forward in 1980–81, capturing the NBA championship, with Bird earning the first of three straight runner-up finishes in the league MVP voting by averaging 21.2 points, 10.9 rebounds, 5.5 assists, and 2 steals per game. Although the Celtics failed to repeat as NBA champions in 1981–82, Bird had another tremendous season, posting averages of 22.9 points, 10.9 rebounds, 5.8 assists, and

1.9 steals per contest. He then began the greatest stretch of his career—an extraordinary six-year run, during which he posted the following numbers:

SEASON	POINTS PER GAME	REBOUNDS PER GAME	ASSISTS PER GAME
1982–83	23.6	11.0	5.8
1983–84	24.2	10.1	5.8
1984–85	28.7	10.5	6.6
1985–86	25.8	9.8	6.8
1986–87	28.1	9.2	7.6
1987–88	29.9	9.3	6.1

In addition to finishing among the league leaders in scoring in five of those seasons, placing as high as second in 1984–85, Bird ranked among the leaders in rebounding four times, while also topping the circuit in free-throw shooting percentage four times, three-point field goals twice, and minutes played per game twice. Bird captured league MVP honors in 1983–84, 1984–85, and 1985–86, joining Bill Russell and Wilt Chamberlain in the process as the only players in NBA history to win the award three straight times. In the last of his MVP campaigns, Bird earned the additional distinctions of being named the *Sporting News* Man of the Year and the Associated Press Male Athlete of the Year. He also received strong MVP consideration in each of the next two seasons, finishing third in the balloting in 1986–87, before placing second in the voting to Michael Jordan the following season. The Celtics made three consecutive NBA Finals appearances during the period, winning the league championship in 1984 and 1986, with Bird being named Finals MVP both times.

Bird's extraordinary all-around play earned him acclaim throughout the league, with longtime NBA referee Norm Drucker stating during a mid-1980s interview that appeared in *From Set Shot to Slam Dunk*, "Oscar Robertson was, and is, the greatest guard I ever saw, and, for a long time, I rated him as the greatest ballplayer. I have changed my mind after watching Larry Bird."

Bird's good friend and foremost rival Magic Johnson said on one occasion, "You cannot believe how good Larry Bird is."

Hall of Fame center Artis Gilmore referred to Bird as "a unique phenomenon."

Bird established himself as one of the greatest outside shooters in NBA history during his time in Boston.
Photo courtesy of George A. Kitrinos.

Celtics legend Bob Cousy commented, "Before Bird, I used to vacillate. The question [of who the game's greatest player was] didn't seem relevant. But Bird came along with all the skills, all the things a basketball player has to do. I think he's the greatest."

Don Nelson proclaimed, "[Bird's] the best player ever to play the game."

Legendary UCLA head coach John Wooden stated, "I've always considered Oscar Robertson to be the best player in the game. Now I'm not so sure that Larry Bird isn't."

Meanwhile, Jerry West, who has always been reluctant to compare players from different eras, noted, "[Bird] is as nearly perfect as you can get in almost every phase of basketball."

Bird perhaps made his greatest impression on others with the completeness of his game. A phenomenal outside shooter with exceptional range, he sometimes practiced three-pointers with his eyes closed. Bird also had the ability to beat his opponent off the dribble by employing a variety of head fakes and pump fakes down low. A superb ball-handler and passer as well, Bird perhaps took a backseat only to Magic Johnson and Isiah Thomas among his contemporaries as a ball-distributor. The 6-foot-9, 225-pound Bird also excelled as a rebounder, doing an outstanding job of positioning himself under the boards. Bird's ability to handle himself inside, along with his passing and ball-handling skills, enabled him to play both forward positions with equal facility over the course of his career. Furthermore, even though Bird lacked superior foot speed and leaping ability, making him just a mediocre defender in one-on-one situations, his extraordinary anticipation and court sense made him an excellent team defender, enabling him to earn three selections to the NBA All-Defensive Second Team.

In commenting on the totality of Bird's game, Red Auerbach stated, "I knew he was a great shooter, but I didn't know how great. I knew he was a great passer and rebounder, but I didn't know how great. And I did not know he would play with injuries . . . Larry was the most self-motivated player I have ever seen." Auerbach added, "The one thing you have to avoid when you talk about Bird is statistics. It's his presence, the total way he commands attention on the court that counts."

As impressive as Bird's statistics tended to be, judging him solely by the numbers he compiled would indeed do him an injustice of sorts. An exceptional leader with a tremendous work ethic, Bird challenged his teammates vocally when he considered it necessary to do so, making them better in the process. He also made them realize that their personal statistics placed a distant second to the ultimate goal of winning. Bird's other intangible qualities included a deep understanding of the game and extraordinary instincts that somehow allowed him to know where his teammates would be on the court at all times. In discussing this last set of attributes, Tommy Heinsohn stated, "Bird reminds me of somebody finding a block of ice in French Lick,

Indiana, chipping away, and out pops a prehistoric basketball player who's got all the skills of yesteryear . . . He reminds me of Bobby Fischer, the chess player. Bird plays chess when everyone else is playing checkers; he's always three moves ahead."

Bird also made a tremendous impact on the NBA as a whole, helping to regenerate interest in a league whose fan base had gradually been diminishing. With few teams of the late 1970s adopting the same selfless approach to the game as their immediate predecessors, fans of the sport found it increasingly difficult to relate to the new one-on-one, run-and-gun philosophy being displayed throughout the league. They found their enthusiasm for the game tempered by persistent rumors of drug abuse among NBA players, and furthermore, a good portion of the white upper-middle-class fan base (those who purchased the vast majority of the tickets) came to feel that the league had simply become "too black." The once-predominantly white NBA had become almost 85 percent black by the late 1970s. Virtually all of the league's stars, and certainly all of its superstars, were African-American. As a result, many white fans simply lost interest in the sport.

The simultaneous arrival of Bird and Magic Johnson in 1979 helped to breathe new life into the game. With Bird joining the Celtics and Johnson taking up residence in Los Angeles, the two young men reemphasized the "team" philosophy that had disappeared from the game. They also brought back into prominence two of the league's most fabled franchises, creating in the process a tremendous rivalry between the two teams. Bird and Johnson also embarked on a personal rivalry second in intensity only to the one that previously existed between Bill Russell and Wilt Chamberlain. And they gave the NBA two great stars to market, one of whom happened to be white.

Unfortunately, fans of the game found themselves unable to marvel at the brilliant all-around play of Bird much beyond the 1987–88 campaign. After missing all but six games in 1988–89 following surgery to remove bone spurs from both heels, Bird returned to the Celtics in 1989–90. However, he subsequently began to feel the effects of a congenital disc problem in his back that he had been diagnosed with a few years earlier. Although Bird played well for the Celtics in 1989–90, posting averages of 24.3 points, 9.5 rebounds, and 7.5 assists per game, he never again performed at quite the same level, spending the remainder of his career playing in constant pain. Forced to sit out 22 games in 1990–91 because of a compressed nerve root in his back, Bird averaged 19.4 points, 8.5 rebounds, and 7.2 assists per contest, before undergoing back surgery during the subsequent off-season.

Able to appear in only 45 games the following season due to lingering back problems, Bird announced his retirement at season's end, concluding his career with 21,791 total points scored, 8,974 rebounds, 5,695 assists, 1,556 steals, a field-goal shooting percentage of 49.6, a free-throw shooting percentage of 88.6, and averages of 24.3 points, 10 rebounds, 6.3 assists, and 1.7 steals per game, with his 24.3 scoring average placing him second in team annals. In addition to leading the NBA in free-throw shooting percentage four times, Bird finished in the league's top 10 in scoring six times, rebounding seven times, and steals twice. He is one of only two players in NBA history (Kevin Garnett being the other) to average more than 20 points, 10 rebounds, and 5 assists per game for as many as five straight seasons.

Following his retirement, Bird spent five years serving as a special assistant in the Celtics' front office before accepting the position of head coach of the Indiana Pacers when the Celtics named Rick Pitino their new president and head coach in 1997. Bird spent the next three seasons coaching the Pacers to an overall record of 147-67, leading them to three consecutive playoff appearances, two Central Division titles, and a berth in the 2000 NBA Finals, en route to earning NBA Coach of the Year honors once. Although Bird resigned as Pacers coach following the conclusion of the 1999–2000 campaign, he returned to the team three years later, after which he spent most of the next 14 seasons serving as the president of basketball operations, taking one year off due to health concerns. Stepping down again in 2017, Bird remained with the team in an advisory capacity.

Still generally considered to be among the handful of greatest players in NBA history, Bird received high praise from former NBA commissioner David Stern upon his retirement, with Stern stating, "Larry Bird helped define the way a generation of basketball fans has come to view and appreciate the NBA."

Meanwhile, Magic Johnson expressed his admiration for his greatest rival by proclaiming, "There will never be another Larry Bird."

CELTICS CAREER HIGHLIGHTS

Best Season

Although Bird performed brilliantly throughout his entire career, he played his best ball for the Celtics from 1984 to 1988. En route to leading Boston to the NBA championship in 1985–86, Bird became just the second player

Bird retired having led the Celtics to three NBA championships.
Photo courtesy of George A. Kitrinos.

in NBA history (after Cliff Hagan in 1960) to finish in the league's top 10 in five different statistical categories, placing among the leaders in scoring (25.8 ppg), rebounding (9.8 rpg), steals (2.0 spg), free-throw accuracy

(89.6%), and three-point shooting (42.3%). In addition to being named league MVP at season's end, Bird earned *Sporting News* Man of the Year and Associated Press Male Athlete of the Year honors.

A strong case could certainly be made for either 1986–87 or 1987–88, as well—seasons in which Bird became the first player to shoot at least 50 percent from the field and 90 percent from the free-throw line in the same year. Although Bird saw his three-year reign as NBA MVP come to an end in the first of those campaigns, he posted exceptional numbers, averaging 28.1 points, 9.2 rebounds, 1.8 steals, and a career-high 7.6 assists per game, while leading the league in free-throw shooting percentage (91%) and minutes played per contest (40.6). He followed that up by posting marks of 29.9 points, 9.3 rebounds, 6.1 assists, and 1.6 steals per game in 1987–88, while shooting 91.6 percent from the free-throw line and a career-best 52.7 percent from the field.

Nevertheless, I decided to go with Bird's 1984–85 campaign, one in which he earned league MVP honors for the second time by averaging 28.7 points, 10.5 rebounds, 6.6 assists, 1.6 steals, and a career-high 1.2 blocked shots per contest, while shooting 52.2 percent from the field, 88.2 percent from the foul line, and averaging a league-leading 39.5 minutes per game. In addition to placing second in the league in scoring, Bird finished eighth in rebounding, fourth in three-point field goals (56), second in three-point field-goal shooting percentage (42.7), and sixth in free-throw shooting percentage. He also led the league with a player efficiency rating of 26.5 that represented the second-highest mark of his career.

Memorable Moments / Greatest Performances

An outstanding team defender, Bird recorded a franchise record 9 steals during a 110–94 win over the Utah Jazz on February 18, 1985. He also scored 30 points, pulled down 12 rebounds, and assisted on 10 baskets during the contest, leaving him just one steal shy of recording a quadruple-double.

Bird also amassed 8 steals in one game twice, doing so for the first time during a 113–109 overtime loss to the Nets in the 1985–86 regular-season opener. He accomplished the feat again during a 129–117 victory over the Nets on January 3, 1986.

An excellent rebounder as well, Bird scored 36 points and pulled down 19 rebounds, in leading the Celtics to a 126–112 win over the Denver Nuggets on December 12, 1982.

Later that same season, on February 4, 1983, Bird recorded 23 points and 20 rebounds during a 102–93 victory over the Indiana Pacers.

Bird led the Celtics to a 105–104 win over the Philadelphia 76ers on January 13, 1984, by scoring 29 points, collecting 19 rebounds, and assisting on 8 baskets.

Bird turned in another exceptional all-around effort five weeks later, on February 19, 1984, when he tallied 34 points, pulled down 18 rebounds, and collected 9 assists during a 107–101 victory over the Portland Trail Blazers.

Bird played a tremendous all-around game on March 22, 1985, when he led the Celtics to a 129–117 win over the Cleveland Cavaliers by scoring 36 points and assisting on 15 baskets.

Some two weeks later, on April 7, 1985, Bird recorded 38 points and 15 rebounds during a 114–102 victory over the Knicks.

Bird turned in two of his finest all-around performances the following year just 10 days apart, scoring 36 points and pulling down 14 rebounds during a 118–101 win over the 76ers on March 16, 1986, before leading the Celtics to a 121–115 victory over the Bucks on March 26 by hitting for 35 points, collecting 12 rebounds, assisting on 6 baskets, and recording 3 blocked shots.

Nearly one year later, on March 15, 1987, Bird scored 35 points, pulled down 15 rebounds, and collected 7 assists during a 113–104 victory over the Knicks.

Although the Celtics lost their December 30, 1987, matchup with the Seattle SuperSonics by a score of 111–105, Bird played a tremendous all-around game, scoring 36 points, collecting 15 rebounds, and assisting on 8 baskets during the contest.

Bird continued his exceptional play in the new year, leading the Celtics to a 104–97 victory over the Bulls on January 12, 1988, by scoring 38 points, pulling down 9 rebounds, and collecting 8 assists.

Bird also had a big game against the 76ers later that month, scoring 29 points and pulling down 17 rebounds during a 100–85 Celtics win on January 31, 1988.

Other standout performances that season included a 39-point, 10-rebound, 6-assist outing against Dallas on February 12, 1988; a 36-point, 13-rebound effort against San Antonio on March 9; and a 37-point, 14-rebound, 8-assist outing against Washington on March 23, all of which resulted in Boston victories.

After missing virtually all of the previous season due to injury, Bird made a memorable return to the Celtics in the opening game of the

Bird scored more than 50 points in a game on four separate occasions. Photo courtesy of MearsOnlineAuctions.com.

1989–90 campaign, scoring 32 points and collecting 8 rebounds during a 127–114 win over the Milwaukee Bucks.

Later that season, on February 13, 1990, Bird turned in an exceptional all-around effort, leading the Celtics to a 107–94 victory over the Houston Rockets by scoring 38 points, pulling down 14 rebounds, and assisting on 8 baskets.

Although the Celtics lost their March 4, 1990, matchup with the Chicago Bulls by a score of 118–114, Bird performed brilliantly during the contest, tallying 38 points, collecting 11 rebounds, and recording 9 assists.

Bird played another great game a little over one month later, when he scored 37 points, pulled down 9 rebounds, and collected 10 assists during a 115–105 win over the Miami Heat on April 7, 1990.

Bird led the Celtics to a 135–132 double-overtime victory over the Chicago Bulls on March 31, 1991, by tallying 34 points, collecting 15 rebounds, and assisting on 8 baskets.

Bird scored at least 40 points in one game a total of 47 times over the course of his career, with his first such effort coming on February 13, 1980, when he hit for 45 points during a 135–134 loss to the Phoenix Suns.

Other notable 40-point outings his first few years in the league included a 41-point, 14-rebound performance during a 115–106 win over Portland on December 2, 1983, a 48-point, 14-rebound effort during a 128–127 victory over Atlanta on December 9, 1984, and a 48-point outburst that led the Celtics to a 128–127 win over Portland on January 27, 1985.

Bird continued his fabulous 1984–85 campaign by scoring 48 points, pulling down 15 rebounds, and collecting 7 assists during a 134–120 victory over the Houston Rockets on March 17, 1985, before hitting for 47 points and recording 14 rebounds during a 115–113 overtime loss to Milwaukee on April 12, 1985.

Bird turned in one of his finest all-around efforts the following season on November 27, 1985, when he led the Celtics to a 132–124 win over the Detroit Pistons by scoring 47 points and pulling down 12 rebounds.

Bird topped the 40-point mark several times during the second half of his career as well, doing so on April 12, 1987, when he led the Celtics to a 119–107 victory over the Knicks by hitting for 47 points, collecting 7 rebounds, assisting on 8 baskets, and recording 4 steals.

The following season, on November 7, 1987, Bird tallied 47 points, pulled down 8 rebounds, and collected 7 assists during a 140–139 double-overtime win over Washington.

Just four days later, on November 11, 1987, Bird hit for 42 points and pulled down 20 rebounds, in leading the Celtics to a 120–106 victory over the Indiana Pacers.

Bird continued his prolific scoring in the New Year, tallying 49 points during a 106–100 win over Washington on January 27, 1988, before scoring 44 points and collecting 15 rebounds during a 129–120 loss to Houston on February 9. He also surpassed 40 points two other times in February, leading the Celtics to a 107–106 victory over Phoenix on February 15 by scoring 49 points, before hitting for 44 points during a 113–112 win over Portland on February 24.

Bird concluded the 1987–88 campaign in style, leading the Celtics to a 126–119 victory over the Chicago Bulls in the regular-season finale by scoring 44 points and pulling down 10 rebounds.

Bird had two of his biggest scoring games of the 1989–90 campaign during the latter stages of the season, hitting for 46 points during a 130–127 win over Orlando on March 16, 1990, before tallying 43 points and collecting 15 rebounds during a 125–106 victory over the New Jersey Nets on April 4, 1990.

Despite being limited to just 60 games in 1990–91 by back problems that forced him to spend the entire season playing in pain, Bird managed to turn in a number of dominant performances, with one of those coming on November 14, 1990, when he led the Celtics to a 135–126 win over the Charlotte Hornets by scoring 45 points, pulling down 8 rebounds, and collecting 8 assists. Bird also scored 43 points, recorded 8 rebounds, and assisted on 13 baskets during a 148–140 victory over the Denver Nuggets on December 5, 1990.

One of only four Celtics players to score as many as 50 points in one game, Bird accomplished the feat on four separate occasions, doing so for the first time on March 30, 1983, when he tallied 53 points during a 142–116 win over the Indiana Pacers. Two years later, on March 12, 1985, Bird established a franchise record that still stands when he led the Celtics to a 126–115 victory over the Atlanta Hawks by hitting for a career-high 60 points. Bird again reached the 50-point mark almost exactly one year later, tallying 50 points during a 116–115 loss to the Dallas Mavericks on March 10, 1986. He accomplished the feat for the fourth and final time in his career on November 10, 1989, when he scored 50 points, pulled down 13 rebounds, and assisted on 7 baskets during a 117–106 victory over the Hawks.

Bird's excellence in all phases of the game enabled him to record 69 triple-doubles during his career, with several of those ranking among his greatest performances ever. One such effort took place on January 13, 1982, when he scored 28 points, pulled down 19 rebounds, and collected 15 assists during a 116–95 victory over the Atlanta Hawks.

Bird turned in another extraordinary all-around effort on May 13, 1984, when he led the Celtics to a 121–104 win over the Knicks by scoring 39 points, collecting 12 rebounds, and assisting on 10 baskets.

Bird recorded six triple-doubles over a two-week period in February 1986, with one of those coming on February 13, when he scored 31 points, pulled down 15 rebounds, and collected 11 assists during a 107–98 win over the Seattle SuperSonics. He followed that up the very next night by scoring 47 points, amassing 14 rebounds, and assisting on 11 baskets, in leading the Celtics to a 120–119 victory over the Portland Trail Blazers. Bird concluded his exceptional stretch of games with a 24-point, 18-rebound, 13-assist performance that led the Celtics to a 91–74 win over the Knicks on February 25.

The following season, Bird recorded a pair of triple-doubles during the first week of April, scoring 30 points, pulling down 17 rebounds, and collecting 15 assists during a 103–86 win over Washington on April 1, 1987, before amassing 39 points, 10 rebounds, and 12 assists during a 106–104 overtime loss to Philadelphia four days later.

Bird turned in one of his finest all-around performances of the ensuing campaign on February 10, 1988, when he tallied 39 points, pulled down 17 rebounds, and assisted on 10 baskets during a 136–120 victory over San Antonio.

Bird posted nearly identical numbers in a pair of December 1989 contests, leading the Celtics to a 109–97 win over Seattle on December 13 by scoring 40 points, collecting 11 rebounds, and recording 10 assists, before amassing 37 points, 11 rebounds, and 10 assists during a 115–112 overtime victory over Sacramento exactly two weeks later.

Later that same season, on March 21, 1990, Bird recorded a career-high 16 assists during a 123–114 win over the Cleveland Cavaliers. He also scored 25 points and pulled down 10 rebounds during the contest.

Bird saved one of his most memorable performances for his final NBA season, when, despite being hampered by a bad back and an injured ankle, he led the Celtics to a 152–148 double-overtime victory over the Portland Trail Blazers on March 15, 1992, by scoring 49 points, pulling down 16 rebounds, assisting on 12 baskets, and recording 4 steals. Bird scored 16 points in the fourth quarter of the nationally televised contest, including Boston's last 9 points and a game-tying three-pointer, with just two seconds remaining in regulation. Portland's Clyde Drexler paid tribute to Bird after the game by telling the *Boston Herald*, "Anytime you have Bird on the floor, anything can happen."

A tremendous performer in pressure situations, Bird posted playoff averages of 23.8 points, 10.3 rebounds, and 6.5 steals per game over the course of his career, saving some of his greatest efforts for postseason play. En route to leading the Celtics to the NBA title in 1984, Bird averaged 27.5 points, 11 rebounds, and 5.9 assists per contest during the playoffs, performing particularly well against the Knicks in the Eastern Conference Semifinals. After scoring 37 points and pulling down 11 rebounds during Boston's 116–102 victory in Game 2, "Larry Legend" led the Celtics to

Bird finished in the league's top five in scoring four times.
Photo courtesy of MearsOnlineAuctions.com.

a 121–104 win in Game 7 by recording 39 points, 12 rebounds, and 10 assists. He then went on to capture NBA Finals MVP honors by averaging 27.4 points and 14 rebounds per game over the course of the series, which the Celtics ended up winning in seven games. Particularly dominant against the Lakers in Games 4 and 5, Bird led the Celtics to a 129–125 overtime win in the first of those contests by scoring 29 points and pulling down 21 rebounds. He followed that up by tallying 34 points and collecting 17 rebounds during Boston's 121–103 Game 5 victory.

Although the Celtics failed to repeat as NBA champions the following year, Bird had another brilliant postseason, averaging 26 points and 9.1 rebounds in Boston's 20 playoff games. Excelling against Cleveland in the first round of the postseason tournament, Bird led the Celtics to a 126–123 win in Game 1 by hitting for 40 points. He then contributed 34 points, 14 rebounds, and 7 assists in the Game 4 clincher, which the Celtics won by a score of 117–115. Bird subsequently helped the Celtics record a six-game victory over Detroit in the 1985 Eastern Conference Finals, turning in his two finest performances in Games 2 and 5. After leading the Celtics to a 121–114 win in the first of those contests by scoring 42 points, pulling down 10 rebounds, and collecting 6 assists, he tallied 43 points and recorded 13 rebounds in Boston's 130–123 win in Game 5.

After earning league MVP honors for the third straight time in 1985–86 by leading the Celtics to an NBA-best 67-15 record over the course of the regular season, Bird had a superb postseason, averaging 25.9 points, 9.3 rebounds, and 8.2 assists per game during the playoffs. En route to leading Boston to a three-game sweep of Chicago in the opening round of the postseason tournament, Bird performed brilliantly in Game 2, scoring 36 points, pulling down 12 rebounds, and recording 8 assists during a 135–131 double-overtime win. He followed that up by leading the Celtics to a five-game victory over Atlanta in the Eastern Conference Semifinals, tallying 36 points during a 119–108 win in Game 2, before hitting for another 36 points during a 132–99 blowout of the Hawks in Game 5. Bird subsequently captured NBA Finals MVP honors for the second time by nearly averaging a triple-double during Boston's six-game victory over Houston, posting marks of 24 points, 9.7 rebounds, and 9.5 assists per contest over the course of the series. In the series finale, which the Celtics won by a score of 114–97, Bird scored 29 points, pulled down 11 rebounds, and assisted on 12 baskets.

Even though the Celtics ended up losing to the Los Angeles Lakers in six games in the NBA Finals the following year, Bird again performed magnificently in the playoffs, posting averages of 27 points, 10 rebounds, and 7.2 assists per game in Boston's 23 postseason contests. Most effective against Milwaukee in the 1987 Eastern Conference Semifinals, Bird topped the 40-point mark twice in that series, hitting for 40 points during Boston's 111–98 win in Game 1, before scoring 42 points in Game 4, in leading the Celtics to a 138–137 double-overtime victory.

The 1988 playoffs featured another memorable performance by Bird, who, despite suffering from bronchial pneumonia, engaged in a thrilling fourth-quarter shootout with Atlanta's Dominique Wilkins in Game 7 of the Eastern Conference Semifinals. Although Wilkins finished the contest with a game-high 47 points, Bird and the Celtics prevailed in the end, with "Larry Legend" leading his team to a 118–116 victory by scoring 20 of his

34 points in the final 12 minutes. Commenting on the events that transpired on the court, Kevin McHale suggested, "It was like two gunfighters waiting to blink. There was one stretch that was as pure a form of basketball as you're ever going to see." Meanwhile, former Celtics guard Don Chaney, then an assistant coach with the Hawks, said of his onetime teammate, "[Bird] wanted it. He wanted the ball, and he came through. That's what superstars are made of."

Yet, the play that perhaps epitomizes Bird as a player more than any other occurred one year earlier, against the Detroit Pistons in Game 5 of the 1987 Eastern Conference Finals. With Detroit holding a one-point lead over the Celtics with just five seconds remaining in regulation, the Pistons needed only to kill off the final few seconds to take a three-games-to-two lead in the series. Isiah Thomas attempted an inbounds pass to one of his teammates, but Bird stole the ball in the backcourt and delivered a perfect pass under the Detroit basket to Dennis Johnson, whose presence there he somehow anticipated. The Boston guard laid the ball in with no time left on the clock, giving the Celtics a 108–107 victory and a 3–2 lead in a series they eventually won in seven games. Although the Celtics subsequently lost to the Lakers in the NBA Finals, Bird's play against Detroit continued to add to his legend.

NOTABLE ACHIEVEMENTS

- Averaged more than 20 points per game 11 times, topping 25 points per contest four times, and 28 points per game on three occasions.
- Averaged more than 10 rebounds per game six times, topping 9 rebounds per contest five other times.
- Averaged more than 5 assists per game 11 times, topping 7 assists per contest three times.
- Averaged 2 steals per game twice.
- Shot better than 50 percent from the field five times.
- Shot better than 90 percent from the free-throw line five times.
- Averaged more than 40 minutes per game once.
- Led NBA in free-throw shooting percentage four times, three-point field goals twice, and minutes played twice.
- Finished in top five in NBA in scoring four times, placing second once and third once.
- Finished in top five in NBA in rebounding once.

Bird's 29.9 ppg scoring average in 1987–88 represents the highest single-season mark in franchise history.
Photo courtesy of George A. Kitrinos.

- Led Celtics in scoring average 11 times; rebounding six times; and assists four times.
- Scored at least 50 points in one game four times.
- Holds share of Celtics record for most points scored in a game (60 vs. Atlanta on 3/12/85).
- Holds share of Celtics single-game record for most steals (9 vs. Utah on 2/18/85).
- Holds Celtics single-season record for highest scoring average (29.9 ppg in 1987–88).
- Ranks among Celtics career leaders in points scored (3rd); scoring average (2nd); assists (3rd); rebounds (4th); steals (2nd); field-goal attempts (3rd); field goals made (2nd); free-throw attempts (7th); free throws made (4th); free-throw shooting percentage (4th); games played (8th); and minutes played (5th).
- 15-time NBA Player of the Week.
- Seven-time NBA Player of the Month.
- 1979–80 NBA Rookie of the Year.
- 1981–82 NBA All-Star Game MVP.
- Two-time NBA Finals MVP (1983–84 and 1985–86).
- Three-time NBA MVP (1983–84, 1984–85, and 1985–86).
- Finished second in NBA MVP voting four other times.
- Nine-time All-NBA First-Team selection (1979–80, 1980–81, 1981–82, 1982–83, 1983–84, 1984–85, 1985–86, 1986–87, and 1987–88).
- 1989–90 All-NBA Second-Team selection.
- Three-time NBA All-Defensive Second-Team selection (1981–82, 1982–83, and 1983–84).
- 12-time NBA All-Star (1980–88 and 1990–92).
- Five-time Eastern Conference champion (1981, 1984, 1985, 1986, and 1987).
- Three-time NBA champion (1981, 1984, and 1986).
- Number 33 retired by Celtics.
- Member of NBA's 50th Anniversary Team.
- Member of NBA's 75th Anniversary Team.
- 1986 *Sporting News* Man of the Year.
- 1986 Associated Press Athlete of the Year.
- Ranked #30 on ESPN's 50 Greatest Athletes of the 20th Century in 1999.
- Inducted into Naismith Memorial Basketball Hall of Fame in 1998.

3

JOHN HAVLICEK

Whether I start or come off the bench makes no difference to me. My game has always been to go as hard as I can, for as long as I can.

—John Havlicek

One of the greatest all-around players in NBA history, John Havlicek excelled in every facet of the game. An outstanding scorer who generally came through in pressure situations, Havlicek averaged more than 20 points per game for eight consecutive seasons, en route to establishing himself as the Celtics' all-time leading scorer. A superb passer, "Hondo," as he came to be known affectionately to his teammates, also ranks second in franchise history only to Bob Cousy in assists. An excellent defender as well, Havlicek earned a total of eight NBA All-Defensive Team nominations, even though the league did not dole out such honors until his seventh season. Havlicek's tremendous versatility enabled him to earn a total of 11 All-NBA selections, 13 All-Star nominations, and a pair of top-five finishes in the league MVP voting. Meanwhile, his character and quiet leadership also contributed significantly to the success Boston experienced over the course of his career, which spanned several eras of Celtic greatness.

Joining the Celtics in Bob Cousy's final year with the team, Havlicek subsequently played with legendary figures such as Bill Russell, Sam Jones, Dave Cowens, and Jo Jo White, before announcing his retirement just one year before Larry Bird arrived on the scene. In all, Havlicek played for eight NBA championship teams in his 16 years in Boston, earning in the process spots on the NBA's 35th, 50th, and 75th Anniversary Teams, and a much-deserved place in the Naismith Memorial Basketball Hall of Fame.

Born to Czechoslovakian immigrant parents in Martins Ferry, Ohio, a small river town on the West Virginia border, on April 8, 1940, John J.

John Havlicek played for eight NBA championship teams during his time in Boston. Photo courtesy of MearsOnlineAuctions.com.

Havlicek began to acquire the extraordinary endurance for which he later became so well noted by running to school and back as a youngster. After enrolling at local Bridgeport High School, Havlicek soon developed a reputation as an exceptional all-around athlete, earning All-State honors in football, baseball, and basketball. Yet, even though he also received numerous scholarship offers to play quarterback and the outfield in college, Havlicek decided to concentrate exclusively on basketball after he enrolled at Ohio State University, where he teamed up with future NBA stars Jerry Lucas and Larry Siegfried to lead the Buckeyes to the 1960 National Championship and an overall record of 78-6 over the course of the next three seasons. Havlicek's lone regret over his collegiate career remains his inability to earn a spot on the 1960 US Olympic team, which he expressed when he recalled, "I felt that I played well enough during the trials to make the team. Unfortunately, the coaches and selection committee didn't see it the same way. I know it sounds cliché, but playing for my country would have been the highlight of my career, and that's why it bothered me so much."

Selected by the Celtics with the seventh overall pick of the 1962 NBA Draft following his graduation from Ohio State, Havlicek made an immediate impact in Boston, averaging 14.3 points, 6.7 rebounds, 2.2 assists, and 27.5 minutes per game as a rookie. Gradually assuming the role of "sixth man" over the course of the campaign, Havlicek used his rare combination of basketball skills to excel at both the small forward and shooting guard positions, although he perhaps felt a bit more comfortable playing in the frontcourt. A consummate team player, Havlicek fit in seamlessly with the rest of the squad, doing whatever his coach asked of him. Whether providing the Celtics instant offense off the bench or applying constant pressure to his man on the defensive end, Havlicek inspired the other players around him, making a great team even better, as the Celtics captured their unprecedented fifth consecutive NBA title at season's end.

Although Havlicek continued to function in the role of "sixth man" the next four seasons, he established himself during that time as one of the team's most significant contributors, helping the Celtics win three more NBA championships and earning All-Star honors in both 1965–66 and 1966–67. And, even though Havlicek began most contests on the bench, he garnered the playing time of a starter, averaging more than 30 minutes per game in three of those four seasons, while posting scoring averages of 19.9, 18.3, 18.8, and 21.4 points per contest. In discussing his role on the team, Havlicek commented, "Whether I start or come off the bench makes no difference to me. My game has always been to go as hard as I can, for as long as I can."

Years later, Havlicek further explained the attitude he brought with him to the court his first few years in the league by stating:

Coming off the bench never bothered me because basketball is a team game. It takes a total team effort, and it takes everyone buying into their role and playing it to the best of their ability. The sixth man role is very important to a ball club—it was back then, and it is equally as important today. I had confidence in my game, and I knew that I had the ability to start, which is something that evolved over time, but joining a team loaded with talent meant that I would have to wait my turn. We had Tom Heinsohn, Satch Sanders, Frank Ramsey, Jim Loscutoff, and Gene Guarilia. All of these guys played the forward position, and all of them had the NBA experience that I lacked as a rookie. So coming off the bench didn't affect me in a negative way. Like I said, I was confident in my ability to play the game of basketball. Besides, one thing I learned from Red Auerbach was that it's not who starts the game, but who finishes it, and I generally was around at the finish.

Havlicek finally broke into the Celtics' starting five in 1967–68, continuing his streak of eight straight seasons in which he averaged more than 20 points per game, and 13 consecutive seasons in which he earned All-Star honors. Here are the numbers he compiled over the course of the next seven seasons:

SEASON	POINTS PER GAME	REBOUNDS PER GAME	ASSISTS PER GAME
1967–68	20.7	6.7	4.7
1968–69	21.6	7.0	5.4
1969–70	24.2	7.8	6.8
1970–71	28.9	9.0	7.5
1971–72	27.5	8.2	7.5
1972–73	23.8	7.1	6.6
1973–74	22.6	6.4	5.9

In addition to finishing second in the NBA in scoring in 1970–71, Havlicek placed third in the league in that category the following season. He also placed among the league leaders in assists all seven years, averaged more minutes per game than any other player in the league twice, earned All-NBA honors each season and a pair of top-five finishes in the league MVP voting, and made either the NBA All-Defensive First or Second Team in each season the squads were announced during that period. The Celtics finished first in the Atlantic Division in each of the final three seasons, winning their 12th NBA championship in 1974, with Havlicek being named

After beginning his career as the Celtics' sixth man, John Havlicek eventually established himself as one of the NBA's greatest players.
Photo courtesy of MearsOnlineAuctions.com.

Finals MVP. Extremely durable as well, Havlicek missed a total of only 10 games over that seven-year stretch, appearing in every game for the Celtics in three different seasons.

Much of Havlicek's success lay in his outstanding athleticism, which helped make him one of the game's most versatile players. Blessed with excellent foot speed, Hondo blanketed his man on defense and ran the court extremely well on offense, proving to be a superb finisher in the transition game. Operating with an economy of motion, he tended to run with quick, short strides when dribbling the ball, allowing him to change directions quickly. Away from the ball, Havlicek used his speed to distance himself from his defender, always moving, cutting, and looking for an opening.

Commenting on the problems Havlicek's athleticism posed to his opponents, *Sports Illustrated*'s Frank Deford wrote in 1966, "Havlicek is one of those rare players who force rivals to alter their regular methods in deference to him. He is 6 feet 5½ and weighs 205 pounds, and he has unusual speed, strength, and agility for a man that size. He is too fast for most forwards and too big for most guards to cope with."

One of the game's top scorers for much of his career, Havlicek shot the ball well from the outside and drove to the basket extremely well, often employing a running one-handed bank shot that he typically released from somewhere in the 10- to 15-foot range. He also excelled at setting up his man for the backdoor cut and easy lay-in. In addition, Havlicek handled the ball quite well and had superb peripheral vision, allowing him to do an excellent job of distributing the ball to his teammates. In fact, he placed in the league's top 10 in assists a total of seven times. A solid rebounder as well, Havlicek made good use of his body under the basket, averaging more than 7 rebounds per game in five different seasons, including a career-high mark of 9 boards per contest in 1970–71.

The totality of Havlicek's game prompted Bill Russell to say of his longtime teammate in 1974, "He was the best all-around player I ever saw."

Meanwhile, speaking in a 1974 *Sports Illustrated* article written by John Underwood and dedicated to Havlicek, Bobby Knight, who served as a backup on the Ohio State teams for which Havlicek played, stated, "For my money, John is the greatest basketball player who ever lived, bar none. I'm not saying he has more ability; I'm saying he's the greatest player because he can beat you so many ways, and nobody, nobody goes as hard for as long as he does."

Havlicek's ability to push himself beyond the limits of most men proved to be another of his greatest assets. Known for his extraordinary endurance, Havlicek remained in almost perpetual motion, literally running his opponent into submission. New York Knicks forward Bill Bradley commented, "Guarding John Havlicek is the most difficult job I have in a season. Havlicek's every movement has a purpose." Meanwhile, in addressing what should be done to Havlicek after he retired to explain his tireless energy on the court, Portland guard Geoff Petrie suggested, "Take his body apart and see what's in it."

Havlicek's great stamina also helped make him one of the league's top defenders, allowing him to participate in the full-court press Boston liked to employ. In discussing the constant pressure Havlicek put on his man, Milwaukee's Jon McGlocklin remarked, "He's right in your shirt whether you're 5 feet from the basket or 20. He's harder to get shots on than anybody."

In paying homage to Havlicek, legendary Knicks coach Red Holzman said, "On stamina alone, he'd be among the top players who ever played the game. It would've been fair to those who had to play him or those who had to coach against him if he had been blessed only with his inhuman endurance. God had to compound it by making him a good scorer, smart ball-handler, and intelligent defensive player with quickness of mind, hands, and feet."

Although Havlicek's opponents marveled at his astonishing level of endurance, he himself found nothing particularly unusual about it, claiming on one occasion, "Over the years, I have pushed myself mentally, and I have pushed myself physically. A lot of people say, 'John Havlicek never gets tired.' Well, I get tired. It's just a matter of pushing myself. I say to myself, 'He's as tired as I am; who's going to win this mental battle?' It's just a matter of mental toughness."

Known also for his humility, tireless work ethic, and old-fashioned values, Havlicek revealed the quality of his character when he suggested, "If you are honest with yourself and can look into a mirror and believe that you have given 100 percent, you should feel proud. If you cannot, then there is more work to be done."

A tremendous competitor with a great deal of drive and determination, Havlicek had the respect of everyone in the league. Sam Jones said of his former teammate, "He came to play every night. You know, there are some players who'll have this let-down . . . No, Havlicek wanted to win every game."

Jerry West commented, "People look at players, watch them dribble between their legs, and they say, 'There's a superstar.' Well, John Havlicek is a superstar, and most of the others are figments of writers' imagination."

Havlicek's string of consecutive seasons with a scoring average in excess of 20 points per game ended in 1974–75, when he posted a mark of 19.2 points per contest. Nevertheless, by also averaging 5.9 rebounds, 5.3 assists, and 1.3 steals per game, Havlicek earned his sixth All-NBA Second-Team selection and his fourth straight NBA All-Defensive First-Team nomination. He made both those teams again the following season after averaging 17 points, 4.1 rebounds, 3.7 assists, and 1.3 steals per game for a Celtics team that captured the 13th NBA Championship in franchise history.

Havlicek remained in Boston another two years, missing a total of only three games during that time, while posting scoring averages of 17.7 and 16.1 points per contest, before announcing his retirement at the conclusion of the 1977–78 campaign. He ended his career with 26,395 points scored, making him the third-leading scorer in NBA history at the time (he has since slipped to 17th). Havlicek also amassed 8,007 rebounds and 6,114 assists, posted averages of 20.8 points, 6.3 rebounds, and 4.8 assists per game, shot 43.9 percent from the field, and connected on 81.5 percent of his shots from the free-throw line. His total of eight NBA championships as a player ties him for third on the all-time list, behind only longtime teammates Bill Russell (11) and Sam Jones (10).

In summing up Havlicek's career, Bob Ryan wrote in the *Boston Globe*, "There is no argument that he wasn't the greatest sixth man in NBA history. He was an amazing, astonishing player."

Sportscaster Brent Musburger commented, "John Havlicek was as big a star as there was in the NBA at that time. He epitomized what the Boston Celtics were all about."

Unfortunately, Havlicek spent his final years suffering from Parkinson's disease before passing away on April 25, 2019, just 17 days after celebrating his 79th birthday. Upon learning of his passing, Bill Bradley issued a statement that read: "For 10 years, John Havlicek was my toughest opponent in the biggest rivalry in the league. Night after night, he was the epitome of constant motion. He only needed half a step to beat me, which he usually did. He was the quintessential Celtic—unselfish and loyal—and through the players' union, he helped make the game more just by ending the reserve clause. The only thing he loved more than the game was his family. He'll always be with them."

Some four decades earlier, Red Auerbach perhaps paid Havlicek his greatest compliment when he stated during a halftime salute to the longtime Celtic in his final game at Boston Garden, "He epitomizes everything good. If I had a son like John, I'd be the happiest man in the world."

CELTICS CAREER HIGHLIGHTS

Best Season

Havlicek performed brilliantly for the Celtics in 1971–72, leading them to a 56-26 record and earning All-NBA First-Team honors and a fourth-place finish in the league MVP voting by averaging 27.5 points, 8.2 rebounds, 7.5 assists, and a league-leading 45 minutes per game. In addition to topping the circuit in minutes played, Havlicek finished third in scoring and fifth in assists. However, even though Boston's 44-38 showing the previous season prevented Havlicek from garnering any support for league MVP, he actually posted slightly better overall numbers. In addition to establishing career-high marks in scoring (28.9 ppg) and rebounding (9 rpg), "Hondo" again averaged 7.5 assists per contest and led the league with 45.4 minutes played per game. His 28.9 scoring average placed him second in the NBA to league MVP Lew Alcindor (Kareem Abdul-Jabbar), and he also finished fourth in the league in assists. It's an extremely close call, but, all things considered, Havlicek had the finest all-around season of his career in 1970–71.

Memorable Moments / Greatest Performances

Havlicek had the highest scoring game of his rookie season on March 2, 1963, when he tallied 32 points during a 122–117 win over the Knicks.

Havlicek turned in a pair of extraordinary efforts the following season, hitting for a career-high 43 points on December 17, 1963, in leading the Celtics to a 131–114 victory over the Baltimore Bullets, and scoring 40 points during a 119–117 overtime loss to the Cincinnati Royals on February 2, 1964.

Although the Celtics lost to the Bullets by a score of 122–114 on February 3, 1965, Havlicek hit for a season-high 38 points during the contest.

Havlicek turned in another exceptional effort in a losing cause the following season, pouring in 41 points during a 125–115 loss to the Lakers on November 17, 1965.

Havlicek had a pair of huge games just four days apart in late February 1968, scoring 38 points during a 141–137 win over the Seattle SuperSonics on February 24, before leading the Celtics to a 135–110 victory over the San Francisco Warriors four days later by hitting for a season-high 41 points.

Havlicek went on a three-game scoring binge the following season, tallying 36 points during a 117–113 overtime victory over the Philadelphia 76ers on November 30, 1968, leading the Celtics to a 137–115 win over Milwaukee in their next game by scoring 41 points, and then hitting for 36 points during a 132–118 victory over the Detroit Pistons on December 6.

Havlicek turned in a number of memorable performances the following year, with the first of those coming on November 18, 1969, when he led the Celtics to a 120–119 win over Phoenix by scoring 41 points. Particularly hard on Seattle, Havlicek led the Celtics to a pair of victories over the SuperSonics, first hitting for 42 points during a 122–112 triple-overtime win on December 26, 1969, before dropping 39 points against the Sonics

Havlicek ended his playing career as the third-leading scorer in NBA history.

during a 127–117 victory on February 6, 1970. Havlicek also scored 36 points, in leading the Celtics to a 147–124 win over the San Diego Rockets on February 25. Although the Celtics ended up losing their March

8 matchup with the Milwaukee Bucks by a score of 138–134, Havlicek equaled his career high by tallying 43 points during the contest.

Excelling throughout his banner season of 1970–71, Havlicek helped the Celtics gain their first win of the campaign after suffering three defeats by scoring 38 points during a 133–115 victory over Portland on October 18, 1970. Later that month, "Hondo" began an exceptional run during which he topped 30 points six straight times. Highlights of the streak, which lasted from October 30 to November 11, included a pair of 37-point efforts that propelled the Celtics to victories over Philadelphia and Cincinnati, on November 4 and 7, respectively.

Havlicek had another big game on November 30, tallying 38 points during a 109–106 win over the Buffalo Braves. He followed that up by scoring 39 points during a 118–107 victory over Cleveland on December 4, before leading the Celtics to a 101–97 win over Chicago the very next night by hitting for a game-high 38 points.

Havlicek continued his outstanding play in the New Year, scoring 39 points, in leading the Celtics to a 122–114 win over the Phoenix Suns on January 8, 1971, before hitting for another 39 points during a 119–116 loss to Phoenix on February 16.

Nearly as dominant the following season, Havlicek led Boston to a 117–107 win over Houston on December 4, 1971, by scoring 38 points. He also scored 37 points during a 120–114 victory over Portland on January 7, 1972, before tallying 40 points eight days later, in leading the Celtics to a 122–106 win over Atlanta. Havlicek, though, had his biggest game of the year nearly one month later, scoring a season-high 42 points during a 128–123 win over Seattle on February 6. He also scored 41 points on March 12, in leading the Celtics to a 112–109 victory over the Knicks, before following that up with a 38-point performance against Golden State during a 124–110 loss two nights later.

Havlicek scored 40 points for the last time in his career during a 128–110 win over Portland on November 6, 1974.

Averaging 22 points per game in 172 playoff contests, Havlicek proved to be an exceptional postseason performer over the course of his career. En route to posting averages of 23.6 points, 9.1 rebounds, and 4.1 assists per game during the 1966 playoffs, Havlicek averaged 25.4 points per contest against Philadelphia in the Eastern Division Finals, including a 32-point effort in the Game 5 clincher. Although Philadelphia returned the favor the following season, eliminating the Celtics in five games in the Eastern Division Finals, Havlicek performed brilliantly, posting a scoring average of 30 points during the series.

Havlicek excelled as a shooter, passer, and ball-handler.
Photo courtesy of MearsOnlineAuctions.com.

Havlicek excelled once again throughout the 1968 playoffs, averaging
25.9 points, 8.6 rebounds, and 7.5 assists in Boston's 19 postseason contests. Highlights of Havlicek's outstanding postseason included a 35-point
effort against Detroit in Game 4 of the Eastern Division Semifinals, a
35-point performance against Philadelphia in Game 1 of the Eastern Division Finals, and a 40-point performance against the Lakers in Game 6 of
the NBA Finals, which clinched the series for Boston.

Havlicek continued his exceptional postseason play the following
year, averaging 25.4 points, 9.9 rebounds, 5.6 assists, and, amazingly,
47.2 minutes per game, in helping the Celtics capture their 11th NBA

Championship in 13 years. Havlicek's superb postseason run included a 35-point effort against Philadelphia in Game 1 of the Eastern Division Semifinals and 37-, 43-, and 34-point performances against the Lakers in the first three games of the NBA Finals.

Although the Celtics ended up losing to the Knicks in five games in the 1972 Eastern Conference Finals, Havlicek had another brilliant postseason, averaging 27.4 points, 8.4 rebounds, 6.4 assists, and 47 minutes per game in Boston's 11 playoff contests, which included a 43-point effort against Atlanta in Game 2 of the Conference Semifinals.

En route to averaging 27.1 points per game during the 1974 playoffs, Havlicek turned in another 43-point performance, doing so in Game 3 of the Eastern Conference Semifinals, when he led the Celtics to a 120–107 victory over the Buffalo Braves. Although the Celtics lost Game 6 of the NBA Finals to Milwaukee by a score of 102–101 in double-overtime, Havlicek played a tremendous all-around game, pulling down 9 rebounds and scoring 36 points, including 9 in the second OT. "Hondo" ended up being named Finals MVP after averaging 26.4 points, 7.7 rebounds, 4.7 assists, and 1.9 steals per game during the series.

Havlicek, though, turned in the greatest postseason performance of his career in Game 1 of the 1973 Eastern Conference Semifinals (which the Celtics won in six games), when he scored a career-high 54 points, in leading Boston to a 134–109 victory over Atlanta. Havlicek's 54 points represented, at the time, the fourth-highest single-game total in NBA playoff history. Meanwhile, his 24 field goals remain a playoff record.

Nevertheless, the highlight of Havlicek's playoff career is one that reveals his greatness as an all-around player. With the Celtics and 76ers engaged in a battle of attrition in Game 7 of the 1965 Eastern Division Finals, Boston held a slim one-point lead with just five seconds remaining in regulation. Needing only to successfully inbound the ball underneath their own basket to secure a berth in the NBA Finals, the Celtics seemed to have matters under control. However, things took a sudden turn for the worse when Bill Russell's inbounds pass struck a wire suspended from the ceiling that helped support the basket. With the 76ers subsequently given possession of the ball, Hal Greer attempted to make an inbounds pass to Chet Walker, who found himself guarded by Havlicek. Standing with his back to Greer, Havlicek quickly spun, leaped high in the air, and tipped the pass to Sam Jones, leading to Boston announcer Johnny Most making the most famous call of his career:

Greer is putting the ball in play. He gets it out deep and Havlicek steals it! Over to Sam Jones! Havlicek stole the ball! It's all over . . . It's all over! Johnny Havlicek is being mobbed by the fans! It's all over! Johnny Havlicek stole the ball!

Veteran referee Earl Strom, who discussed the play in his memoir, *Calling the Shots*, called Havlicek's reaction one of the greatest plays he ever saw in his 32 years as a professional official.

NOTABLE ACHIEVEMENTS

- Averaged more than 20 points per game eight times, topping 27 points per contest twice.
- Averaged more than 18 points per game four other times.
- Averaged more than 5 assists per game eight times, topping 7 assists per contest twice.
- Averaged 9 rebounds per game in 1970–71.
- Averaged more than 40 minutes per game five times, topping 45 minutes per contest twice.
- Played in 569 out of a possible 573 games from 1966 to 1973, appearing in every Celtics game in 8 of 16 seasons.
- Led NBA in games played and minutes played twice each.
- Finished second in NBA in scoring average once, placing third another time.
- Led Celtics in scoring average eight times, assists six times, and rebounding once.
- Holds Celtics single-season records for most points scored (2,338 in 1970–71); field-goal attempts (1,982 in 1970–71); and minutes played (3,698 in 1971–72).
- Holds Celtics career records for most: points scored (26,395); field-goal attempts (23,930); field goals made (10,513); games played (1,270); and minutes played (46,471).
- Ranks among Celtics career leaders in scoring average (6th); assists (2nd); rebounds (5th); free-throw attempts (2nd); and free throws made (2nd).
- Finished in top five of NBA MVP voting twice.
- 1973–74 NBA Finals MVP.

- Four-time All-NBA First-Team selection (1970–71, 1971–72, 1972–73, and 1973–74).
- Seven-time All-NBA Second-Team selection (1963–64, 1965–66, 1967–68, 1968–69, 1969–70, 1974–75, and 1975–76).
- Five-time NBA All-Defensive First-Team selection (1971–72, 1972–73, 1973–74, 1974–75, and 1975–76).
- Three-time NBA All-Defensive Second-Team selection (1968–69, 1969–70, and 1970–71).
- 13-time NBA All-Star (1966–78).
- Six-time Eastern Division champion (1963, 1964, 1965, 1966, 1968, and 1969).
- Two-time Eastern Conference champion (1974 and 1976).
- Eight-time NBA champion (1963, 1964, 1965, 1966, 1968, 1969, 1974, and 1976).
- Number 17 retired by Celtics.
- Member of NBA's 35th Anniversary Team.
- Member of NBA's 50th Anniversary Team.
- Member of NBA's 75th Anniversary Team.
- Ranked #17 on *SLAM* magazine's Top 50 NBA Players of All-Time list in 2009.
- Inducted into Naismith Memorial Basketball Hall of Fame in 1984.

4

BOB COUSY

When I drew Cousy, I could have fallen to the floor.
—Celtics owner, Walter Brown

One of the NBA's first true superstars, Bob Cousy helped to revolutionize the game of basketball with his superb passing and ball-handling skills. Nicknamed the "Houdini of the Hardwood" for his creativity on the court, which greatly influenced future generations of players, Cousy had no peers when it came to distributing the ball to his teammates. En route to establishing himself as one of the greatest point guards in NBA history, "The Cooz," as he came to be known, dominated his position for nearly a decade, leading the league in assists eight straight times at one point. An extremely proficient scorer as well, Cousy placed in the league's top five in scoring on four separate occasions, posting a scoring average in excess of 20 points per game four times, and averaging at least 18 points per contest for 11 consecutive seasons. Cousy earned one league MVP Award, two All-Star Game MVP trophies, 12 All-NBA selections, and All-Star honors in each of his 13 seasons in Boston, helping the Celtics capture six NBA championships in the process.

Born in New York City on August 9, 1928, just a few weeks after his parents emigrated from France, Robert Joseph Cousy grew up in poverty on Manhattan's East Side, spending much of his youth playing stickball and stealing hubcaps. Introduced to the game of basketball as a teenager after moving with his family to the St. Albans section of Queens, Cousy quickly developed an affinity for the still-growing sport, although he failed to make the Andrew Jackson High School junior varsity squad both times he tried out for the team. As fate would have it, though, an accident helped to pave the way for the youngster's future in basketball. Falling out of a

Bob Cousy earned All-Star honors in each of his 13 NBA seasons.
Photo courtesy of MearsOnlineAuctions.com.

tree at the age of 13, Cousy broke his right arm, forcing him to learn how to shoot and dribble with his other arm. After watching the ambidextrous teenager subsequently compete in local leagues, Andrew Jackson's coach suggested that he try out for the varsity squad, which desperately needed a playmaking guard.

Despite playing just one and a half years of high school ball, Cousy became a much-sought-after commodity following his graduation after winning the city scoring championship as a senior. Turning down scholarship offers from Dartmouth and Boston College, Cousy instead chose to attend the College of the Holy Cross in Worcester, Massachusetts, some 40 miles outside of Boston. Although Cousy initially experienced philosophical differences with his college coach, Alvin "Doggie" Julian, who objected to his flashy on-court maneuvers, which included his patented behind-the-back dribble, twice-around pass, behind-the-back transfer, and pass off the dribble, the talented young man went on to earn All-America honors in each of his final three seasons, leading his team to 26 consecutive victories and a second-place finish in the National Invitation Tournament as a senior.

Yet, in spite of Cousy's outstanding play at the collegiate level, NBA scouts remained uncertain as to whether or not his unconventional style of play would successfully translate to the pro game. In evaluating Cousy prior to the 1950 NBA Draft, one pro scout wrote, "The first time he tries that fancy Dan stuff in this league, they'll cram the ball down his throat." Celtics coach Red Auerbach, who held the rights to the first overall pick in that year's draft, certainly had his doubts, choosing to bypass Cousy in favor of Charlie Share, a 6-foot-11 center from Bowling Green, who ended up having a rather mediocre career for three different teams over the course of nine NBA seasons. In explaining his decision at the time, Auerbach stated, "We need a big man. Little men are a dime a dozen. I'm supposed to win, not go after local yokels."

Subsequently selected by the Tri-Cities Blackhawks with the third overall pick, Cousy found himself being dealt to the Chicago Stags shortly thereafter. But, with the Stags folding before the 1950–51 season got under way, the names of three Chicago players—Cousy, Andy Phillip, and high-scoring guard Max Zaslofsky—were tossed into a hat, from which the owners of the Celtics, Knicks, and Philadelphia Warriors were each asked to make a selection. Revealing years later the disappointment he felt at the time over picking Cousy, Celtics owner Walter Brown said, "When I drew Cousy, I could have fallen to the floor."

Boston's good fortune in winding up with Cousy became apparent his first year in the league, when he earned the first of his 13 consecutive All-Star selections by averaging 15.6 points, 4.9 assists, and a career-high 6.9 rebounds per game, in helping the Celtics improve their record from 22-46 to 39-30. The 23-year-old point guard took his game to the next level the following year, though, when his adroit handling of Boston's offense enabled the Celtics to become the first NBA team to average 100 points per game. With Red Auerbach making better use of his skills by installing more of a fast-break offense, Cousy earned All-NBA First-Team honors for the first of 10 straight times by finishing in the league's top three in both scoring and assists, averaging 21.7 points and 6.7 assists per contest.

Cousy clearly established himself as the NBA's top playmaker the following season, beginning in 1952–53 an eight-year run as the league's assists champion. These are the numbers he compiled over the course of those eight seasons:

SEASON	POINTS PER GAME	REBOUNDS PER GAME	ASSISTS PER GAME
1952–53	19.8	7.7	6.3
1953–54	19.2	7.2	5.5
1954–55	21.2	7.8	6.0
1955–56	18.8	8.9	6.8
1956–57	20.6	7.5	4.8
1957–58	18.0	7.1	5.0
1958–59	20.0	8.6	5.5
1959–60	19.4	9.5	4.7

In addition to leading the NBA in assists each season, Cousy finished second in the league in scoring in both 1953–54 and 1954–55. He also won league MVP honors in 1956–57, when the Celtics captured the first of the six NBA titles they won in his final seven years with the team.

Cousy, who stood 6-foot-1 and weighed 185 pounds, could attribute at least part of his success to his large palms and long fingers that enabled him to manipulate the ball with ease. He also possessed extraordinary peripheral vision, superb instincts, and tremendous basketball intelligence. When driving to the basket, he knew precisely when to dish off, and to whom. Meanwhile, his exceptional dribbling ability enabled him to protect the ball from defenders long enough to allow plays to develop. He also had the ability to hit the outside shot and beat his defender to the hoop off the dribble.

In assessing his former teammate's passing skills, Tom Heinsohn told the *Boston Herald* in 1983: "Cooz was the absolute offensive master. What Russell was on defense, that's what Cousy was on offense: a magician. Once that ball reached his hands, the rest of us just took off, never bothering to look back. We didn't have to. He'd find us. When you got into a position to score, the ball would be there."

Bob Cousy (left), seen here with backcourt mate Bill Sharman, earned league MVP honors in 1956-57, when he led the Celtics to their first NBA championship. Photo courtesy of LegendaryAuctions.com.

In another interview some years later, Heinsohn stated, "He was the ultimate creator. Let me put it in perspective—if you think Magic Johnson could pass, if you think John Stockton can pass, multiply them by 10 and you have Bob Cousy."

Contemporary Bob Davies spoke of his rival's ability as a ball-handler: "Cousy was the best dribbler I played against. Trying to take the ball away from him was very difficult."

Former teammate Ed Macauley discussed Cousy's all-around game in *From Set Shot to Slam Dunk*: "Cousy was a phenomenal passer. In his early

In addition to leading the NBA in assists eight straight times, Cousy finished second in the league in scoring twice.
Photo courtesy of Boston Public Library, Leslie Jones Collection.

days, he had a tendency to try to dominate play at the end of the game. He changed his game as he went along. He developed an outside shot. He had a great running hook shot. He was good on the layup, but he never did develop the jump shot. But he was a phenomenal scorer who made things happen."

Even though Cousy finished "just" third in the league in assists for the first of three straight times in 1960–61, he continued his string of 10 consecutive All-NBA First-Team selections by averaging 18.1 points and 7.7 assists per game. He earned Second-Team honors in each of the next two seasons, posting averages of 15.7 points and 7.8 assists per game in 1961–62 and 13.2 points and 6.8 rebounds per contest in 1962–63 for Celtics teams that won their fourth and fifth straight championships.

Having grown weary of the long seasons, constant travel, significant amount of time spent away from his wife and two daughters, and the manner in which the NBA treated its players, Cousy chose to make the 1962–63 campaign his final season. He retired from the game with career totals of 16,955 points scored, 4,781 rebounds, and 6,945 assists, which represented an NBA record at the time. Cousy averaged 18.4 points, 7.5 assists, and 5.2 rebounds per game over the course of his career.

Following his retirement as an active player, Cousy remained in the game, spending the next six seasons coaching at Boston College before making a brief comeback in 1969 as player-coach of the Cincinnati Royals, for whom he appeared in 7 games. Cousy remained coach of the team after it relocated to the midwest and renamed itself the Kansas City-Omaha Kings, continuing in that capacity until November 1973, when he relinquished his duties after leading the club to an overall record of 141-209 in his four-plus seasons in charge. During that time, the Naismith Memorial Basketball Hall of Fame opened its doors to Cousy, who gained admittance in 1971. Cousy subsequently served as commissioner of the American Soccer League from 1974 to 1979, before returning to the Celtics as a color analyst and, later, as a marketing consultant.

Longtime Celtics owner Walter Brown, who once regretted drawing the now 94-year-old Cousy's name from a hat, said of the legendary guard many years later, "He made basketball in this town. If he had played in New York, he would have been the biggest thing since Babe Ruth. I think he is anyway."

CELTICS CAREER HIGHLIGHTS

Best Season

Cousy performed extremely well for the Celtics over the course of the 1951–52 campaign, earning the first of his 10 straight All-NBA First-Team selections by finishing second in the league with an average of 6.7 assists per game, while also posting a career-high scoring average of 21.7 points per contest that placed him third in the league rankings. He had another outstanding season in 1954–55, continuing his streak of leading the league in assists by averaging 7.8 assists per game, while finishing second in the circuit with a 21.2 scoring average and posting a career-best .397 field-goal shooting percentage. Cousy earned NBA MVP honors in 1956–57, when he averaged 20.6 points and a league-leading 7.5 assists per contest, in helping the Celtics capture their first NBA title. However, it could be argued that rookie Bill Russell had more value to the team, even though he appeared in only the final 48 games of the regular season.

The feeling here is that Cousy actually played his best ball for the Celtics from 1958 to 1960. In addition to leading the league with an average of 8.6 assists per game in 1958–59, Cousy averaged 20 points and 5.5 rebounds per contest. The following season, he topped the circuit with a career-high average of 9.5 assists per game, while also averaging 19.4 points and 4.7 rebounds per contest. Statistically, it's awfully close, especially when it is considered that Cousy shot .384 percent from the field, averaged 2.4 more assists per game than the league runner-up, and finished fourth in the NBA MVP voting each year. In the end, I elected to go with the 1958–59 campaign, since Cousy performed better in the playoffs that year, averaging 19.5 points, 10.8 assists, and 6.9 rebounds in Boston's 11 postseason contests, as opposed to the marks of 15.3 points, 8.9 assists, and 3.7 rebounds per game he posted the following year.

Memorable Moments / Greatest Performances

Despite being known more for his passing and ball-handling skills, the "Houdini of the Hardwood" proved himself to be an extremely effective scorer over the course of his career. Cousy topped the 30-point mark for the first time on January 13, 1951, tallying 34 points during a 97–87 win over the Philadelphia Warriors. He surpassed that total some six weeks later, on February 25, when he scored a season-high 39 points, in leading the Celtics to a 93–83 victory over the Warriors.

Cousy scored his season high in points the following year on February 6, 1952, when he led the Celtics to a 99–88 win over the Syracuse Nationals by tallying 33 points. Although the Celtics lost their best two-out-of-three first-round playoff matchup with the Knicks later that year, Cousy performed brilliantly. After hitting for 31 points in leading the Celtics to a 105–94 win in the series opener, Cousy scored 28 points in Game 2, and 34 points in Boston's heartbreaking 88–87 double-overtime loss in the series finale.

However, Cousy turned in the most memorable playoff performance of his career in Game 2 of the 1953 Eastern Division Semifinals, when he scored 50 points to lead the Celtics to a thrilling 111–105 quadruple-overtime victory over the Syracuse Nationals that earned them a spot in the Eastern Division Finals. Despite nursing an injured leg, Cousy scored 25 points during regulation, before recording 6 of his team's 9 points in the first overtime session, including a clutch free-throw in the closing moments. He then scored all 4 points the Celtics scored in the second overtime period, before tallying another 6 in the third overtime session, among them a dramatic long-range buzzer-beater. Cousy then put the game away in the final overtime period by scoring 9 of Boston's 12 points. Playing a

The "Houdini of the Hardwood" retired as the NBA's all-time assists leader.

total of 66 minutes, Cousy finished the game with 50 points, converting a single-game record 30 of 32 free-throw attempts.

Cousy continued to display his ability to score in the clutch the following season, hitting for 35 points during a 113–108 double-overtime win over the Knicks on December 10, 1953. He also scored 42 points, in leading the Celtics to a 111–110 triple-overtime victory over the Baltimore Bullets on February 22, 1954, before tallying 35 points during a 97–95 double-overtime win over the Philadelphia Warriors on March 12.

Cousy topped 30 points in back-to-back victories over Milwaukee during the early stages of the 1954–55 campaign, leading the Celtics to 118–99 and 101–90 wins over the Hawks by scoring 34 and 31 points, respectively.

Cousy went on a scoring binge later that season, hitting for more than 30 points four straight times in early February 1955, averaging 32.8 points per contest over that stretch of games. Ironically, the Celtics won only two of the four contests. However, he had his biggest game of the year on March 8, when he scored a season-high 40 points during a 112–103 victory over the Philadelphia Warriors.

Cousy began the 1956–57 campaign in style, scoring 35 points during a 115–112 victory over the Knicks in the regular-season opener. He also finished the season strong, averaging 20.2 points and 9.3 rebounds per game during the playoffs, including a huge 31-point effort against St. Louis in Game 4 of the NBA Finals—a 123–118 Boston win that evened the series at two games apiece.

Cousy surpassed the 30-point mark on a number of occasions the following season as well, doing so on December 14, 1957, when he led the Celtics to a 112–94 victory over the Philadelphia Warriors by scoring 36 points. He also tallied 39 points during a 111–101 win over the St. Louis Hawks on January 29, 1958, before hitting for 38 points during a 109–91 victory over the Cincinnati Royals a little over one week later.

Cousy had another big game against Cincinnati on November 15, 1959, when he led the Celtics to a 134–128 win over the Royals by scoring a game-high 38 points. He turned in his finest performance of the season, though, on February 7, 1960, when he scored a regular-season career-high 46 points during a 142–135 loss to the Knicks.

Still, it is for his playmaking ability that Cousy is best remembered, and he certainly did a superb job of distributing the ball to his teammates over the course of his career. On November 24, 1956, he set a new franchise record by collecting 19 assists during a 114–99 win over the Syracuse Nationals. Cousy broke his own team record some two and a half years later, on February 27, 1959, when he assisted on 28 baskets during a 173–139 victory over the Minneapolis Lakers. His 28 assists remain the third-highest single-game total in NBA history. During the game, Cousy also established a still-standing mark by collecting 19 assists in one half. He also scored 31 points during the contest.

Cousy proved to be too much for the Lakers to handle in the playoffs as well, setting an NBA Finals record for a four-game series by amassing 51 assists during Boston's four-game sweep of the Lakers in the 1959 NBA Finals.

Cousy turned in one of his finest all-around performances on December 21, 1960, when he scored 25 points and accumulated 21 assists, in leading the Celtics to a 120–108 win over the St. Louis Hawks. He again performed brilliantly on February 19, 1963, scoring 15 points and collecting 19 assists during a 129–126 victory over the Cincinnati Royals.

Cousy turned in the last dominant performance of his career in Game 7 of the 1963 Eastern Division Finals, when he scored 21 points and assisted on 16 baskets during Boston's series-clinching 142–131 win over Cincinnati.

NOTABLE ACHIEVEMENTS

- Averaged more than 20 points per game four times, topping 18 points per contest six other times.
- Averaged more than 7 assists per game 10 times, surpassing 8 assists per contest three times and 9 assists per game once (9.5 in 1959–60).
- Averaged more than 40 minutes per game twice.
- Led NBA in assists eight straight times.
- Finished second in NBA in assists once, placing third on three other occasions.
- Finished second in NBA in scoring average twice, placing third one other time.
- Led Celtics in assists 13 times and scoring average three times.
- Holds NBA record for most assists in one half (19 vs. Lakers on 2/27/59).
- Holds NBA Finals record for most assists in a four-game series (51 vs. Lakers in 1959).
- Holds Celtics single-game record for most assists (28 vs. Lakers on 2/27/59).
- Holds Celtics career record for most assists (6,945).
- Ranks among Celtics career leaders in points scored (6th); scoring average (10th); field-goal attempts (4th); field goals made (7th); free-throw attempts (3rd); free throws made (3rd); games played (6th); and minutes played (6th).

- Two-time NBA All-Star Game MVP (1954 and 1957).
- 1956–57 NBA MVP.
- 10-time All-NBA First-Team selection (1951–52 and 1960–61).
- Two-time All-NBA Second-Team selection (1961–62 and 1962–63).
- 13-time NBA All-Star (1951–63).
- Seven-time Eastern Division champion (1957–63).
- Six-time NBA champion (1957, 1959, 1960, 1961, 1962, and 1963).
- Number 14 retired by Celtics.
- Member of NBA's 25th Anniversary Team.
- Member of NBA's 35th Anniversary Team.
- Member of NBA's 50th Anniversary Team.
- Member of NBA's 75th Anniversary Team.
- Inducted into Naismith Memorial Basketball Hall of Fame in 1971.

5

PAUL PIERCE

He's a heckuva player. If you play for one team as long as he has,
with what he's been able to accomplish, then you're going to get
the rewards, and that's basically what he's done; and rightfully so.
I mean, he went through some tough times when he didn't have as
good a team, and he just kept on getting it himself. There weren't any
complaints at all. You've got to admire a guy that way.

—Former Celtics forward Paul Silas

An exceptional scorer, strong defender, and outstanding team leader, Paul Pierce spent 15 seasons in Boston, establishing himself during that time as one of the greatest players in Celtics history. A 10-time NBA All-Star and four-time All-NBA selection, Pierce averaged more than 20 points per game eight times, topping 25 points per contest on five separate occasions, en route to compiling the second-highest scoring total in franchise history. Pierce also did a solid job on the boards and on defense, amassing more steals over the course of his career than any other Celtics player. Boston's unquestioned leader his last several seasons in Beantown, Pierce served as the driving force behind the team's successful run to the NBA championship in 2007–08, when, after taking center stage for much of his career, he put aside his ego, welcomed fellow superstars Kevin Garnett and Ray Allen, and captained his team to the league's best record during the regular season. Pierce then outplayed both LeBron James and Kobe Bryant during the playoffs, en route to being named NBA Finals MVP.

Born in Oakland, California on October 13, 1977, Paul Anthony Pierce spent most of his youth in Inglewood, California, where he grew up rooting for the Los Angeles Lakers. A huge fan of college basketball as well,

Paul Pierce earned 10 All-Star selections during his time in Boston.
Photo courtesy of Keith Allison.

Pierce dreamed of one day starring in the Final Four, before moving on to the NBA, where he fantasized about playing for his beloved Lakers.

Somewhat overweight as a teenager, Pierce worked tirelessly to improve his speed and stamina after being cut from Inglewood High School's varsity basketball team as a freshman and sophomore. Taller and thinner by his junior year, Pierce spent his last two seasons at Inglewood starring for the Sentinels, earning McDonald's All-American and 1995 California Player of the Year honors as a senior by averaging 24.5 points, 11.5 rebounds, and 4 assists per game.

After being courted by several major colleges following his graduation from Inglewood, Pierce ultimately elected to leave Southern California, spurning UCLA for the University of Kansas. Pierce ended up spending three seasons at Kansas playing for Hall of Fame coach Roy Williams, during which time he averaged 16.4 points and 6.3 rebounds per contest. A First-Team All-America selection as a junior, Pierce also earned MVP honors in the Big 12 Conference Tournament in both his sophomore and junior years. Choosing to turn pro with one year of college eligibility still remaining, Pierce entered the 1998 NBA Draft, where the Boston Celtics selected him with the 10th overall pick.

Supremely confident in his own abilities, Pierce entered the NBA with a huge chip on his shoulder, believing that he should have been selected much earlier in the draft. In fact, he invented a shooting drill during which he moved to different points along the perimeter, all the while attempting to swish shots from long range. Each time Pierce released the ball, he called out the name of a player that had been picked ahead of him.

Despite having his rookie campaign shortened to 50 games by a labor disagreement, Pierce played well his first year in the league, posting averages of 16.5 points and 6.4 rebounds per contest, en route to earning NBA All-Rookie First-Team honors. He followed that up by averaging 19.5 points, 5.4 rebounds, and a team-leading 2.1 steals per game in 1999–2000, placing second in the league in the last category in the process. Yet, just as Pierce appeared to be on the verge of joining the NBA's elite, both his career and life nearly ended prematurely in September 2000 when three men attacked him at a Boston nightclub. Saved from further damage by the heavy leather jacket that helped protect him, Pierce nevertheless suffered numerous injuries at the hands of his assailants, who stabbed him multiple times in the face and neck.

Following his life-threatening ordeal, Pierce took his game to the next level in 2000–01, finishing eighth in the NBA with a scoring average of 25.3 points per game while also averaging 6.4 rebounds, 3.1 assists, and 1.7 steals per contest. Still, the Celtics continued to struggle as a team, posting a losing record for the eighth consecutive season, even though Pierce combined with Antoine Walker to give them arguably the league's top forward tandem.

The duo of Pierce and Walker finally managed to lead Boston to a winning record the following season, with the Celtics posting a mark of 49-33 that earned them their first playoff berth in seven years. Surpassing Walker as the team's top offensive threat and best all-around player, Pierce established new career highs in scoring (26.1 ppg), rebounding (6.9 rpg), and assists (3.2 apg), earning in the process the first of five straight All-Star selections and All-NBA Third-Team honors for the first of three times. Pierce continued to build on the success he experienced the previous two years in subsequent seasons, posting some of the best numbers of his career over the course of the next five campaigns:

SEASON	POINTS PER GAME	REBOUNDS PER GAME	ASSISTS PER GAME
2002–03	25.9	7.3	4.4
2003–04	23.0	6.5	5.1
2004–05	21.6	6.6	4.2
2005–06	26.8	6.7	4.7
2006–07	25.0	5.9	4.1

Although the Celtics experienced very little success as a team those five seasons, compiling a winning record just twice and failing to advance beyond the second round of the playoffs in any single campaign, Pierce's star shone brightly, with the 6-foot-7, 235-pound forward developing a reputation as one of the league's best players and top clutch performers. In addition to finishing among the NBA's leading scorers in three of those seasons, Pierce twice ranked among the league leaders in steals, earning four more All-Star selections and another All-NBA Third-Team nomination.

Capable of taking over a game on offense, Pierce, in his youth, possessed a varied offensive arsenal that included an accurate long-range jumper, an assortment of twisting, mid-range shots, and slashing drives to the basket that made him a frequent visitor to the foul line. An extremely underrated defender as well, Pierce had the quickness to stay with most of the league's speedier forwards and the strength to battle his opponents down low and under the basket. A very hard worker, Pierce also did his due diligence off the court by constantly studying films of his opponents.

Raef LaFrentz, who spent three seasons playing alongside Pierce in Boston, praised his former teammate by saying, "There is not much that can stop him. He can really do some great things."

Phil Jackson, who spent several years devising defensive schemes against Pierce as head coach of the Lakers, acknowledged the truth of LaFrentz's statement, noting, "His matchup is difficult. He's strong. He's able to make some step-throughs or some pivots that get him by our defenders."

Kobe Bryant added, "I enjoy watching him play, and I enjoy playing against him. He's fantastic."

Still, in spite of his excellence as an all-around player, Pierce often clashed with Boston head coach Doc Rivers, who assumed control of the team in 2004. With the Celtics instituting a youth movement shortly after Rivers took over, Pierce angered his coach by telling the *Boston Globe* that he considered his situation in Boston to be a classic example of "a great player on a bad team." Yet, in spite of their philosophical differences, Rivers remained convinced that Pierce had the ability to be an exceptional team player, continuing to express to him his desire to have him share the ball with his teammates and bring a more positive outlook to the court.

With the Celtics coming off a 2006–07 campaign in which they compiled a record of just 24-58, the situation in Boston changed dramatically when the team acquired veteran stars Kevin Garnett and Ray Allen during the subsequent off-season. Surrounded by other talented players for the first time in years, Pierce, who had missed more than 30 games the previous season with a stress fracture in his foot, quickly displayed a willingness to share the spotlight with his new teammates. Choosing to subjugate his own game for the betterment of his team, the Celtics' captain took it upon himself to assume a less prominent role on offense in 2007–08. Yet, he still led the squad with a scoring average of 19.6 points per game while also averaging 5.1 rebounds and 4.5 assists per contest, earning in the process his third All-NBA Third-Team selection and the first of another five consecutive All-Star nominations. Furthermore, Pierce did an excellent job of containing his man on defense, performing particularly well during the playoffs, when he blanketed both LeBron James and Kobe Bryant, en route to earning NBA Finals MVP honors.

Former Celtics forward Paul Silas expressed his admiration for the manner in which Pierce conducted himself during his time in Boston prior to winning the NBA title, stating, "He's a heckuva player. If you play for one team as long as he has, with what he's been able to accomplish, then you're going to get the rewards, and that's basically what he's done; and rightfully so. I mean, he went through some tough times when he didn't have as good a team, and he just kept on getting it himself. There weren't any complaints at all. You've got to admire a guy that way."

Pierce earned Finals MVP honors in 2008, when he led the Celtics to the NBA championship. Photo courtesy of Keith Allison.

Pierce had another outstanding season for the Celtics in 2008–09, earning his lone All-NBA Second-Team selection and a seventh-place finish in the league MVP voting by posting averages of 20.5 points, 5.6 rebounds, and 3.6 assists per game for a Boston team that finished first in the Atlantic Division with a record of 62-20 before losing to the Orlando Magic in seven games in the Eastern Conference Semifinals. He followed that up with four more productive seasons in Boston, averaging better than 18 points per game each year, and leading the Celtics back to the NBA Finals in 2010, when they lost to the Los Angeles Lakers in seven games.

After the 35-year-old Pierce expressed an interest in leaving Boston following the departure of Doc Rivers as head coach at the end of the 2012–13 campaign, the Celtics included him in a nine-player trade they completed with the Nets on July 12, 2013, that also sent Kevin Garnett, Jason Terry, and D. J. White to Brooklyn, in exchange for five players and three future first-round draft picks. Pierce left Boston with career totals of 24,021 points scored, 6,651 rebounds, 4,305 assists, and a franchise-record 1,583 steals. He also shot 44.7 percent from the field and 80.6 percent from the free-throw line during his time in Beantown, while averaging 21.8 points, 6.0 rebounds, 3.9 assists, and 1.4 steals per game.

Pierce spent just one season in Brooklyn, averaging only 13.5 points per contest in 2013–14 before signing with the Washington Wizards as a free agent during the subsequent off-season. After averaging 11.9 points per game as a starter for the Wizards in 2014–15, Pierce assumed a backup role with the Los Angeles Clippers the next two seasons before retiring following the conclusion of the 2016–17 campaign with career totals of 26,397 points scored, 7,527 rebounds, 4,708 assists, and 1,752 steals. Over the course of 19 NBA seasons, Pierce averaged 19.7 points, 5.6 rebounds, 3.5 assists, and 1.3 steals per contest.

CELTICS CAREER HIGHLIGHTS

Best Season

Although Pierce earned his lone All-NBA Second-Team selection and top-10 finish in the league MVP voting in 2008–09, he posted significantly better numbers for the Celtics in several other seasons. Pierce performed exceptionally well in 2001–02, when, in addition to averaging 6.9 rebounds and 3.2 assists per game, he placed among the league leaders with averages of 26.1 points and 1.9 steals per contest, while also topping the circuit in total points scored (2,144). Pierce followed that up by averaging 25.9 points, 4.4 assists, 1.8 steals, and a career-high 7.3 rebounds per game in 2002–03. However, the feeling here is that Pierce had his finest all-around season for the Celtics in 2005–06, when he averaged a career-high 26.8 points per game, while also averaging 6.7 rebounds, 4.7 assists, and 1.4

steals per contest. Pierce also shot 47.1 percent from the field, which far surpassed the marks of 44.2 percent and 41.6 percent he posted the other two seasons.

Memorable Moments / Greatest Performances

An underrated defender, Pierce tied Larry Bird's franchise record on December 3, 1999, when he recorded 9 steals during a 96–84 win over the Miami Heat. He also scored 26 points during the contest.

Pierce turned in another outstanding all-around effort some six weeks later, on January 17, 2000, when he scored 34 points and recorded 5 steals, in leading the Celtics to a 105–101 victory over the Washington Wizards.

Nearly two months later, on March 13, 2000, Pierce hit for a season-high 38 points during a 124–115 loss to the Detroit Pistons.

Pierce topped the 40-point mark 21 times during his career, doing so a total of 8 times in 2000–01 alone. He accomplished the feat for the first time on November 24, 2000, when he led the Celtics to a 103–98 overtime win over Orlando by tallying 41 points. Pierce topped that figure later in the season, on January 15, 2001, scoring 42 points during a 107–102 victory over the Minnesota Timberwolves. He subsequently hit for 40 points during a 102–95 win over the Detroit Pistons on February 2, 2001, before beginning an exceptional stretch of games in mid-March that saw him surpass the 40-point mark four times over a two-week period. Pierce began his extraordinary run by tallying 42 points during a 112–107 loss to the Lakers on March 13. He followed that up two days later by hitting for 42 points, in leading the Celtics to a 105–101 victory over Phoenix. Pierce then scored 44 points during a 113–98 win over the Nets on March 22, before tallying another 41 points during a 115–112 overtime victory over Atlanta on March 27. Pierce topped the 40-point mark for the final time that season on April 11, when he hit for 41 points during a 102–97 loss to the Miami Heat.

Pierce established a new career high the following season, when he scored 48 points, in leading the Celtics to a 105–98 overtime win over the Nets on December 1, 2001.

Nearly two weeks later, on December 14, 2001, Pierce scored 38 points and pulled down 12 rebounds during a 107–101 victory over the Chicago Bulls.

Pierce turned in one of his finest all-around performances of the campaign on December 29, 2001, when he led the Celtics to a 105–103

Pierce averaged more than 25 points per game five times for the Celtics.
Photo courtesy of Keith Allison.

overtime win over the Los Angeles Clippers by scoring 35 points, collecting 10 rebounds, and assisting on 6 baskets.

Although the Celtics lost their January 18, 2002, matchup with the Houston Rockets by a score of 104–101, Pierce had another tremendous all-around game, tallying 38 points, pulling down 11 rebounds, and recording 6 assists.

Pierce also performed extremely well against Washington on March 11, 2002, leading the Celtics to a 104–99 victory by scoring 37 points and collecting 9 rebounds.

Pierce nearly equaled his then-career-high scoring total the following season, when, on November 2, 2002, he hit for 46 points during a 117–107 win over the Knicks.

Nine days later, on November 11, 2002, Pierce recorded 35 points, 7 rebounds, 9 assists, 3 steals, and 3 blocked shots, in leading the Celtics to a 112–95 victory over the Utah Jazz.

Pierce continued his outstanding month of November on the 22nd, when he led the Celtics to a 105–98 double-overtime win over the Atlanta Hawks by scoring 36 points and pulling down 14 rebounds.

Pierce had another big game on December 20, 2002, when he tallied 42 points and collected 14 rebounds during a 108–99 victory over the Minnesota Timberwolves.

Exactly one month later, on January 20, 2003, Pierce led the Celtics to a 100–99 win over the Philadelphia 76ers by hitting for a game-high 40 points.

Pierce followed that up four days later by scoring 45 points and collecting 10 rebounds during a 77–58 victory over the Denver Nuggets.

Pierce recorded the first triple-double of his career in his very next game, on January 26, 2003, when he scored 27 points, pulled down 13 rebounds, and assisted on 13 baskets, in leading the Celtics to a 91–83 win over the Orlando Magic.

Pierce also turned in a pair of exceptional efforts the following month, scoring 36 points during a 100–92 victory over Portland on February 13, 2003, before hitting for 35 points, in leading the Celtics to a 92–84 win over the Clippers just two days later.

Pierce had his last big game of the season on April 4, 2003, when he scored 40 points during a 93–92 loss to the Sacramento Kings.

Pierce hit for a season-high 41 points during a 105–98 victory over the Cleveland Cavaliers on December 13, 2003.

Pierce had another big game later that season, on March 13, 2004, when he led the Celtics to a 111–102 win over the Washington Wizards by scoring 37 points and collecting 12 rebounds.

Almost exactly one year later, on March 11, 2005, Pierce scored a season-high 38 points and pulled down 12 rebounds during a 115–113 double-overtime victory over the Detroit Pistons.

Pierce twice scored 43 points in defeat the following season, reaching that mark for the first time during a 106–102 loss to the Chicago Bulls on December 2, 2005, before again hitting for 43 points during a 118–111 loss to the Seattle SuperSonics on December 26.

The Celtics wasted another strong outing by Pierce on February 1, 2006, when they lost to the Phoenix Suns by a score of 102–94, even though their best player tallied 40 points during the contest.

Shortly thereafter, Pierce went on a 14-game tear during which he scored at least 30 points 13 times. Although the Celtics lost their February 15, 2006, matchup with Cleveland by a score of 113–109 in double-overtime, Pierce hit for a career-high 50 points during the contest. Other highlights of the scoring spree included a 37-point outing against Portland on February 24 and a 39-point explosion against the Lakers on February 26, both of which led to Celtics victories. Pierce also scored 38 points during a 103–96 loss to Miami on March 1, before tallying 31 points, collecting 12 rebounds, and assisting on 10 baskets during a 104–101 win over Philadelphia on March 8. The latter contest featured an off-balance buzzer-beater by Pierce that proved to be the game-winner.

Although the Celtics lost their 2006–07 regular-season opener to the New Orleans / Oklahoma City Hornets by a score of 91–87, Pierce had a big game, scoring 19 points and pulling down a career-high 19 rebounds.

Pierce also performed extremely well on November 8, 2006, when he led the Celtics to a 110–108 overtime victory over the Charlotte Bobcats by tallying 35 points and collecting 13 rebounds.

Pierce turned in another outstanding effort on November 18, 2006, when he scored 39 points during a 122–118 win over the Knicks.

Nearly one month later, on December 15, 2006, Pierce led the Celtics to a 119–114 victory over the Denver Nuggets by scoring 38 points, recording 8 rebounds, and assisting on 9 baskets.

The following year, Pierce scored a season-high 37 points during a 104–96 win over the Seattle SuperSonics on December 27, 2007.

Outstanding performances the following season included a 39-point effort against Toronto on January 12, 2009, a 36-point outing against Minnesota on February 1, 2009, and a 36-point effort against Miami on March 18, 2009, all of which led to Boston victories.

Although the Celtics lost their April 17, 2012, matchup with the Knicks by a score of 118–110, Pierce hit for 43 points during the contest.

Pierce reached the 40-point mark for the last time on December 19, 2012, when he led the Celtics to a 103–91 victory over Cleveland by scoring 40 points.

Pierce led the Celtics in scoring 13 times. Photo courtesy of Keith Allison.

Later that season, on February 10, 2013, Pierce turned in an exceptional all-around effort, leading the Celtics to a 118–114 triple-overtime win over Denver by scoring 27 points, pulling down 14 rebounds, and collecting 14 assists.

Displaying an ability to perform well under pressure throughout his career, Pierce had a number of memorable postseason games as a member of the Celtics, with the first of those coming in the first round of the 2002 playoffs, when he scored 46 points during Boston's series-clinching 120–87 Game 5 victory over the Philadelphia 76ers.

Although the Celtics failed to make it past the second round of the postseason tournament the following year, losing to the New Jersey Nets in four straight games in the Eastern Conference Semifinals, Pierce had a tremendous postseason, averaging 27.1 points, 9 rebounds, and 6.7 assists in Boston's 10 playoff games. Particularly effective during Boston's six-game victory over Indiana in the opening round, Pierce led the Celtics to a 103–100 win in Game 1 by scoring 40 points, pulling down 11 rebounds, and recording 4 steals. He again performed brilliantly in Game 4, leading the Celtics to a 102–92 win by scoring 37 points, collecting 10 rebounds, and assisting on 7 baskets.

Yet, even though Pierce averaged "only" 19.7 points per game during the 2008 playoffs, he will always be remembered most fondly by Boston fans for the manner in which he led the Celtics to their first NBA title in more than two decades. Pierce's first heroic performance came against LeBron James and the Cleveland Cavaliers in Game 7 of the Eastern Conference Semifinals, when he led the Celtics to a 97–92 win by scoring 41 points. Pierce then established himself as the club's undisputed leader prior to Game 6 of the Eastern Conference Finals, when he announced that the Celtics had no intention of returning to Boston for a potential Game 7, and that they planned to close out the series in Auburn Hills. He subsequently backed up his words by leading the Celtics to a memorable fourth-quarter comeback against the Detroit Pistons during which they erased a double-digit deficit, en route to recording an 89–81 victory that earned them a spot in the NBA Finals. Pierce finished the game with 27 points and 8 rebounds.

Pierce subsequently reached legendary status against the Lakers in Game 1 of the NBA Finals, when, after twisting his knee and being helped off the court by two teammates during the early stages of the contest, he returned to the fray at the start of the second half to hit three consecutive three-pointers from virtually the same spot on the court. Playing through pain and swelling, Pierce ended up leading the Celtics to a 98–88 win by scoring 22 points, with 15 of those coming in the second half.

Pierce continued to create a permanent place for himself in Celtics lore in Game 4, when he helped his team overcome an 18-point halftime deficit by taking upon himself the task of guarding Kobe Bryant. With Pierce playing stifling defense on Bryant, the Celtics came back to win the game by a score of 97–91, taking in the process a commanding three-games-to-one lead in the series. Continuing to guard Bryant in the next two contests as well, Pierce outscored his opponent, 55 to 47, earning in the process NBA Finals MVP honors.

NOTABLE ACHIEVEMENTS

- Averaged more than 20 points per game 8 times, topping 25 points per contest on five occasions.
- Averaged more than 5 assists per game once (5.1 in 2003–04).
- Averaged more than 2 steals per game once (2.1 in 1999–2000).
- Averaged more than 40 minutes per game once.
- Led NBA in total points scored once (2,144 in 2001–02).
- Finished in top five in NBA in scoring average three times.
- Finished second in NBA in steals per game once.
- Led Celtics in scoring average 13 times; rebounding twice; and assists twice.
- Scored 50 points vs. Cleveland on February 15, 2006.
- One of only four players in Celtics history to score as many as 50 points in one game (50 vs. Cleveland on 2/15/06).
- Holds Celtics records for most free throws made in a season (627 in 2005–06); game (20 vs. New York on 11/02/02); and half (15 vs. Miami on 3/01/06).
- Holds share of Celtics single-game record for most steals (9 vs. Miami on 12/03/99).
- Holds Celtics record for highest scoring average in one month (33.5 ppg in February 2006).
- Holds Celtics career records for most steals (1,583); three-point field goals made (1,823); most free-throw attempts (7,979); and most free throws made (6,434).
- Ranks among Celtics career leaders in: scoring average (4th); points scored (2nd); assists (5th); rebounds (7th); blocked shots (4th); field-goal attempts (2nd); field goals made (3rd); games played (3rd); and minutes played (3rd).
- 17-time NBA Player of the Week.
- Four-time NBA Player of the Month.
- 1998–99 NBA All-Rookie First-Team selection.
- 2007–08 NBA Finals MVP.
- 2008–09 All-NBA Second-Team selection.
- Three-time All-NBA Third-Team selection (2001–02, 2002–03, and 2007–08).
- 10-time NBA All-Star (2002–06 and 2008–12).
- Two-time Eastern Conference champion (2007–08 and 2009–10).
- 2007–08 NBA champion.
- Number 34 retired by Celtics.
- Member of NBA's 75th Anniversary Team.
- Inducted into Naismith Memorial Basketball Hall of Fame in 2021.

6

DAVE COWENS

There is no player with greater desire than Dave Cowens.
—CBS analyst and Hall of Fame forward Rick Barry

Identified by longtime Boston sportswriter Bob Ryan as one of four pivotal players in Celtics history (the other three being Bob Cousy, Bill Russell, and Larry Bird), Dave Cowens bridged the gap between the Russell and Bird eras, leading the Celtics to a pair of NBA titles along the way. Playing with an intensity few others in the history of the game could match, the 6-foot-9, 230-pound Cowens compensated for his lack of size at the center position by outhustling and outworking his larger opponents. Displaying tremendous tenacity and determination, Cowens ran from one end of the court to the other, setting picks, blocking shots, participating in full-court presses, and diving after loose balls. Paul Silas, who spent four seasons playing alongside Cowens in the Boston frontcourt, described his initial reaction to his teammate thusly: "I thought he was a wild man. I'd never seen anybody with that much talent play that aggressively."

Though somewhat undersized in an era of seven-foot centers, Cowens did indeed possess the kind of talent that helped make him one of the elite players at his position. Blessed with excellent offensive skills, outstanding quickness, leaping ability, and strength, and a will second-to-none, Cowens more than held his own against the league's other big men. En route to earning one league MVP award, three All-NBA nominations, and eight All-Star selections, Cowens averaged more than 20 points per game twice, topping the 18-point mark four other times. He also averaged at least 40 minutes of playing time per game five times, 4 assists per contest six times, and 15 rebounds per game on five separate occasions, placing in the league's top three in the last category a total of five times. A solid defender as well,

Cowens earned three NBA All-Defensive Team selections over the course of his career. In the end, Cowens' talent, desire, spirit, and will to excel helped lead the Celtics to five consecutive Atlantic Division titles and two NBA championships, earning him in the process spots on the NBA's 50th and 75th Anniversary Teams and a place in the Naismith Memorial Basketball Hall of Fame.

Born in Newport, Kentucky, on October 25, 1948, David William Cowens attended Newport Catholic High School, where a five-inch growth spurt between his sophomore and junior years helped him to become a star on the basketball court. Despite being heavily recruited by nearly every college in the Ohio Valley Conference following his graduation from Newport, Cowens felt snubbed when legendary Kentucky coach Adolph Rupp chose not to pursue him. Electing to leave his home state as a result, Cowens enrolled at Florida State University, a school not previously known for its basketball program.

After forming a bond with FSU's head coach, Hugh Durham, who promised him a starting spot as a sophomore, Cowens gradually helped turn the Seminoles into a national power, improving their record over the course of his three seasons on the team from 11-15, to 18-8, and, finally, to 23-3. In describing Cowens's play when he first joined the squad, coach Durham later said, "He wasn't a great scorer. But he could rebound, and that's what we needed."

Cowens ended up amassing a total of 1,340 rebounds during his three varsity seasons in Tallahassee, finishing seventh in the nation in that category as a senior. He also developed into a solid scorer over time, averaging 19 points per game during his collegiate career, while shooting nearly 52 percent from the field. Cowens's stellar all-around play, which also included blocking shots, diving for loose balls, and filling the lane on the fast break, earned him *Sporting News* Second-Team All-America honors in his senior year.

Commenting years later on the impression Cowens made on him the first time he saw him play, Celtics general manager Red Auerbach stated, "He scared me the first time I saw him. He was so good that I kept hoping he'd make a mistake."

In an effort to discourage other teams from drafting Cowens before the Celtics had an opportunity to do so, Auerbach left a Seminoles game early when scouting him for Boston, presumably because the redheaded center failed to make a particularly favorable impression on him. Auerbach's psychological ploy ended up working, as Bob Lanier, Rudy Tomjanovich, and Pete Maravich all came off the board before the Celtics selected Cowens

Dave Cowens led the Celtics to two NBA titles with his hustle and determination. Photo courtesy of LegendaryAuctions.com.

with the fourth overall pick of the 1970 NBA Draft. In explaining his selection of Cowens at the time, Auerbach said, "He's a very dedicated kid. A dedicated kid isn't unheard of, but there aren't as many around as we would like. But our problem with Cowens is telling him when to lay off. He does too much."

Not originally expected to play center when he first arrived in Boston, Cowens initially found himself penciled in at the power forward position, with fellow rookie, Garfield Smith, slated to play center. In fact, former Celtics coach Bill Fitch once said that Cowens could have developed into the best power forward in history. But with Smith failing to impress in training camp, and with Cowens needing the challenge of excelling against men who typically stood at least two or three inches taller than himself, Celtics coach Tom Heinsohn moved the man who became known as "Big Red" into the pivot and devised a system in which Cowens functioned as a "point-center," drawing his counterpart away from the basket and distributing the ball to his teammates from the top of the key. Commenting on the strategy he employed, Heinsohn suggested, "Letting him play outside some on the offensive end was our best chance. Defensively, he battled."

Embracing the role of undersized center, Cowens had an outstanding rookie season, averaging 17 points and 15 rebounds per game, en route to earning the distinction of being named NBA Co-Rookie of the Year—an honor he shared with Portland guard Geoff Petrie. Cowens improved upon his performance the following season, helping the Celtics win the first of their five consecutive Atlantic Division titles, and earning All-Star honors for the first of seven straight times by averaging 18.8 points and 15.2 rebounds per contest, while hitting on 48.4 percent of his shots from the field, which represented the second-highest mark of his career.

Cowens's exceptional play his first two seasons made a strong impression on several of his opponents, with New York Knicks center Willis Reed later saying, "Dave was one of my favorite guys to play against. He was very quick, fast, strong, smart, skilled, and a great competitor."

Meanwhile, Detroit Pistons guard Dave Bing stated, "When he first came into the league, I didn't think Cowens would last that long, diving around like that. Big men didn't do those things."

Diving after loose balls, setting picks, making heady passes, participating in full-court presses, and muscling his way close to the basket for tip-ins, Cowens made a general nuisance of himself to opposing teams. He also had a soft touch on his left-handed jump shot, a reliable hook, and superb timing for rebounds. And, in spite of his lack of size, Cowens's ability to run the floor and operate on the perimeter often allowed him to frustrate some of the league's most outstanding big men, such as Kareem Abdul-Jabbar, Wilt Chamberlain, and Bob Lanier. In fact, at one point, Cowens had a personal 10-game winning streak against Abdul-Jabbar.

Cowens posted the best numbers of his young career in 1972–73, concluding the campaign with averages of 20.5 points, 16.2 rebounds, and 4.1 assists per game, en route to leading the Celtics to a league-best 68-14 record during the regular season. His fabulous performance earned him league MVP honors and the first of his three All-NBA Second-Team selections (Kareem Abdul-Jabbar earned First-Team honors). Cowens followed that up by averaging 19 points, 15.7 rebounds, and 4.4 assists per game in 1973–74, finishing second in the league in rebounding for the first of three straight times in the process. With the Celtics capturing their third consecutive division title en route to winning the NBA Championship, Cowens earned a top-five finish in the league MVP voting, placing fourth in the balloting.

Despite missing 15 games with a broken foot, Cowens had another big year in 1974–75, averaging 20.4 points, 14.7 rebounds, 4.6 assists, and 1.3 steals per game, en route to earning a runner-up finish to Buffalo's Bob McAdoo in the league MVP voting, All-NBA Second-Team honors, and a spot on the NBA's All-Defensive Second Team. He continued to perform exceptionally well the following year, leading the Celtics to another NBA title by averaging 19 points and 16 rebounds per contest. Cowens's spirited play earned him a third-place finish in the MVP balloting, the last of his three All-NBA Second-Team selections, and his lone NBA All-Defensive First-Team nomination. While watching Cowens go all out during the 1976 NBA Finals, CBS analyst and Hall of Fame forward Rick Barry commented, "There is no player with greater desire than Dave Cowens."

Unfortunately, the intensity with which Cowens played the game began to take its toll on him by the conclusion of the 1975–76 campaign, prompting him to take a two-month leave of absence from the team at the start of the following season. Later explaining that he was "suffering from burnout," Cowens spent those two months driving a cab before returning to the Celtics for the final 50 games, during which time he averaged 16.4 points and 13.9 rebounds per contest—the lowest marks of his career to that point.

Rejuvenated somewhat by the start of the 1977–78 season, Cowens earned his seventh-consecutive All-Star selection by averaging 18.6 points, 14 rebounds, and 4.6 assists per game, while shooting a career-best 49 percent from the field. Serving as Boston's player-coach for most of the ensuing campaign, Cowens labored through a season that saw him average 16.6 points and 9.6 rebounds per game for a Celtics team that finished just 29-53. Although the arrival of Larry Bird dramatically improved the fortunes of the ball club in 1979–80, Cowens continued to lose his thirst for the game, averaging just 14.2 points and 8.1 rebounds over 66 contests.

Citing a diminished enthusiasm for the game, Cowens elected to retire during training camp the following year, abruptly making his announcement on the team bus one afternoon. Enlisting one of the Boston beat

Cowens earned a top-five finish in the league MVP voting four straight times during the 1970s, winning the award in 1972–73.
Photo courtesy of Robert Kingsbury through Wikipedia.

writers to edit the statement he had written, Cowens told his teammates, "I wouldn't feel guilty about the amount of money I would earn under these circumstances if I thought I could play even as well as I did last year. But I can't."

Looking back years later on the timing of his announcement, Cowens suggested, "That was a little too much, probably. I was almost at the point where I didn't care anymore, and I hated that feeling. I figured there had to be something else out there for me because I believed this wasn't getting it done for me."

After having his number 18 retired by the Celtics on February 8, 1981, Cowens attempted a brief comeback with the Milwaukee Bucks nearly two years later, appearing in 40 games with them over the second half of the 1982–83 campaign. However, he failed to display the same level of intensity that had become his trademark earlier in his career, prompting him to retire for good at the end of the year. Cowens ended his career with 13,516 points scored, 10,444 rebounds, and 2,910 assists, averages of 17.6 points, 13.6 rebounds, and 3.8 assists per game, a field-goal shooting percentage of 46.0, and a free-throw shooting percentage of 78.3. Cowens's rebounding average of 13.6 boards per contest ranks as the eighth-highest in NBA history. In his years with the Celtics, he scored 13,192 points, pulled down 10,170 rebounds, assisted on 2,828 baskets, and averaged 18.2 points, 14 rebounds, and 3.9 assists per contest.

Following his playing days, Cowens became the athletic director for Regis College, a liberal arts college for women in the Boston area. He subsequently served as the chairman / executive director of the New England Sports Museum, before eventually assisting in the development of the NBA Retired Players' Association.

Longing to return to the sport he loved, Cowens spent one season in the mid-1980s coaching the Continental Basketball Association's Bay State Bombardiers, before joining the coaching staff of the San Antonio Spurs as an assistant in 1994. After two years in San Antonio, Cowens moved on to Charlotte, where he spent three seasons serving as head coach of the Charlotte Hornets. Cowens also had brief tours of duty as head coach of the Golden State Warriors and the WNBA's Chicago Sky before accepting an assistant coaching position with the Detroit Pistons. After moving into the Detroit front office, where he served as a special assistant to Pistons president of basketball operations Joe Dumars, Cowens remained with the organization until Stan Van Gundy replaced Dumars as head man in Detroit in 2014.

In 1991, some eight years after he appeared in his last NBA game, Cowens was accorded the honor of being inducted into the Naismith Memorial Basketball Hall of Fame. In making his acceptance speech, Cowens said, "I never thought of myself as a superstar. I represent the working class of the NBA. I'm honored they've selected me because I could name a whole lot of guys who were better than Dave Cowens. You have to play with the right people and get picked by the right team. Let's face it, I was pretty lucky."

Five years later, Cowens received the additional honor of being named one of the 50 greatest players in NBA history.

Henry Finkel, who spent most of his career serving as a backup to Cowens in Boston, expressed his admiration for the man who kept him on the bench much of the time by saying, "To this day, people ask me who was the toughest guy to play against, and I tell them nobody was tougher than Dave Cowens. Fortunately for me, he got in a few foul problems, so they kept me around for security. He was going to play his aggressive way no matter what, whether he fouled out in three minutes or played the entire game."

Finkel added, "We used to play these benefit games, and I quit playing because Cowens is running 100 miles per hour and I was going to have a heart attack. He played the same in any kind of game, whether you were 20-up or 30-down. You'll never, ever see another Dave Cowens in your life."

Meanwhile, John Havlicek, who spent his first seven seasons in Boston playing with Bill Russell before spending his final eight playing alongside Cowens, stated, "No one ever did more for the Celtics than Dave Cowens."

CELTICS CAREER HIGHLIGHTS

Best Season

Cowens played his best ball for the Celtics from 1972 to 1976, earning three All-NBA selections and four consecutive top-five finishes in the league MVP voting during that time. In addition to averaging at least 19 points each year, Cowens topped 14.7 rebounds and 4 assists all four seasons, placing in the NBA's top three in rebounding each time. Nevertheless, the 1972–73 campaign would have to be considered the finest of his career. En route to earning league MVP honors, Cowens established career-high marks in scoring (20.5 ppg) and rebounding (16.2 rpg), while also averaging 4.1 assists per game. In addition to finishing third in the league in rebounding behind Wilt Chamberlain and Nate Thurmond, Cowens started all 82 games for the Celtics, logging 41.8 minutes of playing time per night. Particularly effective against Chamberlain and Western Conference Champion Los Angeles, Cowens led the Celtics to a perfect 4-0 record against the Lakers by averaging 31 points and 19 rebounds against them. Most proud of the fact that his fellow players voted him league MVP, Cowens told *HOOP* magazine in 1992, "Being named the MVP by my peers meant a lot to me. I was always out to gain the respect of the players. They are the only ones who understand your work habits."

Memorable Moments / Greatest Performances

Although the Celtics lost to the eventual world-champion Milwaukee Bucks by a score of 111–99 on February 28, 1971, Cowens turned in arguably the finest performance of his rookie campaign, scoring a season-high 36 points, outscoring league MVP Kareem Abdul-Jabbar by a margin of 36–26 in the process.

Cowens had another big game against Abdul-Jabbar and the Bucks the following season, hitting for 37 points, in leading the Celtics to a 125–114 win over Milwaukee on October 29, 1971. Still, it should be noted that Jabbar scored 43 points himself during the contest.

Cowens played one of his finest all-around games later that season, scoring 32 points and pulling down 21 rebounds during a 115–108 victory over the Baltimore Bullets on February 1, 1972.

Cowens turned in a number of exceptional performances over the course of his 1972–73 MVP campaign, scoring a season-high 38 points during a 115–106 win over the Knicks on December 26, 1972. He had another big game some three weeks later, tallying 35 points during a 117–99 victory over the Portland Trail Blazers on January 17, 1973. Saving some of his finest efforts for Wilt Chamberlain and the Lakers, Cowens led the Celtics to a 113–112 overtime victory over Los Angeles on February 7 by hitting for 34 points, in a battle of teams holding the league's two best records. Cowens again proved to be a thorn in the side of Chamberlain and the Lakers a little over one month later, scoring another 34 points during a 119–111 Boston win over Los Angeles on March 9.

Cowens continued his outstanding play against the Lakers the following season, scoring a season-high 35 points during a 115–110 victory over Los Angeles on December 16, 1973.

Cowens put together a pair of extraordinary efforts just two days apart the following year, scoring 32 points during a 101–90 win over the Lakers on December 4, 1974, before hitting for a season-high 38 points, in leading the Celtics to a 120–114 overtime victory over the Houston Rockets, on December 6. He had another big game later that season, tallying 33 points during a 107–106 win over Kareem Abdul-Jabbar and the Milwaukee Bucks on February 28, 1975.

Cowens turned in one of his finest performances of the ensuing campaign on December 5, 1975, when he led the Celtics to a 104–93 victory over the New Orleans Jazz by scoring 34 points. Some six weeks later, on January 16, 1976, Cowens scored a career-high 39 points, in leading the Celtics to a 118–110 win over the Philadelphia 76ers. He had another strong effort against the 76ers later in the year, tallying 33 points during a 108–100 Boston victory on March 21.

After taking a two-month leave of absence earlier in the season, Cowens gradually worked his way back into top condition by the second half of the 1976–77 campaign, hitting for a season-high 33 points during a 126–125 overtime win over the Kansas City Kings on February 17, 1977.

In arguably his finest game of the ensuing campaign, Cowens scored a season-high 36 points, in leading the Celtics to a 114–111 overtime victory over the New Jersey Nets on January 13, 1978.

Boasting averages of 18.9 points and 14.4 rebounds per game in postseason play over the course of his career, Cowens proved to be an outstanding playoff performer. Turning in one of his finest all-around efforts in his very first postseason, Cowens scored 26 points and pulled down 20 rebounds in Game 6 of the 1972 Eastern Conference Semifinals, in leading the Celtics to a 127–118 victory over the Atlanta Hawks that clinched the series for Boston.

The loss of John Havlicek for the final four games of the 1973 Eastern Conference Finals following an injury he sustained in Game 3 contributed greatly to Boston's seven-game defeat at the hands of the rival New York Knicks. Nevertheless, Cowens performed brilliantly throughout the series, posting a scoring average of 24.4 points per contest. Particularly effective in Games 4, 5, and 6, Cowens scored a combined 91 points in those three contests, nearly bringing the Celtics all the way back from a three-games-to-one deficit in the series.

Although the Celtics ended up losing to the Philadelphia 76ers in seven games in the 1977 Eastern Conference Semifinals, Cowens turned in a heroic effort in Game 4, helping Boston even the series at two games apiece by scoring 37 points during a 124–119 victory.

Yet, it was Cowens's play in two other series that came to epitomize his career. Even though he fouled out in the first overtime of a thrilling double-OT loss to the Milwaukee Bucks in Game 6 of the 1974 NBA Finals, scoring only 13 points on just 5 of 19 shooting from the field along the way, Cowens left an indelible image of himself in the minds of most fans before leaving the contest. Switching off his man on defense to guard Oscar Robertson, Cowens poked the ball away from the "Big O" toward the Bucks backcourt. Pursuing the ball with reckless abandon, Cowens outsprinted the smaller Robertson, who looked on incredulously as his opponent dove for the loose ball and slid some 10 or 12 feet on the old Boston Garden parquet floor, leaving a trail of perspiration behind him. While the Bucks argued that Cowens never gained full possession of the loose sphere, the

Cowens more than held his own against centers who typically stood 2 or 3 inches taller. Photo courtesy of MearsOnlineAuctions.com.

referees correctly ruled that the 24-second clock had expired, thereby giving the Celtics possession of the ball. After Cowens's subsequent departure from the contest due to foul trouble helped Milwaukee to tie the series at three games apiece, he redeemed himself in Game 7 by scoring 28 points and pulling down 14 rebounds, in leading the Celtics to a 102–87 win that clinched their 12th NBA title.

Cowens similarly displayed his incredible determination in Game 6 of the 1976 NBA Finals, when he willed his team to victory over a younger and healthier Phoenix Suns squad by scoring seven of the nine points Boston scored during a 9–4 fourth-quarter run that put the game away for the Celtics. Making the key play of the game with only minutes remaining in regulation, Cowens tipped the ball away from NBA Rookie of the Year Alvan Adams. He then gathered up the loose ball and roared up court, leading the Celtics on a two-on-one fast break. As he approached the basket, the left-handed Cowens crossed over to the right side and gave a slight head fake that temporarily froze Suns defender Garfield Heard. Cowens then laid in a twisting backhanded layup over his shoulder while being fouled. He then completed the three-point play by hitting a free throw that gave the Celtics a four-point lead they never relinquished. Boston went on to record an 87–80 victory that gave them their 13th NBA championship.

Although far less significant in terms of overall team success, another incident took place during a game against the Houston Rockets that demonstrated Cowens's commitment to the game, as well as his fierce competitiveness. With the Celtics playing the Rockets on February 25, 1976, Cowens grew increasingly disturbed with the antics of Houston guard Mike Newlin, who twice drew fouls against him by stepping in front of him and flopping to the court. Having always maintained that players should adhere to an unwritten code of conduct that Newlin had blatantly violated, Cowens later recalled, "I said to myself, 'Okay, I have to put an end to this. I foul out enough without having this crap.'" Choosing to take matters into his own hands, Cowens charged at Newlin as he trotted up court on a Houston possession shortly thereafter, leveling him with two high forearms. He then turned toward referee Bill Jones and shouted, "Now that's a foul!"

NOTABLE ACHIEVEMENTS

- Averaged more than 20 points per game twice, topping 18 points per contest four other times.
- Averaged more than 14 rebounds per game seven times, topping 15 rebounds per contest on five occasions, and surpassing 16 rebounds per game twice.
- Averaged 5 assists per game once.

- Averaged more than 40 minutes per game five times.
- Led NBA in games played in 1972–73.
- Finished in top five in NBA in rebounding six times, placing second on three occasions.
- Led Celtics in rebounding six times, scoring average three times, and assists once.
- Ranks among Celtics career leaders in points scored (9th); scoring average (12th); total rebounds (3rd); assists (10th); steals (tied for 10th); field-goal attempts (10th); field goals made (10th); and minutes played (8th).
- Ranks eighth in NBA history in rebounding average (13.6 rpg).
- 1970–71 NBA Co-Rookie of the Year.
- 1972–73 NBA All-Star Game MVP.
- 1972–73 NBA MVP.
- Finished in top five in NBA MVP voting three other times, placing second once and third once.
- Three-time All-NBA Second-Team selection (1972–73, 1974–75, and 1975–76).
- 1975–76 NBA All-Defensive First-Team selection.
- Two-time NBA All-Defensive Second-Team selection (1974–75 and 1979–80).
- Eight-time NBA All-Star (1972–78 and 1980).
- Two-time Eastern Conference champion (1974 and 1976).
- Two-time NBA champion (1974 and 1976).
- Number 18 retired by Celtics.
- Member of NBA's 50th Anniversary Team.
- Member of NBA's 75th Anniversary Team.
- Inducted into Naismith Memorial Basketball Hall of Fame in 1991.

7

KEVIN McHALE

He was the best player I ever played against because he was unstoppable offensively, and he gave me nightmares on defense.

—Charles Barkley

One of the greatest post-up players in NBA history, Kevin McHale used his long arms, exceptional quickness, and seemingly endless array of moves down low to thwart opposing defenders, making him one of the most difficult individual matchups in the league over the course of his career. Despite spending his first few seasons coming off the Celtics' bench, McHale ended up averaging well in excess of 20 points per game five straight times, leading all NBA players in field-goal shooting percentage on two separate occasions. The gangly McHale also did a superb job on the defensive end of the floor, averaging more than 2 blocked shots per contest five times, en route to earning NBA All-Defensive honors a total of six times. After being named NBA Sixth Man of the Year twice during the early stages of his career, McHale went on to earn seven All-Star selections while teaming up with Larry Bird and Robert Parish to form one of the most potent front lines in NBA history. McHale's stellar all-around play helped lead the Celtics to five Eastern Conference championships and three NBA titles, eventually earning him spots on the NBA's 50th and 75th Anniversary Teams and a place in the Naismith Memorial Basketball Hall of Fame.

Born in Hibbing, Minnesota, on December 19, 1957, Kevin Edward McHale attended local Hibbing High School, where he experienced a growth spurt of more than a foot that left him standing 6 feet, 10 inches tall. Learning to gain control over his gawky frame by competing one-on-one against his coach, Gary Addington, McHale later credited Addington with the development of his overall skills, telling *Sports Illustrated*, "I could

Kevin McHale teamed up with Larry Bird and Robert Parish to form arguably the greatest front line in NBA history. Photo courtesy of MearsOnlineAuctions.com.

have gotten into a rut, scoring 30 points a game with my back to the basket, but Gary forced me to learn the whole game."

Subsequently offered scholarships by the universities of Utah and Minnesota, McHale chose the latter, spending his first two seasons with the Gophers playing forward alongside future NBA center Mychal Thompson.

McHale emerged as a top pro prospect following Thompson's graduation, earning All-Big Ten honors in 1979 and 1980, and leading his team to the NIT Championship Game as a senior by averaging 17.4 points per game while shooting 56.7 percent from the field. Over the course of his four years at Minnesota, McHale averaged 15.2 points and 8.5 rebounds per contest, establishing himself in the process as the second-leading scorer (1,704 points) and rebounder (950 rebounds) in school history.

Having personally scouted McHale at Minnesota, Celtics president and general manager Red Auerbach elected to make a blockbuster trade just prior to the 1980 NBA Draft, in which he sent the number-one overall pick and another first-round selection to the Golden State Warriors, in exchange for young center Robert Parish and the third overall pick, which he then used to select McHale. By adding Parish and McHale to a roster that already included Larry Bird and Cedric Maxwell, Auerbach instantaneously gave the Celtics the league's most formidable front line.

However, upon his arrival in Boston, McHale first had to be persuaded to accept the role of "sixth man" previously filled by legendary players such as Frank Ramsey and John Havlicek. Bill Fitch, who coached the Celtics McHale's first few years in the league, later recalled, "Making him the sixth man and selling him on it was important. You've got to have those bench points, and have them every night. Kevin got them."

Not only did McHale accept his new role, but he thrived in it. After averaging 10 points, 4.4 rebounds, and 1.8 blocked shots in just over 20 minutes of action per game as a rookie, McHale gradually established himself as the NBA's top bench player over the course of the next few seasons, as he saw his playing time continue to increase each year. Serving as Boston's primary backup at the center and power forward positions in each of the next four seasons, McHale posted scoring averages of 13.6, 14.1, 18.4, and 19.8 points per game, while also averaging more than 6.5 rebounds and 1.5 blocked shots per contest each year. Particularly effective in 1983–84 and 1984–85, McHale earned NBA Sixth Man of the Year honors both seasons by posting averages of 18.4 points, 7.4 rebounds, and 1.5 blocked shots in the first of those campaigns, before averaging 19.8 points, 9 rebounds, and 1.5 blocked shots in the second. He also made his first All-Star appearance in 1984, after earning NBA All-Defensive Second-Team honors for the first of three times the previous season.

Yet, ironically, the Celtics almost lost McHale's services during that period when the New York Knicks signed him to a free-agent offer sheet following the conclusion of the 1982–83 campaign. Red Auerbach ended New York's brief flirtation with McHale, though, when he responded by inking three of the Knicks' top free agents to offer sheets. The Knicks subsequently gave up their pursuit of McHale, choosing instead to re-sign their own players.

After breaking into the Celtics' starting five during the latter stages of the 1984–85 campaign following an injury to Cedric Maxwell, McHale finally became the team's regular starting power forward the following year, when Boston dealt Maxwell to the Los Angeles Clippers for Bill Walton. Despite being plagued by a sore Achilles tendon that limited him to just 68 games and 62 starts, McHale ended up posting the best numbers of his career to that point, earning All-Star and NBA All-Defensive First-Team honors by averaging 21.3 points, 8.1 rebounds, and 2 blocked shots per contest, while shooting 57.4 percent from the field. He continued his outstanding play in the postseason, helping the Celtics capture the NBA championship by posting averages of 24.9 points, 8.6 rebounds, and 2.4 blocked shots in Boston's 18 playoff games.

McHale followed that up by beginning an exceptional four-year run during which he compiled the following numbers:

SEASON	POINTS PER GAME	REBOUNDS PER GAME	ASSISTS PER GAME
1986–87	26.1	9.9	2.2
1987–88	22.6	8.4	1.4
1988–89	22.5	8.2	1.2
1989–90	20.9	8.3	1.9

In addition to finishing sixth in the NBA in scoring en route to earning his lone All-NBA First-Team selection in the first of those campaigns, McHale led the league in field-goal shooting percentage twice during the period, topping the circuit in both 1986–87 and 1987–88, with identical marks of 60.4 percent. He also earned All-Star and NBA All-Defensive honors all four seasons, making it onto the First and Second Defensive Teams two times each.

Having perfected his post-up game during the earlier stages of his career as "sixth man" in Boston, McHale emerged as one of the NBA's most difficult men to guard down low. Standing 6-foot-10 and weighing close to 230 pounds, McHale had extremely long legs and arms that gave him the reach of a significantly larger man. He possessed too much quickness for opposing centers and too much height for opposing forwards, with the length of his arms giving his shots a release point that made them virtually

McHale averaged more than 20 points per game five straight times for the Celtics.
Photo courtesy of MearsOnlineAuctions.com.

impossible for even taller defenders to block. That last fact, in conjunction with the variety of head-fakes, pump-fakes, fade-away shots, shovel shots, and jump hooks he employed from the low post, made him a defender's worst nightmare. Furthermore, McHale possessed exceptional balance and good range on his jump shot, which he had the ability to hit either from the baseline or from the top of the key.

In discussing McHale, Charles Barkley said, "He was the best player I ever played against because he was unstoppable offensively, and he gave me nightmares on defense."

In analyzing the problems McHale presented to opposing teams, Hubie Brown told the *Boston Globe*, "He became the most difficult low-post player to defend—once he made the catch—in the history of the league. He was totally unstoppable because of his quickness, diversification of moves, and the long arms that gave him an angle to release the ball over a taller man or more explosive jumper."

Heaping additional praise on his onetime teammate, Bill Walton suggested, "He [McHale] was the second-best low-post player of all time, after Jabbar. In his strategy against bigger guys he was brilliant—subtle finesse, deft fakes, and all."

Red Auerbach added, "He had the strength, he had the quickness, and he had the mobility; but, above all, he had the smarts."

Yet, even though McHale continued to post outstanding numbers year after year, he eventually found his performance being compromised to some degree by an injury he suffered during the latter stages of the 1986–87 campaign, when he broke the navicular bone in his right foot. Despite being warned by doctors that the injury might end up threatening his career, McHale subsequently averaged 39 minutes per game during the playoffs, enduring so much pain while competing against the Lakers in the NBA Finals that he used a patio chair from the hotel pool as a walker in between contests. Forced to undergo surgery during the off-season, McHale began the 1987–88 campaign on the injured list, although he eventually went on to earn the third of his six consecutive All-Star selections.

Plagued by numerous foot and ankle problems over the course of the 1990–91 campaign, McHale saw his scoring average dip to 18.4 points per game, which represented his lowest mark since he became a starter. He also missed 14 games and averaged fewer minutes per contest, with both trends continuing the next two years. After averaging only 10.7 points and 5 rebounds per game in a backup role in 1992–93, McHale elected to announce his retirement at season's end, concluding his career with 17,335 points scored, 7,122 rebounds, 1,670 assists, 1,690 blocked shots, a field-goal shooting percentage of 55.4, and a free-throw shooting percentage of 79.8. In his 13 seasons with the Celtics, McHale averaged 17.9 points, 7.3 rebounds, 1.7 assists, and 1.7 blocked shots per contest. His career field-goal shooting percentage of 55.4—which places him third on the Celtics all-time among players with at least 1,500 attempts—ranks as the third-highest mark ever posted by an NBA forward.

Following McHale's retirement, the Celtics did not wait long to retire his uniform number 32, doing so during an 18-minute halftime ceremony at Boston Garden on January 30, 1994. In discussing his years with the Celtics,

McHale later told the *Boston Globe*, "We played the game, I thought, the way it should have been played. Those were absolutely the best days of my life."

After leaving Boston, McHale returned to his home state, where he spent one year serving as a television analyst and special assistant for the Minnesota Timberwolves before being promoted to the position of assistant general manager. Following a one-year stint in that role, McHale became Minnesota's vice president of basketball operations—a position he held until he took over as the team's head coach in December of 2008. However, after McHale led the Timberwolves to a record of just 20-43 the rest of the season, ownership elected to relieve him of his duties. McHale subsequently spent the next two years working as a television analyst for NBA games before accepting the position of head coach of the Houston Rockets on June 1, 2011. Experiencing considerably more success in Houston, McHale led the Rockets to a winning record in each of the next four seasons and a berth in the Western Conference Finals in 2015. Nevertheless, Houston management decided to replace him at the helm after the Rockets began the 2015–16 campaign winning just 4 of their first 11 games. Since leaving Houston, McHale has been working with Turner Sports as a basketball analyst.

CELTICS CAREER HIGHLIGHTS

Best Season

McHale clearly played his best ball for the Celtics in 1986–87, prior to suffering a broken bone in his foot that ended up somewhat affecting his performance for the remainder of his career. In addition to posting career-high marks in scoring (26.1 ppg), rebounding (9.9 rpg), and minutes played (39.7 mpg), McHale averaged 2.2 blocked shots per contest, led the NBA with a field-goal shooting percentage of 60.4, and shot 83.6 percent from the free-throw line, becoming in the process the first player ever to shoot better than 60 percent from the floor and 80 percent from the foul line. McHale's exceptional performance earned him a fourth-place finish in the league MVP voting and his lone All-NBA First-Team selection. NBA coaches also named him the league's best defensive player.

Memorable Moments / Greatest Performances

An outstanding shot-blocker over the course of his career, McHale recorded a franchise-record 9 blocks in one game on two separate occasions,

McHale's quickness, long arms, and wide array of moves made him extraordinarily difficult to defend down low.
Photo courtesy of George A. Kitrinos.

accomplishing the feat for the first time during a 113–96 loss to the New Jersey Nets on April 16, 1982. McHale duplicated his earlier effort on January 21, 1983, when he blocked 9 shots and also scored 22 points during a 117–106 win over the Chicago Bulls.

McHale reached the 30-point mark for the first time in his career on December 3, 1982, when he scored 30 points during a 115–112 loss to the Milwaukee Bucks. He surpassed that figure for the first time on February 5, 1984, when he helped lead the Celtics to a 137–134 overtime victory over the Detroit Pistons by tallying 33 points.

However, both those performances paled by comparison to the effort McHale turned in on March 3, 1985, when he scored a career-high 56 points during a 138–129 win over Detroit. Shooting 22 of 28 from the field and 12 of 13 from the free-throw line, McHale established a new Celtics single-game scoring record, which Larry Bird ironically ended up breaking just nine days later. Nevertheless, with McHale tallying 42 points in his very next game, a 110–102 victory over the Knicks, he continues to hold the franchise record for most points scored (98) in consecutive games.

McHale turned in a pair of exceptional all-around efforts in December 1985, scoring 34 points, collecting 10 rebounds, and blocking 4 shots during a 108–102 loss to Philadelphia on December 21, before tallying 22 points and pulling down a career-high 18 rebounds, in helping the Celtics record a 125–103 victory over the Los Angeles Clippers on December 30.

McHale also had a pair of big games in December 1986, scoring 34 points and collecting 13 rebounds during a 105–98 win over the Washington Bullets on December 13, before hitting for 32 points, amassing 15 rebounds, and assisting on 7 baskets during a 122–112 victory over the Phoenix Suns the day after Christmas.

Continuing his strong play in the New Year, McHale scored 38 points, pulled down 10 rebounds, and blocked 5 shots, in leading the Celtics to a 133–128 overtime win over Cleveland on January 16, 1987. He had another tremendous all-around game on February 10, 1987, when he tallied 36 points, collected 14 rebounds, and recorded 4 blocks during a 119–105 victory over Denver. McHale followed that up three days later by hitting for 37 points during a 131–116 win over Portland.

Less than two weeks later, on February 23, 1987, McHale went on a scoring spree that saw him average 30.7 points per game over the course of the next nine contests, while also averaging 10 rebounds per game and shooting a composite 71.7 percent from the field. Particularly noteworthy performances included a 38-point, 14-rebound outing against the Pistons on March 1 (a 112–102 Boston win) and a 36-point, 14-rebound effort against Phoenix on March 11 (a 118–109 Celtics win, in which McHale shot 15 of 19 from the field and 6 of 6 from the free-throw line).

McHale turned in one of his last truly dominant performances for the Celtics on March 16, 1989, when he led them to a 111–99 win over the Indiana Pacers by scoring a season-high 36 points and collecting 9 rebounds.

Saving some of his finest performances for postseason play, McHale averaged more than 20 points per game in the playoffs in six of seven seasons at one point, twice compiling an average in excess of 24 points per contest. En route to posting averages of 22.1 points and 9.9 rebounds per game over the course of the 1984–85 postseason, McHale played particularly well against the Lakers in the NBA Finals, averaging 26 points and 10.7 rebounds per contest in a losing cause, with his best effort coming in Game 6, when he scored 32 points and pulled down 16 rebounds.

McHale again performed brilliantly in the 1985–86 playoffs, helping the Celtics capture the NBA title by averaging 24.9 points and 8.6 rebounds in their 18 postseason contests, while shooting 58 percent from the field. After posting averages of 28 points and 10 rebounds per game during Boston's three-game sweep of Chicago in the opening round, McHale concluded his exceptional postseason by badly outplaying Houston's Ralph Sampson during the NBA Finals. While Sampson averaged only 14.8 points per game and shot just 44 percent from the field over the course of the six-game series, McHale averaged 25.8 points per contest, on 57.3 percent shooting.

McHale had another tremendous postseason in 1988, averaging 25.4 points and 8 rebounds per game, before Detroit eliminated the Celtics from the playoffs by defeating them in six games in the Eastern Conference Finals.

Yet, the postseason play for which McHale is perhaps best remembered took place in Game 4 of the 1984 NBA Finals, when, with the Celtics trailing the Lakers in both the game and the series, he clotheslined Kurt Rambis as the latter headed toward the basket, flinging him down by the throat in the process. The physical play touched off a bench-clearing brawl, after which the Celtics came back to win the game and, eventually, the series.

NOTABLE ACHIEVEMENTS

- Averaged more than 20 points per game five times, topping 18 points per game three other times.
- Averaged more than 8 rebounds per game six times, topping 9 rebounds per contest twice.
- Averaged more than 2 blocked shots per game five times.
- Shot better than 50 percent from the field in 12 of 13 seasons.

- Led NBA in field-goal shooting percentage twice and games played twice.
- Led Celtics in scoring average once.
- Scored 56 points vs. Detroit on 3/03/85.
- Holds share of Celtics single-game record for most blocked shots (9—twice).
- Ranks among Celtics career leaders in points scored (5th); rebounds (6th); "official" blocked shots (2nd); field-goal attempts (9th); field goals made (5th); field-goal shooting percentage (3rd); free-throw attempts (5th); free throws made (5th); games played (4th); and minutes played (7th).
- Two-time NBA Sixth Man of the Year (1983–84 and 1984–85).
- Finished fourth in NBA MVP voting in 1986–87.
- 1986–87 All-NBA First-Team selection.
- Three-time NBA All-Defensive First-Team selection (1985–86, 1986–87, and 1987–88).
- Three-time NBA All-Defensive Second-Team selection (1982–83, 1988–89, and 1989–90).
- Seven-time NBA All-Star (1984, 1986, 1987, 1988, 1989, 1990, and 1991).
- Five-time Eastern Conference champion (1981, 1984, 1985, 1986, and 1987).
- Three-time NBA champion (1981, 1984, and 1986).
- Number 32 retired by Celtics.
- Member of NBA's 50th Anniversary Team.
- Member of NBA's 75th Anniversary Team.
- Inducted into Naismith Memorial Basketball Hall of Fame in 1999.

8

BILL SHARMAN

Bill Sharman was, without a doubt, one of the greatest human beings I have ever met, and one of my all-time favorite individuals, both as a competitor and as a friend. He was the epitome of class and dignity and, I can assure you, we find few men of his character in this world.

—Jerry West

The finest outside shooter of his time, Bill Sharman formed with Bob Cousy what has been referred to as "the first modern backcourt." With Cousy running the Boston offense and Sharman serving as the team's primary scoring threat from the perimeter, the Celtics won five Eastern Division titles and four NBA championships. Possessing an extremely soft shooting touch, Sharman led the NBA in free-throw percentage in 7 of his 10 seasons in Boston, while also consistently ranking among the league leaders in field-goal percentage and scoring. In addition to averaging more than 20 points per game in three different seasons, Sharman typically posted a field-goal shooting percentage that exceeded the league average by some 7 or 8 points. An outstanding defender as well, Sharman proved to be one of the NBA's finest all-around guards for nearly a decade, earning eight All-Star nominations and seven All-NBA selections, before retiring from the game and beginning an equally successful career in coaching.

Born in Abilene, Texas, on May 25, 1926, William Walton Sharman spent most of his youth in central California after moving with his family to the city of Porterville as a child. Following his graduation from Porterville High School, where he starred in baseball and basketball, Sharman spent three years serving his country as a member of the United States Navy during World War II. After leaving the service in 1946, Sharman enrolled

Bill Sharman combined with Bob Cousy to form what has been referred to as "the first modern backcourt."

at the University of Southern California, where he resumed his athletic career, earning All-America honors twice in basketball, and excelling to such a degree on the diamond that the Brooklyn Dodgers signed him to a professional contract. However, after toiling in the Brooklyn farm system for five years while simultaneously playing in the NBA, Sharman elected to concentrate solely on basketball in 1955.

The 6-foot-1, 175-pound Sharman began his career in pro basketball with the Washington Capitols, who selected him in the second round of the 1950 NBA Draft. After averaging just over 12 points per contest in 31 games with the Capitols as a rookie in 1950–51, Sharman became a member of the Fort Wayne Pistons via a dispersal draft at season's end, following the dissolution of the Washington franchise at midseason. However, prior to the start of the ensuing campaign, the Boston Celtics worked out a deal with the Pistons in which they acquired Sharman for center Charlie Share, who they had selected with the first overall pick in the previous year's draft.

Sharman spent his first season in Boston coming off the bench, averaging just under 11 points per game, while shooting nearly 39 percent from the field. He began to hit his stride the following year after Red Auerbach inserted him into the starting lineup alongside backcourt mate Bob Cousy. In addition to posting a scoring average of 16.2 points per game that placed him sixth in the league rankings in 1952–53, Sharman finished among the league leaders with a .436 field-goal shooting percentage and topped the circuit for the first of five straight times in free-throw shooting percentage, successfully converting 85 percent of his free-throw attempts. Sharman's strong performance earned him All-NBA Second-Team honors for the first of three times and the first of his eight consecutive All-Star selections. He posted extremely similar numbers the following season as well, averaging 16 points per contest, shooting 45 percent from the field, and converting just under 85 percent of his free-throw opportunities.

While the numbers Sharman compiled over the course of his first two seasons as a starter might appear modest to some, it must be remembered that he spent his first few years in Boston playing under the adverse conditions that existed in the NBA during the league's formative years. Not only had the league not yet introduced the 24-second clock, but it also failed to properly mold the basketballs it used in its games until the late 1950s, greatly diminishing the shooting accuracy of its players. When it is considered that Sharman's field-goal percentage generally ranged somewhere between 40 and 45 percent at a time when the league average typically stood at about 35 percent, his greatness as a shooter becomes quite evident.

Fellow guard Bob Davies praised Sharman in *From Set Shot to Slam Dunk*, saying of his adversary, "The toughest player I had to play against was Bill Sharman . . . When he got his hands on the ball, he would always set up to shoot. He was by far the most accurate basketball shooter of all time."

Meanwhile, Wilt Chamberlain called Sharman (who later coached him in Los Angeles) "a near-perfect guard who might have been the greatest shooter of all time."

One of the first players to eschew the traditional two-handed set shot, Sharman released the ball quickly with one hand, making it difficult for defenders to block his shot. He also possessed the quickness and athleticism

(From left to right) Bill Sharman, Bob Cousy, Ed Macauley, and Red Auerbach.
Photo courtesy of Boston Public Library, Leslie Jones Collection.

to take the ball to the hoop when the opportunity presented itself. Perhaps
the most overlooked aspect of Sharman's game, though, was his defense, as
former teammate Ed Macauley suggested in *From Set Shot to Slam Dunk*,
when he stated, "Sharman was just an incredible shooter with great con-
centration, great practice habits. He was a very good defensive player, and
people didn't give him credit for that."

Even though Sharman likely could have played at least one or two
more years, he elected to make the 1960–61 campaign his final season,
announcing his retirement after averaging 16 points per game for a Celtics
team that won its fourth NBA championship in five years. He ended his
career with totals of 12,665 points scored, 2,793 rebounds, and 2,101
assists, accumulating the vast majority of those numbers while playing for
the Celtics. Sharman averaged 17.8 points, 3.9 rebounds, and 3 assists per
game over the course of his 11 years in the league. His career free-throw
shooting percentage of 88.3 remains the 15th best in NBA history.

Five years after Sharman retired, the Celtics honored him by retiring his number 21. He later received the additional honors of being named to the NBA's Silver Anniversary Team in 1970, being inducted into the Naismith Memorial Basketball Hall of Fame in 1976, and being awarded spots on both the NBA's 50th and 75th Anniversary Teams. In discussing his long-time teammate in 2007, Tom Heinsohn said, "He deserves the ultimate accolade; he was a winner. He was an incredible athlete, a great competitor, a tenacious defender, and a terrific offensive player."

The following season, Sharman began an outstanding four-year run during which he posted scoring averages of 19.9, 21.1, 22.3, and 20.4 points per game. In addition to finishing among the league leaders in scoring each season, Sharman placed near the top of the league rankings in assists and field-goal percentage twice each. He also topped the circuit in free-throw shooting percentage in three of those four seasons, setting a new NBA record (since broken) in 1958–59 by successfully converting 93.2 percent of his foul shots. Sharman earned All-NBA First-Team honors in each of those four seasons, helping the Celtics capture the NBA title in both 1957 and 1959. He had another excellent season in 1959–60, earning a spot on the All-NBA Second Team and his final All-Star selection by averaging 19.3 points per game and shooting a career-best 45.6 percent from the field.

Still in peak condition at 34 years of age heading into the 1960–61 campaign, Sharman owed much of his longevity to his daily training regimen that included stretching, exercise, and practice. Competing in an era when players rarely took proper care of themselves, Sharman treated his body as a temple, as Bill Reynolds wrote in *Rise of a Dynasty*:

> He drank shakes he claimed gave him energy. He always had vitamins in his suitcase. He drank tea on the afternoon of games. He did calisthenics in front of his locker before games, as the rest of his teammates sat there and thought he was a wacko. He ran on days he wasn't practicing, sometimes jogging behind a car driven by his wife. And on the morning of game days he would go to a local high school gym and shoot by himself, his way of preparing for the evening's games.

Even though Sharman likely could have played at least one or two more years, he elected to make the 1960–61 campaign his final season, announcing his retirement after averaging 16 points per game for a Celtics team that won its fourth NBA championship in five years. He ended his career with totals of 12,665 points scored, 2,793 rebounds, and 2,101 assists, accumulating the vast majority of those numbers while playing for the Celtics. Sharman averaged 17.8 points, 3.9 rebounds, and 3 assists per game over the course of his 11 years in the league. His career free-throw shooting percentage of 88.3 remains the 15th best in NBA history.

Five years after Sharman retired, the Celtics honored him by retiring his number (21). He later received the additional honors of being named to the NBA's Silver Anniversary Team in 1970, being inducted into the Naismith Memorial Basketball Hall of Fame in 1976, and being awarded spots on both the NBA's 50th and 75th Anniversary Teams. In discussing his long-time teammate in 2007, Tom Heinsohn said, "He deserves the ultimate accolade; he was a winner. He was an incredible athlete, a great competitor, a tenacious defender, and a terrific offensive player."

After retiring as an active player, Sharman spent the next 13 years coaching in the college and professional ranks, during which time he became the first coach to emphasize film study and in-depth scouting reports, employ game-day "shoot-arounds," and win championships in three different pro leagues, leading the Cleveland Pipers to the American Basketball League (ABL) title in 1962, the Utah Stars to the ABA crown in 1971, and the Los Angeles Lakers to the NBA championship in 1972. Choosing to retire from coaching following the conclusion of the 1975–76 campaign, Sharman moved seamlessly into the Lakers' front office, spending the next 14 years serving them first as general manager, and then as president. He later became a special consultant for the team, a position he maintained for more than two decades until he suffered a stroke in October 2013 that led to his death one week later. Sharman passed away at the age of 87, on October 25, 2013.

In paying tribute to his onetime opponent and former coach, co-executive, and close friend, Jerry West stated, "Bill Sharman was as competitive a guy as you'd ever want to play against. As a coach, he had a great way with players and people; I rarely saw him get upset. His years coaching the Lakers were probably the happiest of my playing career."

West added, "Bill Sharman was, without a doubt, one of the greatest human beings I have ever met, and one of my all-time favorite individuals, both as a competitor and as a friend. He was the epitome of class and dignity and, I can assure you, we find few men of his character in this world."

Lakers president Jeanie Buss echoed West's sentiments, stating, "His knowledge and passion for the game were unsurpassed, and the Lakers and our fans were beneficiaries of that. Despite his greatness as a player, coach, and executive, Bill was one of the sweetest, nicest, and most humble people I've ever known. He was truly one of a kind."

Earl Lloyd, the first African-American player to appear in an NBA game, played briefly with Sharman when the two men broke into the league together as members of the Washington Capitols in 1950. Lloyd's recollection of Sharman many years later perhaps provides the greatest insight into him, both as a man and as a player:

> I've been asked, of all the players from those days, if there was one I admire most. Let me tell you, it was Bill Sharman . . . He was my friend, and think of what that meant at the time. Of course, when that Washington team folded, he'd end up in Boston and I'd be in Syracuse, and we were fierce competitors on teams that were fierce rivals. But the respect never went away. To this day, we're glad when we get the chance to see each other. Remember, Washington was in the South in the back-of-the-bus days. Here's a guy, when he found out I didn't have an automobile and was riding the bus to training camp, who told me he would pick me up every day at Georgia Avenue and Columbia Road in Washington. And he did.

CELTICS CAREER HIGHLIGHTS

Best Season

Sharman performed very well for the Celtics in his next-to-last season, concluding the 1959–60 campaign with a scoring average of 19.3 points per game and a career-high .456 field-goal shooting percentage. Nevertheless, he played his best ball from 1955 to 1958, earning three of his four All-NBA First-Team selections during that period. Sharman posted career-high marks in scoring (22.3) and rebounding (4.7) in 1957–58, placing fifth in the league in the first category in the process. However, he also averaged only 2.7 assists per contest and shot just slightly over 42 percent (42.4) from the field. Sharman finished sixth in the league in scoring the previous season, with a mark of 21.1 points per game, while also averaging 3.5 assists and 4.3 rebounds per contest and shooting 41.6 percent from the field. The feeling here, though, is that Sharman had his finest all-around season in 1955–56, when, in addition to finishing sixth in the league in scoring with an average of 19.9 points per game, he averaged 3.6 rebounds and a

Sharman played for four NBA championship teams during his time in Boston.

career-high 4.7 assists per contest. He also shot just under 44 percent (43.8) from the field, earning in the process a fifth-place finish in the NBA MVP voting, which represented his best showing ever.

Memorable Moments / Greatest Performances

Sharman turned in the first dominant offensive performance of his career on December 11, 1952, leading the Celtics to a 94–88 win over the

Baltimore Bullets by scoring a season-high 42 points. He had another big game nearly one month later, on January 7, 1953, scoring 34 points during a hard-fought 84–82 victory over the Philadelphia Warriors. Sharman again topped the 30-point mark on February 4, when he tallied 32 points during a 105–92 win over the Syracuse Nationals.

Sharman hit for 37 points twice in 1955, doing so during a 119–110 victory over the Fort Wayne Pistons on January 11, before duplicating that effort during a 105–103 loss to the Rochester Royals on March 12.

Sharman reached his high-water mark in scoring the following season on February 2, 1956, when he tallied 35 points during a 102–101 win over the Minneapolis Lakers.

Sharman put together a number of big games early in 1957, scoring 33 points in leading the Celtics to a 126–117 victory over the St. Louis Hawks on January 18, hitting for another 33 points during a 116–98 win over the Knicks on February 3, and tallying a game-high 32 points in leading Boston to a 92–77 win over the Rochester Royals on February 26. He also proved to be a key figure in the Celtics' seven-game victory over St. Louis in the NBA Finals later that year, scoring 36 points in their 125–123 double-overtime loss to the Hawks in Game 1, before hitting for 32 points in a 124–109 Game 5 win. Sharman finished the series with a scoring average of 21.9 points per game, in helping the Celtics capture their first NBA championship.

Sharman continued his high-scoring ways early the following season, scoring 34 points during a 122–110 victory over the Cincinnati Royals on November 8, 1957, hitting for another 34 points during a 118–112 win over the Syracuse Nationals three weeks later, scoring 41 points in leading the Celtics to a 140–119 victory over the Minneapolis Lakers on December 21, and recording a career-high 44 points during a 120–110 win over the Knicks on December 26. Although New York gained a measure of revenge by defeating the Celtics 136–123 two weeks later, Sharman had another huge game, tallying 39 points during the contest.

Sharman topped the 30-point mark for the final time in his career on March 23, 1961, when he led the Celtics to a 133–110 victory over the Syracuse Nationals in Game 3 of the Eastern Division Finals by scoring a game-high 30 points. He continued his outstanding play against the Nationals in each of the next two contests as well, helping the Celtics close out the series in five games by putting up 21 and 27 points in his team's 120–107 and 123–101 victories.

NOTABLE ACHIEVEMENTS

- Averaged more than 20 points per game three times, topping 18 points per contest three other times.
- Shot better than 90 percent from free-throw line three times.
- Led NBA in free-throw percentage seven times.
- Finished second in NBA in field-goal percentage once.
- Led Celtics in scoring average four times.
- First NBA player to make 50 consecutive free throws.
- Ranks among Celtics career leaders in free-throw percentage (5th) and free throws made (8th).
- 1954–55 NBA All-Star Game MVP.
- Four-time All-NBA First-Team selection (1955–56, 1956–57, 1957–58, and 1958–59).
- Three-time All-NBA Second-Team selection (1952–53, 1954–55, and 1959–60).
- Eight-time NBA All-Star (1953–1960).
- Five-time Eastern Division champion (1957–61).
- Four-time NBA champion (1957, 1959, 1960, and 1961).
- Number 21 retired by Celtics.
- Member of NBA's 25th Anniversary Team.
- Member of NBA's 50th Anniversary Team.
- Member of NBA's 75th Anniversary Team.
- Inducted into Naismith Memorial Basketball Hall of Fame in 1976.

9

SAM JONES

He had a stutter step that would kind of halt your defense and then,
all of a sudden, he just glides by you. He did that to me in a scrimmage
and it just totally blew my mind that he was so smooth with that.

—K. C. Jones

An outstanding scorer, strong defender, and tremendous clutch shooter, Sam Jones served as one of the central figures on Boston Celtics teams that won 10 out of a possible 11 NBA championships between 1959 and 1969. Tasting playoff defeat just twice over the course of his 12-year NBA career, Jones established a legacy of winning second only to fellow Celtic Bill Russell, who once identified his longtime teammate as the best player he ever played with. Making good use of his patented bank shot and exceptional quickness, Jones gradually emerged as an elite scorer during his time in Boston, leading the Celtics in scoring in five out of six seasons at one point, after spending his first few seasons in Beantown coming off the bench. Meanwhile, Jones's cool demeanor, which enabled him to thrive in pressure situations, prompted many of his peers to refer to him as "Mr. Clutch," a moniker more commonly associated with one of his fiercest rivals, Jerry West.

Born in Wilmington, North Carolina, on June 24, 1933, Samuel Jones grew up some 100 miles northwest, in the small town of Laurinburg, North Carolina, during a segregated period in Southern history. Although Jones excelled in both baseball and basketball while attending Laurinburg High School, he never anticipated pursuing a career in professional sports, hoping instead to use his athletic prowess to obtain a scholarship that might afford him an opportunity to eventually become a teacher.

However, Jones began to reevaluate his position after he started to make a name for himself while playing basketball at North Carolina Central University, a small black National Association of Intercollegiate Athletics (NAIA) school located in Durham. Playing for the legendary John McClendon, who had learned the game from Dr. James Naismith, Jones averaged 17.7 points per game over a six-year period (he served two years in the US Army between his junior and senior seasons), earning in the process All-Conference honors three times.

Jones's outstanding play at Central so impressed former Celtic Bones McKinney that the latter recommended him to Boston coach Red Auerbach, who subsequently went against his usual practice of drafting only those players he had seen perform in person. Selecting Jones in the first round of the 1957 NBA Draft with the eighth overall pick, Auerbach shocked the many scouts in attendance, some of whom knew nothing about the 24-year-old guard. Jones, himself, never expected to end up in Boston, believing that his small-college background made him a long shot to make the roster of the defending NBA champions. Recounting the consternation he felt at the time, Jones later revealed, "I never felt so miserable in my life when I got the news. I really thought it was the end of my basketball career. Sure, I was thrilled with the honor . . . I never thought I'd be able to break into the game, let alone into the lineup."

The extremely sagacious Auerbach, though, immediately saw something special in Jones. After wondering at first if the rookie possessed the heart and mental toughness to survive training camp, well-known to be the most demanding in the league, Auerbach took note of his exceptional endurance and conditioning, as well as his willingness to help the team in any way possible, recalling years later, "When he arrived, there were three other guys almost just like Sam who were trying to make the team. The difference was the other three just thought about shooting. After a couple of days, Sam started handing out some nice passes and blocking out so other guys could shoot. You could see that he was committed to becoming a complete player."

After making the Celtics' roster, Jones saw very little action as a rookie, averaging just under 11 minutes, 5 points, and 3 rebounds per game as Bill Sharman's primary backup at the shooting guard position. Playing both small forward and shooting guard in each of the next two seasons, Jones saw significantly more playing time, enabling his production to increase dramatically. Averaging a little over 20 minutes per game each season, Jones averaged 10.7 points and a career-high 6 rebounds per contest in 1958–59, before posting marks of 11.9 points and 5.1 rebounds per game in 1959–60.

Sam Jones's total of 10 NBA championships ranks second only to longtime teammate Bill Russell in league history.
Photo courtesy of LegendaryAuctions.com.

Although the 6-foot-4, 205-pound Jones generally gave away an inch or two in height to his opponent whenever he manned the small forward position, he found that Boston's fast-paced style of play suited him perfectly, as Red Auerbach explained in *Pro Sports Weekly*: "Our style of play at that time started the use of smaller, fast forwards. It was up-tempo, and, because it put a smaller team on the floor, we had to go to the press more often. See, Sam understood his role in this perfectly. He would race the length of the court on the wing, and on defense he knew how to pressure his man. Sam was a smart basketball player."

Bob Cousy added, "In Sam's case, he was even easier to feed in an open court situation than Sharman because of his speed and quickness. Normally people associate basketball players with height, but, in my judgment, speed and quickness are what separate the men from the boys."

With Sharman in his final season in 1960–61, Jones assumed an even more prominent role on the team, averaging 15 points, 5.4 rebounds, and 2.8 assists per game, in 26 minutes of action. Looking back at his state of mind at the time, Jones recalled, "I knew I was ready, but, in my mind, the backcourt still belonged to Bob Cousy and Bill Sharman. They were great, great players who had earned their right to start. Replacing Bill as the starter at that point, well, that was by necessity. He was hurting and the team needed me to step up."

A full-time starter for the first time in his career the following season, Jones established himself as one of the league's top shooting guards, earning the first of his five All-Star selections by averaging 18.4 points, 5.9 rebounds, and 3 assists per game. He followed that up with two more similarly productive seasons, posting averages of 19.7 points, 5.2 rebounds, and 3.2 assists per contest in 1962–63, before averaging 19.4 points, 4.6 rebounds, and 2.7 assists per game in 1963–64, en route to earning All-Star honors for the second time and a ninth-place finish in the league MVP voting.

As Jones rose to prominence in the NBA, his reputation as an outstanding clutch performer began to grow. Although he never averaged as many as 20 points per game in any of his first three seasons as a starter, he topped the 20-point mark each postseason, averaging more than 23 points per contest during both the 1963 and 1964 playoffs. In fact, Jones compiled a higher scoring average in the playoffs than he did during the regular season six straight times at one point, concluding his career with a postseason mark of 18.9 that exceeded his average in regular season play (17.7) by more than a point. The Celtics went 9-0 in Game 7s during Jones's tenure in Boston, with four of those victories taking place in the NBA Finals. Over the course of those nine contests, Jones averaged 27.1 points per game, scoring as many as 47 points, and no fewer than 18.

Jones took his game to the next level in 1964–65, when he averaged a career-high 25.9 points per game, becoming in the process the first Celtics player to score as many as 2,000 points in a season. He also averaged 5.1 rebounds and 2.8 assists per contest, en route to earning a fourth-place finish in the league MVP voting and All-NBA Second-Team honors for the first of three-straight times. Subsequently asked by the media to discuss his scoring prowess, Jones displayed his "team-first" mentality by suggesting, "That doesn't mean a thing. Every guy on this team has the ability to score 2,000 points if that's what he's asked to do. There's a lot of unselfishness by others in those 2,000 points I scored."

Jones followed up his exceptional 1964–65 campaign with three more outstanding seasons, earning a fifth-place finish in the MVP balloting in 1965–66 by averaging 23.5 points, 5.2 rebounds, and a career-best 3.2 assists per game, before posting marks of 22.1 points, 4.7 rebounds, and 3.0 assists per game in 1966–67, and 21.3 points, 4.9 rebounds, and 3.0 assists per contest in 1967–68.

Jones owed much of the success he experienced during that period to his exceptional quickness and varied offensive arsenal that included a long two-handed set shot, a short- to mid-range hook shot, and his signature bank shot, which he preferred to take from somewhere between 15 and 18 feet out. In discussing his favorite maneuver, Jones explained, "I started shooting the bank shot in high school. I wasn't a great outside shooter, and I struggled a little making layups, so I worked on my shooting technique and I focused on using the backboard. I picked out my target and I'd shoot for hours. I got to the point where I could really trust that shot, and it helped the rest of my game."

Making Jones's bank shot an even more potent offensive weapon were his quickness, intelligence, and knack for finding the open spot on the court, which he explained thusly:

> You simply can't stand still. When the ball is shot, the defender has to turn his head to see where the rebound is going. When I see we have the rebound, I immediately go to another position on the court. The man who is guarding me has his back to me now and he doesn't know I've moved. He has to turn around and look for me. It doesn't have to be much—just an opening. That's all you need, because you only need a split second to get a shot off.

In discussing his longtime teammate's ability to free himself for an open shot, K. C. Jones said, "He had a stutter step that would kind of halt your defense and then, all of a sudden, he just glides by you. He did that to me in a scrimmage and it just totally blew my mind that he was so smooth with that."

A personal favorite of Red Auerbach, who included his speed, touch, reflexes, and attitude among his special attributes, Jones received further praise from his coach, who stated, "He'll do anything you ask him. He's always in shape and ready to play, and nobody works any harder at basketball than he does."

On another occasion, Auerbach told the *Sporting News*, "I wouldn't put [Jones] in quite the same class as Oscar Robertson and Jerry West, who do more things well. But, as a shooter, he's every bit as tough to guard."

Jones spent one more season in Boston, averaging 16.3 points, 3.8 rebounds, and 2.6 assists per game in 1968–69, before announcing his retirement after he helped the Celtics win their 10th NBA championship in 11 years. Jones ended his playing career with 15,411 points scored, 4,305 rebounds, 2,209 assists, and averages of 17.7 points, 4.9 rebounds, and 2.5 assists per game. He shot 45.6 percent from the field and 80.3 percent from the free-throw line over the course of his career. Jones continues to rank among the franchise's all-time leaders in numerous statistical categories, including points scored (7th), field goals made (6th), and games played (10th). In addition to having his number 24 retired by the Celtics, Jones earned spots on the NBA's 25th, 50th, and 75th Anniversary Teams, as well as a place in the Naismith Memorial Basketball Hall of Fame, which opened its doors to him in 1984. Displaying his typical humility during his induction speech, Jones said, "It would have made me very happy if the Celtics had gone in as a team, because that's what we were—a great team, not great individuals."

Following his retirement, Jones became the athletic director and head basketball coach at Federal City College in Washington, D.C., which eventually became the University of the District of Columbia. He later coached at his alma mater, North Carolina Central, before briefly serving as an assistant on the coaching staff of the New Orleans Jazz. Jones lived until December 30, 2021, when he passed away at a hospital in Boca Raton, Florida, at the age of 88. Upon news of his passing, the Celtics issued a statement that read: "Sam Jones was one of the most talented, versatile, and clutch shooters for the most successful and dominant team in NBA history. His scoring ability was so prolific, and his form so pure, that he earned the simple nickname, 'The Shooter.' He was also known as 'Mr. Clutch.' Only Bill Russell won more championships in his NBA career. The Jones family is in our thoughts as we mourn his loss and fondly remember the life and career of one of the greatest champions in American sports."

In assessing his former teammate's capabilities some years earlier, Bill Russell commented, "In the years that I played with the Celtics, in terms of total basketball skills, Sam Jones was the most skillful player that I ever played with. At one point, we won a total of eight consecutive NBA championships, and six times during that run we asked Sam to take the shot that meant the season. If he didn't hit the shot, we were finished—we were going home empty-handed. He never missed."

CELTICS CAREER HIGHLIGHTS

Best Season

Jones had an excellent all-around season for the Celtics in 1965–66, averaging 23.5 points, 5.2 rebounds, and a career-best 3.2 assists per game, while shooting 46.9 percent from the field, which represented the second-highest mark of his career. However, he performed even better one year earlier, concluding the 1964–65 campaign with a career-high 25.9 scoring average that placed him fifth in the league rankings. He also shot 45.2 percent from the field and averaged 5.1 rebounds and 2.8 assists per contest, en route to earning a fourth-place finish in the league MVP voting and the first of three consecutive All-NBA Second-Team nominations. Jones continued his outstanding play in the postseason, leading the Celtics to their seventh straight NBA title by posting a scoring average of 28.6 points per game over the course of their 12 playoff contests.

Memorable Moments / Greatest Performances

Having spent his first three seasons in Boston coming off the bench, Jones did not have his first "monster" game for the Celtics until January 13, 1961, when he scored 34 points during a 123–121 overtime win over the Philadelphia Warriors. He topped that performance in the regular-season finale two months later, scoring 44 points, in leading the Celtics to a 136–134 overtime victory over the Syracuse Nationals on March 12.

Jones turned in a pair of exceptional performances against the Warriors in December 1961, leading the Celtics to 123–113 and 116–111 wins over their Philadelphia counterparts on December 13 and 30 by scoring 35 and 36 points, respectively.

Jones had a pair of big games two weeks apart early in 1963, tallying 37 points during a 149–148 overtime loss to the Nationals on January 19, before hitting for 35 points, in leading the Celtics to a 137–128 win over the Detroit Pistons on February 3.

Jones performed brilliantly on a number of occasions over the course of the ensuing campaign, with the first such instance taking place on December 19, 1963, when he scored 36 points during a 143–140 win over the Knicks. He again proved to be too much for the Knicks to handle on February 8, 1964, leading the Celtics to a 135–114 victory by tallying 35 points. Jones again scored 35 points during a 115–108 win over the Pistons three weeks later.

Jones played arguably the best ball of his career in December 1964, scoring more than 30 points in 7 of the 17 games the Celtics played that month. He began his extraordinary run by tallying 37 points during a 117–113 overtime win over the Knicks on the first of the month. Other particularly outstanding efforts included a 40-point performance against the Pistons on December 27, and a 37-point outing against the Baltimore Bullets three days later, with the Celtics winning those games by scores of 112–106 and 121–114, respectively.

Jones continued to compile outstanding numbers later that season, putting together a string of games in mid-February 1965, during which he scored more than 30 points four straight times. After leading the Celtics to a 94–92 overtime win over the Knicks on February 12, by tallying 34 points, Jones hit for 44 points during a 123–113 loss to New York and 35 points during a 126–111 victory over the Baltimore Bullets. He concluded that four-game stretch by scoring 32 points on February 17, in leading the Celtics to a 121–114 win over the St. Louis Hawks.

Jones had another big game early the following month, hitting for 38 points during a 128–124 overtime loss to the Bullets on March 5, 1965.

Jones also turned in a number of exceptional performances over the course of the ensuing campaign, with his finest effort coming on October 29, 1965, when he scored a career-high 51 points during a 108–106 loss to the Detroit Pistons. He also tallied 37 points, in leading the Celtics to a 123–120 overtime win over the Knicks on December 22, 1965, before scoring another 37 points during a 100–98 loss to the St. Louis Hawks on New Year's Day. Jones then led the Celtics to 115–111 and 100–95 wins over the Lakers and Knicks in late February 1966 by scoring 35 and 36 points, respectively.

Jones continued to be a force to be reckoned with the following year, scoring 38 points during a 118–106 win over the 76ers on January 24, 1967, leading the Celtics to a 135–120 victory over the Baltimore Bullets on February 22 by hitting for a season-high 42 points, and tallying 39 points during a 130–119 win over the St. Louis Hawks four days later.

Jones approached 40 points for one of the last times in his career on November 10, 1967, when he led the Celtics to a 115–114 victory over the Baltimore Bullets by scoring 39 points.

Yet, in spite of the many brilliant regular-season performances Jones turned in over the course of his career, Celtics fans will always remember him most for his exceptional postseason play. Jones gave the earliest indication of his ability to excel under pressure in Game 7 of the 1962 Eastern

Jones finished fourth in the league MVP voting in 1964–65, when he became the first Celtics player to score 2,000 points in one season.
Photo courtesy of MearsOnlineAuctions.com.

Division Finals, when he scored a team-high 28 points and delivered the game-winning basket in the closing seconds of a 109–107 victory over the Philadelphia Warriors that clinched a berth in the NBA Finals for the Celtics. Jones scored the game's final two points with just two seconds remaining in regulation, hitting a jump shot over the outstretched arms of Wilt Chamberlain, who called him the Celtics' best player following the contest.

Jones continued to come up big for the Celtics in that year's NBA Finals, helping Boston overcome a 3–2 deficit in the series to Los Angeles by scoring 35 and 27 points in the final two games, which the Celtics won by scores of 119–105 and 110–107. Jones averaged 22.1 points per contest over the course of the seven-game series.

Jones again proved his mettle in Game 7 of the 1963 Eastern Division Finals, when he led the Celtics to a 142–131 win over the Cincinnati Royals by scoring 47 points, winning in the process his personal battle with Oscar Robertson, who scored 43 points for the losing team.

Jones had another tremendous postseason in 1965, averaging just over 29 points during Boston's seven-game victory over the Philadelphia 76ers in the Eastern Division Finals, including a 40-point performance in a Game 2 loss and a 37-point effort in Game 7, which the Celtics won by a score of 110–109. He subsequently averaged 27.8 points per game during Boston's five-game victory over the Los Angeles Lakers in the NBA Finals, concluding the postseason with a scoring average of 28.6 points per contest.

Jones performed extremely well in all three rounds of the 1966 Playoffs, leading the Celtics to a five-game win over the Royals in the opening round by averaging 26.6 points per contest, including a 42-point effort in Boston's 132–125 victory in Game 2. He subsequently posted a scoring average of just under 26 points per game during the Celtics' five-game win over Philadelphia in the Eastern Division Finals, before averaging just under 23 points per contest during Boston's seven-game victory over Los Angeles in the NBA Finals.

Jones turned in one of the greatest performances of his career in Game 4 of the 1967 Eastern Division Semifinals, when he helped the Celtics eliminate the Knicks, three games to one, by scoring 51 points during Boston's 118–109 series-clinching win.

The following year, Jones helped the Celtics overcome a seemingly insurmountable 3–1 deficit to the powerful Philadelphia 76ers in the Eastern Division Finals by scoring a game-high 37 points during a 122–104 Celtics victory in Game 5 that put them back in the series.

Nevertheless, Jones likely will always be remembered more for one shot than any other. With the Celtics trailing Los Angeles two games to one in the 1969 NBA Finals, and with the Lakers holding a one-point lead in Game 4 with only seven seconds remaining in regulation, Boston called a time-out. Player-coach Bill Russell then entrusted Jones with taking the last-second shot, which he hit, to even the series at two games apiece. Recalling his game-winning shot, Jones later said, "I knew that last shot was good from the moment it left my hand. There never was any doubt because I had time to release the shot properly, and I trusted my technique completely. That took the pressure off. The ball rolled right over the cylinder. We won that game, and then we went on to win the championship."

NOTABLE ACHIEVEMENTS

- Averaged more than 20 points per game four times, topping 25 points per contest once (25.9 in 1964–65).
- Averaged more than 18 points per game three other times.
- Averaged more than 20 points per game during playoffs in seven straight seasons.
- Led NBA in games played once (80 in 1964–65).
- Led Celtics in scoring average five times.
- First Celtics player to score 2,000 points in a season (2,070 in 1964–65).
- Scored 51 points vs. Detroit on October 29, 1965.
- Ranks among Celtics career leaders in points scored (7th); field-goal attempts (5th); field goals made (6th); free-throw attempts (8th); free throws made (9th); games played (10th); and minutes played (10th).
- Finished in top five of NBA MVP voting twice.
- Three-time All-NBA Second-Team selection (1964–65, 1965–66, and 1966–67).
- Five-time NBA All-Star (1962, 1964, 1965, 1966, and 1968).
- 11-time Eastern Division champion (1958–66, 1968, and 1969).
- 10-time NBA champion (1959–66, 1968, and 1969).
- Number 24 retired by Celtics.
- Member of NBA's 25th Anniversary Team.
- Member of NBA's 50th Anniversary Team.
- Member of NBA's 75th Anniversary Team.
- Inducted into Naismith Memorial Basketball Hall of Fame in 1984.

10

ROBERT PARISH

It's hard for me to even believe how good we were. Some nights I'd be
out there just kicking some guy's butt, really feeling it, and then I'd
look over and see what Kevin was doing, and what Larry was doing,
and I'd say, "Man, this is something. This is special."

—Robert Parish

The third and final member of arguably the greatest frontcourt in NBA
history, Robert Parish combined strength, agility, and remarkable
endurance to establish himself as one of the finest centers of his era.
Displaying extraordinary consistency over the course of his career, which
covered 21 seasons and more games than any other player in league history,
Parish averaged at least 16 points and 9 rebounds per game in 10 of 11
seasons at one point, while also shooting better than 50 percent from the
field all but once during that period. Particularly effective in his 14 years
in Boston, Parish averaged at least 18.9 points per game four straight times
for the Celtics, using his exceptional mid-range jumper and strong post-up
game to score the fourth-most points in team annals. A solid rebounder and
defender as well, Parish topped 10 rebounds per game eight times and 2
blocked shots per contest twice as a member of the team, giving the Celtics
an intimidating low-post presence. In all, Parish earned nine All-Star selections and two All-NBA nominations during his time in Boston, in helping
the Celtics capture nine Atlantic Division, five Eastern Conference, and
three NBA championships.

Born in Shreveport, Louisiana, on August 30, 1953, Robert Lee Parish attended local Woodlawn High School before enrolling at Louisiana's
Centenary College, where he spent the next four years leading the Gents

Robert Parish appeared in more games than any other player in NBA history. Photo courtesy of MearsOnlineAuctions.com.

to an overall record of 87-21 by averaging 21.6 points and 16.9 rebounds per game. Between his junior and senior years at Centenary, Parish also played for the US national team at the 1975 Pan American Games, serving as captain of a squad that ended up winning the gold medal. Yet, in spite of his outstanding play in college, professional scouts remained unconvinced as to his ability to succeed at the next level, with one talent evaluator suggesting during his senior season, "The jury is still out as to whether Parish can win games for a pro team. He can definitely play in the pros, and he's going to get a lot of money, but that doesn't mean he's going to be another Abdul-Jabbar."

After previously being selected by the San Antonio Spurs in the 1975 ABA draft, Parish elected to sign with Golden State when the Warriors made him the eighth overall pick of the 1976 NBA Draft. Parish subsequently played relatively well for the Warriors in a backup role his first two years in the league, posting averages of 9.1 points and 7.1 rebounds per game as a rookie, before averaging 12.5 points and 8.3 rebounds per contest in his second season. He improved his output dramatically after he became a member of the Warriors' starting five in 1978–79, averaging better than 17 points and 10 rebounds per game in each of the next two campaigns, while shooting right around 50 percent from the field each year. Nevertheless, whispers began to circulate within the organization concerning Parish's lack of proper motivation, which often manifested itself in his failure to work as hard as the team's coaching staff would have liked.

Fully aware of Golden State's dissatisfaction with the talented but somewhat enigmatic Parish, Boston GM Red Auerbach engineered a trade with the Warriors just prior to the 1980 NBA Draft in which he dealt the number-one overall pick and an additional first-rounder to Golden State for Parish and the third overall pick, which he then used to select Kevin McHale. The deal ended up turning Boston into a championship ball club, with Parish and McHale joining Larry Bird to give the Celtics the NBA's most formidable front line.

Parish also benefited greatly from the trade, developing a superior work ethic and a newfound intensity under second-year head coach Bill Fitch, a former Marine drill sergeant who drove his players exceptionally hard in training camp. Commenting on Fitch's methods at one point, Parish stated, "That man liked to kill me." Yet, Parish also admitted, "I was lazy when I got here." Under Fitch, Parish improved his speed and stamina to the point where he ran the floor as well as any center in the league. He also emerged as one of the sport's most durable players, lasting 21 seasons and appearing in an NBA record 1,611 games.

Meanwhile, after playing for a Golden State team riddled with chemistry issues and personality problems, Parish found the atmosphere in Boston refreshing, saying of the trade that made him a member of the Celtics, "It was like going from the outhouse to the penthouse." Parish also acquired a new moniker after he arrived in Beantown, with teammate Cedric Maxwell nicknaming him "Chief," since he believed that the stoic center resembled, in both appearance and demeanor, the strong, quiet Native American character that figured prominently in the 1970s Jack Nicholson movie, *One Flew Over the Cuckoo's Nest.*

Reaching his full potential in Boston, Parish began in 1980–81 an outstanding four-year run that proved to be the finest of his career. Here are the numbers he posted during that stretch of time:

SEASON	POINTS PER GAME	REBOUNDS PER GAME	BLOCKED SHOTS PER GAME
1980–81	18.9	9.5	2.6
1981–82	19.9	10.8	2.4
1982–83	19.3	10.6	1.9
1983–84	19.0	10.7	1.5

Displaying remarkable consistency throughout the period, Parish placed among the league leaders in rebounding and blocked shots two times each, while shooting between 54 and 55 percent from the field and earning All-Star honors each season.

Blessed with an excellent turnaround jump shot, which he liked to release from the left baseline from somewhere in the 14- to 18-foot range, Parish drew praise from Hall of Fame center Bill Walton, who said of his onetime teammate, "He's probably the best medium-range shooting big man in the history of the game." Parish typically released his high-trajectory jumper from well over his head, making it almost impossible to block. He also possessed a good jump hook and surprising mobility for a big man, making him an excellent finisher on the fast break. Parish also ran the pick-and-roll to perfection with Larry Bird, stating following the conclusion of his playing career, "I probably got at least 5,000 points off passes from Larry." Parish did an excellent job off the boards and on defense as well, serving as the backbone of Boston's defense.

Parish continued to perform well for the Celtics in his 10 remaining seasons with them, earning another five All-Star selections, averaging more than 14 points per game eight more times, and more than 8 rebounds per contest nine more times, while also shooting well over 50 percent from the field all but once. Particularly effective in 1984–85, 1986–87, and 1988–89, Parish posted averages of 17.6 points and 10.6 rebounds, 17.5 points and 10.6 rebounds, and 18.6 points and 12.5 rebounds per game, respectively, in those three seasons.

Parish possessed one of the best mid-range jump shots of any center ever to play the game. Photo courtesy of George A. Kitrinos.

With Parish's playing time and productivity gradually diminishing over the course of the previous few seasons, the Celtics chose not to offer him a new contract when he became a free agent following the conclusion of the 1993–94 campaign. The 41-year-old center subsequently signed with the

Charlotte Hornets, with whom he spent the next two years coming off the bench, before winning his fourth NBA championship as a backup for the Chicago Bulls in his final season. Announcing his retirement in typically understated fashion during an off-season television interview on August 25, 1997, Parish stated, "I think it's time. I know in my heart that it's time to walk away."

Parish ended his playing career with 23,334 points scored, 14,715 rebounds, 2,180 assists, 2,361 blocked shots, 1,219 steals, a 53.7 field-goal shooting percentage, and a 72.1 free-throw shooting percentage. Over the course of 21 NBA seasons, he averaged 14.5 points, 9.1 rebounds, 1.4 assists, 1.5 blocked shots, and .8 steals per game. In Parish's 14 years with the Celtics, he scored 18,245 points, accumulated 11,051 rebounds, 1,679 assists, 1,703 blocked shots, and 873 steals, shot 55.2 percent from the field and 73 percent from the free-throw line, and posted averages of 16.5 points, 10 rebounds, 1.5 assists, 1.5 blocked shots, and .8 steals per game.

In addition to holding the NBA record for most games played, Parish ranks among the league's all-time leaders in offensive rebounds (2nd), defensive rebounds (5th), total rebounds (8th), and blocked shots (10th). Extremely durable as well, Parish missed a total of only 42 games during his time in Boston, averaging 79 games per season over that 14-year stretch. Parish's many accomplishments prompted the Celtics to retire his number 00 jersey in 1998. He also earned spots on the NBA's 50th and 75th Anniversary Teams and a place in the Naismith Memorial Basketball Hall of Fame, which opened its doors to him in 2003. Parish currently holds a dual position within the Celtics' organization, serving the team as a consultant and a mentor for current big men.

Although the quiet and reserved Parish tended to shy away from the limelight during his career, preferring instead to let his play do his talking, his teammates knew how important he was to the success of the Celtics, with Larry Bird once stating, "We don't win any of those three NBA titles without Robert."

Meanwhile, in discussing Parish's two most notable attributes, Boston sportswriter Bob Ryan said, "He had the great turnaround jump shot and incredible ability to run the floor."

Always one to focus more on the team than himself, Parish preferred to reflect on the success Boston's "Big Three" experienced together, commenting, "It's hard for me to even believe how good we were. Some nights I'd be out there just kicking some guy's butt, really feeling it, and then I'd look over and see what Kevin was doing, and what Larry was doing, and I'd say, 'Man, this is something. This is special.'"

Parish then added, "I will always be a Celtic at heart. That's where my career took off."

CELTICS CAREER HIGHLIGHTS

Best Season

The 35-year-old Parish performed extremely well for the Celtics in 1988–89, averaging 18.6 points, 1.5 blocked shots, and a career-high 12.5 rebounds per game, while also shooting 57 percent from the field. However, he played the best ball of his career from 1980 to 1984, never averaging less than 18.9 points, 9.5 rebounds, or 1.5 blocked shots per contest over the course of those four seasons. While a legitimate argument could be waged on behalf of any of those seasons, I ultimately settled on the 1981–82 campaign. In addition to averaging a career-high 19.9 points per game, Parish posted marks of 10.8 rebounds and 2.4 blocked shots per contest, while hitting on 54.2 percent of his shots from the field. He finished eighth in the NBA in rebounding and fifth in blocked shots, earning in the process his lone All-NBA Second-Team selection and a fourth-place finish in the league MVP voting. Although the Celtics failed to earn a return trip to the NBA Finals, Parish also had the best postseason of his career, averaging 21.3 points, 11.3 rebounds, and 4 blocked shots in Boston's 12 playoff games.

Memorable Moments / Greatest Performances

Parish recorded his first 30-point game as a member of the Celtics on December 3, 1980, when he helped lead them to a 106–101 win over the Atlanta Hawks by scoring 33 points. He matched that mark a little over one month later, tallying another 33 points during a 120–113 victory over the Cleveland Cavaliers on January 14, 1981. However, Parish saved his biggest scoring output of the season for a February 17, 1981, meeting with the San Antonio Spurs, when he erupted for a career-high 40 points, in leading the Celtics to a 128–116 victory.

Parish turned in a number of outstanding all-around efforts over the course of the ensuing campaign, with the first of those coming on January 8, 1982, when he scored 18 points and pulled down 20 rebounds during a 96–90 win over the Philadelphia 76ers. He had another big game on February 19, 1982, when he scored 27 points, collected 18 rebounds, and assisted on 6 baskets during a 127–117 victory over Portland. Later that month, on February 28, Parish helped lead the Celtics to a 106–102 win over Milwaukee by tallying 29 points and amassing 17 rebounds. During a 113–109 victory over Atlanta on March 17, Parish scored 15 points and set a franchise record by blocking 9 shots. Just four days later, Parish played perhaps his finest all-around game of the year when he scored 37 points, pulled down 21 rebounds, and blocked 5 shots during a 123–111 win over Philadelphia.

Parish also turned in a pair of exceptional performances the following month, scoring 36 points during a 106–103 victory over the New Jersey Nets on April 9, 1982, before tallying 31 points and pulling down 16 rebounds during a 119–99 blowout of the Knicks in the regular-season finale nine days later.

Continuing his outstanding play in that year's postseason, Parish helped the Celtics advance to the 1982 Eastern Conference Finals by scoring 33 points during a 131–126 double-overtime victory over Washington in the Game 5 clincher of the Conference Semifinals.

Parish turned in one of his most dominant performances the following year on January 23, 1983, when he helped lead the Celtics to a 105–91 win over the Cleveland Cavaliers by scoring 26 points and pulling down 19 rebounds. He topped that effort some three weeks later, though, when he scored a season-high 36 points and collected 20 rebounds during a 121–114 loss to Portland on February 17.

Continuing to torment the Cavaliers the following season, Parish scored 30 points and collected 16 rebounds during a 110–108 win over Cleveland on December 14, 1983. He had another big game against the Nets on January 3, 1984, when he led the Celtics to a 105–103 victory by tallying 27 points and pulling down 19 rebounds. A little over one month later, on February 5, Parish scored a season-high 36 points, in leading the Celtics to a 137–134 overtime win over the Detroit Pistons.

However, it was during the 1984 NBA Finals that Parish made two of the biggest plays of his career, first making a critical steal against Lakers forward Bob McAdoo in the final seconds of overtime in Game 2 to help protect a one-point Boston lead, and then sending Game 4 into overtime by converting a three-point play and making another critical steal, this time of a Magic Johnson pass to James Worthy, in the final minute of regulation. The Celtics ended up winning both contests, en route to defeating Los Angeles in seven games.

Parish came back to haunt his former team, Golden State, on February 15, 1985, when he scored 15 points and pulled down 22 rebounds during a 107–100 victory over the Warriors. The following month, on

March 17, Parish scored a season-high 38 points during a 134–120 win over the Houston Rockets.

Although the Celtics lost their March 8, 1986, matchup with the Washington Bullets by a score of 110–108 in overtime, Parish played an outstanding all-around game, scoring 16 points, blocking 4 shots, and collecting 25 rebounds, which proved to be the highest total he ever amassed during his time in Boston (he once recorded 32 rebounds while with Golden State). Parish turned in another dominant performance the following month, leading the Celtics to a 122–106 victory over the Detroit Pistons on April 2 by scoring 30 points and pulling down 18 rebounds.

Parish had a big game against the Chicago Bulls on November 14, 1986, when he led the Celtics to a 110–98 win by scoring 27 points and collecting 18 rebounds. He followed that up the very next night with a brilliant all-around performance against Detroit, leading the Celtics to a 118–111 victory by scoring 34 points, pulling down 19 rebounds, assisting on 9 baskets, and blocking 5 shots. Parish also excelled against Sacramento on the evening of January 9, 1987, tallying 28 points and collecting 25 rebounds during a 109–99 win over the Kings.

Although the Celtics ended up losing to the Lakers in the 1987 NBA Finals, Parish performed heroically for them throughout the postseason, averaging 18 points and 9.4 rebounds per game during the playoffs, despite playing on two severely injured ankles. After scoring 30 points, pulling down 16 rebounds, and blocking 4 shots during a 129–124 loss to Milwaukee in Game 5 of the Eastern Conference Finals, Parish found himself unable to take the court for Game 6. However, playing with two ankle sprains, he subsequently helped the Celtics advance to the Conference Finals by accumulating 23 points, 19 rebounds, and 4 blocks during a 119–113 win in Game 7. Parish then starred for the Celtics in Game 1 of their Conference Final series against Detroit, leading them to a 104–91 victory by collecting 9 rebounds and scoring 31 points, on 10 of 12, shooting from the field.

Parish got off to an excellent start in 1988–89, scoring 21 points and pulling down 22 rebounds during a 122–115 overtime victory over the Knicks in the regular-season opener. He topped that performance later in the year, though, tallying 34 points and collecting 19 rebounds during a 112–99 win over San Antonio on December 30, 1988. Parish also had a pair of big games against Charlotte, scoring 24 points and pulling down 24 rebounds during a 107–94 Boston victory on February 1, 1989, before tallying 21 points and collecting 22 rebounds, in leading the Celtics to a 113–108 overtime win over the Hornets on April 17. In between, he scored

Parish ranks among Boston's all-time leaders in numerous statistical categories, including points scored (4th) and rebounds (2nd).
Photo courtesy of George A. Kitrinos.

27 points and pulled down 22 rebounds during a 107–106 victory over the Dallas Mavericks on March 3.

Parish turned in his last truly dominant performance for the Celtics on December 8, 1989, when he scored 38 points and pulled down 12 rebounds during a 103–102 loss to the Denver Nuggets.

Yet, in spite of his many in-game heroics, the usually placid Parish will always be remembered equally by Celtics fans for the one time he lost his temper on the court. Taking exception to Bill Laimbeer's overly aggressive play under the boards in Game 5 of the 1987 Eastern Conference Finals, Parish responded by delivering three well-aimed blows to the Detroit center's face, breaking his nose in the process. Although the referees calling the game chose not to assess a technical foul to Parish due to Laimbeer's notorious reputation as an on-court instigator, the league ended up suspending him for Game 6.

NOTABLE ACHIEVEMENTS

- Averaged more than 15 points per game nine times, topping 18 points per contest five times.
- Averaged more than 10 rebounds per game eight times, topping 12 rebounds per contest once.
- Averaged more than 2 blocked shots per game twice.
- Shot better than 50 percent from the field 13 straight times.
- Finished third in NBA in rebounding in 1988–89 (12.5 rpg).
- Finished in top five in NBA in blocked shots three times.
- Finished in top five in NBA in field-goal shooting percentage four times, placing second twice.
- Led Celtics in rebounding eight times.
- Holds Celtics single-season record for most blocked shots (214 in 1980–81).
- Holds share of Celtics single-game record for most blocked shots (9 vs. Atlanta on 3/17/82).
- Holds Celtics career record for most "official" blocked shots (1,703).
- Ranks among Celtics career leaders in points scored (4th); rebounds (2nd); steals (5th); field-goal attempts (6th); field goals made (4th); field-goal shooting percentage (6th); free-throw attempts (6th); free throws made (6th); games played (2nd); and minutes played (4th).
- Ranks first in NBA history in games played (1,611).
- Ranks among NBA career leaders in offensive rebounds (2nd); defensive rebounds (5th); total rebounds (8th); and blocked shots (10th).
- Four-time NBA Player of the Week.
- Finished fourth in NBA MVP voting in 1981–82.
- 1981–82 All-NBA Second-Team selection.

- 1988–89 All-NBA Third-Team selection.
- Nine-time NBA All-Star (1981–87, 1990, and 1991).
- Five-time Eastern Conference champion (1981, 1984, 1985, 1986, and 1987).
- Three-time NBA champion (1981, 1984, and 1986).
- Number 00 retired by Celtics.
- Member of NBA's 50th Anniversary Team.
- Member of NBA's 75th Anniversary Team.
- Inducted into Naismith Memorial Basketball Hall of Fame in 2003.

11

KEVIN GARNETT

Kevin Garnett is the prototype for the NBA player of the future. He's already one of the greatest players to have played the game.
—Bill Walton

Already an established star by the time he joined the Celtics prior to the start of the 2007–08 campaign, Kevin Garnett arrived in Boston with a reputation as one of the NBA's finest all-around players. An outstanding scorer, superb rebounder, brilliant defender, and excellent passer, Garnett earlier became the first player in NBA history to average at least 20 points, 10 rebounds, and 5 assists per game for six straight seasons as a member of the Minnesota Timberwolves, with whom he spent the previous 12 seasons. During that time, Garnett averaged more than 20 points and 10 rebounds per game nine times each, led the NBA in rebounding four times, and earned 10 All-Star selections, eight All-NBA nominations, eight NBA All-Defensive selections, and one league MVP Award, placing second in the balloting on two other occasions.

Although age and injuries prevented Garnett from performing at quite the same lofty level for the Celtics for most of the next six seasons, the man known as "The Big Ticket" nevertheless made a huge impact in Boston, helping to lead his new team to five division titles, two NBA Finals appearances, and one league championship. Earning five more All-Star selections, four more NBA All-Defensive nominations, one more All-NBA selection, and 2007–08 NBA Defensive Player of the Year honors during his time in Boston, Garnett helped make the Celtics perennial contenders for the NBA title, with his intensity and leadership also helping to restore Celtics pride and tradition.

Kevin Garnett helped lead the Celtics to five division titles and one NBA championship. Photo courtesy of Keith Allison.

Born in Greenville, South Carolina, on May 19, 1976, Kevin Maurice Garnett moved with his family to nearby Mauldin at the age of 12. After first developing an interest in the game of basketball while attending Hillcrest Middle School, Garnett got his first taste of organized ball at Mauldin High School, whose team he spent three years anchoring. However, Garnett ultimately chose to leave Mauldin after he became involved in a racially charged incident between black and white students that occurred during the summer prior to his senior year of high school. Fearful of being targeted as a result of his actions, Garnett decided to transfer to Farragut Career Academy in Chicago, Illinois, where he spent his senior year earning National High School Player of the Year honors from *USA Today* by leading

Farragut to a 28-2 record. After also being named the Most Outstanding Player at the McDonald's All-American Game, Garnett declared himself eligible for 1995 NBA Draft, where the Minnesota Timberwolves selected him with the fifth overall pick.

Entering the NBA at only 19 years of age, Garnett experienced a moderate amount of success his first year in the league, averaging just over 10 points and 6 rebounds per game as a part-time starter, en route to earning NBA All-Rookie Second-Team honors. He improved upon those numbers in each of the next two seasons, posting averages of 17 points and 8 rebounds per game in 1996–97, before averaging 18.5 points and 9.6 rebounds per contest in 1997–98. After posting marks of 20.8 points, 10.4 rebounds, and 4.3 assists per game during the abbreviated 1998–99 campaign, Garnett began an exceptional six-year run during which he became the first player in NBA history to average more than 20 points, 10 rebounds, and 5 assists per contest six straight times. Garnett had arguably his two best seasons for the Timberwolves in 2002–03 and 2003–04, averaging 23 points, 6 assists, and 13.4 rebounds per game in the first of those campaigns, before averaging 24.2 points, 5 assists, and a league-leading 13.9 rebounds per contest in the second. After finishing runner-up in the MVP voting the previous year, Garnett earned league MVP honors in 2003–04.

Garnett evolved into an exceptional all-around player over the course of those six seasons, gradually developing both a fine outside shot and a strong post-up game on offense. He also possessed an explosive first step, great quickness and agility, and an ability to run the floor well and finish on the fast break. Meanwhile, although Garnett added a considerable amount of bulk over time to the skinny 6-foot-11, 218-pound frame with which he first entered the league, he never tipped the scales at much more than 240 pounds. Yet, in spite of his slender physique, he used his deceptive strength, long arms, and exceptional quickness to eventually establish himself as one of the league's premier rebounders and defenders, topping the circuit in rebounding four straight times, while typically averaging close to 2 blocked shots per contest. He also developed into an exceptional passer, averaging more than 4 assists per game in 10 straight seasons at one point.

Commenting on Garnett's unique physical gifts, former NBA coach Doug Collins suggested, "He's a genetic freak. All the great ones are."

Former New York Knicks guard Allan Houston marveled, "God has really put something together with him. His size and his ability—he's probably one of the most unique players in the world."

NBA Hall of Famer Elgin Baylor noted, "When I first saw him, he had the best athletic skills for his size of anyone I had ever seen at that stage.

He's really thin, but it doesn't matter. With his agility and coordination, he can give people trouble at the power forward, small forward, and center positions."

Jerry West added, "Offensively, he has that wonderful turnaround jump shot and those follow-ups around the basket. He's one of those guys who, because of his size and athletic ability, create real difficult defensive matchups."

Bill Walton proclaimed, "Kevin Garnett is the prototype for the NBA player of the future. He's already one of the greatest players to have played the game."

In addition to his extraordinary physical talent, Garnett possessed several intangible qualities statistics fail to reveal. An extremely intense and driven individual, Garnett played the game with unmatched fervor, exhibiting tremendous dedication to his profession in everything he did. Former Minnesota Timberwolves general manager Kevin McHale commented, "He reminds me of how basketball should be played—with passion, hard work, and discipline."

Former NBA coach Rudy Tomjanovich noted, "This guy has as much energy as anyone I've ever seen. He attacks the boards like he's in a gym all by himself."

The late Flip Saunders, who served as Garnett's first NBA coach, once said, "Even if Kevin's shot isn't on, it's the other things he does—the rebounds he gets, the ones he tips to the other people, the blocked shots, the intimidation inside, just knowing what to do—that makes him so special."

Garnett also drew praise from Magic Johnson, who suggested, "His know-how for the game, his feel for the game—that's something you can't teach. You either got it or you don't. He's got it."

Garnett spent two more extremely productive seasons in Minnesota, averaging close to 22 points and 13 rebounds per game in both 2005–06 and 2006–07, before the Timberwolves elected to trade him to the Celtics for a pair of future first-round draft picks and a package of five players that included Al Jefferson, Theo Ratliff, and Ryan Gomes. After acquiring Garnett on July 31, 2007, Celtics general manager Danny Ainge proclaimed, "Winning a championship is now a legitimate and realistic goal."

Joining longtime Celtics star Paul Pierce and fellow newcomer Ray Allen in Boston, Garnett gave the team an extremely formidable "Big Three" that ended up leading the Celtics to their first NBA championship since 1986. Certainly, all three players made significant contributions to the success the Celtics experienced over the course of the 2007–08 campaign. But, even though Pierce led the team in scoring and retained his position of "official" team leader, it could be argued that Garnett's intensity, exceptional play at both ends of the court, and unselfish approach to the game made the greatest overall impact on a club that finished with one of the NBA's worst records just one year earlier.

In addition to averaging 18.8 points and 9.2 rebounds per game, Garnett earned NBA Defensive Player of the Year honors and inspired his teammates with his dedication, determination, and ability to lead by example. Garnett's stellar all-around play earned him the 11th of his 15 All-Star selections, his fourth and final All-NBA First-Team nomination, and a third-place finish in the league MVP balloting. Garnett also performed extremely well for the Celtics in the postseason, posting averages of 20.4 points and 10.5 rebounds per game in Boston's 26 playoff contests. Subsequently asked to evaluate the deal that brought Garnett to Boston, Danny Ainge replied, "Was he worth it? Absolutely; he won us a championship. He changed our culture."

Garnett continued to play well for the Celtics throughout much of the ensuing campaign, averaging 15.8 points and 8.5 rebounds per game over 57 contests. However, after straining his right knee during a game against the Utah Jazz on February 19, 2009, Garnett appeared in only four more games the rest of the season, with his absence from the Boston lineup ultimately proving to be critical, since it contributed greatly to a seven-game defeat at the hands of the Orlando Magic in the Eastern Conference Semifinals. Yet, despite having his season cut short by injury, Garnett earned the eighth of his nine NBA All-Defensive First-Team selections.

Despite appearing in only 69 games and having his minutes reduced somewhat, to just under 30 minutes per contest the following season, the 33-year-old Garnett helped the Celtics capture their third consecutive Atlantic Division title by averaging 14.3 points and 7.3 rebounds per game, en route to earning his 13th All-Star selection. He followed that up with three more solid seasons for the Celtics, posting averages of 14.9 points and 8.9 rebounds per game in 2010–11, 15.8 points and 8.2 rebounds per contest in 2011–12, and 14.8 points and 7.8 rebounds per game in 2012–13, earning in the process his last two All-Star nominations.

The 2012–13 campaign ended up being Garnett's last in Boston. Convinced by teammate Paul Pierce to waive the no-trade clause in his contract, Garnett subsequently accepted a deal agreed upon by the Celtics and Brooklyn Nets on July 12, 2013, that sent Garnett, Pierce, Jason Terry, and D. J. White to Brooklyn for Keith Bogans, MarShon Brooks, Kris Humphries, Kris Joseph, Gerald Wallace, and three future first-round draft

Garnett won NBA Defensive Player of the Year honors his first season in Boston.
Photo courtesy of Keith Allison.

picks. Garnett left the Celtics having scored 6,233 points, amassed 3,301 rebounds, 1,078 assists, 460 steals, and 394 blocked shots, and averaged 15.7 points, 8.3 rebounds, and 2.7 assists per game as a member of the team. He also shot 52 percent from the field and 82.7 percent from the free-throw line over the course of his six seasons in Boston.

Garnett spent most of the next two seasons in Brooklyn, averaging fewer than 7 points, 7 rebounds, and 21 minutes per contest during that time, before being traded back to Minnesota during the latter stages of the 2014–15 campaign. Although Garnett saw his playing time similarly reduced by the Timberwolves in 2015–16, he assumed the important role of serving as mentor to Karl-Anthony Towns, the rookie center selected first overall by Minnesota in the 2015 NBA Draft. Choosing to announce his retirement at the end of the year, Garnett ended his playing career with 26,071 points scored, 14,662 rebounds, 5,445 assists, 1,859 steals, and 2,037 blocked shots, and averages of 17.8 points, 10 rebounds, and 3.7 assists per game. In addition to holding the NBA record for most defensive rebounds (11,453), Garnett ranks among the league's all-time leaders in total rebounds (9th), games played (7th), and minutes played (5th).

CELTICS CAREER HIGHLIGHTS

Best Season

Garnett clearly played his best ball for the Celtics in his first season in Boston, when, in addition to being named 2007–08 NBA Defensive Player of the Year, he earned a third-place finish in the league MVP voting and his lone All-NBA First-Team selection as a member of the team by averaging 18.8 points, 9.2 rebounds, 3.4 assists, 1.4 steals, and 1.3 blocked shots per game, while shooting a career-best 53.9 percent from the field.

Memorable Moments / Greatest Performances

Garnett got off to an excellent start with the Celtics, leading them to a 103–83 win over Washington in his first game with the team on November 2, 2007, by scoring 22 points, pulling down 20 rebounds, assisting on 5 baskets, blocking 3 shots, and recording 3 steals.

Garnett turned in another outstanding performance exactly one week later on November 9, 2007, when he scored 27 points on 12 of 16 shooting from the field, and collected 19 rebounds during a 106–83 victory over the Atlanta Hawks.

Garnett had another big game against Atlanta on March 2, 2008, when he led the Celtics to a 98–88 win over the Hawks by scoring 20 points and pulling down 16 rebounds. Garnett also starred in the very next game, tallying a season-high 31 points during a 90–78 victory over the Detroit Pistons on March 5, 2008.

Garnett turned in perhaps his finest all-around performance the following season on December 7, 2008, when he led the Celtics to a 122–117 overtime win over Indiana by scoring 17 points and collecting 20 rebounds. Garnett put up extremely similar numbers against the Bulls on December 3, 2010, leading the Celtics to a 104–92 victory over Chicago by scoring 20 points and recording 17 rebounds. Some three months later, on March 2, 2011, Garnett pulled down 11 rebounds and hit for a season-high 28 points during a 115–103 win over the Phoenix Suns.

Excelling for the Celtics throughout the 2007–08 postseason, Garnett came up big against Cleveland in Game 5 of the Eastern Conference Semi-finals, scoring 26 points and collecting 16 rebounds during a 96–89 win over the Cavaliers.

Garnett also had a huge Game 5 against Detroit in the 2008 Eastern Conference Finals, leading the Celtics to a 106–102 victory over the Pistons by scoring 33 points.

Garnett subsequently helped the Celtics claim their 17th NBA championship by scoring 26 points and pulling down 14 rebounds during Boston's 131–92 Game 6 victory over Los Angeles in the NBA Finals.

Although the Celtics lost their 2011 Eastern Conference Semifinal series with the Miami Heat in five games, Garnett played a huge role in their 97–81 win in Game 3, scoring 28 points and collecting 18 rebounds.

Garnett helped the Celtics close out their 2012 first-round playoff matchup with Atlanta by tallying 28 points and pulling down 14 rebounds during their series-clinching 83–80 victory over the Hawks in Game 6.

Garnett followed that up by averaging 20 points and 11 rebounds per contest against Philadelphia in the 2012 Eastern Conference Semifinals, which the Celtics won in seven games.

NOTABLE ACHIEVEMENTS

- Averaged more than 15 points per game three times, topping 18 points per contest once.
- Averaged more than 8 rebounds per game four times.
- Shot better than 50 percent from the field 5 times.
- Led Celtics in rebounding five times and blocked shots once.
- Holds NBA career record for most defensive rebounds (11,453).*
- Five-time NBA Player of the Week.
- Finished third in NBA MVP voting in 2007–08.
- 2007–08 NBA Defensive Player of the Year.
- 2007–08 All-NBA First-Team selection.
- Three-time NBA All-Defensive First-Team selection (2007–08, 2008–09, and 2010–11).
- 2011–12 NBA All-Defensive Second-Team selection.
- Five-time NBA All-Star (2008, 2009, 2010, 2011, and 2013).
- Two-time Eastern Conference champion (2007–08 and 2009–10).
- 2007–08 NBA champion.
- Member of NBA's 75th Anniversary Team.

* Note: The NBA did not distinguish between offensive and defensive rebounds in its record books prior to the 1973–74 season.

12

TOM HEINSOHN

He is the keeper of the tradition and pride. There is nothing better than hearing once again how they had to bail Red out of jail, how terrible a bus driver Red was, and on and on.... When you get to know Tommy, you understand exactly what made the Celtics the greatest example of teamwork and pride there has ever been.

—Team owner Wycliffe Grousbeck

The only person involved with the Celtics in an official team capacity in each of their 17 championship seasons, Tom Heinsohn spent nearly 60 years fulfilling one role or another within the organization. A high-scoring forward on Celtics teams that won eight championships during his playing career, which lasted from 1956 to 1965, Heinsohn subsequently coached the Men in Green to another two titles during the 1970s. After relinquishing his coaching duties, Heinsohn moved into the broadcast booth, where he enlightened and entertained fans in the New England area for more than 35 years.

Heinsohn, though, made this list strictly on the strength of his considerable playing ability, which earned him four All-NBA Second-Team selections and six All-Star nominations. An elite scorer with a soft shooting touch, a variety of moves around the basket, and superb body control, Heinsohn averaged more than 20 points per game in three of his nine seasons in Boston, topping 16 points per contest in all but his final campaign. A hard-nosed defender and outstanding rebounder as well, Heinsohn averaged at least 9.5 rebounds per game in each of his first six seasons, surpassing 10 boards per contest on two separate occasions. Heinsohn's offensive versatility, tenacious rebounding, and solid defensive play made him one of

Tom Heinsohn served the Celtics in one capacity or another in each of their 17 championship seasons. Photo courtesy of Boston Public Library, Leslie Jones Collection.

the premier power forwards of his era, and a key contributor to the Celtics dynasty that began with his arrival in Boston in 1956.

Born in Jersey City, New Jersey, on August 26, 1934, Thomas William Heinsohn moved with his family to nearby Union City while still in grade school. Introduced to the game of basketball as a sixth-grader at St. Joseph's Elementary School, Heinsohn subsequently developed into an outstanding player while attending Union City's St. Michael's High School, earning All-County honors as a junior and high school All-America honors as a senior. The recipient of more than 40 scholarship offers following his graduation from St. Michael's, Heinsohn ultimately settled on the College of the Holy Cross—the same institution from which future Celtics teammate Bob Cousy had graduated a few years earlier. Heinsohn continued his success at the collegiate level, setting a new Holy Cross record as a senior by averaging 27.4 points per game, en route to earning a spot on almost every All-America team.

Subsequently selected by the Celtics as a territorial pick in the 1956 NBA Draft, Heinsohn arrived in Boston the same year as Bill Russell, although the latter missed the first two months of the campaign while leading the US Men's Basketball Team to victory in the 1956 Olympics. With Russell's initial absence likely being the deciding factor, Heinsohn ended up beating out his teammate for NBA Rookie of the Year honors, concluding his first year in the league with averages of 16.2 points and 9.8 rebounds per contest, en route to earning his first All-Star selection. He punctuated his outstanding rookie season by averaging 22.9 points and 11.7 rebounds during the playoffs, including a fabulous 37-point, 23-rebound performance in Game 7 of the NBA Finals, which the Celtics won to capture their first league championship.

Heinsohn continued his strong play in his sophomore campaign of 1957–58, averaging 17.8 points and 10.2 rebounds per game for a Boston team that eventually lost to the St. Louis Hawks in the NBA Finals. After helping the Celtics capture their second NBA title the following year by averaging 18.8 points and 9.7 rebounds per contest, Heinsohn began an exceptional three-year run that saw him post the best numbers of his career. In addition to averaging 21.7 points per game in 1959–60, Heinsohn averaged a career-high 10.6 rebounds per contest. He followed that up by posting averages of 21.3 points and 9.9 rebounds per game in 1960–61, before averaging 22.1 points and 9.5 rebounds per contest in 1961–62. The Celtics emerged victorious in the NBA Finals all three years, with Heinsohn earning All-Star and All-NBA Second-Team honors in both 1960–61 and 1961–62.

The formula for success Boston coach Red Auerbach employed throughout the period had Heinsohn serving as the team's designated shooter, Bob Cousy distributing the ball to his teammates, and Bill Russell dominating the backboards and defensive end of the court. Heinsohn, who stood 6-foot-7 and weighed close to 220 pounds, possessed a varied offensive arsenal that included a long-range jumper he felt most comfortable taking from the corners and from the top of the key. He also boasted a one-handed set shot, a right-handed hook shot that he typically released anywhere from 5 to 15 feet out, a short-range left-handed hook, and several types of driving layups.

Nicknamed "Tommy Gun" for his willingness to shoot, Heinsohn sometimes drew criticism from the media for the emphasis he seemed to place on scoring. The writers also censured him at times for taking a relatively high number of low-percentage shots. Yet, Heinsohn retained the full support of his teammates, with Bob Cousy telling the *Saturday Evening Post* on one occasion, "Sure, he takes a few bad shots now and then, but, over the long haul, the confident player is the one who takes the initiative and wins games for you."

Bill Sharman added, "There are better shooters, I suppose, but Tommy's ability and his exceptional body control give him a big advantage."

Meanwhile, a former New York Knicks coach suggested that Heinsohn would "take five miserable shots that'll make you sick. But then he'll turn around and hit with five or six straight. Even on a bad night, he'll get his 17 or 18 points."

In addition to leaning heavily on Heinsohn for his scoring, Auerbach depended on his thick-skinned power forward to shoulder much of the criticism he doled out to the rest of the team. Fully aware that several other players on the squad possessed egos too fragile to be severely reprimanded, Auerbach often delivered his messages through Heinsohn, who later told the *Boston Globe*, "[Auerbach] knew that some of the big guys had sensitive egos—egos that didn't like it if Red started to get on them verbally. So, when he wanted to get on someone to stir up things in the dressing room, he got on me. He knew I could take it. I was his whipping boy. I understood what he was doing, so I could handle it."

To illustrate his point, Heinsohn recounted one particular incident that took place during halftime of a game in which he had scored more than 20 points and pulled down a dozen rebounds in the first half. Auerbach, who remained unhappy with the performance of the rest of the team, lit into Heinsohn during the intermission, screaming at him in front of his teammates. After silently weathering Auerbach's attack for several minutes, a puzzled Heinsohn asked, "Red, what the hell have I done wrong tonight?," to which his coach responded with a straight face, "Tommy, you warmed up lousy."

The poorly conditioned Heinsohn, who Auerbach once said had the "oldest 27-year-old body in the history of sports," also served as the Celtics' foremost prankster, often cutting a teammate's shoelaces just enough so that they broke when being tied. On one particular occasion, he even took it upon himself to exact a measure of revenge against Auerbach, who previously had given him an exploding cigar. However, deceiving his coach proved to be quite a challenge, since the shrewd Auerbach, suspecting retaliation from the team's resident practical joker, refused to accept cigars from him. Heinsohn finally got Auerbach to let his guard down by offering him perfectly good cigars several times. During a subsequent press conference before a playoff game with Syracuse, Auerbach lit a cigar Heinsohn had given him, only to have it blow up in his face in front of the horde of reporters assembled before him.

Also an ace mimic who possessed the ability to imitate the speech and mannerisms of his teammates, Heinsohn brought levity to the Celtics'

Heinsohn spent much of his time in Boston serving as
the Celtics' designated shooter.
Photo courtesy of MearsOnlineAuctions.com.

clubhouse in any number of ways, as Bill Sharman revealed when he told
the *Saturday Evening Post,* "Before a game, Heinsohn bursts into the dressing room and, no matter how important the game is, he'll get one of the
guys in some give-and-take that relaxes the tension."

Heinsohn had a far more serious and cerebral side, though, which he
demonstrated by assuming an important leadership role in the NBA Players
Association. In fact, while serving as president of the organization following
the retirement of former group head Bob Cousy one year earlier, Heinsohn
proved to be extremely instrumental in the owners' creation of a pension
plan for the players, spearheading a revolt by his fellow All-Stars, who
threatened not to participate in the 1964 All-Star Game.

After averaging more than 20 points per game in each of the three previous seasons, Heinsohn posted a scoring average of 18.9 points per contest
in 1962–63, earning in the process his third straight All-NBA Second-Team
selection. He earned his final Second-Team nomination the following year,
when he helped the Celtics capture the sixth of their eight consecutive NBA
titles by averaging 16.5 points per game.

An "old" 30 heading into the 1964–65 campaign, Heinsohn waxed
philosophic prior to the start of the season, stating, "As the wonderful
agony begins for 1964–65, I sometimes wonder why I do it. I've got an
insurance business going on the side, and it is starting to grow nicely.
Selling insurance fulfills me, in a way, like basketball. But basketball keeps
calling me back. I suppose I'll play until I can't keep up with the kids any
longer."

However, after suffering through an injury-riddled season that saw
him post career-low marks in scoring (13.6) and rebounding (6.0), Heinsohn elected to announce his retirement following the conclusion of the
campaign. Over the course of nine NBA seasons, he scored 12,194 points,
pulled down 5,749 rebounds, and assisted on 1,318 baskets, averaging 18.6
points, 8.8 rebounds, and 2.0 assists per game during that time. Heinsohn
appeared in nine NBA Finals as a member of the Celtics, with the team
emerging victorious eight times.

One year after Heinsohn ended his playing career, Red Auerbach asked
him to take over as head coach in Boston so that he could concentrate
exclusively on his duties as general manager. "And I said no," Heinsohn
recalled, "because Russell was still playing and I knew I couldn't handle
Russell. I knew nobody was going to handle Russell. So I said to Red,
'Why don't you make Russell the coach? He's got so much damn pride,
he'll handle himself.'"

Following Russell's retirement three years later, Auerbach presented
the same opportunity to Heinsohn, who this time accepted the position.
Although the Celtics struggled in Heinsohn's first year at the helm, concluding the 1969–70 campaign with a disappointing record of 34-48, they
gradually developed into a dominant team under his leadership, winning
five straight Eastern Division titles and capturing the NBA championship
in both 1974 and 1976.

Choosing to relinquish his coaching duties midway through the 1977–
78 season after the Celtics got off to a horrendous 11-23 start, Heinsohn
joined Mike Gorman as color commentator in the team's TV broadcast
booth some three years later, beginning in the process a lengthy relationship
that saw the two men become one of the longest-tenured tandems in sports

broadcasting history. For a time during the 1980s, Heinsohn also served as an analyst on CBS's NBA playoff coverage, calling four Finals from 1984 to 1987, three of which pitted the Celtics against the Los Angeles Lakers.

Inducted into the Naismith Memorial Basketball Hall of Fame as a player in 1986, Heinsohn joined an extremely select group of individuals in 2015 when he entered the Hall for a second time as a coach. Heinsohn lived until November 9, 2020, when he died at his home from kidney failure at the age of 86.

In discussing Heinsohn's place in Celtics' history some years earlier, team owner Wycliffe Grousbeck suggested, "He is the keeper of the tradition and pride. There is nothing better than hearing once again how they had to bail Red out of jail, how terrible a bus driver Red was, and on and on. . . . When you get to know Tommy, you understand exactly what made the Celtics the greatest example of teamwork and pride there has ever been."

CELTICS CAREER HIGHLIGHTS

Best Season

Heinsohn played his best ball for the Celtics from 1959 to 1962, averaging more than 21 points and 9.5 rebounds per game in each of those three seasons. En route to earning a sixth-place finish in the league MVP voting in 1960–61, Heinsohn averaged 21.3 points and 9.9 rebounds per contest. He followed that up by averaging a career-high 22.1 points per game in 1961–62, while also averaging 9.5 rebounds per contest and shooting a career-best 42.9 percent from the field. Heinsohn's outstanding play earned him All-Star and All-NBA Second-Team honors both seasons. Yet, even though Heinsohn did not receive either honor in 1959–60, he probably had his finest all-around season. In addition to finishing in the league's top 10 in scoring for the only time in his career by averaging 21.7 points per game, he posted a rebounding average of 10.6 that represented the highest mark of his career. Heinsohn also shot 42.3 percent from the field, en route to earning a 10th-place finish in the NBA MVP balloting.

Memorable Moments / Greatest Performances

Heinsohn had his breakout game for the Celtics on November 28, 1956, when he scored 24 points during a 105–93 win over the Minneapolis Lakers. He topped 30 points for the first time in his career some two weeks

Heinsohn ranks among Boston's all-time leaders in both scoring and rebounding. Photo courtesy of RMYAuctions.com

later, on December 11, leading the Celtics to a 113–97 victory over the Fort Wayne Pistons by tallying a game-high 34 points. Heinsohn nearly duplicated that effort on February 21, 1957, when he scored 32 points during a 125–112 win over the St. Louis Hawks. Although the Celtics lost to the Knicks in overtime by a score of 122–121 one week later, Heinsohn had another big game, scoring 35 points during the contest. Heinsohn turned in another exceptional effort in a losing cause on March 5, recording a season-high 41 points during a 104–102 loss to St. Louis.

Heinsohn continued his success in the 1957 playoffs, scoring 30 points in Boston's 120–105 win over Syracuse in Game 2 of the Eastern Division Finals, before turning in a performance for the ages in Game 7 of the NBA Finals, when he led the Celtics to a 125–123 double-overtime victory over the Hawks by scoring 37 points and pulling down 23 rebounds. Reflecting back on Heinsohn's brilliant effort, teammate Bill Sharman said, "What a show Tommy put on. I never saw anyone play like that under pressure . . . let alone a rookie." Recalling the events that transpired during the contest, Heinsohn recounted, "I was just able to play footloose and fancy-free. The guys who had been here all that time trying to win a championship, Bob Cousy and Bill Sharman, they were so anxious they couldn't get out of their own way that day. I just went out and played."

Heinsohn proved to be a thorn in the side of the Lakers throughout the 1958–59 campaign, outscoring Elgin Baylor, 38–30, in their personal battle, in leading the Celtics to a 117–108 win over Minneapolis on January 12, 1959. Heinsohn again torched the Lakers some six weeks later, scoring 43 points during a 173–139 win over Minneapolis on February 27. Heinsohn subsequently helped lead the Celtics to a four-game sweep of the Lakers in the NBA Finals by averaging 24.3 points and 8.8 rebounds per game during the series.

Heinsohn turned in a number of outstanding efforts early in 1960, scoring 40 points during a 114–113 loss to the Syracuse Nationals on January 3, tallying 43 points during a 144–126 win over the Knicks on January 20, and leading the Celtics to a 122–120 victory over the Philadelphia Warriors on February 13 by hitting for 39 points. He had another big game on March 6, when he scored 37 points during a 126–117 win over the Nationals.

Heinsohn had a huge game against Syracuse on December 25, 1961, celebrating Christmas by scoring a career-high 45 points, in leading the Celtics to a 127–122 victory over the Nationals. He continued his success in the New Year, scoring 43 points during a 124–120 loss to Detroit on January 21, 1962, before tallying 42 points during a 148–115 win over the Chicago Packers on February 11.

Heinsohn topped 40 points for the final time in his career on January 2, 1963, when he hit for 41 points during a 135–120 overtime win over the San Francisco Warriors.

Heinsohn subsequently performed extremely well throughout the 1963 playoffs, helping the Celtics begin their successful postseason run by averaging just under 26 points per game against Cincinnati in the Eastern Division Finals, including a 34-point effort in Game 5 and a 31-point performance in Game 7. He then helped the Celtics record a six-game victory over Los Angeles in the NBA Finals by averaging 23.3 points per game during the series, which included a 35-point performance by Heinsohn in Boston's 108–105 Game 4 win.

Yet, Heinsohn feels that he experienced the greatest moment of his career in Game 6 of the 1960 Eastern Division Finals, when his tip-in at the final buzzer gave the Celtics a 119–117 victory over Wilt Chamberlain and the Philadelphia Warriors. Reflecting back on the basket, which gave him 22 points for the game and clinched a spot for Boston in the NBA Finals, Heinsohn told the *Saturday Evening Post* that it was "the biggest thrill I've had from basketball."

NOTABLE ACHIEVEMENTS

- Averaged more than 20 points per game three times, topping 22 points per contest once (22.1 in 1961–62).
- Averaged more than 17 points per game three other times.
- Averaged more than 10 rebounds per game twice, topping 9.5 rebounds per contest four other times.
- Led NBA in games played in 1956–57.
- Led Celtics in scoring average three times.
- Ranks among Celtics career leaders in points per game (9th); rebounds per game (7th); and total rebounds (9th).
- 1956–57 NBA Rookie of the Year.
- Four-time All-NBA Second-Team selection (1960–61, 1961–62, 1962–63, and 1963–64).
- Six-time NBA All-Star (1957, 1961, 1962, 1963, 1964, and 1965).
- Nine-time Eastern Division champion (1957–65).
- Eight-time NBA champion (1957 and 1959–65).
- Number 15 retired by Celtics.
- Inducted into Naismith Memorial Basketball Hall of Fame in 1986.

13

JO JO WHITE

I was a Marine, so I had been through all the physical and mental challenges that come with military training. Plus, I was in excellent condition because of my military obligation, so I feel that this gave me an added advantage.

—Jo Jo White

An outstanding guard whose offensive repertoire included one of the NBA's best off-the-dribble pull-up jumpers, Jo Jo White spent the better part of 10 seasons in Boston, establishing himself during that time as one of the league's most consistent and durable players. Appearing in a franchise-record 488 consecutive games at one point, White averaged better than 18 points per contest for seven consecutive seasons, topping the 20-point mark on two separate occasions. Excelling at running the Celtics fast break from his point guard position, White also averaged more than 5 assists per game six straight times, surpassing 6 assists per contest twice. An exceptional postseason player as well, White averaged 21.5 points and 5.7 assists per game in his six playoff appearances with the Celtics, earning 1976 NBA Finals MVP honors by leading the Men in Green to a hard-fought six-game victory over the Phoenix Suns. In all, White made seven All-Star teams and earned two All-NBA Second-Team nominations during his time in Boston, en route to earning the additional distinction of having his number (10) retired by the Celtics following the conclusion of his playing career.

Born in St. Louis, Missouri, on November 16, 1946, Joseph Henry White spent his youth rooting for the St. Louis Hawks, after first learning how to play the game of basketball himself at the age of six. Following his graduation from local McKinley High School, White enrolled at the University of Kansas, where he began an extremely successful collegiate career that saw him earn three All-Big Eight team selections and a pair of NCAA All-American Second-Team nominations. After college, White helped lead an undermanned US Men's Basketball Team to an unexpected gold medal at the 1968 Olympic Games in Mexico City, Mexico, recalling years later, "Going into the Olympic Games, we weren't the overwhelming favorites to win the gold medal. We weren't even considered the strongest team in the tournament. That billing went to the Russians, who were upset by Yugoslavia in the semifinals. But we were the more determined team, and I think that's what set us apart."

An outstanding all-around athlete who also played football and baseball in college, White subsequently found himself drafted by the Dallas Cowboys, Cincinnati Reds, and Boston Celtics, who selected him with the ninth overall pick of the 1969 NBA Draft. Quite fortunate that White fell to them at number nine due to a mandatory two-year military commitment, Boston further benefited when Red Auerbach had the young guard's tour of duty shortened to just a few months, enabling him to participate in the 1969–70 NBA season. Joining the Celtics in training camp, White later suggested that his short stint in the military helped him to prepare for the rigors of the NBA season, stating, "I was a Marine, so I had been through all the physical and mental challenges that come with military training. Plus, I was in excellent condition because of my military obligation, so I feel that this gave me an added advantage."

Joining a Celtics squad that had lost longtime stars Bill Russell and Sam Jones to retirement during the previous off-season, White suffered through an unsuccessful 1969–70 campaign that saw the team post its first losing record (34-48) since 1950. Nevertheless, the 6-foot-3, 195-pound guard had a solid rookie season, averaging 12.2 points and 2.4 assists per game, in 22 minutes of action, en route to earning All-NBA Rookie First-Team honors.

The additions of White and NBA Co-Rookie of the Year Dave Cowens to the Boston starting five the following season helped to dramatically improve the fortunes of the club, with White earning NBA All-Star honors for the first of seven straight times by averaging 21.3 points, 4.8 assists, and 5 rebounds per game. He improved upon those numbers in 1971–72, posting career-high marks in scoring (23.1 ppg) and rebounding (5.6 rpg), while also averaging 5.3 assists per contest. The following year, White averaged 19.7 points and a career-high 6.1 assists per game, beginning in the process a string of five consecutive seasons in which he played in every

Jo Jo White set a franchise record by appearing in 488 consecutive games for the Celtics during the 1970s.

Celtics game. Along the way, White set a franchise record by appearing in 488 consecutive contests. In fact, between 1970 and 1977, he missed a total of only 10 games, making him one of the NBA's true "iron men."

Whether driving to the basket or employing his patented pull-up jumper, White proved to be one of the Celtics' most reliable scorers during his time in Boston, averaging fewer than 18 points per game just once in his eight full seasons as a starter. He also did an excellent job of running the fast break, using his tremendous quickness and superior passing skills to create many easy scoring opportunities for his team. Although the ball-distribution skills of teammates John Havlicek and Dave Cowens prevented White from ever finishing any higher than sixth in the NBA in assists, he managed to place in the league's top 10 in that category five straight times during the mid-1970s, averaging as many as 6 assists per game on two separate occasions. An underrated defender as well, White made good use of his outstanding foot speed, applying constant pressure to his man whenever the Celtics elected to employ the full-court press.

After helping the Celtics capture their first championship in five years in 1974 by averaging 18.1 points and 5.5 assists per game during the regular season, White earned All-NBA Second-Team honors for the first of two times in 1974–75 by posting marks of 18.3 points, 5.6 assists, and 1.6 steals per contest. He followed that up by averaging 18.9 points and 5.4 assists per game in 1975–76, in helping the Celtics compile the NBA's second-best record over the course of the regular season. White then averaged 22.7 points and 5.4 assists per game during the playoffs, en route to earning NBA Finals MVP honors.

White had one more very productive year for the Celtics, earning his second All-NBA Second-Team selection in 1976–77 by averaging 19.6 points and 6 assists per game, before an injury he suffered the following season caused his skills to diminish somewhat. Limited to just 46 games in 1977–78, White averaged only 14.8 points and 4.5 assists per contest—his lowest numbers since his rookie campaign of 1969–70.

With the aging Celtics in a state of flux and White experiencing a further drop-off in production through the first 47 games of the ensuing campaign, Boston elected to trade him to the Golden State Warriors for a first-round pick in that year's draft. White left the Celtics with career totals of 13,188 points scored, 3,686 assists, and 3,071 rebounds, averages of 18.4 points, 5.1 assists, and 4.3 rebounds per game, a field-goal shooting percentage of 44.2, and a free-throw shooting percentage of 83.3.

Describing the disappointment White felt over having to leave Boston, Bob Ryan of the *Boston Globe* wrote:

> [B]eing a Celtic, and, specifically, being a part of the Celtic mystique, meant a lot to Jo Jo White. In fact, being a part of the Celtics family, and being able to come in and exchange quips with Red Auerbach, and being able to identify oneself as a "Celtic" probably meant more to Jo Jo White than to any [other] Celtic in the modern era. Circumstances dictated that he leave, but leaving Boston was far from painless.

White ended up spending one and a half seasons in Golden State, before moving on to Kansas City, where he finished out his career in 1980–81 as a backup with the Kings. He retired having scored 14,399 points, assisted on 4,095 baskets, pulled down 3,345 rebounds, and compiled averages of 17.2 points, 4.9 assists, and 4 rebounds per game.

Following his playing days, White returned to the University of Kansas, where he spent one season serving as an assistant coach before attempting a brief comeback as a player-assistant coach with the Topeka Sizzlers of the Continental Basketball Association. During that time, the Celtics honored him by retiring his uniform number 10, raising it to the rafters at the Boston Garden on April 9, 1982. Some 18 years later, White became director of special projects and community relations of the Boston Celtics, a position he held for most of the next two decades. Additionally, in 2009, White and his wife opened a restaurant in Maynard, Massachusetts, that declared bankruptcy and closed just one year later with criminal allegations and litigation against restaurant partner Chris Barnes. Shortly thereafter, White underwent a procedure to remove a tumor on the back of his brain. Following the operation, former Boston Celtics Coach Doc Rivers commented, "When you saw him the first couple of times, you were extremely worried. But we jokingly said that Jo Jo could make sick cool. He really is a cool dude and a great human being."

To assist White's recovery, his attorney elicited memories from him which he subsequently incorporated into a biography he authored entitled *Make It Count: The Life and Times of Basketball Great Jo Jo White*, which was released in 2012. Later that year, White started the Jo Jo White Foundation to provide support for brain cancer research.

Unfortunately, White found himself being plagued by another brain tumor in 2017 that ultimately led to his demise. Developing pneumonia after having the tumor removed, White died at the age of 71 on January 16, 2018, less than three years after the Naismith Memorial Basketball Hall of Fame finally opened its doors to him. The Celtics subsequently paid tribute to White by spending the rest of the season playing with a black stripe stitched onto their jerseys.

CELTICS CAREER HIGHLIGHTS

Best Season

White earned All-NBA honors for the only two times in his career in 1974–75 and 1976–77, posting averages of 18.3 points, 5.6 assists, and 3.8 rebounds per game in the first of those campaigns, before averaging 19.6 points, 6 assists, and 4.7 rebounds per contest in the second. However, he compiled better overall numbers in both 1970–71 and 1971–72. En route

White earned NBA Finals MVP honors in 1976, when he led the Celtics to their 13th league championship. Photo courtesy of Boston Public Library.

to earning the first of seven consecutive All-Star selections in 1970–71, White averaged 21.3 points, 4.8 assists, and 5 rebounds per game, while also shooting 46.4 percent from the field, which represented his highest mark as a member of the Celtics. White, though, posted even better numbers the following season, concluding the 1971–72 campaign with career-high averages in points (23.1) and rebounds (5.6) per game, while also averaging 5.3 assists per contest.

Memorable Moments / Greatest Performances

White had a number of outstanding offensive games in his first season as a full-time starter, with the first of those coming on December 1, 1970, when he helped lead the Celtics to a 117–116 overtime win over the Buffalo Braves by scoring 37 points. He also hit for 35 points twice, doing so during a 102–93 victory over the Braves on December 17, before duplicating that effort during a lopsided 138–108 victory over the San Francisco

Warriors five days later. However, White had his biggest game of the season on February 26, 1971, when he scored 38 points, in leading the Celtics to a 136–129 overtime win over the Atlanta Hawks.

White turned in one of his finest offensive performances of the ensuing campaign on October 22, 1971, when he tallied 34 points during a 115–108 victory over the Atlanta Hawks. He topped that effort some three weeks later, on November 14, when he scored a season-high 36 points during a 128–115 loss to the Los Angeles Lakers.

En route to earning his third straight All-Star selection in 1972–73, White had a number of big offensive games, with his first such effort coming on October 21, 1972, when he led the Celtics to a 104–101 win over the Baltimore Bullets by scoring 36 points. White also turned in a pair of exceptional performances in February 1973, hitting for a season-high 38 points during a 123–115 victory over the Philadelphia 76ers on February 4, before tallying 36 points during a 112–105 win over the Portland Trail Blazers on February 16.

White had his biggest game of the ensuing campaign on December 9, 1973, when he scored a season-high 37 points during a 118–114 victory over Buffalo. He also tallied 35 points on March 24, 1974, in helping the Celtics defeat the Houston Rockets by a score of 109–106 in overtime.

White turned in several outstanding offensive performances en route to earning his final All-Star selection in 1976–77, with the first of those coming on November 27, 1976, when he led the Celtics to a 123–109 win over the Knicks by scoring 36 points. He had another big game one week later, tallying 38 points during a 115–109 overtime victory over the Chicago Bulls on December 3. White saved his finest performance of the season for March 20, 1977, however, when he scored a career-high 41 points, in leading the Celtics to a 118–110 overtime win over the Kansas City Kings.

An exceptional postseason performer over the course of his career, White first displayed his ability to excel under pressure in the 1973 Eastern Conference Semifinals, when he averaged 25.7 points per contest during Boston's six-game victory over the Atlanta Hawks. Particularly effective in the opening and closing games of the series, White scored 34 points in Game 1 before hitting for another 33 points in the clinching Game 6. Although the Celtics subsequently lost to the Knicks in seven games in the Eastern Conference Finals, White played extremely well, averaging 23.6 points per game during the series.

Starring throughout the 1976 playoffs, White began his exceptional postseason run by averaging just under 24 points per contest during

Seen here shooting over Buffalo's Ernie DiGregorio, Jo Jo White made the All-Star team seven straight times while playing for the Celtics.

Boston's six-game victory over Buffalo in the Eastern Conference Semi-finals. He continued his success against the Cleveland Cavaliers in the Eastern Conference Finals, posting a scoring average of 22.5 points per game, in leading the Celtics to another six-game victory. White subsequently earned NBA Finals MVP honors by averaging 21.7 points per game during Boston's six-game victory over the Phoenix Suns, including an epic performance during the Celtics' 128–126 triple-overtime win in Game 5, when he played 60 minutes and led both teams with 33 points and 9 assists.

Although the Celtics ended up losing to the 76ers in seven games in the 1977 Eastern Conference Semifinals, White turned in arguably the finest postseason performance of his career in Game 6, when he led the Celtics to a 113–108 win by scoring a personal playoff-best 40 points.

Yet, White truly showed what he was made of some three years earlier, shortly after the Celtics clinched their 12th NBA title with a victory over the Milwaukee Bucks in Game 7 of the 1974 NBA Finals. Author Mark C. Bodanza recounts the events that transpired at the time in his biography of White, *Make It Count: The Life and Times of Basketball Great Jo Jo White*:

> It was a goal that Jo Jo White had once only dreamed of. As the celebration subsided, Jo Jo's thoughts turned to the years of preparation, to mentors and to heroes. He found his way to the Milwaukee locker room and approached Oscar Robertson. It was a reverent moment for White. He revealed to Robertson what he meant to him as a boy. It was time to drop the stony silence of game-time competition and replace it with a bit of candor from the heart. Jo Jo told Robertson that "he was the best I ever played against." It was a moment he dreamed of growing up on the courts in St. Louis, and all the reality of the NBA championship brought back a flood of memories. White felt very fortunate for the path that brought him to that moment, and the coaches and mentors who helped make it all possible.

White's show of admiration and respect to Robertson revealed the quality of his character and the strength of his leadership, both of which contributed significantly to two NBA championships during his time in Boston.

NOTABLE ACHIEVEMENTS

- Averaged more than 20 points per game twice, topping 18 points per contest five other times.
- Averaged more than 5 assists per game six times, topping 6 assists per contest twice.
- Averaged more than 5 rebounds per game three times.
- Averaged more than 40 minutes per game twice.
- Led NBA in games played twice.
- Led Celtics in scoring average once and assists four times.
- Holds Celtics record for most consecutive games played (488—from 1/21/72 to 1/29/78).
- Ranks among Celtics career leaders in: points scored (10th); assists (7th); field-goal attempts (8th); field goals made (9th); and minutes played (9th).
- 1975–76 NBA Finals MVP.
- 1969–70 All-NBA Rookie First-Team selection.
- Two-time All-NBA Second-Team selection (1974–75 and 1976–77).
- Seven-time NBA All-Star (1971–77).
- Two-time Eastern Conference champion (1974 and 1976).
- Two-time NBA champion (1974 and 1976).
- Number 10 retired by Celtics.
- Inducted into Naismith Memorial Basketball Hall of Fame in 2015.

14

ED MACAULEY

The worst blizzard of the season hit NYU in the form of a 6-foot-8 string bean named Ed Macauley.

—*New York Post*

Even though Ed Macauley is perhaps best remembered for being one of the players the Celtics sent to the St. Louis Hawks in exchange for Bill Russell, the lanky center accomplished a great deal over the course of his Hall of Fame career. Spending most of his peak seasons in Boston, Macauley averaged more than 20 points per game twice for the Celtics, becoming in 1950–51 the first player in franchise history to accomplish the feat. A top offensive threat, Macauley never averaged less than 17.5 points per contest in any of his six seasons in Boston, en route to earning four All-NBA selections and six All-Star nominations. A solid rebounder and excellent passer out of the pivot as well, Macauley also surpassed 8 rebounds and 3.5 assists per game five times as a member of team, placing among the league leaders in each category at different times. Although the Celtics failed to capture their first league championship until after Macauley left Boston, they remained consistent contenders in the NBA's Eastern Division throughout the first half of the 1950s, due primarily to the play of Macauley and fellow Hall of Famers Bob Cousy and Bill Sharman.

Born in St. Louis, Missouri, on March 22, 1928, Charles Edward Macauley Jr. spent his prep-school days at St. Louis University High School, where he starred in basketball. Recruited by such notable institutions as the University of Kentucky and Boston College following his graduation, Macauley instead chose to attend St. Louis University. While in college, Macauley began to draw national attention with his ability to score on a consistent basis in spite of his skinny, 6-foot-8, 185-pound frame, with

Time magazine suggesting early in his college career, "At 19, he looks like an overgrown altar boy." Meanwhile, after Macauley led his team to a 41–24 victory over New York University in the 1948 NIT championship game by scoring 24 points, the *New York Post* reported that "the worst blizzard of the season hit NYU in the form of a 6-foot-8 string bean named Ed Macauley." The following year, Macauley earned AP College Basketball Player of the Years honors.

Macauley also acquired the nickname "Easy Ed" while in college. Although many people naturally assumed the moniker stemmed from either his laid-back manner or seemingly effortless style on offense, Macauley later revealed that it dated back to an incident that took place during his sophomore year at St. Louis University, when he led the team onto the court from the basement locker room after being appointed captain. Macauley explained, "But nobody followed me when I ran down the court and made a layup. Then I heard people shout, 'Take it easy, Ed.' I didn't realize it, but they were playing the National Anthem."

Subsequently picked by the struggling St. Louis Bombers as a territorial selection in the 1949 BAA Draft, Macauley had a solid rookie season, leading the team with a scoring average of 16.1 points per game after it joined the NBA following the merger of the two leagues. However, with the Bombers folding at season's end, Macauley found himself forced to leave his hometown for the first time in his playing career. Seeking to acquire his services, the New York Knicks attempted to purchase the Bomber franchise for $50,000. But, with the NBA vetoing the deal, Macauley ended up going to the Celtics in a special draft.

Macauley found Boston very much to his liking, concluding his first season with the Celtics with a scoring average of 20.4 points per game that placed him third in the league rankings. He also averaged 9.1 rebounds per game and finished second in the league with a field-goal shooting percentage of .466, earning in the process All-NBA First-Team honors for the first of three straight times and the first of his seven consecutive All-Star selections.

Macauley continued his outstanding play in 1951–52, helping the Celtics to become the first team to average better than 100 points per game for a full season by posting a scoring average of 19.2 points per contest that placed him fourth in the league. He followed that up by averaging 20.3 points, 9.1 rebounds, and a career-high 4.1 assists per game in 1952–53, while also leading the NBA with a .452 field-goal shooting percentage.

Teaming up with Bob Cousy and Bill Sharman, Macauley helped give the Celtics the league's most explosive and dynamic offense. While Cousy and Sharman did most of their damage from the outside, Macauley excelled

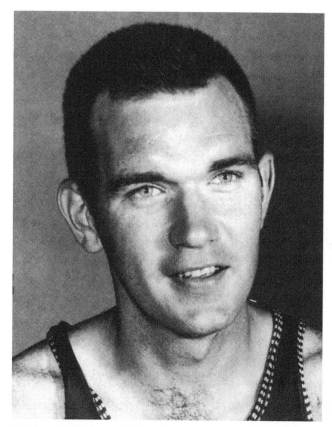

Ed Macauley earned All-Star honors in each of his six seasons with the Celtics, before being included in the deal with St. Louis that brought Bill Russell to Boston.
Photo courtesy of StLouisSportsHallofFame.com.

in the pivot, frustrating opponents with his outstanding hook shot and deft passing. In *From Set Shot to Slam Dunk*, Sharman described his former teammate as "the most talented center in the league" when Sharman first joined the Celtics in 1951. The Hall of Fame guard went on to say, "He was extremely smooth and a great passer and shooter, with outstanding running speed. However, he lacked the physical strength to bang around with some of the bigger centers in the league, such as Charlie Share, Larry Foust, and George Mikan."

Macauley earned All-NBA honors for the final time in 1953–54, receiving a Second-Team nomination after averaging 18.9 points and 8 rebounds per game, while leading the league in field-goal shooting percentage for the second straight time with a career-high mark of .486. He followed that up with two more solid seasons, averaging 17.6 points and 8.5 rebounds per game in 1954–55, before posting marks of 17.5 points and 5.9 rebounds per contest in the ensuing campaign.

However, due primarily to their porous defense, the Celtics found themselves unable to advance beyond the Eastern Division Finals in any of Macauley's six seasons in Boston. Seeking to improve themselves on that end of the floor, the Celtics elected to trade Macauley and Cliff Hagan to St. Louis when the Hawks offered them Bill Russell in return shortly after they selected him with the second overall pick of the 1956 NBA Draft. Although Walter Brown initially balked at the idea of trading away his popular center, Macauley made his decision much easier when he informed the Celtics' owner that he would welcome a return to St. Louis since it would provide him with more of an opportunity to care for his disabled son, who had recently been stricken with spinal meningitis and subsequently suffered brain damage. Looking back at that troubled period in his life, Macauley recalled, "We had a one-year-old son whose brain could not function, and I didn't know if I could play in Boston the next year."

After agreeing to the terms of the deal, Brown expressed to Macauley his sadness over having to part ways with perhaps his favorite player, stating in a letter to him, "What this means for the Boston Celtics, God only knows. You have heard me say many times that as long as I have Ed Macauley, I have a ball club. Well, now I don't have Ed Macauley. This is the hardest letter I ever tried to write."

Macauley ended up spending three seasons with the Hawks, performing his best for them in 1956–57, when he earned the last of his seven All-Star selections by averaging 16.5 points and 6.1 rebounds per game. Ironically, he won the only championship of his career the following year, when St. Louis defeated the Celtics in six games in the NBA Finals. After appearing in only 14 games in 1958–59, Macauley announced his retirement to accept the dual role of head coach and vice president of the Hawks. He concluded his playing career with 11,234 points scored, 4,325 rebounds, 2,079 assists, a 17.5 scoring average, and a 7.5 rebounding average. In Macauley's six seasons with the Celtics, he scored 7,882 points, pulled down 3,367 rebounds, and accumulated 1,521 assists, averaging in the process 18.9 points, 8.1 rebounds, and 3.7 assists per contest. Macauley entered the Basketball Hall of Fame just one year after he retired, making him, at age 32, the youngest male player ever to be admitted. The Celtics later honored him as well by retiring his uniform number (22).

After serving as head coach and vice president of the Hawks through the end of the 1959–60 campaign, Macauley became a television commentator and director in St. Louis. He later chose to devote himself to causes like counseling prisoners and fighting abortion before becoming a deacon in the Roman Catholic Church, where he remained until he developed Alzheimer's disease. Macauley lived until November 9, 2011, when he passed away in a St. Louis retirement home at the age of 83.

CELTICS CAREER HIGHLIGHTS

Best Season

Macauley performed extremely well for the Celtics in 1953–54, averaging 18.9 points and 8 rebounds per game, while posting a league-leading .486 field-goal shooting percentage that represented the highest mark of his career. However, he had his two best all-around years in 1950–51 and 1952–53, compiling virtually identical numbers those two seasons. En route to finishing third in the league in scoring in the first of those campaigns, Macauley averaged 20.4 points per game, becoming in the process the first Celtics player to post a scoring average in excess of 20 points per contest. He also averaged 9.1 rebounds and 3.7 assists per game, finishing ninth in the NBA in the first category. Meanwhile, his .466 field-goal shooting percentage placed him second in the league. Macauley posted eerily similar numbers two years later, concluding the 1952–53 campaign with averages of 20.3 points, 9.1 rebounds, and 4.1 assists per contest, while shooting a league-leading .452 percent from the field. In addition to once again finishing third in the NBA in scoring, Macauley placed seventh in the league in assists and second in the circuit with a career-high average of just over 42 minutes played per game. It's an awfully close call, but since the Celtics won seven more games in 1952–53, we'll go with that season.

Memorable Moments / Greatest Performances

Macauley turned in his first dominant performance for the Celtics on December 31, 1950, when he scored 33 points during a 100–90 win over the Knicks. He had another big game just a few days later, leading the Celtics to a hard-fought 84–82 victory over the Tri-Cities Blackhawks by tallying 28 points. Although the Celtics lost their February 13, 1951, matchup with the Philadelphia Warriors by a score of 104–98, Macauley played exceptionally well, scoring 32 points during the contest. However,

Ed Macauley became the first player in Celtics history to average
more than 20 points per game in a season in 1950-51.

he had his best game of the year eight days later, scoring a season-high 36
points during an 87–85 overtime win over the Knicks.

Even though New York defeated the Celtics by a score of 93–92 on
November 18, 1951, Macauley continued to be a thorn in the side of
the Knicks, tallying a game-high 35 points during the contest. Macauley
also performed extremely well against the Knicks in the playoffs later that
season, averaging 23.3 points and 11 rebounds during Boston's first-round
playoff loss to New York, including a 36-point outburst in Game 2.

Although the Celtics lost to the Minneapolis Lakers by a score of 94–91 in the second game of the 1952–53 regular season, Macauley badly outplayed his primary nemesis, George Mikan, tallying 37 points to Mikan's 13.

Macauley turned in a pair of notable performances early in 1953, leading the Celtics to a 99–83 win over the Knicks on January 18, and a 101–98 overtime victory over the Baltimore Bullets on February 7, by scoring 33 points in each contest. He saved his biggest game of the year, though, for George Mikan and the Lakers, tallying a career-high 46 points during a 100–85 Boston win over Minneapolis on March 6.

Macauley had another outstanding game on December 6, 1953, leading the Celtics to a 102–95 overtime win over Baltimore by scoring 35 points.

The following season, on December 14, 1954, Macauley scored 37 points during a 115–108 victory over the Lakers.

Macauley also distinguished himself in the first-ever NBA All-Star Game, earning game MVP honors by scoring 20 points and pulling down 6 rebounds.

NOTABLE ACHIEVEMENTS

- Averaged more than 20 points per game twice, topping 17 points per contest four other times.
- First Celtics player to average more than 20 points per game in a season (20.4 in 1950–51).
- Led NBA in field goal percentage twice.
- Finished third in NBA in scoring three times, placing fourth on another occasion.
- Led Celtics in scoring average twice and rebounding four times.
- Ranks among Celtics career leaders in scoring average (8th) and free-throw attempts (9th).
- 1950–51 NBA All-Star Game MVP.
- Three-time All-NBA First-Team selection (1950–51, 1951–52, and 1952–53).
- 1953–54 All-NBA Second-Team selection.
- Six-time NBA All-Star (1951, 1952, 1953, 1954, 1955, and 1956).
- Number 22 retired by Celtics.
- Inducted into Naismith Memorial Basketball Hall of Fame in 1960.

15

DENNIS JOHNSON

He was one of the most underrated players in the history of the game, in my opinion, and one of the greatest Celtic acquisitions of all time. DJ was a free spirit and a fun personality who loved to laugh and play the game.

—Danny Ainge

A winner wherever he went, Dennis Johnson played for only one losing team in his 14 NBA seasons, helping to improve the fortunes of three different franchises during his career. A member of seven division, six conference, and three NBA championship teams, Johnson provided consistent scoring, outstanding ball-handling, and superb defense to his squads, establishing himself as arguably the finest defensive guard of his era. En route to earning five All-Star selections, two All-NBA nominations, and spots on nine NBA All-Defensive Teams, Johnson left a lasting impression on several of the game's greats, with Magic Johnson calling him "the greatest backcourt defender of all time." Meanwhile, Larry Bird, with whom Johnson spent his final seven seasons in Boston, referred to him in his autobiography, *Drive: The Story of My Life*, as "the best teammate I ever had."

Born in San Pedro, California, on September 18, 1954, Dennis Wayne Johnson grew up in nearby Compton, where he attended Dominguez High School. A huge fan of New York Knicks guard Walt Frazier as a teenager, Johnson fantasized about one day playing in the NBA, although, at only 5-foot-9, he seemed to have little hope of making his dream become a reality. However, after taking a job as a forklift operator following his graduation from high school, Johnson grew some six inches in less than a year

Referred to by Larry Bird as "the best teammate I ever had," Dennis Johnson helped the Celtics capture two NBA championships.
Photo courtesy of MearsOnlineAuctions.com.

and developed the exceptional leaping ability for which he became so well-known during the early stages of his professional career.

After being discovered by Los Angeles Harbor College head coach Jim White while competing in a pickup game, Johnson enrolled at the junior college, which he led to a state title by averaging 18.3 points and 12 rebounds per game over the course of the next two seasons. Still, in spite of the success he experienced on the court, Johnson developed a reputation as a troublemaker, often clashing with White, who suspended him from the team on three separate occasions.

Following his two-year stay at LAHC, Johnson received scholarship offers from just two universities—Azusa Pacific University and Pepperdine University. Choosing to attend the latter, Johnson spent just one full year in college, leading his school into the NCAA tournament's "Sweet 16" by averaging 15.7 points, 5.8 rebounds, and 3.3 assists per game, before declaring himself eligible for the 1976 NBA Draft as a hardship case.

Subsequently selected by the Seattle SuperSonics in the second round of that year's draft with the 29th overall pick, Johnson spent his first pro season coming off the bench, averaging 9.2 points, 3.7 rebounds, and 1.5 assists in just under 21 minutes of action per contest. Inserted into the starting lineup during the early stages of the ensuing campaign, Johnson averaged 12.7 points and 2.8 assists per game, in helping the SuperSonics advance to the NBA Finals, where they lost to the Washington Bullets in seven games. Increasing his scoring output to 15.9 points per game in 1978–79, Johnson earned his first All-Star selection and the first of his six NBA All-Defensive First-Team nominations. He then went on to lead the Sonics to a five-game victory over Washington in their NBA Finals rematch, earning Finals MVP honors in the process by posting averages of 22.6 points, 6 rebounds, and 6 assists per contest, while playing his typically tenacious brand of defense. Johnson followed that up by having his finest statistical season for Seattle in 1979–80, averaging 19 points, 4.1 assists, 5.1 rebounds, and 1.8 steals per game, en route to earning All-NBA Second-Team honors. Yet, despite performing well on the court, Johnson became somewhat complacent, gained some weight, began shooting too much, and openly defied Seattle head coach Lenny Wilkens, causing the Hall of Fame player-coach to label him a "cancer."

Subsequently dealt to the Suns for high-scoring guard Paul Westphal during the off-season, Johnson spent the next three years in Phoenix, during which time he played some of the best ball of his career. Posting scoring averages of 18.8 and 19.5 points per game in his first two seasons with the Suns, Johnson earned a pair of All-Star selections, two NBA All-Defensive First-Team nominations, and his lone All-NBA First-Team selection. However, after experiencing a precipitous drop-off in production in 1982–83 and having his name mentioned in a Maricopa County drug sting operation, Johnson came to be viewed by many around the league as damaged goods, with several scouts suggesting that he had slowed down and criticizing him for what they perceived to be his temperamental personality.

With Johnson's best days apparently behind him, Phoenix elected to trade him to the Celtics for little-used backup center Rick Robey and a pair of draft picks. Hoping that a change in scenery might help to resuscitate

Johnson's career, Boston general manager Red Auerbach also believed that Johnson's leadership skills and ability to perform well under pressure would help make the Celtics more formidable come playoff time.

Auerbach's gamble ended up paying huge dividends for the Celtics. Although no longer blessed with the same speed and superior jumping ability that he had had earlier in his career, Johnson still possessed several exceptional qualities that enabled him to make significant contributions to the Celtics in the years that followed. In spite of his expanding waistline, Johnson remained an elite perimeter defender whose intelligence, long arms, and lengthy 6-foot-4 frame served as a constant deterrent to big guards such as Magic Johnson, Andrew Toney, and Sidney Moncrief, who previously feasted against the Celtics' defense.

Furthermore, Johnson's offensive versatility, which included an ability to either post up his defender, hit from the outside, crash the boards, or set up his teammates for open shots, enabled him to adapt his game to fit the needs of his new team. After spending his years in Seattle and Phoenix functioning primarily as a shooting guard, Johnson turned himself into a point guard in Boston, doing an outstanding job of running the Celtics' offense and distributing the ball to his teammates. After failing to average more than 5 assists per game in any of his first seven seasons, Johnson surpassed 6 assists per contest in five of his seven years in Beantown, assisting on more than 7 baskets per game on two separate occasions.

Viewing his acquisition by the Celtics as "a dream come true," Johnson also developed into a consummate pro as a member of the team, experiencing none of the personality clashes that had haunted him at each of his previous two stops. In fact, Johnson quickly built a strong relationship with Red Auerbach, to whom he referred as "living history," and a tremendous rapport with Larry Bird, who once referred to him as "the best player I ever played with . . . and probably the one guy as intense, or more intense, about winning than me."

Johnson posted relatively modest numbers his first season in Boston, concluding the 1983–84 campaign with averages of 13.2 points and 4.2 assists per game. Nevertheless, his steady play and exceptional defense, which earned him NBA All-Defensive honors for the sixth of nine straight times, proved to be key factors in the Celtics winning the NBA title. Particularly effective against the Lakers in the NBA Finals, Johnson averaged 17.6 points per contest during the seven-game series, while also playing smothering defense against his counterpart, Magic Johnson. In fact, "DJ," as he came to be known by Celtics fans, performed so well against Johnson that the Lakers legend later called him "one of the best individual defensive players probably to ever play in the league."

Johnson assumed a more prominent role in the Celtics' offense over the course of the next five seasons, increasing his scoring output while also gradually establishing himself as the team's floor general. En route to earning the last of his five All-Star selections in 1984–85, Johnson averaged 15.7 points and 6.8 assists per game. He followed that up by posting marks of 15.6 points and 5.8 assists per contest for Boston's 1985–86 championship team. Although the Celtics failed to win another title with Johnson serving as a member of their starting backcourt, he continued to do an excellent job of running their offense, averaging 13.4 points and 7.5 assists per game in 1986–87, before posting marks of 12.6 points and a career-high 7.8 assists per contest the following season.

Even though Johnson remained an effective player for the Celtics the next two seasons, his playing time and on-court production gradually fell off somewhat, prompting the Celtics to refrain from offering him a new contract following the conclusion of the 1989–90 campaign. Johnson subsequently announced his retirement, ending his career with 15,535 points scored, 5,499 assists, 4,249 rebounds, 1,477 steals, and 675 blocked shots, making him one of only 11 players at that time to amass more than 15,000 points and 5,000 assists. Meanwhile, Johnson's 675 blocked shots remain one of the highest totals in NBA history by a guard. Johnson also shot 44.5 percent from the field and 79.7 percent from the free-throw line, while averaging 15.6 points, 5.5 assists, 4.3 rebounds, and 1.5 steals per game over the course of his career. In his seven seasons with the Celtics, Johnson scored 6,805 points, accumulated 3,486 assists, 1,757 rebounds, and 654 steals, and averaged 12.6 points, 6.4 assists, 3.2 rebounds, and 1.2 steals per contest.

Following his playing days, Johnson remained with the Celtics, serving them as a scout for three seasons, during which time the organization retired his number 3 jersey. Johnson then began a lengthy career as an assistant coach, first with the Celtics and, later with the Los Angeles Clippers, for whom he also briefly served as an interim head coach in 2002–03. Johnson left Los Angeles in 2004 to become head coach of the NBA Development League's Florida Flame, after which he assumed the same position with Boston's league affiliate, the Austin Toros.

While serving as coach of the Toros on February 22, 2007, the 52-year-old Johnson died after suffering a heart attack following a practice at the Convention Center in Austin, Texas. Toros spokeswoman Perri Travillion later revealed that she and Johnson were engaged in a conversation on the sidewalk outside the Convention Center when he collapsed. Travillion called 911, but Johnson never regained consciousness, even after paramedics spent nearly a half-hour trying to revive him.

Upon learning of his former teammate's passing, Danny Ainge said, "He was one of the most underrated players in the history of the game, in my opinion, and one of the greatest Celtic acquisitions of all time. DJ was a free spirit and a fun personality who loved to laugh and play the game."

Then-Dallas Mavericks head coach Rick Carlisle, who also played with Johnson in Boston, stated, "DJ will be remembered as one of the key figures in the resurgence of the NBA in the late 1970s and early 1980s. He redefined the shooting guard position by becoming one of the first true 'stoppers' in the modern era. Dennis had a great passion for the game of basketball as a player, and loved to teach the game as a coach. He will forever be remembered by his teammates and opponents as one of the great winners and money players in NBA history."

Former Celtics coach K. C. Jones, who guided the team to titles in 1984 and 1986, said, "Larry Bird was totally in awe of Dennis. Dennis was just an awesome player. He played hard and he took the big shots."

Even hated foe Bill Laimbeer of the rival Detroit Pistons praised Johnson, calling him "a great player on a great ball club." Laimbeer added, "He played with passion and grit. It was fun to play games like that. You always enjoyed it. It made for not only great games, but great entertainment."

Posthumously inducted into the Naismith Memorial Basketball Hall of Fame in 2010, Johnson received an honor long overdue in the minds of many people, including outspoken former teammate Bill Walton, who considered his earlier exclusion to be a travesty.

CELTICS CAREER HIGHLIGHTS

Best Season

Even though Johnson averaged a career-high 7.8 assists per game for the Celtics in 1987–88, he played his best ball for them three seasons earlier. In addition to posting his highest marks in scoring (15.7 ppg), rebounding (4 rpg), and shooting percentage (46.2) as a member of the team in 1984–85, Johnson averaged 6.8 assists and 1.2 steals per contest, while also shooting 85.3 percent from the free-throw line and averaging a career-high 37.2 minutes per game.

Memorable Moments / Greatest Performances

Johnson got off to a good start in 1984–85, scoring 29 points and collecting 9 assists during a 130–123 victory over the Detroit Pistons in the regular-season opener. He also had a number of other outstanding all-around games that season, with one of those coming on December 18, 1984, when he scored 21 points and handed out 12 assists during a 126–108 win over the Knicks. Johnson helped lead the Celtics to a 142–123 victory over the Kansas City Kings on February 1, 1985, by tallying 20 points and assisting on 13 baskets. He established a career high in assists later in the year, amassing 17 assists and scoring 15 points during a 126–115 win over the Atlanta Hawks on March 12.

Johnson reached the 30-point mark for the first time as a member of the Celtics on November 13, 1985, when he helped lead them to a 118–114 win over the Indiana Pacers by scoring 30 points, handing out 4 assists, and recording 6 steals.

Johnson turned in an exceptional all-around effort against the Washington Bullets in the 1986–87 regular-season opener, scoring 26 points and assisting on 7 baskets during a 120–102 Celtics victory. He also performed brilliantly against Philadelphia and Chicago later in the season, scoring 27 points and collecting 12 assists during a 108–106 win over the 76ers on December 5, 1986, and tallying 26 points and handing out 10 assists during a 132–103 blowout of the Bulls on January 28, 1987.

Johnson had another big game against the Bulls on April 21, 1988, when he helped lead the Celtics to a 126–119 victory by scoring 23 points and collecting 15 assists.

After earlier excelling for both Seattle and Phoenix in postseason play, Johnson continued to perform extremely well in the playoffs as a member of the Celtics. A key figure in Boston's march to the 1984 NBA championship, Johnson scored 26 points during a 125–110 win over Milwaukee in Game 2 of the Eastern Conference Finals. He then averaged 17.6 points per game against the Lakers in the NBA Finals, posting a scoring average of 21.5 points per contest over the course of the final four games, three of which the Celtics won. Particularly effective in Game 4, Johnson scored 22 points and handed out 14 assists during Boston's 129–125 overtime win. He also came up big in Game 7, scoring 22 points, holding Magic Johnson to just 5 of 14 shooting from the field, and making a key defensive play during the latter stages of the Celtics' 111–102 win that clinched their 15th NBA title. With the Celtics holding a slim three-point lead and only 45 seconds remaining in the game, Johnson poked the ball away from Magic Johnson,

Johnson led the Celtics in assists four times.
Photo courtesy of MearsOnlineAuctions.com.

chased it down, and dribbled the length of the court, before being fouled on the way to the basket by Michael Cooper. Hitting on both his free-throw attempts, Johnson gave the Celtics a five-point lead they never relinquished.

Continuing to display his penchant for performing well under pressure in the 1985 postseason, Johnson scored 30 points and collected 6 assists during Boston's 130–123 victory over Detroit in Game 5 of the Eastern Conference Semifinals. He then delivered one of the biggest shots of his career against the Lakers in the closing moments of Game 4 of the NBA Finals, when he evened the series at two games apiece by hitting a buzzer-beater that gave the Celtics a 107–105 win. Unfortunately, the Lakers exacted a measure of revenge against their Eastern Conference counterparts by winning the next two contests, clinching the NBA title in the process.

Johnson also turned in a pair of outstanding performances en route to helping the Celtics capture their 16th NBA championship the following year, hitting for 26 points during a 123–104 victory over the Chicago Bulls in Game 1 of their first-round matchup, before scoring 16 points and assisting on 14 baskets during a 103–91 win over the Atlanta Hawks in Game 1 of the Eastern Conference Semifinals.

Although the Celtics failed to repeat as NBA champions in 1987, Johnson had a tremendous postseason, averaging 18.9 points and 8.9 assists in Boston's 23 playoff games. He began his exceptional playoff run by averaging 22.1 points per contest during the Celtics' seven-game victory over Milwaukee in the Eastern Conference Semifinals. Performing particularly well in Boston's Game 3 loss, Johnson scored 32 points and collected 14 assists during the contest.

Johnson also performed brilliantly against the Lakers in the NBA Finals, posting averages of 21 points and 9.3 assists per game, while shooting 48 percent from the field and 89 percent from the foul line. Once again turning in his finest effort in a losing cause, Johnson scored a game-high 33 points, pulled down 10 rebounds, and collected 5 assists during the Celtics' 106–93 loss in Game 6.

Still, Johnson experienced arguably the most seminal moment of his career in that year's Eastern Conference Finals, when he somehow managed to be in exactly the right place on the court when Larry Bird made his memorable steal of Isiah Thomas's inbounds pass in the closing seconds of Game 5, enabling him to convert the game-winning basket as time expired. Instinctively bolting toward the hoop as Bird made his steal, Johnson arrived just in time to receive "Larry Legend's" pass, after which he banked in a difficult layup over his right shoulder that required him to put an inordinate amount of spin on the ball, while also clearing the outstretched hand of Bill Laimbeer. In discussing the events that transpired after he gained possession of the ball, Bird explained, "I just saw the flash of a white jersey and of course it was DEE-jay." Celtics' announcer Johnny Most described the play thusly:

> Now there's a steal by Bird! Underneath to DJ, who lays it in! Right at one second left! What a play by Bird! Bird stole the inbounds pass, laid it up to DJ, and DJ laid it up and in, and Boston has a one-point lead with one second left! Oh my, this place is going crazy!!!

Hall of Fame center Bob Lanier later suggested, "It was like DJ was in Bird's head on that play . . . he knew right where to cut." Johnson, who later called the play the favorite of his career, finished the game with 18 points, 7 rebounds, and 5 assists.

NOTABLE ACHIEVEMENTS

- Averaged more than 15 points per game twice.
- Averaged more than 6 assists per game five times, topping 7 assists per contest twice.
- Led Celtics in assists four times.
- Ranks among Celtics career leaders in assists (8th) and steals (9th).
- 1986–87 NBA All-Defensive First-Team selection.
- Three-time NBA All-Defensive Second-Team selection (1983–84, 1984–85, and 1985–86).
- 1984–85 NBA All-Star.
- Four-time Eastern Conference champion (1984, 1985, 1986, and 1987).
- Two-time NBA champion (1984 and 1986).
- Number 3 retired by Celtics.
- Inducted into Naismith Memorial Basketball Hall of Fame in 2010.

16

FRANK RAMSEY

It's difficult to keep track of a team today because the players change teams. When we were in Boston, you very seldom had a player leave the team, and, when you were there, you were there for life. When you get attached to a team, of course, you get attached to the players.

—Frank Ramsey

The NBA's original "sixth man," Frank Ramsey performed brilliantly in that role over the course of his nine seasons in Boston, providing instant offensive firepower off the bench to Celtics teams that won seven NBA championships. Despite never averaging as many as 30 minutes per game in any single season, Ramsey posted a scoring average in excess of 15 points per contest five different times, making him a key contributor to the success the Celtics experienced between 1957 and 1964. Ramsey's somewhat limited playing time prevented him from ever ranking among the league leaders in any major statistical category, nor did he ever attain All-NBA honors. Nevertheless, fully aware of the overall impact Ramsey made during his time in Boston, the Celtics retired his number (23) after his playing career ended. The Naismith Memorial Basketball Hall of Fame also honored him by admitting him into its ranks in 1981.

Born in Corydon, Kentucky, on July 13, 1931, Frank Vernon Ramsey Jr. grew up some 40 miles south, in the city of Madisonville, where he attended Madisonville High School. After enrolling at the University of Kentucky following his graduation, Ramsey established himself as a multisport star for the Wildcats, excelling in both baseball and basketball. He gained his greatest measure of fame on the hardwood, though, helping to lead Kentucky to the NCAA Championship as a sophomore in 1951, while playing under legendary coach Adolph Rupp.

The NBA's original "sixth man," Frank Ramsey excelled in that role over the course of his nine seasons in Boston.

After being forced to sit out his senior year with the rest of his Wildcat teammates as the result of a 1952 point-shaving scandal involving three other Kentucky players, Ramsey became eligible for the 1953 NBA Draft, where the Boston Celtics selected him in the first round with the fifth overall pick. Ramsey, though, elected to return to Kentucky for one more season—one in which he averaged 19.6 points per game for a Wildcats team that posted a perfect 25-0 record.

Making his professional debut with the Celtics the following year, Ramsey played well as a rookie in 1954–55, averaging 11.2 points, 6.3 rebounds, and 2.9 assists per game in just over 27 minutes of action, while spending most of his time at the small forward position. Subsequently drafted into the US Army, Ramsey missed the entire 1955–56 season, before returning to the Celtics midway through the ensuing campaign. With rookies Bill Russell and Tom Heinsohn having established themselves as two of the three starters in Boston's frontcourt during his absence, Ramsey found himself splitting time with veteran Jim Loscutoff at small forward, while also backing up perennial All-Star shooting guard Bill Sharman in the backcourt. Doing a solid job at both positions, the 6-foot-3, 190-pound Ramsey averaged nearly 12 points and just over 23 minutes of action in the 35 games in which he appeared.

Despite coming off the bench once again the following season, Ramsey assumed a somewhat more prominent role on the team, averaging career-high marks in minutes played (29.7), points scored (16.5), and rebounds (7.4) per game, as he continued to pioneer the role of "sixth man." Although Ramsey remained one of Boston's five best players throughout most of his career, he felt more comfortable coming off the bench, which made him the perfect candidate for head coach Red Auerbach's experiment. Furthermore, Auerbach realized the importance of keeping the clutch-shooting Ramsey fresh and in the lineup at the end of close games, especially after he contributed 10 points in the final 10 minutes of Boston's 125–123 double-overtime win over St. Louis in Game 7 of the 1957 NBA Finals.

Ramsey, who Auerbach usually inserted into contests to provide a burst of energy and score a bushel of points at the most critical of moments, discussed his role on the team many years later, telling Boston.com in December 2004, "You have to realize back when that was happening, the standard was the original Celtics back in the 1940s, and now it seems the standard is the Celtics teams of the late '50s and '60s. It's certainly pleasing to me to be a part of that. . . . I was playing behind two All-Star guards—Bill Sharman and Bob Cousy. I just wanted to get some time to play, and Red [Auerbach] saw fit to use my talents that way. It was great."

Ramsey contributed greatly to Celtics teams that won each of the next four NBA championships, averaging more than 15 points per game each season, from 1958 to 1962. He also averaged close to 7 rebounds per game in both 1958–59 and 1959–60, while establishing himself as a solid and shrewd defender who often employed devious measures such as flopping to gain the upper hand on his opponents. An outstanding postseason performer over the course of his career, Ramsey averaged at least 16.7 points per game four straight years in the playoffs from 1958 to 1961, including a career-high mark of 23.2 points per contest in 1959.

Although the Celtics captured the NBA title in 1963 and 1964 as well, the arrival of John Havlicek forced Ramsey to assume a lesser role on the team, limiting him to fewer than 20 minutes and 11 points per game in each of his last two seasons. He subsequently elected to announce his retirement at the conclusion of the 1963–64 campaign, ending his career with 8,378 points scored, 3,410 rebounds, 1,134 assists, and averages of 13.4 points, 5.5 rebounds, and 1.8 assists per contest.

Following his playing days, Ramsey spent one season (1970–71) coaching in the ABA before returning to his home state of Kentucky, where he became president of the Dixon Bank—a position he held for more than 30 years before retiring to private life. Ramsey lived until July 8, 2018, when he died of natural causes at the age of 86.

Discussing some years earlier the good fortune that was bestowed upon him following the conclusion of his playing career, which included the retirement of his number 23 jersey in Boston and his induction into the Pro Basketball Hall of Fame, Ramsey marveled, "It's unbelievable for a small kid who came out of a town of 5,000—all this stuff has happened to me. It's just fantastic. I have been very fortunate because it couldn't have happened unless I had been associated with the coaches and players I was associated with."

CELTICS CAREER HIGHLIGHTS

Best Season

Ramsey's first full season after returning from his 18-month stint in the military proved to be the finest of his career. Garnering just under 30 minutes of playing time per contest over the course of the 1957–58 campaign, Ramsey posted career-high averages in scoring (16.5) and rebounding (7.3), while also averaging 2.4 assists per game and shooting 42 percent from the field, with each of the last two figures representing the second-highest marks of his career. Although the Celtics failed to capture their second straight league championship, losing to the St. Louis Hawks in six games in the NBA Finals, Ramsey continued his outstanding play in the playoffs, averaging 18.4 points and 8.2 rebounds per game in Boston's 11 postseason contests, while shooting 42.5 percent from the field and 91.5 percent from the free-throw line.

Memorable Moments / Greatest Performances

Ramsey surpassed the 20-point mark for the first time in his career on November 20, 1954, when he helped lead the Celtics to a 117–98 victory over the Knicks by tallying 25 points. Ramsey continued to be a thorn in the side of the Knicks later that season, recording a season-high 27 points during a 113–96 win over the New Yorkers on January 2, 1955. He also hurt the Knicks in that year's postseason, scoring 25 points in his very first playoff game—a 122–101 Celtics victory in a series they went on to win, two games to one.

Ramsey turned in a pair of exceptional performances just days apart late in 1957, establishing a new career high by scoring 35 points during a 124–113 win over the Detroit Pistons on December 3, before leading the Celtics to a 111–97 victory over the St. Louis Hawks by tallying 31 points three days later. Ramsey had another big game against the Pistons two months later, scoring a game-high 32 points during a 119–115 win over Detroit on February 2, 1958. Ramsey equaled his career high in points less than two weeks later, when he hit for 35, in leading the Celtics to a 110–96 victory over the Philadelphia Warriors.

Ramsey topped the 30-point mark three times the following season, recording 33 points during a lopsided 130–105 victory over the Cincinnati Royals on November 15, 1958, hitting for 30 during a 120–111 overtime win over the St. Louis Hawks on January 28, 1959, and tallying 31 points, in leading the Celtics to a 111–106 overtime win over the Detroit Pistons on February 20.

Ramsey recorded his highest scoring output of the 1960–61 campaign on March 9, 1961, when he helped lead the Celtics to a hard-fought 119–118 victory over the Pistons by scoring 31 points.

Although the Celtics lost to New York by a score of 129–121 on January 26, 1962, Ramsey scored a career-high 38 points during the contest. He had another big game one month later, leading the Celtics to a 129–123 overtime win over the Cincinnati Royals on February 28 by tallying 30 points.

An outstanding clutch performer over the course of his career, Ramsey played exceptionally well throughout the 1959 playoffs, scoring 28 points in Boston's 130–125 win over Syracuse in Game 7 of the Eastern Division Finals, en route to averaging a team-leading 23.6 points per game for the series. He followed that up by posting a scoring average of 22.5 points per game against Minneapolis in the NBA Finals, in helping the Celtics record a four-game sweep of the Lakers. Ramsey concluded the postseason with an average of 23.2 points per game, hitting on 49.5 percent of his shots from the field.

Ramsey again came up big against the Lakers in the playoffs after they moved to Los Angeles, leading the Celtics to a 110–107 overtime win in Game 7 of the 1962 NBA Finals by scoring 23 points.

However, Ramsey experienced his finest moment in Game 7 of the 1957 NBA Finals against the St. Louis Hawks, when he hit a last-second, off-balance 20-footer at the buzzer of the second overtime to give the Celtics a 125–123 victory and their first NBA title. He finished the game with 16 points, 10 of which came in the two overtime sessions.

NOTABLE ACHIEVEMENTS

- Averaged more than 15 points per game five times.
- Averaged more than 20 points per game in playoffs once (23.2 in 1959).
- Led NBA in games played twice.
- Eight-time Eastern Division champion (1957–64).
- Seven-time NBA champion (1957, 1959, 1960, 1961, 1962, 1963, and 1964).
- Number 23 retired by Celtics.
- Inducted into Naismith Memorial Basketball Hall of Fame in 1981.

17

RAJON RONDO

I'm a point guard, so I want to see everybody else score and be happy.
I don't necessarily need to score at all. I could be happy with zero
points, as long as it was a team game and everybody contributed.

—Rajon Rondo

Blessed with an exceptionally high basketball IQ, a competitive spirit, and outstanding all-around ability, Rajon Rondo overcame numerous obstacles, including a below-average outside shot and his own stubbornness, to eventually establish himself as one of the NBA's top point guards. After spending his first few years in the league playing in the shadow of Boston's "Big Three" of Paul Pierce, Kevin Garnett, and Ray Allen, Rondo became the Celtics' on-court leader and best all-around player, nearly leading them into the NBA Finals in 2012 by putting on a memorable postseason performance that included three triple-doubles. A solid scorer, superb playmaker, and outstanding defender, Rondo finished in double digits in scoring seven times as a member of the Celtics, while also leading the league in assists twice and steals once. Along the way, he earned four All-Star selections, one All-NBA nomination, four NBA All-Defensive Team selections, and one top-10 finish in the league MVP voting. Unfortunately, Rondo's truculent nature ultimately forced the Celtics to part ways with him, leaving him to ply his trade with several other teams. Otherwise, the enigmatic point guard likely would have remained in Boston much longer than he did.

Born in Louisville, Kentucky, on February 22, 1986, Rajon Pierre Rondo spent much of his youth playing football and baseball, before focusing his attention on basketball while attending local Eastern High

Rajon Rondo earned four All-Star selections during his time in Boston.
Photo courtesy of Aaron Frutman of DGA Productions.

School. After initially clashing with coach Doug Bibby at Eastern High, the headstrong Rondo learned to respect his mentor, leading to the teenager's development into an exceptional all-around player. Averaging 27.9 points, 10 rebounds, and 7.5 assists per game as a junior, Rondo earned All-State and 7th Region Player of the Year honors en route to leading his school to the Louisville Invitational Tournament Championship. He then transferred to Oak Hill Academy in Mouth of Wilson, Virginia, where he spent his senior year earning 2004 McDonald's All-American honors by leading his team to a 38-0 record with averages of 21 points and 12 assists per contest.

Choosing to enroll at the University of Kentucky instead of hometown Louisville following his graduation from Oak Hill Academy, Rondo set a school record as a freshman by recording 87 steals, earning in the process a spot on the SEC All-Freshman Team. Rondo had a solid sophomore campaign as well, posting averages of 11.2 points, 6.1 rebounds, 4.9 assists, and 2.1 steals per game, although he once again found himself experiencing philosophical differences with his head coach, this time Tubby Smith, who objected to his point guard's occasional tendency to ignore his instructions by speeding up the game, rather than directing his squad to a disciplined half-court offense. Electing to forgo his final two years of college eligibility, Rondo entered the 2006 NBA Draft, where the Phoenix Suns selected him in the first round with the 21st overall pick. Phoenix, though, immediately traded him and Brian Grant to the Boston Celtics for a 2007 first-round draft pick.

After arriving in Boston, Rondo spent most of his rookie season splitting time at the point guard spot with Sebastian Telfair and Delonte West, averaging 6.4 points, 3.7 rebounds, 3.8 assists, and 23.5 minutes per game for a Celtics team that finished just 24-58. A poor outside shooter when he first entered the league, Rondo worked extremely hard on improving his jump shot during the subsequent off-season, enabling him to win the starting job prior to the start of the ensuing campaign. Establishing himself as a key member of Boston's 2007–08 NBA championship squad, Rondo earned a top-five finish in the NBA Most Improved Player voting by averaging 10.6 points per game, on 49 percent shooting from the field. He also posted averages of 5.1 assists, 4.2 rebounds, and 1.7 steals per contest, in helping the Celtics to improve their record to 66-16—the biggest single-season turnaround in NBA history. Although Paul Pierce ended up claiming NBA Finals MVP honors after the Celtics defeated Los Angeles in six games, Rondo recorded six steals in the Game 6 clincher, prompting Lakers head coach Phil Jackson to call him the "star" of the contest.

Rondo followed that up by increasing his output to 11.9 points, 8.2 assists, 5.2 rebounds, and 1.9 steals per game during the 2008–09 regular season, while earning NBA All-Defensive Second-Team honors for the first of two times. He then took his game up a notch during the playoffs, nearly averaging a triple-double, as he helped the Celtics to extend the eventual Eastern Conference champion Orlando Magic to seven games in the

Conference Semifinals by posting averages of 16.9 points, 9.8 assists, 9.7 rebounds, and 2.5 steals in Boston's 14 postseason contests.

On equal footing with his three superstar teammates by the start of the 2009–10 campaign, Rondo assumed complete control of the Celtics' offense, averaging 13.7 points and 9.8 assists per game, while also leading the league with 2.3 steals per contest. Rondo's outstanding play earned him All-Star honors for the first of four straight times and the first of his two consecutive NBA All-Defensive First-Team nominations. Despite being limited by injuries to 68 games the following season, Rondo continued to perform well, averaging 10.6 points per contest and finishing second in the league with averages of 11.2 assists and 2.3 steals per game.

Although Rondo gradually evolved into a proficient scorer his first few seasons in Boston, he never developed into anything more than a marginal outside shooter, scoring the vast majority of his points on drives to the basket, offensive rebounds, and foul shots. Yet, Rondo had few peers as a playmaker and a defender. Blessed with exceptional quickness and long arms, the 6-foot-1, 185-pound Rondo did an excellent job of sticking to his man on defense, hounding him all over the court. Meanwhile, his intelligence, superb peripheral vision, and selfless attitude made him arguably the league's top ball-distributor.

In discussing the mentality he brought with him to the court each night, Rondo revealed, "I'm a point guard, so I want to see everybody else score and be happy. I don't necessarily need to score at all. I could be happy with zero points, as long as it was a team game and everybody contributed."

Rondo added, "I feel like nobody can stop me off the dribble. At crunch time, we're looking for somebody to score, and I definitely want to be the guy who has the ball in his hands."

At the same time, Kobe Bryant, who faced Rondo twice in the NBA Finals, expressed his respect for Rondo's basketball acumen by stating, "He knows all the plays, knows all the actions, and can think two, three moves ahead. He's freakishly smart."

Despite missing several games due to injury in 2011–12, Rondo averaged 11.9 points and a league-leading 11.7 assists per game, en route to earning All-NBA Third-Team honors and an eighth-place finish in the league MVP voting. He then played the best ball of his career in the playoffs, nearly leading an aging and injury-riddled Celtics squad into the NBA Finals by averaging 17.3 points, 11.9 assists, and 6.7 rebounds per game during the postseason. Rondo picked up right where he left off the following year, averaging 13.7 points, 5.6 rebounds, and a league-leading 11.1 assists per contest over the first 38 games of the 2012–13 campaign, before a torn anterior cruciate ligament in his right knee brought his season to a premature end in January 2013.

Yet, in spite of Rondo's exceptional on-court performance, he slowly began to wear out his welcome in Boston. Although Celtics head coach Doc Rivers eventually learned to appreciate Rondo's high basketball IQ and competitive nature, he also found himself being put off at times by the point guard's stubbornness and unwillingness to yield to authority. Rondo also alienated several of his teammates with his behavior, with Rivers later admitting that Rondo's contentious relationship with Ray Allen contributed significantly to the latter's decision to leave the Celtics via free agency following the conclusion of the 2011–12 campaign.

One former teammate, Kendrick Perkins, said of Rondo, "He's my friend, but he knows he's too smart. And that's his problem. He knows when he's wrong. It's just getting him to admit it. The problem is, nine times out of 10, he'll be right about what he's saying."

Another Celtics insider held a less favorable impression of Rondo, stating, "He always thinks he's the smartest person in the room, even if he isn't."

Celtics general manager Danny Ainge confided, "He doesn't like to be told what to do. He wants to be coached, but, when you coach him, you'd better know what you're talking about. And, even then, he still may challenge you. The question always was, 'Is he a good enough player to behave the way he does?'"

Although Rondo failed to take the court again for the Celtics until midway through the 2013–14 campaign after undergoing surgery to repair his injured knee, he received the honor during his absence of being named the 15th captain in franchise history. Nevertheless, Ainge, who had grown increasingly impatient with Rondo over time, elected to trade away his team's best player the following season, including him in a five-player deal he completed with the Dallas Mavericks on December 18, 2014, that netted the Celtics three lesser players and a pair of draft picks in return. Rondo left Boston with career totals of 5,783 points scored, 4,474 assists, 2,485 rebounds, and 990 steals, a 47.3 field-goal shooting percentage, and a 61.4 free-throw shooting percentage. He averaged 11 points, 8.5 assists, 4.7 rebounds, and 1.9 steals per game as a member of the Celtics, with his mark of 8.5 assists per contest representing a franchise record.

Rondo spent the remainder of the 2014–15 campaign in Dallas, averaging 9.3 points, 6.5 assists, and 4.5 rebounds per game for the Mavericks, before signing a one-year deal with the Sacramento Kings at season's end. During his relatively brief stay in Dallas, Rondo continued to display his penchant for challenging authority figures, being suspended for one game in February 2015 for conduct detrimental to the team after engaging in a heated on-court exchange with Coach Rick Carlisle one day earlier. After averaging 11.9 points, 6 rebounds, and a league-leading 11.7 assists per game for Sacramento in 2015–16, Rondo split the next six seasons between six different teams, never again performing at an elite level, although he managed to win a second championship as a backup with the Lakers in 2020. A free agent as of this writing, Rondo currently boasts career totals of 9,337 points scored, 7,584 assists, 4,349 rebounds, and 1,518 steals, and averages of 9.8 points, 7.9 assists, 4.5 rebounds, and 1.6 steals per contest.

CELTICS CAREER HIGHLIGHTS

Best Season

Rondo earned his lone All-NBA selection and top-10 finish in the league MVP balloting in 2011–12, when he averaged 11.9 points, 4.8 rebounds, 1.8 steals, and a league-leading 11.7 assists per game, before performing even better in the playoffs. Nevertheless, Rondo had his finest all-around season two years earlier, concluding the 2009–10 campaign with averages of 13.7 points, 9.8 assists, 4.4 rebounds, and 2.3 steals per contest, while shooting a career-best 50.8 percent from the field. In addition to leading the NBA in steals, Rondo finished fourth in assists, establishing in the process Celtics single-season records for most steals (189), most assists (794), and highest assists-per-game average (9.8).

Memorable Moments / Greatest Performances

Although known more for his ability as a playmaker, Rondo had a number of high-scoring games during his time in Boston, with his first effort of more than 30 points coming on February 22, 2009, when he led the Celtics to a 128–109 victory over the Phoenix Suns by scoring 32 points and assisting on 10 baskets.

Rondo turned in another exceptional all-around performance some six weeks later, on April 8, 2009, hitting for 31 points, pulling down 9 rebounds, and recording 5 assists during a 106–104 win over the New Jersey Nets.

Although the Celtics lost their December 28, 2009, matchup with the Golden State Warriors by a score of 103–99, Rondo played a tremendous game, tallying 30 points and collecting 15 assists.

A tenacious defender, Rondo earned four NBA All-Defensive nominations as a member of the Celtics.
Photo courtesy of Keith Allison.

Rondo turned in another extraordinary all-around effort in a losing cause on February 15, 2012, when he scored 35 points, pulled down 5 rebounds, collected 6 assists, and recorded 4 steals during a 98–88 defeat at the hands of the Detroit Pistons.

Rondo began the 2010–11 campaign in style, compiling 17 assists in Boston's regular-season opener, an 88–80 victory over the Miami Heat, before dishing out a career-high 24 assists during a 105–101 win over the Knicks two games later. With 9 assists against Cleveland in between those two efforts, Rondo tied John Stockton's NBA record with 50 total assists through the first three games of the season. Meanwhile, Rondo's 24 assists against the Knicks gave him the second-highest single-game total in franchise history.

Rondo again exhibited his ball-distribution skills on November 9, 2012, when he assisted on 20 baskets and scored 14 points during a 106–100 loss to the Philadelphia 76ers. He handed out another 20 assists just eight days later, doing so during a 107–89 win over the Toronto Raptors on November 17.

Rondo recorded a total of 31 triple-doubles as a member of the Celtics, placing him second only to Larry Bird in franchise history. Rondo's first such effort came on December 3, 2008, when he scored 16 points, pulled down 13 rebounds, and assisted on 17 baskets during a 114–96 win over the Indiana Pacers.

Rondo recorded another triple-double a little over two months later, leading the Celtics to a 99–92 victory over the Dallas Mavericks by tallying 19 points, collecting 15 rebounds, and assisting on 14 baskets.

Other particularly outstanding all-around performances included a 12-point, 10-rebound, 23-assist, 6-steal outing against San Antonio on January 5, 2011, a 32-point, 10-rebound, 15-assist effort against Chicago on February 12, 2012, and an 18-point, 17-rebound, 20-assist outing against the Knicks on March 4, 2012, all of which resulted in Celtics wins.

Rondo also had a big game against Atlanta on April 11, 2012, when he led the Celtics to an 88–86 overtime victory over the Hawks by scoring 10 points, pulling down 10 rebounds, and collecting 20 assists.

Rondo saved several of his finest performances for the playoffs, first exhibiting his ability to raise his level of play in the postseason during the 2009 playoffs, when he nearly averaged a triple-double. Particularly effective against Chicago in the first round of the postseason tournament, Rondo tallied 29 points, pulled down 9 rebounds, and assisted on 7 baskets during Boston's 105–103 overtime loss in Game 1, before leading the Celtics to a 118–115 win in Game 2 by recording 19 points, 12 rebounds, 16 assists, and 5 steals. He again performed brilliantly in Game 5, leading his team to a 106–104 overtime victory by scoring 28 points, pulling down 8 rebounds, and recording 11 assists. Rondo also played extremely well against Orlando in the Eastern Conference Semifinals, with his best effort coming in Game 2, when he scored 15 points, collected 11 rebounds, and assisted on 18 baskets during a 112–94 Celtics win.

Rondo had another tremendous postseason in 2010, helping the Celtics advance to the NBA Finals for the second time in three years by posting averages of 15.8 points and 9.3 assists per game during the playoffs. Most effective against the Cleveland Cavaliers in the Eastern Conference Semifinals, Rondo accumulated 19 assists during Boston's 104–86 win in Game

Rondo's average of 8.5 assists per game as a member of the Celtics represents a franchise record. Photo courtesy of Marissa Gawel.

2, before leading the Celtics to a 97–87 victory in Game 4 by scoring 29 points, pulling down 18 rebounds, and collecting 13 assists. Although the Celtics eventually lost to the Los Angeles Lakers in seven games in the

NBA Finals, Rondo again played extremely well, registering his second triple-double of the postseason in Game 2, when he led his team to a 103–94 win by scoring 19 points, collecting 12 rebounds, and assisting on 10 baskets.

Although the Celtics failed to advance beyond the Eastern Conference Semifinals the following year, losing to the Miami Heat in five games, Rondo continued to perform exceptionally well in the playoffs, posting averages of 14 points and 9.6 assists per game in Boston's nine postseason contests. Dominating the Knicks in the opening round of the 2011 postseason tournament, Rondo led the Celtics to a 96–93 win in Game 2 by scoring 30 points, before recording 15 points, 11 rebounds, and a franchise playoff record 20 assists during a 113–96 victory in Game 3.

However, Rondo reached new heights during the 2012 postseason, when he played arguably the best ball of his career in helping the Celtics advance to the Eastern Conference Finals, where they ultimately lost to the Miami Heat in seven games. En route to posting averages of 17.3 points, 11.9 assists, and 6.7 rebounds per game in the playoffs, Rondo turned in the greatest individual performance of his career in Game 2 of the Conference Finals, when, in addition to playing all 53 minutes of the 115–111 overtime loss to Miami, he scored a career-high 44 points, pulled down 8 rebounds, assisted on 10 baskets, and recorded 3 steals.

NOTABLE ACHIEVEMENTS

- Averaged more than 11 assists per game three times, topping 9 assists per contest three other times.
- Averaged more than 5 rebounds per game four times.
- Averaged more than 2 steals per game twice.
- Shot better than 50 percent from the field twice.
- Led NBA in assists twice and steals once.
- Finished second in NBA in assists once and steals once.
- Led Celtics in assists seven times and steals six times.
- Holds Celtics single-season records for most steals (189 in 2009–10); most assists (794 in 2009–10); and highest assists-per-game average (11.7 in 2011–12).
- Holds Celtics second-highest single-game total for assists (24 vs. New York on 10/29/10).
- Holds Celtics career record for highest assists-per-game average (8.5).

- Ranks among Celtics career leaders in assists (4th) and steals (3rd).
- One-time NBA Player of the Week.
- 2006–07 NBA All-Rookie Second-Team selection.
- 2011–12 All-NBA Third-Team selection.
- Two-time NBA All-Defensive First-Team selection (2009–10 and 2010–11).
- Two-time NBA All-Defensive Second-Team selection (2008–09 and 2011–12).
- Four-time NBA All-Star (2009–10, 2010–11, 2011–12, and 2012–13).
- Two-time Eastern Conference champion (2007–08 and 2009–10).
- 2007–08 NBA champion.

18

JAYSON TATUM

Considered the player most likely to lead the Celtics to their next NBA championship, Jayson Tatum has gradually established himself as one of the league's foremost players since he first arrived in Boston in 2017. A tremendous force on offense, Tatum has led the Celtics in scoring in each of the last four seasons, averaging more than 25 points per contest on three separate occasions. A good rebounder, solid defender, and adept passer as well, Tatum has also led the team in rebounding, steals, and assists at various times, with his outstanding all-around play earning him four All-Star selections and two All-NBA nominations. Currently in the middle of an MVP-type campaign, Tatum serves as the centerpiece of a Celtics team that has high hopes of winning the league championship.

Born in St. Louis, Missouri, on March 3, 1998, Jayson Christopher Tatum grew up in a single-parent household, with his mother giving birth to him when she and his father were both 19-year-old undergraduates. The son of Justin Tatum, a former college basketball player and current gym teacher and basketball coach at Christian Brothers College High School in St. Louis, and Brandy Cole, who, after graduating from Saint Louis University School of Law, became a practicing attorney in the St. Louis area, Tatum came to understand the importance of hard work during his formative years, recalling, "Because I grew up in a single-parent home with my mom, growing up, things weren't always the best. . . . My mom tried not to let me see how much we were struggling, but I noticed it. I think that's what made me work harder. I saw how hard she was working, and I just wanted a better life for both of us."

Developing a fondness for basketball at an early age, Tatum remembered, "When I was, like, four or five, my mom would ask me what I wanted to be when I got older. And I would just be like, 'I wanna be Kobe.' She'd be like, 'You wanna be in the NBA?' 'No, like, I wanna be Kobe.'"

Although Tatum's mother served as his primary caregiver, his father had a huge hand in his early development, particularly as his coach on

Jayson Tatum has led the Celtics in scoring in each of the last four seasons.

the basketball court. While Tatum stated that his dad's tough love helped propel him to the NBA, he also revealed that the two shared a tumultuous relationship, stating, "I was scared of him, and he would grab me by my shirt and pin me up against the wall, and cuss me out in front of everybody, and I would be bawling. But then I would come out at halftime, and I would outscore the rest of the team, and we would win. So, in his mind, he needed to push my buttons to get me to a certain point."

Tatum added, "As a kid, I couldn't separate coach and dad—there was just one. He would always tell me I was soft, I wasn't gonna make it,

I wasn't gonna be anything, and he would take it to the extreme. But part of me working out at 5:30 in the morning was because I wanted to prove him wrong."

Eventually enrolling at Chaminade College Preparatory School in nearby Creve Coeur, Tatum spent four years excelling on the court for the Red Devils, performing especially well in his final two seasons. After earning Second-Team Naismith Trophy All-America honors his junior year by averaging 25.9 points, 11.7 rebounds, and 3.4 assists per game, Tatum garnered McDonald's All-America and 2016 Gatorade National Player of the Year recognition as a senior by averaging 29.6 points and 9.1 rebounds per contest for the Missouri Class 5A state champions.

Subsequently offered scholarships to several colleges, Tatum ultimately chose Duke University over North Carolina, Kentucky, and his mother and father's alma mater, Saint Louis University. Continuing his outstanding play at Duke, Tatum helped lead the Blue Devils to the ACC tournament championship in 2016–17 by averaging 16.8 points and 7.3 rebounds per game, earning in the process a spot on the ACC All-Freshman team. Choosing to forgo his final three years of college, Tatum entered the 2017 NBA Draft, where the Celtics selected him with the third overall pick.

Performing well his first year in Boston after being named to the starting unit prior to the start of the regular season, Tatum earned NBA All-Rookie First-Team honors by averaging 13.9 points, 5.0 rebounds, and 1.6 assists per game, while spending most of his time at the small forward position. Improving upon those numbers the following season, Tatum averaged 15.7 points, 6.0 rebounds, and 2.1 assists per contest for a Celtics team that concluded the campaign with a record of 49-33, before sweeping the Indiana Pacers in the opening round of the playoffs and then losing to the Milwaukee Bucks in five games in the Eastern Conference Semifinals.

Tatum didn't truly begin to thrive, though, until 2019–20, when, following the departure of Kyrie Irving, he became the focal point of the Celtics' offense. Moved to power forward after adding some much-needed bulk onto his slender 6-foot-8-inch, 210-pound frame over the course of the previous two seasons, Tatum averaged 23.4 points, 7.0 rebounds, 3.0 assists, and 1.4 steals per game, earning in the process his first All-Star selection and All-NBA Third-Team honors. Performing even better during the pandemic-shortened 2020–21 campaign, Tatum averaged 26.4 points, 7.4 rebounds, and 4.3 assists per contest. But, with the Celtics compiling a record of just 36-36 during the regular season and then losing to the Brooklyn Nets in five games in the opening round of the playoffs, questions began to arise as to whether Tatum had it in him to be the best player on a championship-level team.

Admitting that such thoughts began to enter his own mind, Tatum later said, "I was 23, playing for the biggest franchise in the NBA, with the expectations of being the best player, being the best leader, being the best teammate, and being the guy that can take a team to a championship. . . . You think about, 'Can I be the best player on a championship team?' because not many guys can. It's only the best of the best of the best, but that is where I aspire to be. And there were moments at the games where I was like, 'This is just not working.' But I think I've always stayed with it."

Tatum certainly has the talent and all the physical tools to lead his team to a championship. Blessed with outstanding quickness and leaping ability, Tatum excels at driving to the basket, shooting over his defender, and finishing on the fast break. He also possesses a soft touch on his mid- to long-range jumper, rebounds well, and does a good job of distributing the ball to his teammates.

Meanwhile, although some have questioned his leadership skills, Tatum responded to his critics by saying, "I feel like I'm very vocal. I might not be the loudest guy—especially in front of the camera. But for the guys in that locker room, when we're in practice or on the plane or on the court, my presence is felt in my voice . . . that's all I try to do when I see something: try to help guys out."

Joining the NBA's elite in 2021–22, Tatum earned All-NBA First-Team honors and a sixth-place finish in the league MVP voting by averaging 26.9 points, 8.0 rebounds, and 4.4 assists per game for a Celtics team that finished first in the Atlantic Division with a regular-season record of 51-31. Tatum subsequently performed well in the first three rounds of the playoffs, helping the Celtics advance to the NBA Finals by posting scoring averages of 29.5 points against Brooklyn, 27.6 points against Milwaukee, and 25.0 points against Miami, with his outstanding all-around play against the Heat gaining him Eastern Conference Finals MVP recognition. However, Tatum faltered against the Warriors in the NBA Finals, averaging only 21.5 points per contest on just 37 percent shooting from the field during Boston's six-game loss to Golden State.

Seemingly on a mission to redeem himself in 2022–23, Tatum has averaged 31.2 points, 8.5 rebounds, and 4.3 assists per game over the first half of the season, in leading the Celtics to the league's best record. If Tatum can continue to perform at the same level the rest of the way, he has an excellent chance of being named league MVP. Meanwhile, the Celtics will likely enter the postseason as one of the favorites to win the NBA championship.

As of this writing, Tatum boasts career totals of 9,011 points scored, 2,794 rebounds, 1,296 assists, 457 steals, and 286 blocked shots. He has also averaged 22.0 points, 6.8 rebounds, 3.2 assists, 1.1 steals, and 0.7 blocks per game.

CELTICS CAREER HIGHLIGHTS

Best Season

After averaging more than 26 points per game in each of the previous two campaigns, Tatum has reached new heights in 2022–23, posting a scoring average of 31.2 points per contest to this point in the season that puts him on pace to establish a new single-season franchise record.

Memorable Moments / Greatest Performances

Tatum led the Celtics to a convincing 119-93 victory over the Charlotte Hornets on December 22, 2019, by scoring 39 points, pulling down 12 rebounds, and blocking three shots.

Tatum contributed to a 140-105 rout of the New Orleans Pelicans on January 11, 2020, by scoring 41 points, going 16-of-22 from the field and 6-of-9 from three-point range.

Tatum helped lead the Celtics to a 141-133 double-overtime win over the Los Angeles Clippers on February 13, 2020, by scoring 39 points and grabbing nine rebounds.

Tatum proved to be the difference in a 126-114 win over the Toronto Raptors on January 4, 2021, scoring 40 points on 11-of-19 shooting from the field and 13-of-13 shooting from the free-throw line.

Tatum reached the 50-point mark for the first time in his career on April 9, 2021, when he scored 53 points during a 145-136 overtime win over the Minnesota Timberwolves.

Eight days later, Tatum led the Celtics to a 119-114 win over the Golden State Warriors by tallying 44 points and pulling down 10 rebounds.

Tatum tied Larry Bird for the franchise record for most points scored in a game when he tallied 60 points during a 143-140 overtime win over the San Antonio Spurs on April 30, 2021.

Tatum led the Celtics to a 118-100 win over the Washington Wizards on May 18, 2021, that earned them a spot in the playoffs by scoring 50 points.

Tatum subsequently led the Celtics to their only win of the 2021 play-offs by scoring 50 points during a 125-119 victory over the Brooklyn Nets in Game 3 of the opening round.

Tatum helped lead the Celtics to a 140-129 overtime win over Charlotte on October 25, 2021, by scoring 41 points and assisting on eight baskets.

Tatum tallied a game-high 42 points during a 117-103 win over Milwaukee on December 13, 2021.

Continuing to perform at an elite level in 2022, Tatum scored 51 points, grabbed 10 rebounds, and collected seven assists during a 116-87 rout of the Washington Wizards on January 23.

Tatum led the Celtics to a 126-120 victory over Brooklyn on March 6, 2022, by tallying 54 points, outscoring Nets forward Kevin Durant by 17 points in the process.

Remaining hot in his next game three days later, Tatum scored 44 points during a 115-101 win over Charlotte, going 16-of-24 from the field and 6-of-6 from the free-throw line.

Tatum led the Celtics to a 109-103 win over the Nets in Game 3 of their opening round 2022 NBA Eastern Conference Playoff series by scoring 39 points.

Tatum subsequently helped the Celtics even their 2022 NBA Eastern Conference Semifinals series with the Bucks at three games apiece by scoring 46 points and gathering in nine rebounds during a 108-95 win in Game 6.

Tatum helped lead the Celtics to a 126-120 win over Orlando on October 22, 2022, by scoring 40 points on 14-of-21 shooting from the field and 8-of-9 shooting from the free-throw line.

Tatum led the Celtics to a 117-108 win over the Pistons on November 12, 2022, by scoring 43 points and pulling down 10 rebounds.

Tatum topped that performance on November 30, 2022, scoring 49 points and grabbing 11 rebounds during a 134-121 win over the Miami Heat.

Tatum helped lead the Celtics to a 122-118 overtime win over the Lakers on December 13, 2022, by scoring 44 points and pulling down nine rebounds.

Tatum led the Celtics to a convincing 139-118 victory over the Bucks on Christmas Day 2022 by outscoring Giannis Antetokounmpo 41 to 27.

Tatum turned in an outstanding all-around effort during a lopsided 124-95 victory over the Dallas Mavericks on January 5, 2023, recording a triple-double by scoring 29 points, grabbing 14 rebounds, and collecting 10 assists.

Tatum led the Celtics to their seventh straight victory on January 16, 2023, by tallying 51 points, pulling down nine rebounds, and assisting on five baskets during a 130-118 win over Charlotte.

Tatum followed that up with another exceptional outing three days later, scoring 34 points and gathering in a career-high 19 rebounds during a 121-118 overtime victory over Golden State.

NOTABLE ACHIEVEMENTS

- Has averaged more than 20 points per game four times, topping 25 points per contest on three occasions.
- Has led Celtics in scoring average four times, rebounding four times, assists once, and steals once.
- Holds share of single-game franchise record for most points scored (60 vs. San Antonio on 4/30/21).
- Has scored at least 50 points in one game seven times.
- Ranks among Celtics career leaders in scoring average (fifth) and three-point field goals (second).
- Nine-time NBA Player of the Week.
- December 2017 NBA Rookie of the Month.
- Two-time NBA Player of the Month.
- 2017–18 NBA All-Rookie First-Team selection.
- 2022 NBA Eastern Conference Finals MVP.
- Finished sixth in 2021–22 NBA MVP voting.
- 2021–22 All-NBA First-Team selection.
- 2019–20 All-NBA Third-Team selection.
- Four-time NBA All-Star selection (2019–20, 2020–21, 2021–22, and 2022–23).
- 2021–22 Atlantic Division champion.
- 2021–22 Eastern Conference champion.

19

REGGIE LEWIS

He kept you off balance all the time. There were a few guys in the league I hated to guard because you didn't know what they were thinking. I'm glad Reggie was my teammate, because he was one of them.

—Larry Bird

His career tragically cut short by a heart attack that took his life at only 27 years of age, Reggie Lewis never attained the greatness for which he appeared headed after his first few seasons in Boston. Blessed with a world of talent, Lewis seemed destined to succeed Larry Bird as the Celtics' franchise player, with onetime teammate Dee Brown suggesting, "He was a guy that people didn't get a chance to see in his prime. He was getting there. He would have been one of the best players to play with the Celtics."

Yet, even though Celtics fans probably never got to see the very best of Lewis, the 6-foot-7 swingman accomplished quite a bit during his relatively brief stay in Boston. Averaging more than 17 points per game in each of his five seasons as a starter, Lewis topped the 20-point mark twice, leading the team in scoring both times. An outstanding defender as well, Lewis surpassed 1.5 steals and 1 blocked shot per contest three times each, en route to earning one All-Star selection. Although Lewis's time with the Celtics proved to be far too short, his stellar all-around play, exceptional leadership, and charisma prompted the team to retire his number-35 jersey following his passing, making him one of only two players in franchise history (Ed Macauley being the other) to be so honored without winning a championship as a member of the team.

Reggie Lewis never fulfilled his enormous potential due to his tragic passing at only 27 years of age. Photo courtesy of George A. Kitrinos.

Born in Baltimore, Maryland, on November 21, 1965, Reginald C. Lewis attended local Paul Laurence Dunbar High School, where he played basketball alongside future NBA notables Muggsy Bogues, David Wingate, and Reggie Williams. The most talented of Dunbar's outstanding quartet of players, Lewis ended up leading the Poets to an overall record of 60-0 over the course of his final two seasons, earning in the process a scholarship to Boston's Northeastern University. Continuing his exceptional play at the collegiate level under legendary coach Jim Calhoun (still in the relatively early stages of his coaching career at that point in time), Lewis amassed a total of 2,708 points in his four years at Northeastern, making him the school's all-time leading scorer. In so doing, he led his team to four consecutive ECAC North championships and four straight NCAA Men's Basketball Tournament appearances, en route to earning America East Player of the Year honors three times.

Subsequently selected by the Celtics in the first round of the 1987 NBA Draft, with the 22nd overall pick, Lewis saw very little action his first year in Boston, averaging only 4.5 points and 8.3 minutes per game as a backup to Danny Ainge at the shooting guard position. However, with Larry Bird missing virtually the entire 1988–89 campaign, Lewis saw his playing time increase dramatically after he took over for Bird at small forward—the same position he played in college. Excelling at his former post, Lewis averaged 18.5 points and 4.7 rebounds per game in his first season as an NBA starter. Shifted back to shooting guard upon Bird's return to the team the following season, Lewis again posted solid numbers as a starter, averaging 17 points, 4.4 rebounds, and 2.8 assists per contest. Lewis then compiled the best numbers of his young career in 1990–91, finishing second on the team to Bird in scoring with an average of 18.7 points per game, while also averaging 5.2 rebounds, 1.2 steals, and 1.1 blocked shots per contest.

Considered to be a very good offensive player from the time he first entered the league, the 6-foot-7, 200-pound Lewis gradually made a name for himself as a solid defender as well, thrusting himself into the national spotlight one evening in late March 1991, when he blocked four Michael Jordan shots during a 135–132 Celtics double-overtime victory over the Chicago Bulls. In discussing his frustrating outing against Lewis, Jordan later admitted, "He was a tough matchup. He had those long arms that really bothered me. I was trying to be aggressive with him. I was trying to take advantage of his passive demeanor, but he didn't back down. He never relinquished his own aggressiveness. He shocked me a little bit."

Lewis also impressed Jordan with his offensive skills, with Jim Calhoun later stating, "I remember talking to MJ about him. Michael said Reggie's first step was the best in the league. That's pretty high praise."

Meanwhile, Joe Dumars addressed Lewis's offensive prowess by noting, "He was long, athletic, smooth; he could raise up over you and shoot. He was a really good defender, too. He was a tough, tough cover. Man, he was a tough guy to guard. He was definitely the one, other than MJ, who was the toughest for me to figure out. He was so long, and you couldn't really get physical with him, because he was so slim, and it always seemed like I was getting called for fouls. He was a great, great player."

Larry Bird added, "He kept you off balance all the time. There were a few guys in the league I hated to guard because you didn't know what they were thinking. I'm glad Reggie was my teammate, because he was one of them."

In addition to his outstanding play at both ends of the court, Lewis contributed to the Celtics with his ability to lead by example. Although quiet and somewhat shy, Lewis conducted himself in an extremely professional manner that tended to rub off on the other players. At the same time, his enthusiasm and infectious smile made him a joy to be around, as Jim Calhoun suggested when he said, "Reggie had a true joy playing basketball that gave comfort to people."

Lewis began to establish himself as one of the NBA's bigger stars in 1991–92, when he earned All-Star honors for the first time by leading the Celtics with a scoring average of 20.8 points per game. After being named captain prior to the start of the following season after Bird announced his retirement, Lewis once again led the team in scoring with an average of 20.8 points per contest. However, the 1992–93 campaign unfortunately ended up being Lewis's final NBA season.

With the Celtics having compiled a record of 48-34 during the regular season, they entered the 1993 playoffs as the Eastern Conference's Number 4 seed. Facing the Charlotte Hornets in the opening round of the postseason tournament, the Celtics got off to a fast start in Game 1 before Lewis inexplicably collapsed while running down the left side of the court midway through the first quarter. Describing the events that transpired to Celtics fans watching on television, Tommy Heinsohn reported, "Reggie is hurt on the other end of the court. I'm not sure exactly what happened, but, boy, he was down and writhing in pain."

Recalling the incident years later, Heinsohn said, "I remember I was broadcasting the game when he went down, and he was playing so great at the time. I just thought he dropped because of his own adrenaline, because he was playing so hard."

Muggsy Bogues, a member of the Hornets at the time, stood only a few feet from the spot where his former high school teammate collapsed, stating many years later, "I see him fall every day. I thought somebody had tripped him, and [Charlotte forward] Johnny Newman was trying to pick him up as he was falling. Then we went back down to the other end, not even knowing how serious it was."

Celtics teammate Kevin Gamble, one of Lewis's closest friends on the squad, also failed to grasp the severity of the situation at that moment, recounting, "During the game, I didn't think anything of it. I just thought he was lightheaded or didn't eat—we didn't know he had the health problem that he had."

Dee Brown added, "I remember it every time I get on the court. We didn't know what was going on against Charlotte. We lost the series, but that wasn't the important thing. Reggie was down—was he okay?"

After leaving the game for only a few minutes, during which time the Boston training staff tended to him, Lewis returned to the contest. However, he left the court again a short time later after complaining of shortness of breath. Lewis missed the remainder of the series after subsequently being diagnosed with a cardiac abnormality initially thought to be life-threatening arrhythmia.

The misdiagnosis proved to be fatal to Lewis, who later received clearance to attempt a comeback. Less than three months later, on July 27, 1993, Lewis collapsed again while shooting hoops with a friend at Brandeis University. After police officers tried unsuccessfully to revive him, Lewis was pronounced dead hours later at a local hospital, with his premature passing at the age of 27 being attributed to hypertrophic cardiomyopathy, a genetic heart defect common in the deaths of young athletes.

Recalling the unhappy events that transpired, Jeff Twiss, Boston's longtime PR man and a close friend of Lewis, said, "I was 15, 20 feet down the hall in the hospital and heard them working on Reggie. I saw [then teammate] Rick Fox come in with tears in his eyes, and I knew we had lost Reggie."

Dee Brown revealed, "The GM at the time, Jan Volk, called me and said, 'You've got to get back to Boston.' From that call, I don't remember one thing. The next season, I don't remember. I can't tell you a highlight I had. I can't tell you a play I played in. I can't tell you my teammates, because the one that I wanted to be playing with wasn't there anymore."

Lewis's passing had a similar impact on the entire city of Boston, with Celtics fans bemoaning the loss of their beloved hero. In addition to starring for the Celtics on the court, Lewis gave back to the community, with one of his more philanthropic gestures being his annual giveaway of hundreds of turkeys to underprivileged families in the area. Lewis's contributions to the team and the city as a whole prompted the Celtics to honor his memory by retiring his number-35 jersey in a special ceremony held at the Boston Garden on March 22, 1995.

Following his passing, many of Lewis's friends and former teammates also chose to express their admiration for him as both a player and a person.

Celtics legend Tommy Heinsohn told Comcast SportsNet, "He was well on the verge of being [in] the upper echelon of players in the NBA, being a perennial All-Star."

Dee Brown stated, "He was our quiet superstar. He was the guy, he was the captain."

Jeff Twiss recalled, "He didn't want to try to be the next Larry Bird, the next Dennis Johnson. Reggie wanted, and was starting to carve, his own place inside the Celtics' lore."

In speaking of his former protégé, Jim Calhoun suggested, "We saw a great player, but I think he was on his way to the Hall of Fame. I think he was that good."

CELTICS CAREER HIGHLIGHTS

Best Season

Although Lewis compiled outstanding numbers the following season as well, posting the same scoring average while assisting on a career-high 3.7 baskets per game, he had his finest all-around season for the Celtics in 1991–92. En route to earning his lone All-Star selection, Lewis appeared in all 82 Celtics games, posting averages of 20.8 points, 4.8 rebounds, 1.5 steals, and 1.3 blocked shots per contest, while also shooting a career-best 50.3 percent from the field. By recording 394 rebounds, 185 assists, 125 steals, and 105 blocked shots, Lewis became the only player in franchise history to surpass the 100-mark in all four categories in the same season.

Memorable Moments / Greatest Performances

Although Lewis built his reputation primarily on his scoring prowess, he used his outstanding athleticism and defensive skills to create one of his most memorable moments. Going head-to-head against Michael Jordan during a March 31, 1991, contest versus the Chicago Bulls, Lewis frustrated Air Jordan as few others ever did, blocking four of his shots, while also holding him to just 12-of-36 shooting from the field. Lewis also scored 25 points during the game, in leading the Celtics to a 135–132 double-overtime victory over the eventual NBA champions.

Lewis reached the 20-point mark for the first time in his career on November 23, 1988, when he scored 20 points during a 114–109 win over the Charlotte Hornets.

An exceptional two-way player, Lewis excelled on both ends of the court.
Photo courtesy of George A. Kitrinos.

Lewis topped 30 points for the first time in his career two weeks later, scoring 33 points during a 105–100 loss to the Chicago Bulls on December 6. Facing Michael Jordan for the first time as a starter, Lewis also pulled down 6 rebounds and assisted on 4 baskets during the contest.

Lewis had a number of other big offensive games over the course of the 1988–89 campaign, with one of those coming on February 3, 1989, when he tallied 32 points during a 117–108 win over the Washington Bullets. Although the Celtics lost their March 28, 1989, matchup with the Philadelphia 76ers by a score of 117–115 in overtime, Lewis scored a season-high 39 points during the game. Lewis hit for another 35 points the very next evening, in leading the Celtics to a 106–97 victory over the Portland Trail Blazers.

Lewis turned in an outstanding all-around effort on January 10, 1990, when he scored 32 points and pulled down 11 rebounds during a 104–97 win over the Detroit Pistons. Some three months later, on April 15, 1990, Lewis scored a season-high 34 points during a 101–94 victory over the Knicks.

Lewis had his biggest game of the ensuing campaign on April 12, 1991, when, after previously topping the 30-point mark five other times during the season, he scored a career-high 42 points, in leading the Celtics to a 119–109 win over the Miami Heat.

Lewis had another huge game on November 25, 1991, when he scored 37 points during a 121–108 win over the Washington Bullets.

Lewis turned in a pair of extraordinary performances just five days apart during the latter stages of the 1991–92 campaign, hitting for 38 points, in leading the Celtics to a 100–97 victory over the Cleveland Cavaliers on April 7, 1992, before scoring 35 points, collecting 9 rebounds, and assisting on 6 baskets during a 128–102 blowout of the Charlotte Hornets on April 12.

Lewis played one of his best games of his final NBA season on December 9, 1992, when he scored 36 points during a 129–119 win over the Denver Nuggets. He topped that mark a few months later, though, hitting for a season-high 37 points during a 106–104 victory over the Portland Trail Blazers on March 21, 1993. Lewis approached the 40-point mark for the final time in his career one week later, on March 28, when he led the Celtics to a 114–113 win over the Washington Bullets by tallying 36 points.

En route to posting a scoring average of 28 points per game during the 1992 playoffs, Lewis turned in a number of exceptional performances for the Celtics, with his first such effort coming in Game 1 of the opening round, when he tallied 36 points during a 124–113 victory over the Indiana Pacers. Lewis hit for another 32 points in the Game 3 clincher, which Boston won by a score of 102–98.

Although the Celtics subsequently came up short in their Eastern Conference Semifinal matchup with Cleveland, losing to the Cavaliers in seven games, Lewis performed brilliantly, posting a scoring average of 28.1 points per contest over the course of the series. Particularly dominant in Boston's 114–112 overtime loss in Game 4, Lewis followed up a 36-point Game 3 performance with a 42-point effort in which he also collected 6 assists and 5 steals, while holding Cleveland's Craig Ehlo to just one point in 45 minutes of action.

NOTABLE ACHIEVEMENTS

- Averaged more than 20 points per game twice, topping 17 points per contest three other times.
- Shot better than 50 percent from the field once (50.3% in 1991–92).
- Finished second in NBA in games played once.
- Led Celtics in scoring average twice.
- Ranks among Celtics career leaders in steals (tied for 10th).
- 1991–92 NBA All-Star.
- Number 35 retired by Celtics.

20

ANTOINE WALKER

Joined by Paul Pierce in the Boston frontcourt the following season, Walker teamed up with the high-scoring Pierce to give the Celtics one of the league's top forward tandems.

Spending much of his time in Boston playing alongside Paul Pierce, Antoine Walker helped make the Celtics relevant once again after initially joining the team in the middle of a rebuilding period. Proving to be an offensive force during his time in Beantown, Walker averaged more than 20 points per game in five of his seven full seasons with the Celtics, while also topping 5 assists per contest twice. A strong rebounder as well, Walker also averaged more than 10 rebounds per game once, en route to earning three All-Star selections as a member of the team. Walker's excellent all-around play helped the Celtics advance to the playoffs in each of his final three seasons with them, after they finished his rookie campaign with an embarrassing record of just 15-67.

Born in Chicago, Illinois, on August 12, 1976, Antoine Devon Walker attended local Mount Carmel High School, where he starred on the hardwood alongside future NFL quarterback Donovan McNabb. After attaining All-State status as a senior, Walker received a scholarship offer to play for Rick Pitino at the University of Kentucky. Excelling as a freshman in college, Walker earned SEC Tournament MVP honors, before garnering All-SEC First Team and All-NCAA Regional Team selections as a sophomore by posting averages of 15.2 points and 8.4 rebounds per game as a starting forward on the Wildcats' national championship team.

Choosing to forgo his final two years of collegiate eligibility, Walker entered the 1996 NBA Draft, where the Celtics selected him with the sixth overall pick, ahead of such other future NBA stars as Kobe Bryant, Steve

Seen here as a member of the Miami Heat, Antoine Walker averaged more than 20 points per game in five of his seven full seasons in Boston.
Photo courtesy of Keith Allison.

Nash, and Jermaine O'Neal. Joining a struggling team in Boston that concluded the previous campaign with a record of just 33-49, Walker found himself unable to improve the fortunes of the club, even though he earned a spot on the NBA All-Rookie First Team by averaging 17.5 points and 9 rebounds per game. However, with Rick Pitino assuming the position of head coach in Boston prior to the start of the 1997–98 season, the Celtics ended up improving their record by 21 games, to 36-46. Thriving under his former college coach after being given more freedom on offense, Walker earned his first All-Star selection by posting averages of 22.4 points and 10.2 rebounds per game.

Joined by Paul Pierce in the Boston frontcourt the following season, Walker teamed up with the high-scoring Pierce to give the Celtics one of the league's top forward tandems. For his part, Walker continued his outstanding production, averaging 18.7 points and 8.5 rebounds per game in 1998–99, before beginning a four-year run during which he topped the 20-point mark each season. Here are the numbers he compiled over that stretch of time:

SEASON	POINTS PER GAME	REBOUNDS PER GAME	ASSISTS PER GAME
1999–2000	20.5	8.0	3.7
2000–01	23.4	8.9	5.5
2001–02	22.1	8.8	5.0
2002–03	20.1	7.2	4.8

In addition to giving the Celtics excellent scoring and solid rebounding throughout the period, Walker gradually improved his ball-distribution skills, surpassing 5 assists per contest on two separate occasions. He also proved to be extremely durable, missing a total of only six games over the course of those four seasons. Walker garnered All-Star honors in both 2001–02 and 2002–03.

Yet, in spite of the outstanding numbers Walker posted year after year, he found himself being criticized at times for taking too many shots, particularly of the low-percentage variety. Ranking among the NBA leaders in field-goal attempts in five of his first seven seasons, Walker led the league in that category once and finished second another time. He also topped the circuit in three-point field-goal attempts three straight times, which baffled many, since his burly 6-foot-8, 240-pound frame made him an effective low-post player. Furthermore, Walker annually placed among the league leaders in turnovers and field goals missed, generally compiling a below-average field-goal shooting percentage that fell somewhere in the 39 to 43 percent range. He also tended to struggle at the foul line, converting more than 65 percent of his free-throw attempts just three times over the course of his career.

Equally maddening to many Celtics fans were Walker's sense of entitlement and poor attitude. Coming off his All-Star campaign of 1997–98 (just his second in the league, and his first under Rick Pitino), Walker refused to attend coach Pitino's summer sessions, telling Michael Holley of the *Boston Globe* at the time, "Let me tell you, no veteran All-Star player shows up for a camp like that. For the rest of my career, I'll never go to a camp like that; never." During that same interview, Walker suggested that he considered himself to be "the most loved player in the NBA," and stated that he wished the Celtics had drafted his college teammate, Nazr Mohammed, instead of Paul Pierce, who, he said, "is a guy who can come off the bench and give scoring to our second unit. But I know what our team needs. We need big people."

In response, the *Boston Globe*'s Bob Ryan penned an article in which he called Walker a "punk . . . an arrogant, misguided, yes, punk; a snotty punk who has no idea what it takes to win a championship at this level." Ryan went on to advise the Celtics against signing Walker to a long-term contract, because "he will immediately take it as a validation of his greatness. He feels no need for improvement."

Walker eventually inked a long-term deal to stay in Boston, after which he continued to post impressive scoring and rebounding totals. Nevertheless, at least some of Ryan's predictions came to fruition, since Walker never developed into anything more than a marginal defensive player, gained a considerable amount of weight, lost much of his athleticism, and regressed into primarily a long-range shooter.

Seeking to cut ties with Walker in spite of his on-court production, the Celtics included him in a six-player trade they completed with the Dallas Mavericks on October 20, 2003, that netted them Raef LaFrentz, Chris Mills, Jiri Welsch, and a 2004 first-round draft pick in return.

Walker subsequently spent the remainder of his career traveling from one city to another, playing for five different teams over the course of his final five years in the league. After averaging 14 points and 8.3 rebounds per game in his one year as a starter in Dallas, Walker split the 2004–05 campaign between the Hawks and Celtics, returning to Boston on February 24, 2005, for a package of four players that included Tom Gugliotta, Gary Payton, Michael Stewart, and a 2006 first-round draft pick. Although Walker played well for the Celtics in his second stint with them, posting averages of 16.3 points and 8.3 rebounds per contest over the final 24 games of the season, his stay in Beantown proved to be short-lived. With the Celtics taking part in a gigantic five-team, 13-player trade that also included Miami, Memphis, Utah, and New Orleans / Oklahoma City, Walker departed for Miami on August 2, 2005, after which he spent the next two seasons serving as a backup for the Heat.

After contributing 12.2 points and 5.1 rebounds per game to Miami's 2005–06 NBA championship team, Walker assumed a somewhat less prominent role the following season, averaging only 8.5 points and 4.3 rebounds per contest. Traded to Minnesota just prior to the start of the 2007–08 campaign, Walker ended his NBA career coming off the bench for the Timberwolves, averaging 8 points, 3.7 rebounds, and 19.4 minutes per game, before being dealt at season's end to the Memphis Grizzlies, who waived him during the early stages of the ensuing campaign after he failed to make an official appearance with them.

Over the course of 12 NBA seasons, Walker scored 15,647 points, amassed 6,891 rebounds, 3,170 assists, and 1,085 steals, shot 41.4 percent from the field and 63.3 percent from the free-throw line, and posted averages of 17.5 points, 7.7 rebounds, 3.5 assists, and 1.2 steals per game. In his seven and a half seasons with the Celtics, he scored 11,386 points, pulled down 4,782 rebounds, accumulated 2,266 assists and 828 steals, and averaged 20.6 points, 8.7 rebounds, 4.1 assists, and 1.5 steals per contest. Walker's 20.6 points-per-game scoring average ranks as the seventh highest mark in franchise history.

Following the conclusion of his NBA career, Walker spent two seasons with the Idaho Stampede of the NBA Development League before officially announcing his retirement in April 2012. During that time, he ran afoul of the law, being arrested by Las Vegas police in July 2009 for writing bad checks related to gambling debts he had incurred at three local casinos. Although a subsequent plea agreement prevented Walker from facing a prison term, he was put on probation and had to work toward repaying the debt. Despite earning more than $108 million over the course of his playing career, Walker experienced other financial difficulties in retirement as well, filing for bankruptcy in May 2010 after losing most of his money in a series of ill-advised real estate investments he made during his time in Boston.

CELTICS CAREER HIGHLIGHTS

Best Season

Walker had a fine statistical season for the Celtics in 2000–01, when he posted career-high marks in scoring (23.4 ppg), assists (5.5 apg), and steals (1.7 spg), while also averaging 8.9 rebounds per game. He again compiled outstanding numbers the following season, averaging 22.1 points, 8.8 rebounds, 5 assists, and 1.5 steals per contest. However, Walker shot just 41.3 percent from the field in the first of those campaigns, after which he shot only 39.4 percent from the floor in the second, while leading the league in both field-goal attempts and field goals missed. Meanwhile, Walker averaged 22.4 points, 3.3 assists, 1.7 steals, and a career-high 10.2 rebounds per game in 1997–98, while hitting on 42.3 percent of his shots from the field. In the process, he earned his first All-Star selection and a 12th-place finish in the NBA MVP voting, receiving MVP consideration for the only time in his career. All things considered, Walker played his best ball for the Celtics in 1997–98.

Memorable Moments / Greatest Performances

Although the Celtics lost both contests, Walker turned in a pair of exceptional all-around efforts in March 1997, scoring 19 points, pulling down a career-high 21 rebounds, and assisting on 5 baskets during a 104–99 loss to the Orlando Magic on March 21, before hitting for 37 points, collecting 14 rebounds, and recording 6 assists during a 113–105 defeat at the hands of the Philadelphia 76ers seven days later.

Walker again starred in defeat on April 4, 1997, tallying 36 points and amassing 12 rebounds and 6 assists during a 117–102 loss to the LA Clippers.

Walker performed extremely well for much of January 1998, with one of his best all-around games coming on January 2, when he scored 27 points and pulled down 18 rebounds, in leading the Celtics to a 93–89 win over the Minnesota Timberwolves. Although the Celtics lost their January 7 matchup with the Washington Wizards by a score of 110–108, Walker hit for a career-high 49 points during the contest. He had another big game on January 30, when he recorded 38 points, 11 rebounds, and 6 assists during a 97–95 loss to the Charlotte Hornets.

Walker turned in another outstanding all-around effort on March 6, 1998, when he scored 35 points and pulled down 13 rebounds, in leading the Celtics to a 108–98 victory over Washington.

Walker reached the 40-point mark for the second time in his career on April 8, 1998, hitting for 43 points during a 117–104 loss to the New Jersey Nets.

Walker had another huge game against the Nets two years later, scoring 39 points and collecting 11 rebounds during a 99–96 Celtics win on January 15, 2000.

Walker continued his success against New Jersey the following season, tallying 21 points, pulling down 19 rebounds, and recording 7 assists, in leading the Celtics to a 99–86 win over the Nets on December 20, 2000. Walker nearly equaled his career-high mark in scoring the following month, when he hit for 47 points and collected 13 assists during a 111–106 loss to the Sacramento Kings on January 17, 2001.

Walker led the Celtics to a 103–82 rout of the Cleveland Cavaliers on February 4, 2001, by scoring 36 points, pulling down 11 rebounds, collecting 8 assists, and recording 3 steals. Walker again tallied 36 points just three days later, in leading the Celtics to a 94–91 victory over the Milwaukee Bucks. He also collected 13 rebounds during the contest.

Walker turned in one of his finest all-around performances of the ensuing campaign on December 11, 2001, when he led the Celtics to a 102–93 win over the Knicks by scoring 42 points, pulling down 9 rebounds, and assisting on 9 baskets. Walker had another big game later that season, on March 15, 2002, when he scored 38 points during a 103–97 victory over the Memphis Grizzlies.

Walker recorded 13 triple-doubles during his time in Boston, with his first such effort coming on February 1, 1998, when he led the Celtics to a 107–96 win over the Houston Rockets by scoring 27 points, pulling down 14 rebounds, and assisting on 10 baskets.

Walker accomplished the feat for the second time in his career on March 8, 2000, when he scored 30 points, collected 19 rebounds, and recorded 10 assists during a 112–101 victory over the Milwaukee Bucks.

Other particularly outstanding efforts included a 30-point, 12-rebound, 14-assist performance during a 110–93 win over Denver on February 12, 2002, and a 30-point, 14-rebound, 10-assist outing against the Lakers one week later that helped the Celtics record a 109–108 victory. Walker also hit for 33 points, pulled down 11 rebounds, and collected 10 assists during a 115–100 win over Cleveland on December 13, 2002.

NOTABLE ACHIEVEMENTS

- Averaged more than 20 points per game five times, topping 17 points per game two other times.
- Averaged more than 10 rebounds per game once, topping 8 rebounds per game five other times.
- Averaged more than 5 assists per game twice.
- Led NBA in three-point field goals once; games played once; and minutes played once.
- Finished in NBA's top-10 in scoring twice and rebounding once.
- Led Celtics in scoring average four times; rebounding five times; and assists three times.
- Holds Celtics single-game (9—twice) and single-season (222 in 2001–02) records for most three-point field goals made.
- Ranks among Celtics career leaders in scoring average (7th); rebounds (10th); and steals (6th).
- Two-time NBA Player of the Week.
- NBA Player of the Month for December 2001.
- 1996–97 NBA All-Rookie First-Team selection.
- Three-time NBA All-Star (1998, 2002, and 2003).

21

PAUL SILAS

It's almost like a collegiate atmosphere in a pro world; an atmosphere of total sacrifice for the good of the team, on and off the court. It's a way of life. You just fall into it.

—Paul Silas

An outstanding defensive player, exceptional rebounder, and excellent team leader, Paul Silas played for five different teams over the course of his 16-year NBA career, helping to improve the fortunes of all five clubs. After learning the tools of his trade from all-time NBA great Bob Pettit while playing for the St. Louis Hawks, Silas went on to star for the Phoenix Suns, before joining the Boston Celtics in 1972. Over the course of the next four seasons, Silas helped lead the Celtics to two NBA championships, earning in the process one All-Star selection and three NBA All-Defensive Team nominations. From Boston, Silas moved on to Denver and, finally, Seattle, where he won his third NBA title as a member of the SuperSonics. Silas, though, will always be remembered most for his time in Boston, where he established himself as one of the greatest "Sixth Men" in franchise history.

Born in Prescott, Arkansas, on July 12, 1943, Paul Theron Silas lived a somewhat nomadic existence as a youth, moving with his family to New York and Chicago, before returning to Arkansas at the age of six. The son of an alcoholic father, with whom he had very little interaction, young Paul traveled to Oakland, California, to live with his grandparents at age eight. Finding race relations in Oakland to be much better than the conditions that existed in Arkansas at the time, Silas later recalled, "I got used to having white teachers and playing with white guys."

Although tall and lanky, Silas knew little about the game of basketball, which he learned how to play the hard way, recounting years later, "I wasn't that tough at that time. Players used to come at me and beat the hell out of me." Silas ended up benefiting greatly from the physical tests he endured on the courts of Oakland, learning to strike back when another player got rough with him, and developing a mean streak that helped him to succeed as his athletic career progressed.

After making the varsity basketball team at McClymonds High School at age 14, Silas went on to average more than 30 points per game as a senior, earning in the process recognition as the best player in the entire state of California. Subsequently offered a scholarship to attend Creighton University in Omaha, Silas continued to star on the court, averaging 21.6 rebounds per game over the course of three seasons, en route to setting an NCAA rebounding record.

Selected by the St. Louis Hawks with the 10th overall pick of the 1964 NBA Draft following his graduation from Creighton, Silas saw very little playing time his first two seasons, serving as a backup to star forwards Bob Pettit, Cliff Hagan, and Bill Bridges. However, Pettit, one of the game's premier interior players, proved to be extremely influential in Silas's development into an elite rebounder, helping him to refine his technique. In discussing the lessons he learned from Pettit, Silas revealed, "He was one of the guys that really taught me how to rebound offensively; to turn my body and put my shoulder on a player, and just hold him there and keep your hands up."

Silas finally earned a starting job in St. Louis following Pettit's retirement, having his best season for the Hawks in 1967–68, when he averaged 13.4 points and 11.7 rebounds per game. Following one more year with the Hawks, Silas became a member of the Suns when Phoenix acquired him in a trade prior to the start of the 1969–70 campaign. Playing under head coach Cotton Fitzsimmons, who encouraged him to shoot more, Silas really came into his own in Phoenix, averaging 12.8 points and 11.7 rebounds in his first season with the Suns, before posting marks of 11.9 points and 12.5 rebounds per contest the following year.

However, the 6-foot-7 Silas performed even better after he shed nearly 30 pounds prior to the start of the 1971–72 campaign. A far more svelte 215 pounds following the weight loss, Silas suddenly found himself able to beat his man down the court for easy baskets, while also getting better lift on his jump shot in the half-court offense. Although Silas never developed into anything more than a marginal outside shooter—admitting himself, "I worked on it and I got better; not really good, but better"—his newfound

Doing all the "little things" to help his team win, Paul Silas made key contributions to two NBA championship teams during his time in Boston.

athleticism enabled him to average a career-high 17.5 points per game. Meanwhile, he continued to play excellent defense and rebound extremely well, averaging 11.9 rebounds per contest, en route to earning All-Star honors for the first time in his career.

Having taken note of Silas's improved play, Red Auerbach elected to trade the NBA Draft rights to Charlie Scott, who had been playing for the ABA's Virginia Squires, to the Suns for the 29-year-old forward on March 14, 1972. Silas, who had grown quite comfortable in Phoenix, initially balked at the idea of moving to Boston, stating years later, "It was difficult. I just didn't want to go, so Red Auerbach started talking to me and whatnot, and I just didn't have much to say. I did not want to go."

Nevertheless, the extremely persistent Auerbach eventually convinced Silas that joining the Celtics would benefit him greatly, with the forward later revealing, "I'd talk to him about basketball; about this, about that; whatever. It was just special. He was so smart, and I began to love being there."

After being warned by Bill Russell of the difficulties that faced black players who lived in the Boston area, Silas learned that many Celtics fans cared more about the color of his jersey than the color of his skin, saying, "We were a good team. People just admired you." Silas also came to view the Celtic "mystique" much differently than he had as an opposing player, suggesting, "To be truthful, I thought it was a lot of nonsense. But when I arrived it was amazing. It's almost like a collegiate atmosphere in a pro world; an atmosphere of total sacrifice for the good of the team, on and off the court. It's a way of life. You just fall into it."

Silas immediately demonstrated his sense of self-sacrifice after he arrived in Boston, accepting the role of "sixth man" presented to him by Celtics coach Tom Heinsohn, who later recalled telling the veteran forward, "Paul, I know this situation here is something that you didn't expect. I'll tell you this: Everybody in this town understands what the role of a sixth man is, and you are the quintessential sixth man. I guarantee you one thing—you will always be in at the end of the game when it is most important."

Although Silas did not particularly care for the idea of coming off the bench at first, Heinsohn revealed that he eventually came to embrace his new role, suggesting, "By the end of the year, even though he was grousing about it at the beginning, he ended up being on the cover of *Sports Illustrated* for being the sixth man. He wasn't a great shooter, but he was such a solid player. He could pass and rebound and defend. In an up-tempo game, he could score as well as anybody. What he did in his career is really max out what he was."

Silas ended up averaging 13.3 points and a career-high 13 rebounds per game in his first season in Boston, in helping the Celtics compile a league-best record of 68-14 during the regular season. He followed that up with a solid 1973–74 campaign in which he posted averages of 11.5 points and 11.2 rebounds per contest for a Celtics team that went on to win the NBA championship.

In discussing the contributions Silas made to the Celtics his first two years with the team, Tom Heinsohn noted, "Silas has played the sixth-man role for the last two years. We don't believe that it's important as to who starts the game—it is important who's in there at the end. And Silas could go up against the opposition's best forward. They know he's coming in 99 out of 100 times. He knows what his job is and how important his role is to our ball club."

Silas's presence did indeed prove to be essential to the success the Celtics experienced in each of his first two seasons in Boston, especially since it enabled Dave Cowens to thrive as never before. Forming a symbiotic relationship with the team's similarly undersized center, Silas employed the same relentless approach to the game as Cowens, who later said, "It's not all about personnel. It's about people playing into a particular comfort zone and being in places where they can do what they do best. Silas allowed me to expand as a perimeter player because he could take care of business inside, and he was a relentless offensive rebounder. Whoever was guarding him was busy all the way through the possession. Nobody was helping off him."

Commenting on the way the two men worked together, Silas stated, "Me and Dave began to just wear teams out—I mean, wear them out."

While Cowens proved to be an effective post-up player, he also scored well from the outside. Silas, though, did most of his damage from the inside, filling the lane well on the fast break and cleaning up the offensive boards. One of the league's top offensive rebounders, Silas used his body exceptionally well, usually starting out on the baseline, often out of bounds, before boxing out his opponent. Doing so gave him more room to maneuver, and more of an opportunity to put himself between his man and the basket.

Silas earned the second All-Star selection of his career in 1974–75, a season in which he averaged 10.6 points and 12.5 rebounds per game for a Celtics team that lost to the Washington Bullets in the Eastern Conference Finals. He also earned his first of two consecutive NBA All-Defensive First-Team nominations, after previously being named to the Second Team three times. Silas followed that up by posting averages of 10.7 points and 12.7 rebounds per contest in 1975–76, in helping the Celtics capture their fifth consecutive Atlantic Division title, before going on to win their 13th league championship.

Unfortunately, the 1975–76 campaign ended up being Silas's last in Boston. Seeking a new contract that would make him the Celtics' highest-paid player, he instead found himself included in a three-team trade that sent him to the Denver Nuggets in exchange for forward Curtis Rowe. Looking back at the events that transpired at the time, Silas recalled, "Red told me that he was going to pay me good money, but I got a whole lot more with Denver. That was the only reason I couldn't stay there. Years after that, I told Red I should've just stayed with them and won more championships."

Silas's departure did not sit well with Dave Cowens, who chose to take a break from the game one year later. Recounting his feelings upon learning of Silas's exit, Cowens said, "I wasn't excited about it because I thought we had something going on. We'd just won a championship in '76, so it's like, why screw around with a good thing? I was a little bit upset at everybody. I was upset at Paul, and I was upset at the Celtics for allowing that to happen."

Silas ended up spending just one season in Denver, before moving on to Seattle, where he helped the SuperSonics advance to the NBA Finals twice and capture one league championship in his three years in the Great Northwest. He announced his retirement following the conclusion of the 1979–80 campaign, ending his career with 11,782 points scored, 12,357 rebounds, 2,572 assists, averages of 9.4 points, 9.9 rebounds, and 2.1 assists per game, and shooting percentages of 43.2 from the field and 67.3 from the free-throw line. In his four years with the Celtics, Silas scored 3,744 points, pulled down 4,004 rebounds, assisted on 864 baskets, and posted averages of 11.5 points, 12.3 rebounds, and 2.7 assists per contest.

Following his playing days, Silas pursued a career in coaching, serving as an assistant on the staffs of the New Jersey Nets, New York Knicks, Phoenix Suns, and Charlotte Hornets, before becoming a head coach, first with the San Diego Clippers, and, later, with the Cleveland Cavaliers. After being relieved of his duties in Cleveland during the latter stages of the 2004–05 campaign, Silas took a job at ESPN, although he eventually returned to coaching, serving as head coach of the Charlotte Bobcats from December 22, 2010 to April 30, 2012.

Mostly unsuccessful over the course of his coaching career, Silas will always be remembered more for the intensity, leadership, and level of professionalism he displayed on the court as a player. Cotton Fitzsimmons, who spent two seasons coaching him in Phoenix, once expressed his admiration for Silas by saying:

> There are three things that make Silas great. The first is character, which is a word that is tossed around loosely these days. Only a few people have great character, and Paul Silas is one of them.
>
> Next there is desire. He has the desire to be the best forward in the league. He may only have been in one All-Star game, but he's an All-Star forward every night in my book. He not only has the desire to play, but also the desire to be the best. And Paul Silas is the best rebounder, inch for inch, in the NBA. Other guys can jump, and other guys are as strong, but Silas has made a science out

of the thing, and he's the one who comes up with the ball when you need it.

Finally, there is attitude. He wants to win. He is only happy when he wins. He can be pretty surly when he's not winning, let me tell you. The reason I'm still in the NBA is guys like Paul Silas. He was the backbone of my team in Phoenix. I respected Dick Van Arsdale and Connie Hawkins, sure, but Silas always delivered. One of the reasons I left there is that Silas was traded away from me.

Summing it up, Paul Silas is a professional. They're all professionals because they take money, but they're not all pros. Paul Silas is a pro.

CELTICS CAREER HIGHLIGHTS

Best Season

Silas played well in each of his four seasons in Boston, placing among the league leaders in rebounding three times, earning two NBA All-Defensive First-Team nominations, and making the All-Star Team once. In helping the Celtics capture the NBA title in 1975–76, Silas averaged 10.7 points and 12.7 rebounds per game, finishing fourth in the league in rebounding in the process, while also topping the circuit with an average of 4.5 offensive rebounds per contest.

Silas, though, had his finest all-around season for the Celtics in 1972–73, when he averaged 13.3 points and a career-high 13 rebounds per game. He also shot a career-best 47 percent from the field and averaged 3.1 assists per contest, which represented the highest mark he posted as a member of the Celtics.

Memorable Moments / Greatest Performances

Although not known for his scoring, Silas turned in a number of outstanding offensive efforts during his time in Boston, with the first of those coming on December 19, 1972, when he scored a season-high 26 points during a 115–112 loss to the Golden State Warriors. Silas matched that total later in the season, when he tallied 26 points during a 125–113 win over the Buffalo Braves on March 4, 1973. He had another outstanding game two weeks later, helping the Celtics record a 109–105 victory over the Kansas

Pictured here guarding Bob McAdoo, Silas earned NBA All-Defensive honors in three of his four seasons with the Celtics.
Photo courtesy of MearsOnlineAuctions.com.

City–Omaha Kings on March 18 by hitting for 24 points. Silas, though, had his biggest offensive game as a member of the Celtics in the 1973–74 regular-season opener, when he helped lead them to a 118–112 win over the Buffalo Braves by scoring 31 points.

Known more for his exceptional rebounding, Silas did some of his best work off the boards for the Celtics in postseason play, averaging just over 15 rebounds per game during the 1973 playoffs. Particularly effective against the Knicks in the Eastern Conference Finals, Silas totaled 71 boards over the first five games, pulling down a total of 43 rebounds in Games 4 and 5 alone. Although he scored just 9 points in Boston's 98–97 victory in Game 5, Silas ended up being the hero of the contest, giving the Celtics their only basket of the final 8 minutes with a desperation 30-foot bank shot, before sinking a pair of free throws with 7 seconds left on the clock to put Boston ahead to stay.

Silas also performed heroically in Game 5 of the 1974 NBA Finals, helping the Celtics defeat the Milwaukee Bucks by a score of 96–87 by pulling down a game-high 16 rebounds. He subsequently came up big against Milwaukee in Game 7 as well, scoring 14 points, recording 9 rebounds, and figuring prominently in Boston's containment of Kareem Abdul-Jabbar. After Jabbar averaged 33.7 points per contest over the course of the first six games with Dave Cowens guarding him one-on-one, the Celtics altered their defensive strategy in Game 7, choosing instead to double-team him with Silas and Cowens. With Silas fronting him much of the time, Jabbar scored "only" 26 points, leading to a convincing 102–87 Boston victory.

Silas again played extremely well throughout the 1976 postseason, averaging 13.7 rebounds per game in Boston's 18 playoff contests. Most effective against the Phoenix Suns in the NBA Finals, which the Celtics won in six games, Silas averaged 12.8 points and 13.8 rebounds per game during the series, scoring 18 points in a 109–107 Game 4 loss, before scoring 17 points and collecting 17 rebounds in Boston's 128–126 triple-overtime win in Game 5.

NOTABLE ACHIEVEMENTS

- Averaged more than 10 rebounds per game four straight times, topping 12 rebounds per contest on three separate occasions.
- Led NBA with 365 offensive rebounds in 1975–76.
- Led NBA in games played in 1973–74.
- Led Celtics in rebounding once.
- Missed only three games in four years with Celtics.
- Two-time NBA All-Defensive First-Team selection (1974–75 and 1975–76).
- 1972–73 NBA All-Defensive Second-Team selection.
- 1974–75 NBA All-Star.
- Two-time Eastern Conference champion (1974 and 1976).
- Two-time NBA champion (1974 and 1976).

22

TOM "SATCH" SANDERS

The name of the game was to let people know you weren't going to be pushed around, and you were going to take a spot if you had to. But I was not going home.

—Tom "Satch" Sanders

he ultimate team player, Tom "Satch" Sanders spent his entire career subjugating his own game for the betterment of his team. Overshadowed over the course of his 13 NBA seasons by more glamorous Boston stars such as Bill Russell, John Havlicek, and Sam Jones, Sanders rarely received the credit he deserved for doing much of the dirty work that helped the Celtics to create the greatest dynasty in the history of professional team sports. Nevertheless, those who played alongside Sanders greatly appreciated the tremendous sense of self-sacrifice he exhibited every night by focusing primarily on rebounding and guarding the opposing team's top offensive forward. By doing so, Sanders became a key contributor to Celtics teams that captured eight NBA championships, establishing himself along the way as one of the finest defensive forwards of his era.

Born in New York City on November 8, 1938, Thomas Ernest Sanders grew up in Harlem, where he spent his early years aspiring to be a baseball pitcher, much like his childhood hero, Satchel Paige. Nicknamed after the Negro League great, Sanders later recalled, "I was tall, thin, and long-armed, and people thought I looked like Satchel Paige."

Advised by a friend to attend Seward Park High School, Sanders recounted, "In those days, you could pick the high school you wanted and go there, providing you could get there and they wanted you. I woke up every morning and rode the train from Harlem to Seward."

Tom "Satch" Sanders contributed to eight NBA championship teams in Boston with his stellar defense and strong rebounding.

Sanders began to abandon his dream of pitching in the Major Leagues while attending Seward, focusing instead on playing basketball—a sport in which he excelled to such a degree that notable institutions such as Duquesne and Seton Hall expressed interest in him as graduation approached. Given an opportunity to break the color barrier at the University of Alabama as well, Sanders ultimately decided to enroll at New York University, stating years later, "That just wasn't me. And NYU did offer me a scholarship."

Sanders's childhood companion and college teammate Cal Ramsey, who played briefly in the NBA, discussed his earliest memories of his long-time friend: "The thing about Satch is, when I first met him in junior high, he couldn't walk and chew gum at the same time. By the time I got him to come to NYU, a year after I got there, we had been playing for years at Morris Park in Harlem and in the Rucker tournament. At NYU, we used

Sanders, seen here battling Bob Pettit for a loose ball. Photo courtesy of LegendaryAuctions.com.

to call him 'Posture,' because he was gangly, with arms down to his knees, and he was always working on his posture. Satch worked hard to become a great player."

After earning Helms Foundation First-Team All-America honors at NYU, Sanders became a member of the Boston Celtics when they selected him with the eighth overall pick of the 1960 NBA Draft. Recalling his feelings at the time, Sanders stated, "I would rather have played for the New York Knicks at that point . . . You have to remember that, back then, New York was the center of college basketball, and it's where everyone wanted to play. Teams wanted to come east and play at Madison Square Garden."

Since the 6-foot-6, 210-pound Sanders played center in college, many people questioned his ability to learn how to play facing the basket, as he needed to do as a forward in the NBA. They also expressed doubts as to whether or not he might be able to take playing time away from established forwards Tom Heinsohn, Jim Loscutoff, and Frank Ramsey. As a result, Sanders arrived in Boston with a huge chip on his shoulder, noting, "I came up very combative, to put it mildly. I felt I had to make this team. I was so

Sanders (#16), receiving pass from K. C. Jones.
Photo courtesy of MearsOnlineAuctions.com.

determined to make the team, I was ready to bump heads and fight with
Loscutoff every chance I could get."

Sanders added, "The name of the game was to let people know you
weren't going to be pushed around, and you were going to take a spot if you
had to. But I was not going home."

Sanders also felt compelled to earn the respect of his new teammates,
since they had previously been so successful together, noting, "A lot of them
had been together and were successful for a number of years. They didn't
need new friends. You had to show them you were going to play hard, dive
for loose balls, and make a difference."

Red Auerbach later recalled his earliest impressions of Sanders, saying,
"When he came to camp, I was shocked. He didn't look like any basketball
player. He wore elbow pads and knee pads halfway up his legs, and glasses.
He must have been carrying 20 pounds of equipment around on him. First
thing I did, I told him to get contact lenses . . . that we'd pay for them. Then
I told Frank Ramsey to steal his knee guards."

Sanders ended up seeing an extremely limited amount of playing time
as a rookie, averaging just 5.3 points, 5.7 rebounds, and 16 minutes per

Sanders, pictured here with Boston Mayor John F. Collins.
Photo courtesy of City of Boston Archives.

game his first year in the league. However, he became a far more significant contributor to the Celtics in his sophomore campaign of 1961–62, helping them capture their fourth consecutive NBA championship by averaging 11.2 points and a career-high 9.5 rebounds per contest, in 29 minutes of action.

Asked to assume a supporting role on the team, Sanders stated, "I had offensive talent. But Auerbach told me he needed me to rebound and play defense. And I could do that. When you played on the playgrounds of New York City, you had to score, but you had to block a shot once in a while, too . . . They had offense when I arrived. Red needed me to play defense, and that's what I did."

Commenting on the level of self-sacrifice Sanders displayed during his time in Boston, Bob Cousy suggested, "As a player, Satch got all the dirty jobs; he never complained; he just went out and did what he had to do."

Sanders continued to assume the same unheralded role in each of the next four seasons, as the Celtics reeled off another four straight league championships. Yet, even though he never averaged more than 12.6 points or 8.3 rebounds per game in any of those campaigns, he remained a huge contributor to the team, doing an exceptional job of guarding the likes of Elgin Baylor, Bob Pettit, Jerry Lucas, and Dave DeBusschere.

Praising his former college teammate for the outstanding level of defensive play he exhibited throughout the period, Cal Ramsey told the *New York Daily News* in April of 2011: "[Sanders] is the best defender I ever played against. Ask Elgin Baylor and Bob Pettit and all those great players from that era. If you saw him play defense, you'd know that stats don't apply in this case. To this day, he's the best defender I've ever seen at the forward position."

An extremely durable player as well, Sanders appeared in more than 450 straight games at one point in his career, missing a total of only 8 contests between 1961 and 1967.

After the Celtics failed to repeat as NBA champions in 1967, Sanders helped them capture the next two league titles by posting averages of 10.2 points and 5.8 rebounds per game in 1967–68, before averaging 11.2 points and 7 rebounds per contest in 1968–69. Sanders's stellar defensive play also enabled him to earn NBA All-Defensive Second-Team honors in the second of those campaigns, which marked the first time the league awarded players for their outstanding play on that end of the court.

Sanders had one more solid season for the Celtics, averaging 11.5 points and 5.5 rebounds per game in 1969–70, before spending his final three campaigns serving strictly as a bench player. After averaging just 2 points, 1.5 rebounds, and 7 minutes played per contest in 1972–73, Sanders announced his retirement, ending his career with 8,766 points scored, 5,798 rebounds, 1,026 assists, and averages of 9.6 points, 6.3 rebounds, and 1.1 assists per game. He shot 42.8 percent from the field and 76.7 percent from the free-throw line over the course of his 13 years in the league. Sanders's eight NBA championships as a player tie him for the third most in NBA history, placing him behind only teammates Bill Russell (11) and Sam Jones (10). The Celtics expressed their gratitude to Sanders for the many contributions he made to them through the years by retiring his number (16) in January of 1973.

Following his retirement, Sanders spent four years coaching at Harvard University before returning to the Celtics for two seasons, first as an assistant and then as head coach. He subsequently began working with NBA rookies and veterans alike to provide guidance to them before, during, and after their playing careers. The programs Sanders founded, which were aimed at helping players to understand and appreciate their status as role models, leaders, and celebrities, eventually prompted the league to assign him the title of NBA vice president and director of player programs. Sanders received the additional honor of being elected to the Naismith Memorial Basketball Hall of Fame as a contributor in 2011.

CELTICS CAREER HIGHLIGHTS

Best Season

Although statistics hardly tell the whole story when it comes to Sanders, the numbers would seem to indicate that he played his best ball for the Celtics from 1961 to 1966. It could certainly be argued that he had his finest season in 1965–66, when he averaged 7.1 rebounds and a career-high 12.6 points per game. Sanders also performed well in each of the three previous campaigns, posting marks of 10.8 points and 7.2 rebounds per game in 1962–63, 11.4 points and 8.3 rebounds per contest in 1963–64, and 11.8 points and 8.3 rebounds per game in 1964–65. However, he probably had his best all-around season in 1961–62, when he averaged 11.2 points and a career-high 9.5 rebounds per contest, in helping the Celtics capture their fourth of eight consecutive NBA championships.

Memorable Moments / Greatest Performances

Sanders had his first big game for the Celtics on February 10, 1961, when he scored 19 points during a 137–134 loss to the Detroit Pistons. He reached the 20-point plateau for the first time in his career nearly one month later, on March 9, when he scored 20 points during a 119–118 win over the Pistons. Sanders, though, turned in the finest performance of his rookie campaign in Game 4 of the 1961 NBA Finals, when he tallied a team-high 22 points, in helping the Celtics defeat the St. Louis Hawks by a score of 119–104.

Receiving significantly more playing time in his sophomore season of 1961–62, Sanders developed into a regular contributor to the Celtics cause. After scoring 22 points during a 141–121 win over the Hawks on November 22, 1961, Sanders tallied 21 points just four days later, in helping Boston record a 107–101 victory over Detroit. He also scored 23 points during a 122–103 win over the Knicks on December 21, before hitting for 24 points during a 131–106 loss to the Philadelphia Warriors on January 27, 1962.

Performing particularly well in the month of February, Sanders scored 22 points during a 138–117 win over the Chicago Packers on February 13, 1962, before hitting for a game-high 26 points during a 115–96 win over the Lakers one week later. He also tallied 24 points, in helping the Celtics register a 129–123 overtime win over the Cincinnati Royals on February 28. Sanders, though, saved his biggest game of the year for the regular-season finale, leading the Celtics to a lopsided 142–110 victory over the Syracuse Nationals by scoring a season-high 30 points.

Sanders continued his solid play early the following season, scoring 26 points during a 127–109 win over the San Francisco Warriors on November 17, 1962, before hitting for a team-high 27 points, in leading the Celtics to a 116–104 victory over the Chicago Zephyrs six days later.

After scoring a season-high 27 points during a 126–113 win over the Knicks on March 19, 1966, Sanders tallied a personal playoff best 28 points, in leading the Celtics to a 120–103 win over the Cincinnati Royals in Game 4 of that year's Eastern Division Semifinals. The Celtics went on to win the series in five games.

NOTABLE ACHIEVEMENTS

- Averaged 9.5 rebounds per game in 1961–62.
- Led NBA in games played four times.
- Played in over 450 consecutive games, appearing in every Celtics game between 1961 and 1965.
- Played in every Celtics game in seven of 13 seasons.
- Ranks among Celtics career leaders in total rebounds (8th) and games played (7th).
- 1968–69 NBA All-Defensive Second-Team selection.
- Eight-time Eastern Division champion (1961–66, 1968, and 1969).
- Eight-time NBA champion (1961–66, 1968, and 1969).
- Number 16 retired by Celtics.
- Inducted into Naismith Memorial Basketball Hall of Fame in 2011.

23

RAY ALLEN

Ray is hands down the best shooter in NBA history. He's an amazing piece of work. It's kind of cool just watching him. Every time he gets the ball, we think it's going in.

—Celtics guard Nate Robinson

Widely considered to be among the best pure shooters in NBA history, Ray Allen established himself as one of the league's most consistent scorers over the course of his career, averaging at least 21.8 points per game eight straight seasons at one point. Second all-time in the NBA in three-point field goals, Allen also ranks among the game's best-ever free-throw shooters, successfully converting nearly 90 percent (89.4) of his foul shots during his 18-year career. An intelligent and unselfish player as well, Allen helped his teams capture two NBA titles and advance to the playoffs a total of 11 times, en route to earning 10 All-Star selections and a pair of All-NBA nominations. In his five seasons in Boston alone, Allen made the All-Star team three times, helping the Celtics win one league championship and make two NBA Finals appearances in the process.

Born at Castle Air Force Base near Merced, California, on July 20, 1975, Walter Ray Allen grew up in a military family, traveling with his parents and siblings to wherever his father's occupation took them. After spending various stages of his youth living in England, Oklahoma, California, and Germany, Allen settled with his family in Dalzell, South Carolina, where he starred in basketball for Hillcrest High School, leading the institution to a state championship as a senior.

Subsequently courted by several colleges, Allen ultimately settled on the University of Connecticut, where he spent the next three years playing

Ray Allen earned All-Star honors in three of his five seasons in Boston.
Photo courtesy of Keith Allison.

for head coach Jim Calhoun. While at UConn, Allen earned First-Team All-America honors and recognition as USA Basketball's Male Athlete of the Year as a sophomore, before being voted Big East Player of the Year and once again being named a First-Team All-American as a junior.

Choosing to forgo his final year of collegiate eligibility, Allen entered the 1996 NBA Draft, where the Minnesota Timberwolves selected him with the fifth overall pick. However, Minnesota immediately traded him and Andrew Lang to Milwaukee for the rights to Stephon Marbury, who the Bucks selected just ahead of Allen with the fourth pick of the draft.

Allen played well his first year in the league, earning a spot on the NBA's All-Rookie Second Team by averaging 13.4 points per game. After posting scoring averages of 19.5 and 17.1 points per contest the next two seasons, Allen developed into a star his fourth year in the league, earning All-Star honors for the first time in his career by averaging 22.1 points per game. He continued to perform well for the Bucks over the course of the next two and a half seasons, averaging well in excess of 20 points per game each year, en route to earning two more All-Star selections and one All-NBA Third-Team nomination. Nevertheless, the Bucks elected to include Allen in a six-player trade they completed with the Seattle SuperSonics on February 20, 2003, that netted them Gary Payton and Desmond Mason in return.

After joining the SuperSonics, Allen enjoyed the greatest individual success of his career, averaging better than 23 points per game in each of his four and a half seasons in Seattle, en route to earning another four All-Star nominations, one All-NBA Second-Team selection, and his lone top-10 finish in the league MVP voting. Allen had his two most productive seasons for the SuperSonics in 2005–06 and 2006–07, posting scoring averages of 25.1 and 26.4 points per game, respectively.

During his years in Milwaukee and Seattle, Allen built his reputation primarily on his exceptional outside shooting and explosive first step that kept defenders back on their heels. Making good use of his dribble-drive, Allen often headed toward the hoop down the left wing, before bouncing back for one of his patented fade-away jumpers. He also proved to be a superb finisher on the fast break and a deadly catch-and-shoot player from medium range.

In discussing Allen's offensive prowess, former Milwaukee Bucks team-mate Glenn Robinson stated, "Ray's got that smooth flow. He's the most natural player I've played with."

George Karl, who spent many years coaching against Allen in Denver, suggested, "[Allen's] more in a style of a George Gervin. He's a fluid player; he's a flow player; he's a finesse player."

A solid rebounder as well, Allen averaged more than 5 rebounds per game three times. Possessing outstanding quickness in his youth, Allen also did an excellent job of sticking to his man on defense, recording more than 1.5 steals per contest twice.

With Allen still seeking his first NBA title as he approached his 32nd birthday, his fortunes changed dramatically when the Boston Celtics traded Delonte West, Wally Szczerbiak, rookie Jeff Green, and a second-round pick in the 2008 NBA Draft to Seattle for him and Glen Davis—the 35th overall pick in the 2007 NBA Draft. After subsequently acquiring Kevin Garnett from the Minnesota Timberwolves as well, the Celtics suddenly found themselves able to field a "Big Three" of Allen, Garnett, and holdover Paul Pierce, unmatched by any other trio of players in the league.

Upon learning of Allen's acquisition, Boston head coach Doc Rivers noted, "Ray is a consummate pro, and the things he brings to the game will resonate in our locker room. That is something I don't think the average fan gets. Players can teach other players about being a pro. Coaches can't do that. So that'll be great to have a guy like him around for that."

While Garnett and Pierce also made personal sacrifices in an effort to bring a championship to the city of Boston, no one subjugated his game more for the betterment of the team than Allen. Accepting a reduced scoring role with the Celtics in deference to the other two members of Boston's "Big Three," Allen spent many nights focusing on playing solid defense and stretching the opposing team's defense with the threat of his outside shot, thereby creating space down low for Pierce and Garnett. Yet, when the Celtics needed him to score, Allen continued to display an ability to fill the basket, finishing his first year in Boston with a scoring average of 17.4 points per game that earned him All-Star honors for the fifth straight time. He then helped the Celtics to secure their first league championship in more than two decades by hitting for a then-Finals record seven three-pointers during a 131–92 victory over the Los Angeles Lakers in the Game 6 clincher of the NBA Finals.

Allen earned his sixth consecutive All-Star selection the following year by averaging 18.2 points per game, while hitting on 48 percent of his shots from the field. The Celtics, though, failed to repeat as NBA champions, losing to Orlando in seven games in the Eastern Conference Semifinals. Boston returned to the NBA Finals in 2010, with Allen posting a scoring average of 16.3 points per contest during the regular season. Once again facing Los Angeles for the title, the Celtics came up a bit short this time, falling to the Lakers in seven games. Nevertheless, Allen turned in an epic performance in Game 2 of the series, leading the Celtics to a 103–94

Allen connected for more three-pointers during his career than any other player in NBA history. Photo courtesy of Keith Allison.

victory by scoring 32 points, with 24 of those coming on a Finals record 8 three-pointers.

Allen's soft touch from the outside and clutch play earned him the admiration and respect of his teammates and coaches, with Paul Pierce stating, "Ray is one of the great shooters of all time—right behind me!"

Celtics guard Nate Robinson gushed, "Ray is hands down the best shooter in NBA history. He's an amazing piece of work. It's kind of cool just watching him. Every time he gets the ball, we think it's going in."

Allen spent two more years in Boston, posting scoring averages of 16.5 and 14.2 points per game, before becoming a free agent following the conclusion of the 2011–12 campaign. Unhappy over losing his starting job to second-year guard Avery Bradley during the latter stages of the season, Allen elected to sign a two-year contract with the rival Miami Heat, who defeated the Celtics in the 2012 Eastern Conference Finals. Subsequently treated with disdain by Celtics fans, Allen came to be viewed as a traitor by many, especially since the Celtics offered him significantly more money than the amount he accepted from Miami.

Yet, head coach Doc Rivers later revealed that Allen had more than just additional championships on his mind when he decided to leave Boston for Miami, suggesting that his decisions to relegate Allen to sixth-man status and turn the offense over to Rajon Rondo ultimately pushed the veteran guard out the door. Accepting much of the blame for Allen's departure, Rivers told Yahoo! Sports:

> People can use all the Rondo stuff—and it was there, no doubt about it—but it was more than Rondo. I'm the guy who gave Rondo the ball. I'm the guy who decided that Rondo needed to be more of the leader of the team. That doesn't mean guys liked that—and Ray did not love that—because Rondo now had the ball all the time.
>
> Think about everything Allen said when he left: "I want to be more of a part of the offense." Everything was back at Rondo. And I look at that and say, "That's not Rondo's fault." That's what I wanted Rondo to do, and that's what Rondo should've done because that's Rondo's ability. He's the best passer in the league. He has the best feel in the league. He's not a great shooter, so he needs the ball in his hands to be effective. And that bothered Ray.
>
> And not starting bothered Ray. I did examine it, and the conclusion I came back to was this: By doing the right things, we may have lost Ray. If I hadn't done that, I would've been a hypocrite. In the opening speech I make every year, I tell the team: "Every decision I make is going to be what's good for the team, and it may not be what's good for the individual."

Allen ended up spending two seasons in Miami, winning his second NBA championship as a member of the Heat in 2013 after averaging 10.9 points per game during the regular season as backup. After averaging a career-low 9.6 points per contest coming off the bench in 2013–14, Allen elected to sit out the ensuing campaign, even though a number of contenders attempted to lure him back onto the court. Ultimately choosing to officially announce his retirement on November 1, 2016, Allen ended his playing career with 24,505 points scored, 5,272 rebounds, 4,361 assists, and 1,451 steals. He also shot 45.2 percent from the field and 89.4 percent from the foul line, while averaging 18.9 points, 4.1 rebounds, 3.4 assists, and 1.1 steals per game over the course of 18 NBA seasons. During his time in Boston, Allen scored 5,987 points, accumulated 1,215 rebounds, 981 assists, and 324 steals, and posted averages of 16.7 points, 3.4 rebounds, 2.7 assists, and .9 steals per contest.

Almost two years after he retired as an active player, Allen released his autobiography, *From the Outside.* He later accepted the position of director of boys' and girls' basketball at Gulliver Preparatory School, where he also serves as the boys' varsity basketball head coach.

CELTICS CAREER HIGHLIGHTS

Best Season

Although Allen performed well his first year in Boston, helping the Celtics compile a league-best record of 66-16 during the regular season by averaging 17.4 points, 3.7 rebounds, and 3.1 assists per game, he played his best ball for the Celtics the following season, concluding the 2008–09 campaign with averages of 18.2 points, 3.5 rebounds, and 2.8 assists per contest, while shooting 48 percent from the field, which represented the second-highest mark of his career.

Memorable Moments / Greatest Performances

Allen quickly ingratiated himself with Celtics fans in just his second game with the team by sinking a game-winning three-pointer with only three seconds remaining in overtime, giving the Celtics a 98–95 victory over the Toronto Raptors. Allen concluded the November 4, 2007, contest with 33 points, surpassing in the process the 17,000-point mark for his career.

Allen had another big game just six days later, leading Boston to a 112–101 win over the New Jersey Nets on November 10, 2007, by scoring 27 points, collecting 10 rebounds, and assisting on 5 baskets.

Allen hit for a season-high 35 points on January 16, 2008, in leading the Celtics to a 100–90 win over the Portland Trail Blazers.

However, Allen saved his two most memorable performances of the 2007–08 campaign for the NBA Finals, with the first of those coming in Game 4, when he helped the Celtics to overcome an early 24-point deficit by playing all 48 minutes and contributing 19 points, 9 rebounds, and 3 steals. Allen's layup with 16.4 seconds remaining in the fourth quarter all but clinched the victory for the Celtics, giving them the largest comeback win in NBA Finals history. Allen came up big again in Game 6, scoring a game-high 26 points, in leading the Celtics to a series-clinching 131–92 victory over the Lakers that included a record-tying seven three-pointers by the sharp-shooting guard.

Allen turned in a pair of extraordinary efforts for the Celtics the following season, hitting for 35 points during a 122–117 overtime win over the Indiana Pacers on December 7, 2008, and tallying 36 points during a 94–88 victory over the Toronto Raptors on January 11, 2009.

Allen displayed his ability to hit from long range during a November 11, 2010, contest against Miami, leading the Celtics to a 112–107 win over the Heat by connecting on 7 of 9 shots from three-point range, en route to scoring a total of 35 points.

Allen reached a milestone later that season, when, during a game against the Los Angeles Lakers on February 10, 2011, he surpassed Reggie Miller as the NBA's all-time leader in three-point field goals made by converting the 2,562nd three-pointer of his career.

Although the Celtics failed to win their second consecutive NBA title in 2008–09, losing to the Orlando Magic in seven games in the Eastern Conference Semifinals, Allen performed brilliantly in their first-round playoff matchup with the Chicago Bulls, leading them to a seven-game victory by averaging 23.4 points per contest. Coming up big in the clutch in Game 2, Allen helped the Celtics to even the series at a game apiece with a 118–115 win, during which he hit the game-winning three-pointer with just two seconds remaining in regulation. Allen finished the contest with 30 points. He topped that performance, though, in Game 6, scoring 51 points during Boston's 128–127 triple-overtime loss. Allen connected on 9 of 18 three-pointers during the contest, setting in the process an NBA playoff record for the most three-point field goals made in one game.

Allen again displayed his long-range shooting prowess in Game 2 of the 2010 NBA Finals when he led the Celtics to a 103–94 victory over the Lakers by hitting 8 of 11 three-point shots, en route to establishing a new NBA Finals record. Allen finished the game with 32 points, scoring 27 of those in the first half.

NOTABLE ACHIEVEMENTS

- Averaged more than 16 points per game four times, topping 17 ppg twice and 18 ppg once.
- Shot better than 90 percent from the free-throw line four times.
- Finished second in NBA in three-point field goals once; three-point field-goal shooting percentage once; and free-throw shooting percentage once.
- Holds Celtics record for most consecutive free-throws made (72—from 12/28/08 to 2/23/09).
- Holds Celtics single-season record for highest free-throw shooting percentage (95.2% in 2008–09).
- Ranks second in NBA history in three-point field goals made (2,973).
- Holds NBA Finals record for most three-point field goals made in one game (8 vs. Lakers—June 6, 2010).
- Holds NBA playoff record for most three-point field goals made in one game (9 vs. Chicago Bulls—April 30, 2009).
- Ranks seventh in NBA history in career free-throw shooting percentage (89.4%).
- Three-time NBA All-Star (2008, 2009, and 2011).
- Two-time Eastern Conference champion (2007–08 and 2009–10).
- 2007–08 NBA champion.
- Member of NBA's 75th Anniversary Team.
- Inducted into Naismith Memorial Basketball Hall of Fame in 2018.

24

NATE ARCHIBALD

Here I was, coming off the most frustrating year of my career, and it was the kids who were counseling me. They kept saying, "Don't worry, Tiny. Don't get down. You can do it. The Celtics need you." I'll never forget them for that.

—Nate Archibald

Considered to be just a shell of his former self by the time he arrived in Boston, Nate "Tiny" Archibald resurrected his career after joining the Celtics in 1978. Although no longer the same dynamic player who once accomplished the unique feat of leading the NBA in scoring and assists in the same season, Archibald proved to be an outstanding floor general for the Celtics over the course of the next five seasons, helping them win one NBA championship and leading them to the league's best regular-season record three straight times. And, even though the diminutive guard never again reached the same lofty status he had attained earlier in his career, he managed to earn three All-Star selections, one All-NBA nomination, and one top-five finish in the league MVP voting during his time in Boston. Combined with the extraordinary play Archibald exhibited earlier as a member of the Cincinnati Royals / Kansas City–Omaha Kings, his years in Boston ended up earning him a spot on the NBA's 50th Anniversary All-Star Team and a place in the Naismith Memorial Basketball Hall of Fame.

Born in the Bronx, New York, on September 2, 1948, Nathaniel Archibald honed his basketball skills on the playgrounds of New York City while growing up in poverty in the South Bronx. In discussing his formative years living in a two-bedroom apartment in the Patterson Projects,

Nate Archibald spent five seasons in Boston, earning three All-Star selections and one top-five finish in the league MVP voting during that time. Photo courtesy of MearsOnlineAuctions.com.

Archibald recalled, "We paid $109 a month rent and got the neighborhood for free. We were overcharged for both."

Finding comfort on the asphalt of the South Bronx, Archibald spent virtually all of his free time playing basketball, competing against older players and peers on the local playgrounds, all the while developing a wide range of offensive moves and an excellent feel for the game. Nicknamed "Nate the Skate" within the basketball community, Archibald nearly dropped out of high school when bad grades and truancy kept him off DeWitt Clinton's varsity team as a sophomore. However, encouraged by Hilton White, a community leader and personal mentor who later became the basketball coach at American International College, Archibald returned to school and dedicated himself to improving his game. Looking back at that particular time in his life, Archibald said, "I had to make changes. I didn't know where I was going; I didn't know I was going to the NBA, going to Texas Western. People saw something in me that I didn't see."

After seeing a limited amount of playing time as a junior, Archibald blossomed into a star in his senior year of high school, earning All-City honors while leading DeWitt Clinton to the city public school title in 1966. Meanwhile, off the court, he attended school regularly and worked hard to improve his grades. Unfortunately, Archibald's poor academic record deterred most colleges from offering him a scholarship, forcing him to enroll at tiny Arizona Western Community College. However, after continuing to apply himself in the classroom while simultaneously excelling on the basketball court, Archibald earned a scholarship to the University of Texas, El Paso, where he spent the next three years playing under legendary coach Don Haskins, who had just delivered an NCAA Championship to the school, which previously bore the name Texas Western.

After averaging more than 20 points per game and setting a new school record by scoring a total of 1,459 points in his three seasons at UTEP, Archibald entered the NBA when Cincinnati Royals head coach and Queens native Bob Cousy selected him in the second round of the 1970 NBA Draft, with the 19th overall pick. Cousy, who also grew up in the projects of New York City and played the point guard position with a great deal of flair, saw a lot of himself in Archibald, who later said of his first professional coach, "I always tell people Cooz is like my stepdad. He gave me a chance to play. In the game of basketball, you need chances."

Cousy did indeed give Archibald a chance to play, immediately turning over control of the Cincinnati offense to him. Rewarding his coach for the faith he placed in him, Archibald had a solid rookie season, averaging 16 points and 5.5 assists per game for a Royals team that finished just 33-49. Although the Royals failed to improve their performance the following season, concluding the 1971–72 campaign with a record of only 31-51, Archibald emerged as an elite player, placing second in the NBA to Kareem Abdul-Jabbar with a scoring average of 28.2 points per game while also finishing third in the league with an average of 9.2 assists per contest en route to earning All-NBA Second-Team honors.

With the Royals relocating the following year and renaming themselves the Kansas City–Omaha Kings, Archibald had a season for the ages, averaging a league-leading 34 points, 11.4 assists, and 46 minutes per game. In the process, he became the only player in NBA history to top the circuit

in both scoring and assists in the same season. Archibald's fabulous performance earned him the first of his three All-NBA First-Team selections, All-
Star honors for the first of six times, a third-place finish in the league MVP
voting, and recognition as the *Sporting News* NBA Most Valuable Player.

Standing just 6-foot-1 and weighing only 160 pounds, Archibald gradually acquired the nickname "Tiny" during his playing days. Yet, in spite of
his lack of size, he established himself as one of the giants of the game with
his incredible quickness that enabled him to break down opposing defenses
better than any player who preceded him in the NBA. A superb penetrator,
Archibald regularly drove past defenders on his way to the basket, leaving
him the option of either laying the ball in himself or kicking it out to an
open shooter. He also possessed an above-average mid-range jump shot,
making him a threat to score from virtually anywhere on the court.

Injuries slowed Archibald for much of the ensuing campaign, limiting
him to only 35 games and a scoring average of 17.6 points per contest in
1973–74. However, he returned to top form the following season, averaging 26.5 points and 6.8 assists per game, before posting marks of 24.8
points and 7.9 assists per contest in 1975–76, earning in the process All-
NBA First-Team honors both years.

Unfortunately, a series of foot and Achilles tendon injuries prevented
Archibald from ever again being a dominant player. After being traded to
the New York Nets for two players and a pair of first-round draft picks on
September 10, 1976, Archibald sustained a severe foot injury just 34 games
into the 1976–77 season that forced him to miss the remainder of the
campaign. Then, after being dealt to the Buffalo Braves (who later became
the San Diego Clippers) at season's end, Archibald tore his Achilles tendon
before the 1977–78 campaign got under way, putting him on the sidelines
for the entire year. Archibald subsequently became a member of the Celtics
when San Diego included him in a nine-player trade they completed with
Boston on August 4, 1978.

Some 20 pounds overweight after his lengthy layoff and lacking the
great quickness he once possessed, Archibald arrived in Boston with most
people expecting little from him. Reflecting back at that point in his career,
Archibald said, "My career was almost over. Red [Auerbach] took me in his
office and he said, 'All I need out of you is leadership. Everybody else gave
up on you.'"

Yet, in spite of Auerbach's words of encouragement, Archibald struggled in his first season with the Celtics, averaging just 11 points and 4.7
assists, in 24 minutes of action per game, as he reacclimated himself to life
in the NBA. Furthermore, Archibald had difficulty blending in with the

Archibald remains the only player in NBA history ever to lead the league in scoring and assists in the same season. Photo courtesy of MearsOnlineAuctions.com.

rest of the team, failing to work cohesively with Jo Jo White in the back-court while often finding himself at odds with player-coach Dave Cowens over playing time.

Following Boston's dismal 29-53 showing in 1978–79, rumors abounded of Archibald's impending release, with one NBA general manager telling *Sport* magazine in 1980, "The sad part is that I'm not sure anyone would have taken Tiny. Heck, he was 30 years old, had a bad reputation, and a huge contract. He seemed to have lost his game."

Archibald, though, drew inspiration from the troubled youngsters in the South Bronx he counseled each summer, recalling years later, "Here I was, coming off the most frustrating year of my career, and it was the kids who were counseling me. They kept saying, 'Don't worry, Tiny. Don't get down. You can do it. The Celtics need you.' I'll never forget them for that."

Returning to a very different Celtics team that featured NBA Rookie of the Year Larry Bird, Archibald experienced something of a renaissance in 1979–80. Focusing more than ever on distributing the ball to his team-mates and providing on-court leadership to them, Archibald helped the Celtics compile the league's best regular-season record for the first of three straight times, leading them to a mark of 61-21. Although he averaged only 14.1 points per game, Archibald finished second in the NBA with an average of 8.4 assists per contest, earning in the process All-Star honors for the fourth time and a fifth-place finish in the league MVP voting.

With the Celtics further improving their roster by adding Robert Parish and Kevin McHale during the subsequent off-season, they went on to win their 14th NBA championship in 1981. Archibald once again con-tributed significantly to the cause by averaging 13.8 points and 7.7 assists per game during the regular season, before posting marks of 15.6 points and 6.3 assists per contest in the playoffs, en route to earning All-NBA Second-Team honors and his fifth All-Star selection. He made the All-Star team for the final time the following season by averaging 12.6 points and 8 assists per game for a Celtics team that won 63 games during the regular season, before losing in seven games to the Philadelphia 76ers in the Eastern Conference Finals.

Archibald spent one more season in Boston, averaging 10.5 points and 6.2 assists per contest in 1982–83 before being waived by the Celtics prior to the start of the ensuing campaign. After signing with the Bucks as a free agent, Archibald spent one year in Milwaukee coming off the bench before announcing his retirement at season's end with career totals of 16,481 points scored, 6,476 assists, and 2,046 rebounds. Over parts of 13 NBA seasons, he averaged 18.8 points, 7.4 assists, and 2.3 rebounds per game, while shooting 46.7 percent from the field and 81 percent from the free-throw line.

In his five years with the Celtics, Archibald scored 4,550 points, assisted on 2,563 baskets, and collected 683 rebounds, averaging in the process 12.5 points, 7.1 assists, and 1.9 rebounds per contest as a member of the team.

Following his playing career, Archibald briefly served as an assistant coach at his alma mater, the University of Texas–El Paso, where he men-tored future NBA star Tim Hardaway. Crediting Archibald with much of the success he later experienced, Hardaway once said, "That's the man right there. He had a lot of flair. That's one of the reasons I went to UTEP, because Nate Archibald went there. He was there for two years as an assistant coach and taught me a lot about how to play the game."

Archibald later coached the New Jersey Jammers of the USBL and a team in the National Basketball Developmental League as well, before taking a position with the NBA's community relations department. He also returned to school to complete his requirements for a bachelor's degree, taught in the New York City public school system, and earned a master's degree in education from Fordham University. Currently working toward acquiring a PhD in education, Archibald, who once nearly quit high school, says, "That would be the championship of my life."

CELTICS CAREER HIGHLIGHTS

Best Season

Archibald earned All-NBA honors for the only time as a member of the Celtics in 1980–81, when he averaged 13.8 points, 7.7 assists, 2.2 rebounds, and .9 steals per game, while shooting a career-best 49.9 percent from the field. Nevertheless, he compiled slightly better overall numbers the previous season, averaging 14.1 points, 8.4 assists, 2.5 rebounds, and 1.3 steals per contest, while connecting on 48.2 percent of his shots from the field. Furthermore, Archibald's unselfish play and on-court leadership helped the Celtics record one of the biggest single-season turnarounds in NBA history, earning him a fifth-place finish in the league MVP voting. All things considered, Archibald had his best season for the Celtics in 1979–80.

Memorable Moments / Greatest Performances

Archibald had his first big game for the Celtics on November 1, 1978, when he scored 25 points during a 118–112 win over the Chicago Bulls.

In addition to doing an outstanding job of directing the Celtics offense and distributing the ball to his teammates in 1979–80, Archibald occasionally chose to demonstrate the fact that he had not completely lost his scoring ability, doing so on one occasion on March 26, 1980, when he led the Celtics to a 129–121 victory over the Knicks by tallying a season-high 29 points.

Archibald also turned in a number of strong offensive performances the following season, with his first such effort coming on December 20, 1980, when he scored 25 points during a 116–97 win over the Phoenix Suns. He also led the Celtics to a 117–111 overtime victory over the Bulls on January 9, 1981, by tallying 25 points, before scoring 26 points during a 117–115 win over the New Jersey Nets the very next night.

However, Archibald proved to be most valuable to the Celtics as a play-maker, recording the third-highest single-game assists total in franchise history on February 5, 1982, when he assisted on 23 baskets during a 145–144 victory over the Denver Nuggets. Archibald also collected 19 assists during a 129–120 loss to the San Antonio Spurs on October 23, 1979, before setting up his teammates 18 times during a 108–100 win over the Seattle SuperSonics on February 16, 1983.

A key contributor during Boston's march to the 1981 NBA title, Archibald scored 27 points, in helping the Celtics defeat Chicago by a score of 106–97 in Game 2 of a 1981 Eastern Conference Semifinal series they swept in four straight games. He then averaged 19 points per contest during Boston's seven-game victory over Philadelphia in the Conference Finals.

NOTABLE ACHIEVEMENTS

- Averaged more than 7 assists per game three times, topping 8 assists per contest twice.
- Shot 50 percent from the field in 1980–81.
- Finished second in NBA in assists in 1979–80 (8.4 apg).
- Led Celtics in assists three times.
- Holds Celtics third-highest single-game total for assists (23 vs. Denver on 2/5/82).
- Holds Celtics single-game record for most free throws made (20 vs. Chicago on 1/16/80).
- 1980–81 NBA All-Star Game MVP.
- Finished fifth in NBA MVP voting in 1979–80.
- 1980–81 All-NBA Second-Team selection.
- Three-time NBA All-Star (1980, 1981, and 1982).
- 1980–81 Eastern Conference champion.
- 1980–81 NBA champion.
- Member of NBA's 75th Anniversary Team.
- Inducted into Naismith Memorial Basketball Hall of Fame in 1991.

25

CEDRIC MAXWELL

Cedric was all arms and legs his rookie year. He learned how to put all of that together, and, some way, it was able to come out as some type of fluidity. Cedric is a great guy—he was a great guy as a rookie, but he was all arms and legs then!

—Celtics guard Charlie Scott

A member of one of the most formidable front lines in NBA history, Cedric Maxwell spent much of his career playing alongside Larry Bird and Robert Parish, starting ahead of Kevin McHale for four seasons. Playing both forward positions over the course of his eight seasons in Boston, Maxwell proved to be a huge asset to the Celtics, surpassing 15 points per game three times and 8 rebounds per contest twice, while hitting on better than 50 percent of his shots from the field on seven separate occasions, en route to compiling a franchise-record 55.9 field-goal shooting percentage. An outstanding postseason performer as well, Maxwell earned 1981 NBA Finals MVP honors by averaging 17.7 points and 9.5 rebounds per contest, in leading the Celtics to a six-game victory over the Houston Rockets. In the process, Maxwell became the only player in NBA history to be named Finals MVP without ever earning the additional distinction of making the All-Star team. In all, Maxwell helped the Celtics capture three Eastern Conference Championships and two NBA titles, leading to the team retiring his number (31) following the conclusion of his playing career.

Born in Kinston, North Carolina, on November 21, 1955, Cedric Bryan Maxwell attended Kinston High School, where he honed his basketball skills before enrolling at the University of North Carolina at Charlotte. It was at UNC that Maxwell acquired the nickname "Cornbread," a moniker that remained affixed to him throughout the rest of his playing career. Maxwell and his college teammate, Melvin Watkins, went to see the movie *Cornbread, Earl and Me*, which focuses on the traumatization of a 12-year-old boy following the murder of his friend, a star basketball player. Believing that Maxwell bore a close resemblance to the title character, Watkins began calling him "Cornbread." However, since Maxwell did not particularly care for the nickname, it did not gain widespread use until he earned MVP honors at the 1976 NIT tournament, when, according to Watkins, "The New York media picked up on it." Playing both center and forward during his time at UNC, Maxwell led his team to the NCAA Final Four as a senior, prompting the Celtics to select him with the 12th overall pick of the 1977 NBA Draft.

Joining a Celtics team in the midst of a rebuilding program, Maxwell assumed a backup role as a rookie, averaging 7.3 points, 5.3 rebounds, and nearly 17 minutes per game over the course of the 1977–78 campaign. Recalling the impression Maxwell made on him his first year in the league, Celtics guard Charlie Scott commented, "Cedric was all arms and legs his rookie year. He learned how to put all of that together, and, some way, it was able to come out as some type of fluidity. Cedric is a great guy—he was a great guy as a rookie, but he was all arms and legs then!"

Emerging as Boston's best player the following season after being inserted into the starting lineup, Maxwell led a Celtics team that finished just 29-53 in scoring (19 ppg) and rebounding (9.9 rpg), while also finishing first in the entire league with a field-goal shooting percentage of 58.4. He followed that up with another extremely productive year in 1979–80, averaging 16.9 points and 8.8 rebounds per game, and once again topping the circuit in field-goal shooting percentage, this time with a mark of 60.9 percent. Maxwell's strong play, along with the addition of NBA Rookie of the Year Larry Bird, helped the Celtics improve their record to 61-21.

In discussing the evolution of Maxwell's game, Charlie Scott noted, "With Cedric, I think he had to figure out how to fit his talent into what the Celtics were trying to do. Fit those talents into the Celtics style. And, when he did that, then those arms and legs became very much a weapon. He had to develop that little jump hook, and he had to learn how to move without the ball. He wasn't used to doing those things in college. Again, Red put together the perfect team. When you look at Larry, Cedric, Kevin McHale, and Robert Parish, it was a perfect foursome."

The Celtics took another step forward in 1980–81, winning the NBA title, with Maxwell contributing to the cause by averaging 15.2 points and 6.5 rebounds per game during the regular season. The 6-foot-8, 215-pound

Cedric Maxwell compiled a franchise-best 55.9 field-goal shooting percentage over the course of his eight seasons in Boston.
Photo courtesy of George A. Kitrinos.

forward proved to be even more of a factor in the NBA Finals, posting averages of 17.7 points and 9.5 rebounds per game, while shooting a series-best 56.8 percent from the field, en route to earning Finals MVP honors. Although the Celtics failed to repeat as NBA champions the following season, Maxwell had another solid year, averaging 14.8 points and 6.4 rebounds per contest, while leading the team in field-goal shooting percentage for the fifth straight time with a mark of 54.8 percent. Maxwell compiled somewhat less impressive numbers in each of the next two campaigns, averaging 11.9 points and 5.3 rebounds per game in 1982–83, before posting marks of 11.9 points and 5.8 rebounds per contest for a Celtics team that captured the NBA championship the following year.

Despite being overshadowed by Bird, Parish, and McHale for much of his time in Boston, Maxwell proved to be one of the Celtics' most complete players, making huge contributions on both ends of the court. Best known on offense for his moves around the basket, Maxwell had an outstanding low-post game, often faking defenders into the air before converting high-percentage shots that included an excellent jump hook. Meanwhile, Maxwell, who played both power forward and shooting forward during his time in Beantown, usually guarded the opposing team's toughest frontcourt player, including the likes of Julius Erving, James Worthy, and Bernard King, allowing Bird to freelance in the passing lanes, looking for steals. Yet, in spite of Maxwell's stellar all-around play, he never earned a spot on the All-Star team.

Still, even though Maxwell generally took a backseat to some of his teammates in the minds of most Celtics fans, he often found a way to push himself to the forefront with his colorful persona. Never one to shy away from controversy, Maxwell talked an endless stream of trash to his opponents, with the most notable instance taking place prior to the start of the 1984 Eastern Conference Semifinals, when he promised to shut down New York Knicks high-scoring forward Bernard King, boldly predicting, "That bitch ain't gettin' 40 [points] on me." Continuing to berate one of the league's top scorers, Maxwell mocked King's distinctive gait, stating, "Ain't no way a guy who walks like this is getting 40 on me." Responding to Maxwell's challenge, King proceeded to surpass the 40-point mark twice in a series the Celtics ended up barely winning in seven games.

On another occasion, Maxwell approached Elvin Hayes before a game and predicted a severe ass-kicking . . . courtesy of Kevin McHale. Maxwell further angered McHale and the rest of his teammates at times by putting forth less than a 100 percent effort against weak teams, trying to pick up fouls quickly so that he could take a seat on the bench. In defending his actions, Maxwell would tell his teammates, "I'm not getting injured playing no junior varsity game."

Maxwell made his biggest mistake, though, when he got on the bad side of Red Auerbach. After injuring his knee during the 1984–85 season,

Maxwell earned NBA Finals MVP honors in 1981 for his performance against the Houston Rockets. Photo courtesy of George A. Kitrinos.

Maxwell, according to some, failed to fully commit himself to his rehab. Then, when Auerbach suggested to him that he attend rookie camp to test the knee, Maxwell balked at the idea, putting him in the general manager's doghouse. Auerbach subsequently traded Maxwell to the Los Angeles

Clippers for Bill Walton prior to the start of the ensuing campaign, ending the forward's eight-year association with the Celtics. He concluded his time in Boston with career totals of 8,311 points scored, 4,023 rebounds, and 1,390 assists, a franchise-best 55.9 field-goal shooting percentage, and a free-throw shooting percentage of 78.3. In his eight seasons with the Celtics, Maxwell averaged 13.7 points, 6.6 rebounds, and 2.3 assists per game.

Maxwell spent one and a half seasons in Los Angeles, playing his best ball for the Clippers in 1985–86, when he averaged 14.1 points and 8.2 rebounds per contest. After being traded to the Houston Rockets midway through the following season, he spent another one and a half years in Houston, finishing out his career as a backup with the Rockets in 1987–88. Choosing to retire prior to the start of the 1988–89 campaign, Maxwell ended his career with 10,465 points scored, 5,261 rebounds, 1,862 assists, a 54.6 field-goal shooting percentage, a 78.4 free-throw shooting percentage, and averages of 12.5 points, 6.3 rebounds, and 2.2 assists per game.

On December 15, 2003, some 18 years after Maxwell played his last game for the Celtics, the team retired his number-31 jersey, ending his lengthy period of estrangement from Red Auerbach. Commenting on the manner in which Auerbach chose to reveal that he had forgiven him for his transgressions, Maxwell noted, "The father should not have to apologize to the son. And Red is the father."

Maxwell later became a radio broadcaster for WRKO-AM in Boston, where he announces Celtics games with Sean Grande. As outspoken as ever, Maxwell drew a considerable amount of criticism for comments he made on the air during a game in 2007, when, unhappy with the officiating of referee Violet Palmer, he told listeners that Palmer should "go back to the kitchen and make me some bacon and eggs." He later apologized for those ill-advised remarks during a subsequent broadcast.

CELTICS CAREER HIGHLIGHTS

Best Season

Maxwell played extremely well for the Celtics in 1979–80, helping them compile an NBA-best record of 61-21 during the regular season by averaging 16.9 points and 8.8 rebounds per game, while shooting a career-high and league-leading 60.9 percent from the field. Nevertheless, he had his finest all-around season one year earlier, posting career-high marks in scoring

(19 ppg), rebounding (9.9 rpg), assists (2.9 apg), and steals (1.2 spg), while hitting on a league-leading 58.4 percent of his shots from the field.

Memorable Moments / Greatest Performances

Maxwell topped the 30-point mark for the first time in his career on December 13, 1978, when he helped lead the Celtics to a 102–96 win over the New Orleans Jazz by scoring 31 points. Maxwell had another big game just nine days later, on December 22, hitting for 33 points during a 124–105 victory over the Atlanta Hawks.

Although the Celtics suffered a 120–99 defeat at the hands of the Kansas City–Omaha Kings on January 17, 1979, Maxwell tallied a season-high 35 points during the contest. He nearly equaled that mark some three weeks later, scoring 33 points during a 106–102 win over the Knicks on February 10.

Maxwell produced his biggest scoring output of the 1980–81 campaign on February 15, 1981, when he led the Celtics to a 120–118 victory over the Denver Nuggets by tallying 34 points. Maxwell also turned in two of his finest performances the following year in the month of February, scoring 31 points during a 129–116 win over the San Diego Clippers on February 12, 1982, before hitting for 31 points again during a 106–102 victory over the Milwaukee Bucks on February 28.

Maxwell played one of his best all-around games the following season on November 24, 1982, when he scored 21 points and pulled down 16 rebounds during a 104–95 win over the Portland Trail Blazers. He also had a big game against the Lakers on February 23, 1983, when he led the Celtics to a 113–104 victory by hitting for a season-high 30 points.

Maxwell scored 30 points for the final time in his career on November 15, 1984, when he tallied 30 points during a 125–105 win over the Chicago Bulls.

Always an outstanding clutch performer, Maxell used his physicality to score 28 points against Houston in Game 5 of the 1981 NBA Finals, prompting teammate Larry Bird to call the effort "one of the greatest football games I've ever seen Cedric Maxwell play." After the Game 6 clincher, Boston head coach Bill Fitch said, "One of the real keys to the game was in the second period when the Rockets decided to use Robert Reid to double up on Max, who was hurting them inside. Once Reid did that, it freed up Larry Bird, who started hitting his outside shot. Maxwell can be that effective, both on offense and defense. And when he gets out in the lanes and really runs, there isn't a forward in the league that can stay with him." Maxwell, who ended up being named Finals MVP, later commented, "Now you kind of marvel in the accomplishment. It was a proud, proud moment."

Maxwell experienced another extremely proud moment in the 1984 NBA Finals, when, after telling his teammates prior to the start of Game 7 to "climb on my back, boys," he went out and scored 24 points, pulled down 8 rebounds, and assisted on 8 baskets, in leading the Celtics to a 111–102 victory over the Los Angeles Lakers.

NOTABLE ACHIEVEMENTS

- Averaged more than 15 points per game three times, posting average of 19 points per game once.
- Averaged 9.9 rebounds per game in 1978–79.
- Shot better than 50 percent from the field seven times, topping 60 percent once (61% in 1979–80).
- Led NBA in field-goal shooting percentage twice.
- Led Celtics in scoring once and rebounding once.
- Ranks third in franchise history in field-goal shooting percentage (55.9%).
- 1980–81 NBA Finals MVP.
- Three-time Eastern Conference champion (1981, 1984, and 1985).
- Two-time NBA champion (1981 and 1984).
- Number 31 retired by Celtics.

26

JAYLEN BROWN

A versatile player who has started for the Celtics at both shooting guard and small forward, Jaylen Brown overcame early struggles with his shooting, ball-handling, and passing skills to establish himself as arguably the NBA's top swingman. After also being criticized early in his career for his lack of discipline, both on and off the court, Brown has since emerged as one of the leaders of Celtic teams that have advanced to the Eastern Conference Finals four times and the NBA Finals once. A two-time NBA All-Star, Brown has averaged more than 20 points and six rebounds per game in each of the last four seasons, combining with Jayson Tatum during that time to give the Celtics a formidable one-two punch.

Born in Marietta, Georgia, on October 24, 1996, Jaylen Marselles Brown first made a name for himself at Wheeler High School, where he led his team to an overall record of 30-3 and the Georgia High School Association Class 6A State Championship as a senior by averaging 28 points and 12 rebounds per contest. Named Gatorade Georgia Boys Player of the Year, *USA Today*'s All-USA Georgia Player of the Year, Class 6A Player of the Year, and Georgia's Mr. Basketball, Brown earned the additional honor of winning a 2014 FIBA Americas Championship gold medal as part of the USA Basketball Men's U18 National Team.

Offered an athletic scholarship to the University of California, Brown spent just one season playing for the Golden Bears, earning Pac-12 Freshman of the Year and First-Team All-Pac 12 honors by averaging 14.6 points, 5.4 rebounds, and 2.0 assists per game, before declaring himself eligible for the 2016 NBA Draft.

Selected by the Celtics in the first round with the third overall pick, Brown spent his first season in Boston coming off the bench, performing well enough in a backup role (he averaged 6.6 points, 2.8 rebounds, 0.8 assists, and 17.2 minutes per contest) to be named to the NBA All-Rookie Second Team. Impressing everyone in the organization with his tremendous athletic ability, the 6-foot-6-inch, 225-pound Brown drew praise during

Jaylen Brown has excelled for the Celtics at both small forward and shooting guard.

the early stages of the campaign from teammate Terry Rozier, who said, "He can jump out of the gym. He's very athletic, so he's gonna see a lot of minutes this year, I feel, and once the game really slows down for him, it's gonna be scary for a lot of people."

Al Horford added, "I always get excited when he gets in the game because I just want to see what he can do, or what he's going to do. It seems like he's always getting a highlight play, and I think that's just a preview of what we're going to see during the season."

Meanwhile, Avery Bradley spoke of Brown's willingness to learn, saying, "He works hard, and he asks questions. I appreciate him for that, being a young guy that has an open mind and wants to work hard, because that has to be your mindset coming into a team like this, with good players like we have. He's going to be a perfect piece for us."

Promoted to the starting unit the following year, Brown spent most of the 2017–18 season at shooting guard, where he averaged 14.5 points,

4.9 rebounds, and 1.6 assists per game, despite missing two weeks with a concussion. Off to a slow start in 2018–19, Brown soon found himself relegated to bench duty, with the *Boston Globe* criticizing him for taking too many long jump shots and exhibiting an overall "lack of focus and discipline." However, following a verbal berating by Kevin Garnett, who stressed to him the strong tradition of the Celtics and the proper way to conduct oneself as a professional, Brown eventually righted himself, enabling him to finish the season with averages of 13 points, 4.2 rebounds, and 1.4 assists per contest.

After spending the entire off-season working on his weaknesses, which included an inability to deliver the ball well to his teammates and to see the floor properly, Brown arrived at training camp in 2019 with a more well-rounded game and a new attitude. Despite missing 15 games due to injury, Brown established himself as one of the league's better all-around shooting guards by averaging 20.3 points, 6.4 rebounds, and 2.1 assists per contest. Performing even better in 2020–21, Brown earned his first All-Star nomination by posting averages of 24.7 points, 6.0 rebounds, and 3.4 assists per game, while also finishing second on the team with 72 steals.

Moved to small forward the following season, Brown displayed his versatility by averaging 23.6 points, 6.1 rebounds, and 3.5 assists per game, before posting extremely similar numbers in 24 postseason contests. Praising Brown for his outstanding playoff performance, *Sports Illustrated* wrote, "Brown is the do-it-all wing every team wishes it had in the postseason. Even with his shaky handle, Brown can score pretty much however you ask him to. He may never be a true No. 1 option, but it would be hard to find many better second ones."

Continuing his outstanding play in 2022–23, Brown has averaged 26.9 points, 7.1 rebounds, and 3.2 assists per game to this point in the season, giving him career averages of 17.4 points, 5.1 rebounds, and 2.1 assists per contest. As of this writing, Brown has also scored 7,746 points, amassed 2,286 rebounds, and collected 953 assists over the course of his career.

Aside from his contributions to the Celtics on the court, the extremely intelligent Brown, whose outside interests include learning Spanish, studying history, meditation, and exploring philosophy, gives back to the community through his work with the Bridge Program at the Massachusetts Institute of Technology, which mentors Greater Boston youth and high school students of color who are interested in pursuing careers in STEM programs. In recent years, Brown has also spoken on the importance of education and technology at Harvard University, the University of California, Berkeley, and Massachusetts Institute of Technology.

CELTICS CAREER HIGHLIGHTS

Best Season

Brown performed exceptionally well during the pandemic-shortened 2020–21 season, earning his first All-Star selection by averaging 24.7 points, six rebounds, 3.4 assists, and 1.2 steals per game. But, barring injury, Brown appears to be headed for his most productive season in 2022–23, posting averages of 26.8 points, 6.9 rebounds, 3.3 assists, and 1.1 steals per contest through the midway point of the campaign.

Memorable Moments / Greatest Performances

Brown led the Celtics to a 129-117 win over the Cleveland Cavaliers on December 27, 2019, by scoring 34 points and grabbing nine rebounds.

Brown reached the 40-point mark for the first time in his career during a 126-107 win over the Memphis Grizzlies on December 30, 2020, finishing the game with 42 points on 15-of-21 shooting from the field, including seven three-pointers.

Brown helped lead the Celtics to a 112-96 win over the Orlando Magic on March 21, 2021, by scoring 34 points, going 12-of-24 from the field and 10-of-19 from three-point range.

Brown displayed his shooting touch during a 121-113 win over the Lakers on April 15, 2021, scoring 40 points by hitting on 17 of his 20 shots from the field, including three from three-point range.

Brown starred in defeat on April 27, 2021, scoring 39 points, pulling down 11 rebounds, and recording four steals during a 119-115 loss to the Oklahoma City Thunder.

Brown followed that up by scoring 38 points and grabbing seven rebounds during a 120-111 win over the Charlotte Hornets the very next day.

Although the Celtics lost to the Knicks in double-overtime by a score of 138-134 in the 2021–22 regular-season opener, Brown performed brilliantly, scoring 46 points, gathering in nine rebounds, and assisting on six baskets.

Brown led the Celtics to a 116-111 overtime win over the Orlando Magic on January 2, 2022, by scoring a career-high 50 points and pulling down 11 rebounds.

Although the Celtics suffered a 109-103 defeat at the hands of the Miami Heat in Game 3 of the 2022 NBA Eastern Conference Finals,

Brown turned in an outstanding effort, scoring 40 points and collecting nine rebounds.

Brown helped lead the Celtics to a 126-117 victory over the 76ers in the 2022–23 regular-season opener by scoring 35 points on 14-of-24 shooting from the field and 3-of-3 shooting from the free-throw line.

Brown led the Celtics to a 130-121 win over the Washington Wizards on November 27, 2022, by scoring a game-high 36 points.

Brown starred during a 120-116 overtime loss to Miami on December 2, 2022, scoring 37 points and pulling down 14 rebounds.

Brown helped the Celtics record a 126-102 victory over the Houston Rockets on December 27, 2022, by scoring a game-high 39 points.

NOTABLE ACHIEVEMENTS

- Has averaged more than 20 points per game four times.
- Scored 50 points versus Orlando on January 2, 2022.
- Two-time NBA Player of the Week.
- 2016–17 NBA All-Rookie Second-Team selection.
- Two-time NBA All-Star selection (2020–21 and 2022–23).
- Two-time Atlantic Division champion (2016–17 and 2021–22).
- 2021–22 Eastern Conference champion.

27

DON NELSON

Although considered unconventional by many, Nelson's tactics helped to keep the Bucks in contention for most of the 1980s, earning him NBA Coach of the Year honors in 1983 and 1985.

Continuing the Celtic tradition of outstanding "sixth men," Don Nelson spent 11 seasons in Boston, establishing himself during that time as one of the NBA's finest role players. Playing both forward positions over the course of his career, Nelson backed up the likes of John Havlicek, Satch Sanders, Bailey Howell, and Paul Silas, helping the Celtics to capture five league championships between 1966 and 1976 in the process. A solid scorer, Nelson posted a scoring average in excess of 10 points per game nine times, even though he never earned a starter's minutes, averaging as many as 25 minutes per contest just four times. "Nellie," as he came to be known, also shot better than 50 percent from the field on three separate occasions, leading the league in field-goal shooting percentage once. An extremely durable player as well, Nelson played in every Celtics game in 6 of his 11 seasons in Boston, at one point appearing in over 450 consecutive contests. Yet, in spite of the many contributions Nelson made to the Celtics through the years, he likely will always be remembered mostly by fans of the team for one shot he made that helped to clinch the franchise's 11th NBA title in 13 years.

Born in Muskegon, Michigan, on May 15, 1940, Donald Arvid Nelson grew up in the state of Illinois, where he starred in basketball for Rock Island High School. After receiving an athletic scholarship to attend the University of Iowa, Nelson earned All-American honors twice, averaging 21.1 points and 10.5 rebounds a game over the course of his collegiate career.

Subsequently selected by the expansion Chicago Zephyrs (who later became the Baltimore Bullets) in the third round of the 1962 NBA Draft, with the 17th overall pick, the 6-foot-6, 210-pound Nelson spent his rookie season coming off the bench for the Zephyrs, averaging 6.8 points and 4.5 rebounds per game, in just over 17 minutes of action. After being released by Chicago prior to the start of the ensuing campaign, Nelson joined the Los Angeles Lakers, with whom he failed to distinguish himself as a backup over the course of the next two seasons.

Released by the Lakers following the conclusion of the 1964–65 campaign, Nelson signed with the Celtics, for whom he immediately assumed a more prominent role. Averaging just under 24 minutes per game while sharing playing time at both forward positions with John Havlicek, Satch Sanders, and Willie Naulls, Nelson posted averages of 10.2 points and 5.4 rebounds per contest, in helping the Celtics capture their eighth straight league championship. After experiencing something of a drop-off in production in 1966–67, Nelson began an eight-year run during which time he established himself as one of the NBA's most consistent and durable players.

Appearing in every Celtics game for the first of five straight times in 1967–68, Nelson averaged 10 points and 5.3 rebounds per contest, in only 18 minutes of action. He finished in double digits in scoring in each of the next seven seasons as well, playing his best ball for the Celtics in 1969–70, 1970–71, and 1974–75. Nelson established career-high marks in both scoring (15.4 ppg) and rebounding (7.3 rpg) in the first of those campaigns, while also shooting 50 percent from the field. He followed that up by averaging 13.9 points and 6.9 rebounds per game in 1970–71, before averaging 14 points and 5.9 rebounds per contest in 1974–75, while shooting a career-best and league-leading 53.9 percent from the field.

During that time, Nelson came to be known for his distinctive one-handed style of shooting free throws. Placing the ball in his shooting (right) hand, he leaned in, almost off balance, and toed the free-throw line with his right foot, his left leg tailing behind. Nelson then pushed the ball toward the basket completely with his right hand, while springing with his right knee and lifting his trailing foot in a sort of hop. Although unorthodox in style, this technique enabled Nelson to compile a lifetime free-throw shooting percentage of 76.5.

Nelson also came to personify the hardworking, blue-collar mentality of his Midwestern roots. A fierce competitor, Nelson made up for whatever he lacked in talent with desire and determination. Acknowledging his own limitations, Nelson once said, "I was just a so-so player anyway. I was lucky

Don Nelson continued the Celtics tradition of outstanding sixth men.

enough to hang around with a great team for a long time. What I brought to the party was in a reserve role. I was just a 25-minute player."

Nevertheless, Nelson proved to be a huge contributor to the Celtics over the course of his career, eventually earning the distinction of being considered one of the best "sixth men" ever to play in the NBA. Nelson perhaps made his greatest contribution to the Celtics in Game 7 of the 1969

NBA Finals when he converted one of the most famous shots in playoff history—a foul-line jumper which dropped through the basket after hitting the back rim and bouncing several feet straight up. The shot, taken with the Celtics holding a one-point lead over Los Angeles with just over one minute left in the game, helped to secure Boston's 11th NBA championship in 13 seasons.

After seeing his playing time diminish greatly in 1975–76, the 36-year-old Nelson elected to announce his retirement, ending his career with 10,898 points scored, 5,192 rebounds, 1,526 assists, and averages of 10.3 points, 4.9 rebounds, and 1.4 assists per game. Over the course of his career, he shot 48 percent from the field and 76.5 percent from the free-throw line. In Nelson's 11 years with the Celtics, he amassed 9,968 points, 4,517 rebounds, and 1,354 assists, and posted averages of 11.4 points, 5.2 rebounds, and 1.6 assists per contest. To show their appreciation to Nelson for the vital role he played in helping them win five NBA championships, the Celtics honored him in 1978 by retiring his uniform number (19), raising it to the Boston Garden rafters.

Following his playing days, Nelson began an extremely successful coaching career that lasted more than three decades. Taking over as general manager and head coach of the Milwaukee Bucks shortly after he retired, Nelson became known for his innovative coaching style that, among other things, ended up pioneering the concept of the point forward, which placed the responsibility of running the offense on the small forward, rather than a member of the backcourt. Although considered unconventional by many, Nelson's tactics helped to keep the Bucks in contention for most of the 1980s, earning him NBA Coach of the Year honors in 1983 and 1985.

Leaving Milwaukee after 10 seasons, Nelson subsequently became coach and vice president of the Golden State Warriors—a dual role he retained for nearly five years, during which time he earned his third NBA Coach of the Year nomination. After leaving the Warriors following a dispute with star forward Chris Webber, Nelson briefly served as coach of the Knicks before moving on to Dallas, where he accepted the position of head coach and general manager of the Mavericks in 1997. While leading the Mavericks to four consecutive 50-win seasons, Nelson continued to display his penchant for thinking outside the box, introducing the "Hack-a-Shaq" defense to the NBA.

Nelson continued to run the Mavericks until 2005, when a bout with prostate cancer prompted him to surrender his coaching duties to Avery Johnson and his responsibilities as general manager to his son, Donnie Nelson, who had previously served as his assistant. After taking a year off, Nelson returned to Golden State, where he spent the next four years coaching the Warriors before being relieved of his duties after failing to lead the team into the playoffs three straight times. During that time, though, Nelson passed Lenny Wilkens for first place on the all-time NBA wins list, having compiled an overall record of 1,335-1,063 over the course of his coaching career. Subsequently named one of the Top 10 coaches in NBA history, Nelson received the additional honor of being inducted into the Naismith Memorial Basketball Hall of Fame in 2012.

CELTICS CAREER HIGHLIGHTS

Best Season

Without a legitimate NBA center on their roster, the Celtics finished just 34-48 in 1969–70. Nevertheless, Nelson had his finest all-around season that year, posting career-high marks in scoring (15.4) and rebounding (7.3), while shooting 50 percent from the field.

Memorable Moments / Greatest Performances

Nelson reached the 20-point plateau for the first time as a member of the Celtics on November 13, 1965, when he scored a game-high 20 points during a 122–93 win over the Detroit Pistons. He topped that mark later in the year, helping the Celtics record a 116–113 victory over the San Francisco Warriors on December 30 by hitting for a season-high 25 points.

Nelson established new career highs in scoring twice during the 1968–69 campaign, tallying 27 points during a 132–118 win over the Pistons on December 6, 1968, before hitting for 28 points, in leading the Celtics to a 121–97 victory over Seattle on January 6, 1969.

Nelson posted the two highest scoring totals of his career the following season, however, hitting for 36 points during a 127–125 win over the SuperSonics on February 20, 1970, before scoring a career-high 40 points just five days later, in leading the Celtics to a 147–124 victory over the San Diego Rockets. Nelson also tallied 36 points on March 14, 1971, leading the Celtics to a 117–104 win over the Chicago Bulls in the process.

Nelson turned in a pair of outstanding offensive efforts one week apart in November of 1974, scoring 35 points during a 124–109 win over Washington on November 16, before hitting for another 35 points during a 98–96 loss to the 76ers seven days later.

Nelson, shown here guarding Walt Frazier of the Knicks, made huge contributions to five NBA championship teams during his time in Boston. Photo courtesy of MearsOnlineAuctions.com.

A solid postseason performer throughout his career, Nelson helped the Celtics take a 3–2 lead over the Lakers in the 1968 NBA Finals by scoring 26 points during a 120–117 overtime win in Game 5. He also came up big for Boston in Game 6 of the 1969 NBA Finals, hitting for 25 points, in helping the Celtics to even their series with Los Angeles at three games apiece, with a 99–90 victory.

However, Nelson unquestionably experienced his most memorable moment in the following contest, when he hit the biggest shot of his career. Having watched the heavily favored Lakers whittle down their once-substantial 17-point fourth-quarter lead to a single point by the closing moments of Game 7, the Celtics found themselves clinging to a 103–102 lead with barely a minute remaining in the contest. With Boston in possession of the ball and time running out on the shot clock, a Los Angeles player knocked the ball away from John Havlicek, right into the hands of Nelson at the free-throw line. Releasing the ball quickly, Nelson put up a shot that hit the back of the rim and got the ultimate shooter's bounce—straight down and through the net. From there, the Celtics held on to win by a score of 108–106, giving them their 11th NBA title in 13 seasons. Nelson finished the contest with 16 points.

NOTABLE ACHIEVEMENTS

- Averaged more than 15 points per game once (15.4 in 1969–70).
- Shot better than 50 percent from the field three times.
- Led NBA in field-goal percentage once and games played twice.
- Played in over 450 consecutive games, appearing in every Celtics game between 1967 and 1972.
- Played in every Celtics game in 6 of 11 seasons.
- Ranks ninth in Celtics history in games played (872).
- Three-time Eastern Division champion (1966, 1968, and 1969).
- Two-time Eastern Conference champion (1974 and 1976).
- Five-time NBA champion (1966, 1968, 1969, 1974, and 1976).
- Number 19 retired by Celtics.
- Inducted into Naismith Memorial Basketball Hall of Fame as player-coach in 2012.

28

BAILEY HOWELL

When Bailey played with Detroit and Baltimore, he used to run up and down my back on the offensive board. The guy really bugged me. And if that wasn't bad enough, he was also from Mississippi and had a Southern accent. But secretly I've always admired the way Howell plays. He never takes anything from anybody. He's been a Celtic-type player for a long time.

—Bill Russell

A consistent winner throughout his NBA career, Bailey Howell played for four different teams in his 12 years in the league, helping his squads advance to the playoffs a total of 10 times. Scoring many "garbage" baskets on fast breaks and offensive rebounds, Howell didn't possess an abundance of offensive moves. Nor did he display much grace or elegance on the court. Nevertheless, his strong work ethic, fierce competitiveness, and willingness to do whatever it took to win helped make him one of the league's top forwards for nearly a decade. In his four years with the Celtics alone, Howell averaged more than 19 points and 8 rebounds per game three times each, in helping them capture a pair of NBA titles. By the time he retired following the conclusion of the 1970–71 campaign, Howell had earned a total of six All-Star selections, compiling over the course of his career the fourth-best scoring average in league history to that point. Howell ranked in the top 10 in eight other statistical categories as well, clearly establishing himself as one of the best all-around forwards of the 1960s.

Born in the small Southern town of Middleton, Tennessee, on January 20, 1937, Bailey E. Howell began playing basketball at an early age, noting years later, "Basketball was a year-round sport back home . . .

Bailey Howell helped the Celtics win two NBA titles during his four years in Boston. Photo courtesy of MearsOnlineAuctions.com.

Basketball was the only sport offered at our high school. There were no football or baseball teams for the students, so we'd play pickup games whenever we could."

Starring on the hardwood for Middleton High School, Howell averaged 31.2 points per game over three seasons, setting in the process an all-time Tennessee Prep scoring record with 1,187 points. Recruited by numerous colleges following his graduation, Howell eventually chose to attend Mississippi State University, where he continued to excel on the court, becoming the first SEC player to reach the 2,000-point, 1,000-rebound plateaus by amassing totals of 2,030 points and 1,277 rebounds during his collegiate career. Particularly effective as a senior, when he earned consensus All-American honors by finishing second in the nation in both scoring (27.5 ppg) and rebounding (15.1 rpg), Howell led the Bulldogs to a record of 24-1 and their first SEC championship, while manning both the center and power forward positions.

Selected by the Detroit Pistons with the second overall pick of the 1959 NBA Draft, Howell ended up spending five extremely productive seasons in Detroit, leading the Pistons in scoring four times and rebounding three times. After averaging 17.8 points and 10.5 rebounds per game as a rookie in 1959–60, the 6-foot-7, 210-pound Howell had his finest statistical season in 1960–61, earning an eighth-place finish in the NBA MVP voting and the first of four consecutive All-Star nominations by placing among the league leaders with averages of 23.6 points and 14.4 rebounds per contest. He also performed extremely well in 1962–63, earning his lone All-NBA Second-Team selection by averaging 22.7 points and 11.5 rebounds per game. Yet, even though Howell had another big year for Detroit in 1963–64, posting averages of 21.6 points and 10.1 rebounds per game, the Pistons elected to include him in an eight-player trade they completed with the Baltimore Bullets at season's end that netted them Terry Dischinger, Don Kojis, and Rod Thorn in return.

Although Howell's numbers fell off somewhat after he arrived in Baltimore, he proved to be one of the Bullets' best players, finishing runner-up on the team in scoring in each of the next two seasons, with averages of 19.2 and 17.5 points per game, while leading the club in rebounding, with an average of 9.9 rebounds per contest in 1965–66. Once again, though, Howell found himself on the move at the end of the 1965–66 season, when Baltimore traded him to the Celtics for 7-foot center / power forward Mel Counts.

Looking back at the deal that sent him to Boston, Howell recalled, "It was a big thrill to go from a club with mediocre success to a team that had won eight NBA championships in a row. I got to play with players like Sam Jones, John Havlicek, and Bill Russell, which was very special for me, because they were such special people."

Howell remained one of the league's premier power forwards after he joined the Celtics, placing second on the team in both scoring and rebounding in each of his first three seasons in Boston. He began his four-year stint in Beantown by averaging 20 points and 8.4 rebounds per game in 1966–67, en route to earning the last of his six All-Star selections. Howell followed that up by posting marks of 19.8 points and 9.8 rebounds per contest in 1967–68, before averaging 19.7 points and 8.8 rebounds per game in 1968–69, in helping the Celtics win back-to-back NBA titles.

In expressing his sentiments toward Howell, a white Southerner who nevertheless respected him more than any other coach he ever played for, Bill Russell commented, "When Bailey played with Detroit and Baltimore, he used to run up and down my back on the offensive board. The guy really bugged me. And if that wasn't bad enough, he was also from Mississippi and had a Southern accent. But secretly I've always admired the way Howell plays. He never takes anything from anybody. He's been a Celtic-type player for a long time."

Russell expounded upon those feelings some years later in his book, *Dynasty's End*, saying of his former teammate:

> We knew Howell was a good player. He had an average of better than 20 points for seven seasons in the NBA, and he played in most of the All-Star games since he's been in the league. Yet, sometimes you don't realize a player's true value until he's on your side for a while. After all, we would see Howell for 9 or 10 times a year at the most. From what he's shown me, I have to say he's a great player. He's got the good offensive drive. He's a real holler-guy on the bench, too. Bailey likes team basketball. Joining the Celtics made him a happy player. He doesn't care how much he scores. He just wants to win.

Red Auerbach echoed Russell's sentiments, stating, "Howell is a real, real pro. There is no such thing as this guy having to be motivated—he comes to play every night. I've always liked him, not just as a player, but for his attitude."

In discussing Howell's attitude, former Cincinnati Royals center Wayne Embry, who also spent two years serving as Howell's teammate in Boston while backing up Bill Russell, told author Terry Pluto in his book, *Tall Tales*, "Bailey would step on your foot, elbow you in the throat. He was a great offensive rebounder, but he'd kick you to get the ball."

A tenacious rebounder, particularly on the offensive boards, Howell worked extremely hard on that aspect of his game, stating, "Hustle made me a pro. I know that I do not have the natural skills of many ballplayers, but I can compensate for any lack with hustle, and it has paid off."

A physical defensive player as well who retired with the fifth most personal fouls in NBA history, Howell believed in doing anything possible to gain an advantage over his opponent—a philosophy that stood in stark contrast to the image he portrayed off the court. A Southern gentleman and religious family man who neither drank nor smoked, Howell proved to be an enigma to many, as teammate John Havlicek later wrote in his autobiography:

> He might be sitting in the locker room brewing a pot of tea, but when the game started he was a terror. A couple of years before he joined the team, he was playing such a rough game against us one night in Providence that our broadcaster, Johnny Most, bellowed, "Bailey Howell's got twelve elbows!" He was the pushingest, shovingest guy I have ever seen. If someone got mad at him for that, he'd just laugh at him. He was a physical player who wouldn't back down from anything, but I never saw him in a fight.

Meanwhile, although Howell lacked finesse and style on offense, he ended up averaging more than 20 points per game in four different seasons due to his offensive rebounding, ability to drive aggressively to the basket, and effective use of the hook shot. Since Howell took the vast majority of his shots from relatively close range, he also consistently ranked among the league leaders in field-goal percentage, shooting better than 50 percent from the field on two separate occasions.

The 32-year-old Howell assumed a somewhat reduced role in Boston in 1969–70, averaging just 12.6 points and 6.7 rebounds per game, in only 25 minutes of action, for a Celtics team that concluded the campaign with a record of just 34-48. Subsequently left unprotected in the expansion draft, Howell briefly became a member of the Buffalo Braves, who immediately traded him to the Philadelphia 76ers. He then spent his final season in Philadelphia, averaging 10.7 points and 5.4 rebounds for the 76ers in a part-time role in 1970–71 before announcing his retirement at season's end. Howell ended his career with 17,770 points scored, 9,383 rebounds, 1,853 assists, and averages of 18.7 points, 9.9 rebounds, and 2 assists per game. He also shot 48 percent from the field and 76.2 percent from the free-throw line over the course of his career. In his four years with the Celtics, Howell scored 5,812 points, pulled down 2,717 rebounds, and assisted on 493 baskets, averaging in the process 18 points, 8.4 rebounds, and 1.5 assists per contest.

Following his playing career, Howell pursued graduate work at Mississippi State University, where he also spent several years serving as an assistant coach. He later went to work for the Converse shoe company, before

Howell finished second on the Celtics in both scoring and rebounding in each of his first three seasons in Boston. Photo courtesy of MearsOnlineAuctions.com.

becoming a member of the Starkville, Mississippi, Church of Christ. He gained induction into the Basketball Hall of Fame in 1997.

Red Auerbach once expressed his feelings toward Howell by proclaiming, "Bailey Howell has been a Celtic all his life. It just took him a lot longer to get the uniform."

Howell, in turn, revealed how special he considered his time in Boston to be when he suggested, "We were a group of guys from different backgrounds. I think we were an example of how people of different backgrounds, different races, or whatever, played together, worked together, and developed a love and respect for each other. Like I say, it's the epitome of what humans can accomplish when you get rid of all those petty things, the vices that you have, the prejudices that you have. . . . Everybody pulled together. It was a great situation to be in."

CELTICS CAREER HIGHLIGHTS

Best Season

Howell earned his only All-Star selection as a member of the Celtics in his first season in Boston, concluding the 1966–67 campaign with averages of 20 points and 8.4 rebounds per game, while shooting just over 51 percent from the field. He also played extremely well in 1968–69, averaging 19.7 points and 8.8 rebounds per contest. However, he had his finest all-around season in Boston in 1967–68, when he averaged 19.8 points and 9.8 rebounds per game, shot 48 percent from the field, and appeared in every game for the Celtics for one of three times, in helping them capture the first of their back-to-back NBA championships.

Memorable Moments / Greatest Performances

Howell turned in a number of outstanding performances in his first season in Boston, with the first of those coming on January 17, 1967, when he scored 30 points during a 109–101 win over the Chicago Bulls. He had another big game 12 days later, leading the Celtics to a lopsided 141–106 victory over the Knicks by tallying a game-high 32 points. Howell hit for a season-high 38 points during a 127–103 win over the Detroit Pistons on March 6, 1967, before scoring another 37 points, in leading the Celtics to a 132–109 victory over Detroit just 10 days later.

Howell had two of his biggest games the following season against Philadelphia, leading the Celtics to a 116–111 win over the 76ers on November 18, 1967, by scoring 33 points, before hitting for a season-high 35 points during a 133–127 loss to the 76ers on March 3, 1968.

Howell, though, turned in probably his most memorable effort as a member of the Celtics in Game 6 of the 1968 NBA Finals, when he scored 30 points and pulled down 11 rebounds during a 124–109 victory over the Lakers that clinched the NBA title for Boston. Commenting on his performance following the contest, Howell stated, "It certainly was my happiest moment in basketball when that final gong sounded. I had spent so many years trying to help clubs stay in the playoffs, like Detroit and Baltimore, and last year we lost out to Philly. This has to be my greatest thrill."

NOTABLE ACHIEVEMENTS

- Averaged 20 points per game once (1966–67), topping 19 points per contest two other times.
- Averaged 9.8 rebounds per game in 1967–68.
- Shot better than 50 percent from the field once (51.2% in 1966–67).
- Led NBA in games played twice.
- 1966–67 NBA All-Star.
- Two-time Eastern Division champion (1968 and 1969).
- Two-time NBA champion (1968 and 1969).
- Inducted into Naismith Memorial Basketball Hall of Fame in 1997.

29

K. C. JONES

This is one of the finest boys I have ever coached; never complains; loyal; unselfish. You've got to keep bugging him or else he won't tell you when he's hurting. Whoever gets that kid to work for him after he retires will get the very best.

—Red Auerbach

Serving the Celtics first as a player, then later as an assistant coach, a head coach, and a front office executive, K. C. Jones spent more than two decades in Boston, contributing to 10 championship teams during that time. An often-overlooked member of Celtics teams that captured the NBA title in each of his first eight years in the league, Jones did an expert job of running the offense, while blanketing the opposing team's top offensive guard. Although Jones provided little in the way of scoring himself, never averaging more than 9.2 points per game in any single season, he distributed the ball to his teammates extremely well, finishing third in the league in assists on two separate occasions. Jones, though, proved to be much more of a factor on the defensive end, establishing himself over the course of his career as the NBA's premier defender at the guard position.

Born in Taylor, Texas, on May 25, 1932, K. C. Jones moved with his mother and siblings to San Francisco at the age of nine after his parents separated. Named after his father, who had been named for the legendary railroad engineer, Casey Jones, young K. C. grew up in poverty, spending his earliest days on the basketball court competing against other inner-city children.

Jones began his athletic career in earnest after enrolling at San Francisco's Commerce High School, where he emerged as a two-sport star, excelling in both basketball and football. Yet, even though he earned All-City

K. C. Jones established himself as the NBA's premier defensive guard during his time in Boston.
Photo courtesy of RMYAuctions.com.

honors in both sports, Jones placed little hope in acquiring a college education, stating years later, "I had only one scholarship offer. I didn't know it
at the time, but my history teacher, Mildred Smith, arranged it. Being from
the ghetto, college was not very familiar to me."

Accepting the lone offer tendered him, Jones enrolled at the University
of San Francisco, where he began a lifelong friendship with fellow recruit Bill
Russell, to whom he would become linked for the remainder of his collegiate
and professional career. The outgoing and gregarious Russell, who spent his
four years of college rooming with Jones, later recalled that his shy and intro-
verted roommate barely spoke to him their first month together on campus,
writing in his book, *Second Wind*, "He'd slap my bunk on the way out of
the room in the mornings, and he'd nod at the salt or sugar during the silent

Jones spent his first five years in Boston backing up Bob Cousy, before joining the starting unit following Cousy's retirement in 1963.
Photo courtesy of LegendaryAuctions.com.

meals we ate in the school cafeteria. That was the extent of our communication, until one day, when he started talking like a normal person."

The tandem of Russell and Jones ended up leading the Dons to 56 consecutive wins and back-to-back NCAA Championships in 1955 and 1956, before earning Gold together at the 1956 Olympic Games. Although neither man possessed superior offensive skills, they both excelled on defense, with the 6-foot-1, 200-pound Jones displaying outstanding strength, quickness, and desire.

Subsequently selected in the second round of the 1956 NBA Draft by Celtics head coach and general manager Red Auerbach, who first took note of him while scouting Bill Russell for his team, Jones spent the next two years serving in the US Army, later expressing the belief that Boston's deep bench might well have prevented him from making the roster as a rookie in 1956–57. Still unconvinced that he had the ability to succeed in the NBA upon his discharge from the service in 1958, Jones briefly flirted with the idea of playing professional football as a member of the Los Angeles Rams, who had selected him in the later rounds of the 1956 NFL draft on the recommendation of former University of San Francisco public relations official and future NFL commissioner Pete Rozelle, who had seen him excel in high school. However, after playing in several exhibition games as a defensive back for the Rams, Jones suffered a leg injury that essentially ended his career in football.

Finally arriving in Boston later in 1958, Jones found himself reunited with Bill Russell, who, in his absence, had led the Celtics to two NBA Finals appearances and one league championship. Yet, unlike his former USF teammate, who had taken the NBA by storm, Jones initially found it extremely difficult to garner a significant amount of playing time. His path to a starting job in the backcourt blocked by future Hall of Famers Bob Cousy and Bill Sharman, the 26-year-old Jones spent his first few seasons in Boston coming off the bench. Revealing years later the first impression that his new teammate made on him, Cousy said, "I just didn't see how a man who shot as poorly as K. C. could stay in the NBA. I really didn't think his other skills would be enough to keep him around. But I was wrong. The man turned out to be amazing on defense, and eventually learned to score enough so that rival teams couldn't afford not to guard him."

Averaging just a little over 12 minutes per game as a rookie, Jones posted averages of only 3.5 points and 1.4 assists per contest, while shooting just 34 percent from the field. Seeing his playing time gradually increase to nearly 26 minutes per game over the course of the next three campaigns, Jones improved upon his numbers each season, eventually reaching marks of 9.2 points and 4.3 assists per contest by 1961–62. Yet, even though Jones slowly improved his shooting percentage as well, averaging just over 40 percent from the field in two of those three seasons, he never developed into anything more than a marginal shooter, typically compiling a mark well below the league average in that category, while also generally shooting only around 65 percent from the free-throw line.

Jones spent one more season coming off the bench, doing so in 1962–63, when he averaged 7.2 points and 4 assists per game in just under 25 minutes of action. He finally became a starter the following year, after Cousy announced his retirement, joining Sam Jones in Boston's starting backcourt. Looking back at the role he assumed his first five years in Boston, Jones recalled, "I played for Red Auerbach. I watched him, listened to him, saw what he did. Cousy was the quarterback of our team and I watched him. I was a bench guy, and I hated being on the bench. But, while I was there, I watched and absorbed, and, when I got out there on the court, I was in heaven."

Working extremely well together, the "Jones Boys," as they came to be known, developed into quite a formidable duo. Serving as a perfect complement to sharp-shooting Sam, who typically averaged more than 20 points per game, K. C. did an excellent job of setting up his teammates, placing among the NBA leaders in assists in four of the next five seasons. He also further established himself as the league's best defensive player at his position, using his quickness and athleticism to apply constant pressure to his man. Invariably assigned the unenviable task of covering the opposing team's top offensive guard, Jones regularly found himself matched up with the likes of Oscar Robertson and Jerry West. Yet, he never wilted under the pressure, sticking to his man like glue, pressing him all over the court, and using his long arms to obscure his view.

Unfortunately, the unquantifiable nature of Jones's game prevented him from ever earning All-Star honors. Nor did he ever make an All-NBA Defensive team, since the league did not begin naming such squads until two years after he retired. Nonetheless, those who watched Jones perform on a nightly basis fully understood the tremendous overall contributions he made to the success of the Celtics over the course of his career. On one occasion, Red Auerbach expressed his appreciation for his point guard by proclaiming, "This is one of the finest boys I have ever coached; never complains; loyal; unselfish. You've got to keep bugging him or else he won't tell you when he's hurting. Whoever gets that kid to work for him after he retires will get the very best."

Meanwhile, in addressing initial concerns that surfaced in Boston over the team's potential inability to repeat as NBA champions following the retirement of Bob Cousy in 1963, former Celtics publicity director Howie McHugh once confided, "I used to read about this and laugh because I knew something that the papers didn't. Russell, as much as he respected Cousy, wanted to show the world two things—that he had always been the main reason the Celtics won, and that his pal, K. C. Jones, was as good as any playmaker in the league. That was the year Russell grabbed almost 2,000 rebounds and was so self-motivated you wouldn't believe it."

The Celtics ended up winning the NBA title in eight of Jones's nine seasons with the team, failing to do so only in his final campaign of 1966–67, when they lost to the Philadelphia 76ers in five games in the Eastern Division Finals. Announcing his retirement shortly after the loss to Philadelphia, Jones ended his career with 5,011 points scored, 2,908 assists, 2,399 rebounds, a field-goal shooting percentage of just 38.7, and a free-throw shooting percentage of only 64.7. He averaged 7.4 points, 4.3 assists, and 3.5 rebounds per game over the course of his career.

Following his playing days, Jones immediately went into coaching, spending the next three years serving as head coach at Bradley University, before returning to the NBA as an assistant under former teammate Bill Sharman in Los Angeles. After winning his ninth NBA championship

After helping the Celtics win eight NBA titles as a player, Jones guided them to another two championships as head coach. Photo courtesy of LegendaryAuctions.com.

with the Lakers in 1972, Jones became head coach of the ABA's San Diego Conquistadores, who folded after just one season. From San Diego, Jones moved on to Washington, where he spent two years coaching the Bullets, leading them to a berth in the 1975 NBA Finals, where they lost to the Golden State Warriors in four games.

Following his two-year stint in Washington, Jones joined the coaching staff of the Milwaukee Bucks before returning to Boston as an assistant under head coach Bill Fitch. After serving under Fitch for two years, Jones assumed control of the team prior to the start of the 1983–84 campaign, leading the Celtics into the NBA Finals four straight times and winning two more championships in his five years in charge. Jones's total of 11 NBA titles ties him with Phil Jackson for third place on the all-time list, placing him behind only Celtics legends Red Auerbach (16) and Bill Russell (11).

Following the conclusion of the 1987–88 season, Jones elected to move into the Boston front office, where he spent the next two years serving as vice president of the Celtics. Upon announcing Jones's decision, team president Red Auerbach stated, "He had the complete respect of the players. Look at the record: He had five seasons. He won two championships. What more could he do? It's time to do something else."

After two years behind a desk, Jones returned to the sidelines as an assistant on the coaching staffs of the Seattle SuperSonics, Detroit Pistons, and Celtics. He later worked for the University of Hartford Athletic Office and did color commentary for that school's Men's Basketball Team until the onset of Alzheimer's disease forced him to enter an assisted living center in Connecticut, where he passed away at the age of 88 on December 25, 2020.

Employing a laid-back approach throughout his coaching career, Jones led his teams to a total of 522 regular-season victories, including an overall record of 308-102 in his five years as head coach in Boston. Jones's squads captured seven division titles, five Eastern Conference titles, and two NBA championships. In recognition of his overall contributions to the game as a player and coach, Jones received the ultimate honor of being inducted into the Naismith Memorial Basketball Hall of Fame in 1989. The Celtics also retired his uniform number (25) and raised it to the rafters at the Boston Garden.

Bill Walton, who spent parts of two seasons playing under Jones in Boston, said of his former coach, "His ability to evoke Celtic pride was incredible. He would always talk about how all the old players called him up after an embarrassing performance and wanted to disassociate themselves from the Celtics. They wanted to mail in their championship rings, wanted their numbers removed from the rafters, and, by this point, there would be tears rolling down our cheeks and we'd want to kill."

In expressing his admiration for his former head coach, Larry Bird once remarked, "He's the kind of person I'd like to be, but I don't have the time to work on it."

CELTICS CAREER HIGHLIGHTS

Best Season

Although not yet a full-time starter, Jones had one of his finest statistical seasons for the Celtics in 1961–62, averaging a career-high 9.2 points per game, assisting on 4.3 baskets per contest, and shooting over 40 percent from the field (40.6%) for one of only two times. He also played well in both 1963–64 and 1964-65, posting averages of 8.2 points, 5.1 assists, and a career-high 4.7 rebounds per game in the first of those campaigns, before averaging 8.3 points and 5.6 assists per contest the following season. Nevertheless, Jones had his finest all-around season in 1965–66, when he helped the Celtics capture their eighth straight NBA championship by averaging 8.6 points per game, while also finishing third in the league with a career-best average of 6.3 assists per contest.

Memorable Moments / Greatest Performances

Jones turned in the top offensive performance of his rookie campaign on March 8, 1959, when he scored 16 points during a 141–131 victory over the Cincinnati Royals.

Nearly two years later, on March 8, 1959, Jones established a new career high by tallying 19 points during a 142–116 win over the Knicks.

Although the Syracuse Nationals defeated the Celtics by a score of 122–110 on February 8, 1962, Jones reached the 20-point mark for the first time in his career, scoring 20 points during the loss.

Jones had two of his biggest offensive games during the 1962–63 season, scoring 22 points during a 126–112 win over the Los Angeles Lakers on December 7, 1962, before leading the Celtics to a 111–109 victory over the St. Louis Hawks on January 24, 1963, with a career-high 27 points.

Jones came up big for the Celtics in Game 5 of the 1965 NBA Finals, scoring a personal playoff high 20 points during a lopsided 129–96 victory over the Los Angeles Lakers that clinched the NBA title for Boston.

Jones topped the 20-point mark for the final time in his career on November 16, 1965, when he helped lead the Celtics to a 108–105 win over the San Francisco Warriors by hitting for a season-high 22 points.

NOTABLE ACHIEVEMENTS

- Averaged more than 5 assists per game four times, topping 6 assists per contest once (6.3 in 1965–66).
- Led NBA in games played twice.
- Finished third in NBA in assists twice.
- Led Celtics in assists three times.
- Ranks ninth in Celtics history in assists (2,904).
- Eight-time Eastern Division champion (1959–66).
- Eight-time NBA champion (1959–66).
- Number 25 retired by Celtics.
- Inducted into Naismith Memorial Basketball Hall of Fame in 1989.

30

MARCUS SMART

The heart and soul of the Celtics for the last several seasons, Marcus Smart has provided leadership and energy to his teammates since he first arrived in Boston in 2014. Spending time at both guard positions, Smart has displayed a willingness to do whatever it takes to win, with his aggressive style of play enabling him to win the NBA Hustle Award twice. A lockdown defender capable of guarding virtually anyone on the opposing team, Smart has also earned three NBA All-Defensive First-Team nominations and one NBA Defensive Player of the Year award. Gradually developing into a solid offensive performer as well, Smart has finished in double digits in scoring six times and averaged more than five assists per game on three separate occasions, with his strong all-around play making him a key contributor to Celtic teams that have won two division titles and one Eastern Conference championship.

Born in Flower Mound, Texas, on March 6, 1994, Marcus Osmond Smart experienced heartbreak at an early age, recalling, "I'm the youngest of four boys, and my eldest brother, Todd, was like a father figure to me. We were very close even though we were 23 years apart. When my parents were working, he was the one there for me. He was diagnosed with lung cancer when he was 15 years old."

After revealing that his oldest sibling lost his battle with the disease in 2004, Smart said, "I could've easily let the passing of my brother control how I live my life. But I was determined not to let him die in vain and to make a negative into a positive."

Developing into a standout basketball player at Edward S. Marcus High School, Smart helped lead his team to an overall record of 115-6 and two 5A state championships, earning McDonald's All-American honors his senior year by averaging 15.1 points, 9.2 rebounds, and 5 assists per game. After accepting an athletic scholarship to Oklahoma State University, Smart continued his exceptional play at the collegiate level, leading the Cowboys to a 24-8 record and a berth in the NCAA Tournament as a freshman by

Marcus Smart earned NBA Defensive Player of the Year honors in 2021-22.

averaging 15.4 points, 5.8 rebounds, and 4.2 assists per contest, while also leading the Big 12 with 99 steals. Following an equally impressive sophomore campaign, Smart chose to forgo his final two years of college and enter the 2014 NBA Draft.

Selected by the Celtics in the first round with the sixth overall pick, Smart ended up spending most of his first season in Boston coming off the bench, performing well enough in a part-time role (he averaged 7.8 points, 3.3 rebounds, 3.1 assists, and 1.5 steals per game) to be named to the NBA All-Rookie Second Team. Hampered by injuries in two of the next three seasons, Smart continued to serve the Celtics as a bench player, although he saw a significant amount of playing time each season. Completely healthy only in 2016–17, Smart posted his best overall numbers during that three-year stretch, averaging 10.6 points, 4.6 assists, 3.9 rebounds, 1.6 steals, and just over 30 minutes per game, while playing mostly shooting guard.

Although Smart finally joined the starting unit in 2018–19, he saw virtually the same amount of action, averaging just under 28 minutes per contest. But even though Smart failed to increase his offensive output, averaging only 8.9 points and 4.0 assists per game, he earned NBA All-Defensive First-Team honors with his spirited play on defense. Improving upon his overall numbers the following year, Smart averaged 12.9 points, 4.9 assists, and 3.8 rebounds per game, while also gaining NBA All-Defensive First-Team recognition for the second straight time.

Moved to point guard in 2020–21, Smart thrived as never before, posting new career-high marks with 13.1 points and 5.7 assists per game, before averaging 12.1 points and 5.9 assists per contest the following year, while also earning his third selection to the NBA All-Defensive First Team.

Although the 220-pound Smart stands just 6-foot-3, he possesses a 6-foot-9-inch wingspan, giving him the ability to guard players considerably taller than himself. Extremely aggressive and physical on defense, Smart pursues his man all over the court, making him feel uncomfortable and often causing turnovers or missed shots. Particularly effective at fighting through screens, Smart drew praise for his tenacious defense from Warriors head coach Steve Kerr, who said, "Smart plays hard, gets underneath players, makes a lot of steals, disruptions."

Also known for diving after loose balls and taking charges, Smart claims that his late brother serves as his inspiration for the type of defense he plays, saying, "I defend just like my brother Todd lived. He taught me how to play defense by the way he lived his life. I defend like every game is my last game, like anything can be taken away at any moment, and that's what my brother taught me. That's what he always preached to me, so that's how I believe the game should be played."

Smart continued, "I pride myself on the defensive end. That's where I earn my keep. . . . I'm a lock-up defender, and I believe strongly in my defense, so I don't need to take cheap shots at guys to get an edge. . . . If you watch me for a long time, you'll really understand and appreciate the way I play."

Though not nearly as proficient on the other end of the court, Smart has gradually improved his outside shooting and developed into more of a threat on offense, saying, "I'm not the best shooter, and I'm not the best scorer, but you do have to respect me because I can go off."

Suggesting that Smart's intensity and excellence in other aspects of the game more than compensate for his shortcomings on offense, then-Celtics head coach Brad Stevens stated in December 2016, "There aren't a lot of guys his age that have impacted winning the way he has. Maybe not from a statistical standpoint, but more so from: You can feel it when he's on the court. You ask anybody in here, and they all know Marcus' value."

Stevens added, "I think toughness, generally, is difficult to quantify. Everybody brings their own levels of skill to the table and everything else, but you have to have a competitiveness and an ability to figure out a way to win that possession. And he's able to do that on a lot of possessions."

Describing the energy that Smart brings to the game, former Celtics teammate Kemba Walker said, "It's exciting. It's energizing. He just gets everybody going. Gets us going, gets the crowd going. Like I said, we just kinda feed off him. He just does so many great things. And he propels our defense each and every night."

Continuing to provide a spark to his teammates over the first half of the 2022–23 season, Smart has helped lead the Celtics to the NBA's best record by averaging 11.4 points and a career-high 7.3 assists per game. As of this writing, Smart boasts career totals of 5,893 points, 2,608 assists, 2005 rebounds, and 874 steals, with the last figure representing the fourth highest mark in team annals. Over parts of nine NBA seasons, Smart has also averaged 10.5 points, 4.7 assists, 3.6 rebounds, and 1.6 steals per game.

CELTICS CAREER HIGHLIGHTS

Best Season

Although Smart averaged one more point per game the previous season, he posted slightly better overall numbers in 2021–22, concluding the campaign with averages of 12.1 points, 5.9 assists, 3.8 rebounds, and 1.7 steals per contest, while also shooting somewhat better from the field (41.8% to 39.8%).

Memorable Moments / Greatest Performances

Smart contributed to a 100-85 win over the Oklahoma City Thunder on November 15, 2015, by scoring a team-high 26 points and gathering in eight rebounds.

Smart turned in an outstanding all-around effort during a 116-108 win over the 76ers on February 15, 2017, scoring 21 points and collecting five rebounds, five assists, and eight steals.

Smart helped the Celtics earn their only victory of the 2017 NBA Eastern Conference Finals in Game 3 by scoring 27 points and collecting seven assists during a 111-108 win over Cleveland.

Although the Celtics lost to the Phoenix Suns, 123-119, on January 18, 2020, Smart scored a career-high 37 points, hitting on 11 of his 22 three-point attempts.

Smart led the Celtics to a 141-133 double-overtime victory over the Los Angeles Clippers on February 13, 2020, by scoring 31 points and recording four steals.

Smart helped lead the Celtics to a 117-102 win over Miami in Game 2 of the 2022 NBA Eastern Conference Finals by scoring 24 points, grabbing nine rebounds, and assisting on 12 baskets.

Smart excelled in Game 7 of that series as well, scoring 24 points, pulling down nine rebounds, and collecting six assists during a 100-96 win that sent the Celtics to the NBA Finals.

Smart led the Celtics to a lopsided 140-105 victory over the Charlotte Hornets on November 28, 2022, by scoring 22 points and dishing out 15 assists.

NOTABLE ACHIEVEMENTS

- Has averaged more than five assists per game three times.
- Finished third in NBA in steals in 2018–19.
- Has led the Celtics in assists three times and steals six times.
- Ranks among Celtics career leaders in steals (fourth).
- February 2015 NBA Rookie of the Month.
- 2014–15 NBA All-Rookie Second-Team selection.
- Two-time NBA Hustle Award winner (2018–19 and 2021–22).
- 2021–22 NBA Defensive Player of the Year.
- Three-time NBA All-Defensive First-Team selection (2018–19, 2019–20, and 2021–22).
- Two-time Atlantic Division champion (2016–17 and 2021–22).
- 2021–22 Eastern Conference champion.

31

DANNY AINGE

With Garnett and Allen joining Paul Pierce in Boston to form a "Big Three," the Celtics compiled a league-best 66-16 record during the 2007–08 regular season, en route to winning their 17th NBA championship. Ainge, who earned NBA Executive of the Year honors as a result, received the additional distinction of being named president of basketball operations for the Celtics, a position he held until June 2, 2021, when he announced his retirement.

An outstanding all-around athlete who played both basketball and baseball at the professional level, Danny Ainge eventually elected to focus solely on furthering his NBA career after failing to distinguish himself as an infielder with the Toronto Blue Jays. Spending parts of eight seasons in Boston, Ainge had most of his best years for the Celtics, serving as a member of their starting backcourt from 1984 to 1988. During that time, Ainge averaged more than 15 points per game twice and 5 assists per contest four times, while also shooting better than 50 percent from the field twice. Along the way, he earned one All-Star nomination and helped the Celtics capture four Eastern Conference and two NBA championships. And, following the conclusion of his playing career, Ainge eventually became the primary decision-maker in Boston's front office, helping the Celtics win two more Eastern Conference championships and another NBA title in that role.

Born in Eugene, Oregon, on March 17, 1959, Daniel Ray Ainge established himself as a legend of sorts while attending North Eugene High School. The only person to be named a high school First-Team All-American in football, basketball, and baseball, Ainge earned All-State honors

Danny Ainge served as a key member of four Eastern Conference and
two NBA championship teams during his time in Boston.

in basketball in both 1976 and 1977 by leading North Eugene to back-
to-back state championships. Also considered to be one of the top prep
football recruits in the state, Ainge earned *Parade* magazine High School
All-American honors as a junior in 1977.

Continuing to star in multiple sports after enrolling at Brigham Young
University, Ainge played both baseball and basketball in college, becoming
a household name after his length-of-the-court drive with seven seconds
remaining in the fourth quarter gave the Cougars a one-point victory over
Notre Dame in the 1981 NCAA Tournament. Ainge's extraordinary effort

capped off a brilliant collegiate career that saw him earn four All-WAC selections and WAC Player of the Year honors as a senior. In his final year at BYU, he also was named National Basketball College Player of the Year and won the John R. Wooden Award, presented annually to the most outstanding male college basketball player. Meanwhile, Ainge's baseball skills prompted the Toronto Blue Jays to select him in the 15th round of the 1977 MLB Draft. However, Ainge proved to be somewhat less talented on the diamond, compiling a batting average of just .220 over parts of three seasons as a backup infielder with the Blue Jays after being promoted by the club to the big leagues in May of 1979.

Choosing to focus exclusively on basketball after Boston selected him with the 31st overall pick in the second round of the 1981 NBA Draft, Ainge abandoned his dream of also playing in the Major Leagues following a lengthy court battle that forced the Celtics to buy out his contract from Toronto. Yet, after starring on the hardwood in both high school and college, Ainge found the road to success far more difficult in the NBA. Encountering numerous problems in his early days in Boston, Ainge failed to make much of an impression on his Celtics teammates, who openly mocked him after he joined them two months into the 1981–82 campaign. In discussing Ainge's performance in his first day of practice, Larry Bird later wrote in his autobiography, *Drive: The Story of My Life*, that the rookie guard "shot 0-2547." Celtics coach Bill Fitch also found Ainge's play to be a source of amusement, saying that his .220 batting average exceeded his shooting percentage on the basketball court.

While Ainge actually shot 35.7 percent from the field over the final 53 games of the season, he ended up contributing very little to a Celtics team that compiled a regular-season record of 63-19, before eventually losing to the Philadelphia 76ers in seven games in the Eastern Conference Finals. Garnering only about 11 minutes of playing time per contest, Ainge posted averages of just 4.1 points and 1.6 assists per game as a rookie. However, displaying the same determination and fierce competiveness for which he later became so well noted, Ainge dramatically improved upon his performance the following year, averaging 9.9 points and 3.1 assists in nearly 26 minutes of action per contest, while shooting just under 50 percent from the field.

After taking a step backward in 1983–84 (he averaged only 5.4 points, 2.3 assists, and 16.3 minutes per game), Ainge emerged as a key member of the Celtics the following season. Joining Dennis Johnson in Boston's starting backcourt, Ainge posted averages of 12.9 points and 5.3 assists per contest, while shooting a career-high 52.9 percent from the field. He followed that up by averaging 10.7 points and 5.1 assists per game for Boston's 1985–86 NBA championship ball club during the regular season, before increasing his scoring output in the playoffs to 15.6 points per contest. Excelling throughout the postseason, Ainge also averaged 5.2 assists and 2.3 steals per game in Boston's 18 playoff contests, while hitting on 55.4 percent of his shots from the field. Picking up right where he left off the previous season, Ainge helped the Celtics capture their fourth consecutive Eastern Conference title in 1986–87 by averaging 14.8 points and 5.6 assists per game before establishing new career highs the following year by posting marks of 15.7 points and 6.2 assists per contest, en route to earning his lone All-Star selection.

Yet, even as Ainge rose to prominence in the NBA, he developed a reputation as one of the league's most disliked players. Although Ainge's opponents very much respected the tenacity and aggressiveness he displayed on the court, they came to resent his cockiness and arrogance, which likely stemmed from the sense of entitlement he developed while starring in multiple sports in high school and college. Furthermore, Ainge became known throughout the league as a whiner who constantly complained to the referees when calls failed to go his way. Ainge's reputation and abrasive personality led to numerous confrontations with opposing players through the years, with perhaps the most notable of those taking place during a 1983 playoff game against the Atlanta Hawks, when the 6-foot-4, 190-pound guard exchanged blows with 7-foot-1, 270-pound center Tree Rollins.

The incident occurred in Game 3 of the Eastern Conference Quarterfinals, when Rollins retaliated for allegedly being called a sissy by elbowing Ainge in the face. In response, Ainge tackled Rollins to the ground, after which the two men began to wrestle. During the fray, Rollins bit Ainge's middle finger so badly that it required stitches to repair. Nevertheless, the referees elected to eject Ainge from the contest, while they chose not to banish Rollins.

The 1987–88 campaign proved to be Ainge's last full season in Boston. With Robert Parish having turned 35 years of age during the previous off-season, the Celtics decided to trade Ainge to the Sacramento Kings for promising young center Joe Kleine and forward Ed Pinckney on February 23, 1989, bringing to an end their nearly eight-year association with the shooting guard. Ainge left Boston with career totals of 6,257 points scored, 2,422 assists, 1,534 rebounds, and 671 steals, a field-goal shooting percentage of 48.7, and an outstanding free-throw shooting percentage of 86.7. He averaged 11.3 points, 4.4 assists, 2.8 rebounds, and 1.2 steals per game as a member of the Celtics.

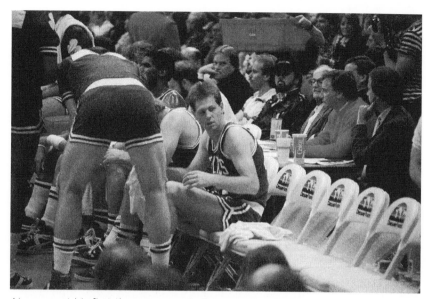

Ainge spent his first three seasons in Boston coming off the bench, before
finally joining Dennis Johnson as a starter in the backcourt.
Photo courtesy of Dave Madeloni.

Ainge spent the remainder of the 1988–89 season and all of the ensuing
campaign in Sacramento, posting a career-high scoring average of 17.9 points
per game for the Kings in 1989–90. However, Sacramento subsequently
dealt him to the Portland Trail Blazers, with whom Ainge spent the next two
seasons coming off the bench. A free agent following the conclusion of the
1991–92 campaign, Ainge signed with the Phoenix Suns, who he helped
advance to the NBA Finals the next year by averaging 11.8 points and 3.3
assists per game in a reserve role. After seeing his playing time gradually
diminish over the course of the next two seasons, Ainge chose to announce
his retirement prior to the start of the 1995 campaign, ending his career with
11,964 points scored, 4,199 assists, 2,768 rebounds, 1,133 steals, a field-goal
shooting percentage of 46.9, a free-throw shooting percentage of 84.6, and
averages of 11.5 points, 4 assists, 2.7 rebounds, and 1.1 steals per game.

Following his playing career, Ainge spent parts of four seasons coaching the Suns, leading them to an overall record of 136-90, before suddenly
handing in his resignation just 20 games into the 1999–2000 campaign.
He subsequently spent some time serving as a commentator for the NBA
on TNT, before accepting the position of Executive Director of Basketball
Operations for the Celtics in 2003. After experiencing little in the way
of success his first few years in that role, Ainge helped return the team to

prominence by making a pair of trades prior to the start of the 2007–08 campaign—one for Minnesota's Kevin Garnett, and the other for Seattle's Ray Allen. With Garnett and Allen joining Paul Pierce in Boston to form a "Big Three," the Celtics compiled a league-best 66-16 record during the 2007–08 regular season, en route to winning their 17th NBA championship. Ainge, who earned NBA Executive of the Year honors as a result, received the additional distinction of being named President of Basketball Operations for the Celtics, a position he held until June 2, 2021, when he announced his retirement. However, some six months later, Ainge returned to the game as the CEO of basketball operations and alternate governor of the Utah Jazz.

CELTICS CAREER HIGHLIGHTS

Best Season

Ainge played well for the Celtics in his first year as a full-time starter, averaging 12.9 points, 5.3 assists, 3.6 rebounds, and 1.6 steals per game in 1984–85, while also shooting a career-best 52.9 percent from the field. However, he had his best season for them in 1987–88, when he posted marks of 15.7 points, 6.2 assists, 3.1 rebounds, and 1.4 steals per contest, earning in the process the only All-Star selection of his career.

Memorable Moments / Greatest Performances

Ainge reached the 20-point mark for the first time in his career on November 17, 1982, when he scored 20 points during a 112–94 win over the Houston Rockets.

Ainge turned in a number of outstanding performances over the course of the 1984–85 campaign after earning a starting job in the Boston backcourt alongside Dennis Johnson. Putting on an exceptional shooting display during a 130–121 victory over the New Jersey Nets on December 11, 1984, Ainge hit on 11 of his 15 shots from the field and both of his free-throw attempts, en route to establishing a new career high with 25 points. He equaled that mark one month later, on January 12, 1985, when he scored a team-high 25 points, in leading the Celtics to a 119–111 win over the Atlanta Hawks. Ainge had another big game some three weeks later, hitting for 26 points during a 142–123 victory over the Kansas City Kings on February 1. Extremely efficient during the contest, Ainge connected on 11 of his 14 shots from the floor and all 4 of his free-throw attempts.

Ainge also came up big for the Celtics in Game 2 of the 1985 Eastern Conference Semifinals, helping them record a 121–114 win over the Detroit Pistons by scoring 25 points and collecting 6 assists.

Ainge played an exceptional all-around game against the Dallas Mavericks on December 18, 1985, scoring 20 points and assisting on 13 baskets during a lopsided 137–117 Celtics victory.

Ainge had one of the highest-scoring games of his career on December 3, 1986, when he tallied a game-high 34 points during a 119–113 win over the Denver Nuggets. Ainge turned in one of his finest all-around performances the following month, when he scored 24 points, collected 8 assists, and pulled down a career-high 11 rebounds during a 117–108 win over Dallas on January 14, 1987.

Although the Celtics lost their March 8, 1987, matchup with the Detroit Pistons by a score of 122–119 in overtime, Ainge established a new career high by scoring 35 points during the contest.

Ainge established another career high later that month, when he assisted on 15 baskets during a 111–106 victory over the Chicago Bulls on March 27, 1987.

Ainge played one of his biggest games of the year in Game 2 of the 1987 Eastern Conference Semifinals, when he helped the Celtics defeat Milwaukee by a score of 126–124 by tallying 30 points.

However, Ainge turned in his greatest performance as a member of the Celtics on December 9, 1988, when he scored a career-high 45 points during a 121–107 win over the Philadelphia 76ers, hitting on 20 of 29 shots, including a pair of three-pointers, and 3 out of 4 free-throw attempts during the contest. Ainge later tallied 45 points as a member of the Sacramento Kings as well.

NOTABLE ACHIEVEMENTS

- Averaged more than 15 points per game twice.
- Averaged more than 5 assists per game four times.
- Shot better than 50 percent from the field twice.
- Shot better than 90 percent from the free-throw line once (90.4% in 1985–86).
- Led NBA with 148 three-point field goals in 1987–88.
- Finished second in NBA with 89.7 free-throw shooting percentage in 1986–87.

Ainge, seen here applying defensive pressure to San Antonio's George Gervin. Photo courtesy of MearsOnlineAuctions.com.

- Ranks among Celtics career leaders in steals (8th).
- 1987–88 NBA All-Star.
- Four-time Eastern Conference champion (1984, 1985, 1986, and 1987).
- Two-time NBA champion (1984 and 1986).

32

DON CHANEY

The fans gave the trophy to Don because Don Chaney still exemplified the blood and guts of sports—no excuses and no crying towels, and certainly no "flops" for the charging call.
>   —former *Boston Globe* writer Walter Haynes

A defensive specialist capable of shutting down the opposing team's top offensive guard, Don Chaney spent parts of 10 seasons in Boston, proving to be the embodiment of Celtics pride during that time. The only Celtics to play with both Bill Russell and Larry Bird, Chaney willingly accepted whatever role his coach assigned to him, doing his job without much fanfare, drawing little attention to himself with his low-key demeanor, and letting his on-court performance do all his talking for him. In the end, though, Chaney gained a degree of notoriety by earning two NBA championship rings and five NBA All-Defensive Second-Team nominations. And, even though Chaney built his reputation primarily on his defense, he contributed to the Celtics on the offensive end as well, finishing in double digits in scoring four straight times between 1970 and 1974.

Born in Baton Rouge, Louisiana, on March 22, 1946, Donald R. Chaney attended local McKinley High School, where he abandoned the idea of playing quarterback at the insistence of his mother, who literally walked onto the football field one day and pulled him to the sidelines. With his mom persuading him to focus on basketball instead due to the extreme physical nature of his first love, young Don spent the rest of high school concentrating exclusively on further developing his basketball skills, succeeding to the point where he received a scholarship offer to attend the University of Houston.

A defensive specialist, Don Chaney spent his time in Boston guarding the likes of Milwaukee's Oscar Robertson. *Photo courtesy of the Milwaukee Bucks.*

After enrolling at Houston, Chaney embarked on an outstanding collegiate career that saw him score 1,133 points and earn Second-Team All-America honors as a senior. Teaming up with future NBA star Elvin Hayes, Chaney helped lead the Cougars to an upset victory over Lew Alcindor and previously undefeated UCLA in the first game ever played in the Houston Astrodome, snapping in the process the Bruins' 47-game winning streak in a nationally televised contest that attracted the largest crowd ever to witness a basketball game to that point.

Subsequently selected by the Celtics with the 12th overall pick of the 1968 NBA Draft, Chaney garnered very little playing time his first two seasons in Boston, appearing in only 20 games as a rookie before averaging just 5 points, 2.4 rebounds, 1.1 assists, and 13 minutes of action in the 63 contests in which he appeared the following year. Chaney finally began to make significant contributions to the Celtics his third year in the league, when he earned a starting job in the backcourt alongside Jo Jo White. Playing the "off-guard" position opposite White, who ran the Boston offense, Chaney posted averages of 11.5 points, 5.7 rebounds, and 2.9 assists, in the 28 minutes of action he saw per game. He compiled extremely similar numbers in 1971–72, averaging 11.9 points, 5 rebounds, and 2.6 assists per contest, while also earning NBA All-Defensive Second-Team honors for the first of four straight times. Chaney followed that up with his finest statistical season in 1972–73, helping the Celtics record the NBA's best regular-season record by averaging 13.1 points, 5.7 rebounds, and 2.8 assists per game.

As Chaney emerged as one of Boston's most reliable players over the course of his first three seasons as a starter, his reputation as a lockdown defender continued to grow. Regularly assigned the task of guarding the opposing team's top-scoring guard, the 6-foot-5, 210-pound Chaney used his quickness and long arms (he had an 82-inch wingspan) to blanket his man, enabling him to gain recognition as one of the league's finest defensive players at his position. Chaney also became known for his loquaciousness and intensity on the court, which differed dramatically from the quiet and mild-mannered demeanor he displayed away from the arena. In explaining his different personas, Chaney stated, "I just felt like I was being paid to play, and not for my opinions."

Chaney again played well for the Celtics in 1973–74, averaging 10.4 points, 4.7 rebounds, and 2.2 assists per game for a team that went on to win the NBA Championship. However, after posting extremely similar numbers the following season, Chaney elected to jump to the St. Louis Spirits of the rival ABA, explaining his decision a year later by saying, "There were things said about my move to St. Louis, and I made statements, and Red Auerbach made statements, and, from what I could tell, most fans seemed to be on his side. But the time was turning. Guys felt they were being used, and the ABA made them feel more independent in their outlook. You started thinking in terms of how much you could get, instead of how much they were willing to give you."

Despite being upset over Chaney's impending departure, the Boston fans presented him with a huge man-size trophy before he left—a gesture that former *Boston Globe* writer Walter Haynes explained thusly: "The fans gave the trophy to Don because Don Chaney still exemplified the blood and guts of sports—no excuses and no crying towels, and certainly no 'flops' for the charging call."

Chaney ended up spending just one season in St. Louis before returning to the NBA as a member of the Los Angeles Lakers. After posting modest numbers for the Lakers as a starter his first year back, Chaney found himself slowed by a knee injury that forced him to undergo surgery prior to the start of the ensuing campaign. With Chaney having appeared in only nine games for them through the midway point of the 1977–78 season, the Lakers agreed on a trade with the Celtics on December 27, 1977, that sent Chaney and forward Kermit Washington to Boston for veteran guard Charlie Scott.

Although Chaney was happy to be back in Boston, he quickly noted the many changes that had taken place in his absence, later revealing, "It was different when I got back; when I left, we were a close team. Everyone was around for a long time; we were a unit. When I got back, the old closeness was gone and guys had gone their separate ways. When you boil it all down, it's the ticket receipts now. It's a new day, and it's all business. I just don't think you're going to see players staying on one team for more than four years. I think everyone is going to be moved around."

Chaney remained in Boston another two and a half years, serving the Celtics as a backup player until he announced his retirement following the conclusion of the 1979–80 campaign. He ended his career with 6,663 points scored, 3,147 rebounds, 1,762 assists, averages of 8.4 points, 4 rebounds, and 2.2 assists per game, a 43.6 field-goal shooting percentage, and a free-throw shooting percentage of 77.6. Over parts of 10 seasons in Boston, Chaney scored 5,689 points, pulled down 2,572 rebounds, assisted on 1,268 baskets, and posted averages of 8.7 points, 3.9 rebounds, and 1.9 assists per contest.

Following his playing days, Chaney spent several seasons coaching in the NBA as both an assistant and a head coach. His coaching career included stints with the Los Angeles Clippers, Houston Rockets, Detroit Pistons, and New York Knicks, with his greatest success coming in Houston, where he earned NBA Coach of the Year honors in 1991. After being replaced as head coach in New York by Lenny Wilkens midway through the 2003–04 campaign, Chaney retired to his home in Houston, where he occasionally does color commentary for Rockets games on their TV network.

CELTICS CAREER HIGHLIGHTS

Best Season

Although Chaney also performed well for the Celtics in each of the two previous seasons, he clearly played his best ball for them in 1972–73, when he established career-high marks in scoring average (13.1 ppg), rebounding average (5.7 rpg), field-goal shooting percentage (48.2), and minutes played (31.5 mpg).

Memorable Moments / Greatest Performances

Doing an excellent job of guarding the likes of Jerry West, Oscar Robertson, Walt Frazier, Dave Bing, and Hal Greer over the course of his career, Chaney built his reputation primarily on his defense. Nevertheless, he proved to be an effective offensive player as well during his time in Boston. Chaney topped 20 points for the first time in his career on November 12, 1969, when he scored 21 points during a 116–107 loss to the Cincinnati Royals.

Chaney had his first big offensive game as a starter with the Celtics on December 19, 1970, when he tallied 28 points during a 134–128 loss to the Baltimore Bullets. He topped that mark later in the season, leading the Celtics to a 140–128 victory over the Atlanta Hawks on January 3, 1971, by hitting for 31 points.

Chaney had his biggest game of the ensuing campaign on January 29, 1972, when he helped the Celtics record a 124–112 win over the Detroit Pistons by scoring 29 points.

Chaney turned in another outstanding offensive performance almost exactly one year later, scoring 26 points during a 94–89 win over the Cleveland Cavaliers on January 31, 1973. He had another big game one month later, when he scored a career-high 32 points, in leading the Celtics to a 118–111 victory over the Golden State Warriors on February 28.

Chaney's highest scoring output of the 1973–74 season turned out to be a 26-point effort he turned in during a 104–88 win over the rival Knicks on March 2, 1974.

Chaney had a similarly impressive game against the Chicago Bulls on December 10, 1974, when he led the Celtics to a 107–89 victory by scoring a season-high 28 points.

Chaney also proved to be a solid playoff performer during his time in Boston, with his biggest offensive game coming against the Houston Rockets in Game 4 of the 1975 Eastern Conference Semifinals, when he scored 29 points during a 122–117 Celtics win. Boston went on to win the series in five games before losing to the Washington Bullets in six games in the Conference Finals.

Yet, Chaney arguably experienced his finest moments as a member of the Celtics against the Milwaukee Bucks in the 1974 NBA Finals—a series that Boston ended up winning in seven games. Assigned the task of guarding an aging Oscar Robertson, who retired at season's end, Chaney pressed the 35-year-old guard all over the court, limiting him to an average of just 12.1 points per contest. And, although the Celtics eventually lost Game 6 by a score of 102–101 in double-overtime, Chaney made one of the most notable plays of the series late in the first overtime, when he recorded a steal that led to a John Havlicek basket that sent the game into an additional OT session.

NOTABLE ACHIEVEMENTS

- Averaged more than 5 rebounds per game three times.
- Led Celtics in field-goal shooting percentage once.
- Missed only eight games between 1970 and 1975.
- Four-time NBA All-Defensive Second-Team selection (1971–72, 1972–73, 1973–74, and 1974–75).
- 1968–69 Eastern Division champion.
- 1973–74 Eastern Conference champion.
- Two-time NBA champion (1969 and 1974).

33

AL HORFORD

An extremely unselfish player whose contributions to his team cannot be measured merely by statistics, Al Horford has proven to be one of the NBA's most overlooked and underappreciated players for the last 16 seasons. A tremendous competitor who cares only about winning, Horford has used his superior all-around ability, intelligence, exceptional court awareness, and outstanding leadership skills to make an enormous impact on teams that have advanced to the playoffs 14 times, the Eastern Conference Finals four times, and the NBA Finals once. After spending his first nine years in the league in Atlanta, Horford joined the Celtics, who he has helped lead to two Atlantic Division titles and one Eastern Conference championship in his two tours of duty with the club. And, although Horford does not generally post the kind of numbers that draw a significant amount of attention, his overall contributions to the success the Celtics have experienced during his five years in Beantown have earned him one NBA All-Star selection and one NBA All-Defensive Second-Team nomination.

Born in Puerto Plata, Dominican Republic, on June 3, 1986, Alfred Joel Horford spent his formative years living with his mother in his homeland before joining his father, Tito, and his stepmother in Lansing, Michigan, at the age of 14. The son of a former NBA player who also spent several years competing in other countries, Horford developed into quite a player himself at Grand Ledge High School, setting seven school records, including most career points (1,239). Particularly outstanding his senior year, Horford earned Class A Player of the Year honors by averaging 21 points, 13 rebounds, and five blocked shots per game, prompting Rivals. com to rank him as the No. 7 power forward and the No. 36 player in the nation in 2004. Continuing to excel on the court after he accepted an athletic scholarship to the University of Florida, Horford spent three seasons playing for head coach Billy Donovan, leading the Gators to the 2005 Southeastern Conference championship and the NCAA championship in each of the next two seasons.

Al Horford has played for teams that have advanced to the playoffs 14 times.

Subsequently selected by the Hawks with the third overall pick of the 2007 NBA Draft, Horford immediately laid claim to the starting center job upon his arrival in Atlanta, after which he went on to earn NBA All-Rookie First-Team honors and a runner-up finish in the Rookie of the Year voting by averaging 10.1 points, 9.7 rebounds, and 0.9 blocked shots per contest. Steadily improving upon those numbers in each of the next three seasons, Horford gained All-Star recognition in 2009–10 and 2010–11 by posting averages of 14.2 points and 9.9 rebounds in the first of those campaigns before averaging 15.3 points and 9.3 rebounds per game in the second. Remaining one of the league's better big men the next five seasons, Horford earned two more All-Star nominations, performing especially well in 2012–13, when he averaged 17.4 points and a career-high 10.2 rebounds per game, and 2013–14, when he posted averages of 18.6 points and 8.4 rebounds per contest.

Choosing to leave Atlanta when the Celtics offered him a four-year contract worth $113 million in July 2016, Horford headed for Boston, where he spent the next three seasons starting at center for teams that won one division title and advanced to the Eastern Conference Finals each year. Despite missing nine games with a concussion in 2016–17, Horford made huge contributions to the Atlantic Division champions by averaging 14 points, five assists, and a team-high 6.8 rebounds and 1.3 blocks per game. En route to earning NBA All-Defensive Second-Team honors and his lone All-Star selection as a member of the Celtics the following season, Horford posted averages of 12.9 points, 7.4 rebounds, 4.7 assists, and 1.1 blocks per contest. Although hampered by a sore left knee for much of the 2018–19 campaign, Horford averaged 13.6 points, 6.7 rebounds, 4.2 assists, and 1.3 blocked shots per game, in helping the Celtics compile a record of 49-33 that represented the fourth-best mark in the Eastern Conference.

Standing 6-feet-9 and weighing close to 250 pounds, Horford possesses good size and strength, making him a solid rebounder and an excellent low-post defender. A good shooter, capable ball-handler, and adept passer as well, Horford has the ability to hit the mid-range jumper, shoot from three, or deliver the ball to one of his teammates in prime shooting position.

In discussing the totality of Horford's game, former Celtics big man Tyler Zeller stated, "He really doesn't have any weaknesses. He kind of does a little bit of everything."

Expressing similar sentiments, former Houston Rockets head coach Mike D'Antoni said, "He's a really good player. It'd be nice if he wasn't, but he is. I mean, he's got everything. He's got every skill set you want. . . . He shoots threes and can drive, and whatever you need from him. He's really good."

Portland Trail Blazers center Meyers Leonard told Bleacher Report, "He can go down to the block if you try to switch a pick-and-roll. He's comfortable in the mid-range. He's comfortable at three. Good passer, kind of making plays in that little window, as we call it, on the short roll in the free-throw line area. So, he's very talented, a guy that's been around the league and knows what it takes to win."

Perhaps Horford's greatest strengths, though, are his selfless attitude, leadership skills, and ability to make the other players around him better. In discussing his older half-brother, Jon Horford stated, "He's the ultimate glue guy—the guy who does all the little things on the floor. . . . He does all those things because of how competitive he is, because winning is all that matters to him, and he knows those plays are needed to win."

Speaking of Horford during the 2017 playoffs, then-Celtics head coach Brad Stevens said, "His ability to make people around him better has been very helpful to our team, obviously. . . . His presence makes unselfish basketball contagious."

Horford also received high praise from two of his most prominent teammates, with Marcus Smart stating, "We love Al. Best vet we've ever had. He comes in. Never changes, good or bad. Nine times out of 10, it's going to work in our favor. . . . He understands what he brings to the game and to this team, and we need every last bit of it on every night we can."

Meanwhile, Jayson Tatum said toward the end of the 2021–22 season, "Al is our leader. I've been fortunate to have Al as a teammate for three years. He's been great for me and my development—just the ultimate professional."

Yet, despite Horford's importance to the team, the Celtics chose not to match the four-year, $97 million contract the Philadelphia 76ers offered him when he became a free agent following the conclusion of the 2018–19 campaign. Horford subsequently spent one season in Philadelphia before being dealt to Oklahoma City on December 8, 2020. Reacquired by the Celtics, essentially for Kemba Walker on June 18, 2021, Horford has spent the last two seasons providing solid play and outstanding leadership to one of the NBA's strongest teams. After averaging 10.2 points, 7.7 rebounds, 3.4 assists, and 1.3 blocked shots per game for a Celtics squad that advanced to the NBA Finals in 2021–22, Harford has posted similar numbers over the first half of the 2022–23 campaign, giving him totals of 3,856 points, 2,210 rebounds, 1,286 assists, and 378 blocked shots, and averages of 12.3 points, 7.1 rebounds, 4.1 assists, and 1.2 blocks per game as a member of the team. As of this writing, Horford also boasts career totals of 13,340 points, 7,998 rebounds, 3,239 assists, and 1,162 blocked shots, and averages of 13.5 points, 8.1 rebounds, 3.3 assists, and 1.2 blocked shots per contest. And, with the Celtics, who currently hold the league's best record and are being considered one of the favorites to win the NBA championship, Horford may finally capture the title that has eluded him all these years.

CELTICS CAREER HIGHLIGHTS

Best Season

Horford posted extremely comparable numbers in each of his first three seasons in Boston. But since Horford earned NBA All-Defensive Second-Team honors and his only All-Star selection as a member of the Celtics in 2017–18 by averaging 12.9 points, 7.4 rebounds, and 4.7 assists per game, we'll identify that as his finest season in Beantown.

Memorable Moments / Greatest Performances

Horford helped lead the Celtics to a 97-92 win over the Sacramento Kings on December 2, 2016, by scoring 26 points, grabbing eight rebounds, blocking six shots, and collecting two steals.

Horford helped the Celtics take a 3-2 series lead over the Bulls in the opening round of the 2017 NBA Eastern Conference Playoffs by scoring 21 points, pulling down seven rebounds, and assisting on nine baskets during a 108-97 win.

Horford turned in a similarly impressive performance in Game 1 of the 2017 NBA Eastern Conference Semifinals, scoring 21 points, grabbing nine rebounds, and collecting 10 assists during a 123-111 victory over the Washington Wizards.

Horford contributed to a 96-89 win over the Milwaukee Bucks on October 26, 2017, by scoring a season-high 27 points while also collecting nine rebounds and four assists.

Horford punctuated a 22-point, 10-rebound effort on February 4, 2018, by hitting a 15-foot fadeaway jumper at the buzzer that gave the Celtics a 97-96 win over the Portland Trail Blazers.

Horford helped lead the Celtics to a 113-107 win in Game 1 of their first-round playoff matchup with the Bucks in 2018 by scoring 24 points, grabbing 10 rebounds, and blocking three shots.

Horford came up big for the Celtics in Game 7 of that series as well, helping them advance to the ensuing round by scoring 26 points and pulling down eight rebounds during a 112-96 victory.

Continuing his strong play in Game 1 of the 2018 NBA Eastern Conference Semifinals, Horford scored 26 points during a 117-101 win over the 76ers.

Horford made huge contributions to the Celtics 115-114 win in Game 1 of their opening round playoff matchup with the Brooklyn Nets in 2022, scoring 20 points and collecting 15 rebounds.

Horford led the Celtics to a 116-108 victory over the Bucks in Game 4 of the 2022 NBA Eastern Conference Semifinals by scoring 30 points, 16 of which came in the final period. Expressing his admiration for his teammate, who hit on 11 of his 14 shots from the field and five of his seven three-point attempts, Marcus Smart issued a message on Twitter after the game that read: "When I'm almost 36 years old, please Lord, please let me be just a fraction of the player that Al Horford is! I mean—what an absolute amazing teammate and player."

NOTABLE ACHIEVEMENTS

- Has averaged five assists per game once.
- Has shot better than 50 percent from the field once.
- Has led the Celtics in rebounding twice, blocked shots three times, and assists once.
- Ranks among Celtics career leaders in blocked shots (eighth).
- 2017–18 NBA All-Defensive Second-Team selection.
- 2017–18 NBA All-Star selection.
- Two-time Atlantic Division champion (2016–17 and 2021–22).
- 2021–22 Eastern Conference champion.

34

ISAIAH THOMAS

A quality scorer who also did an excellent job of distributing the ball to his teammates, Isaiah Thomas proved to be one of the NBA's most exciting players the first half of his career, before injuries prevented him from being much of a factor his last few years in the league. Reaching elite status during his time in Boston, the diminutive Thomas spent parts of three seasons with the Celtics, helping them advance to the playoffs three times and win one division title by averaging more than 19 points and five assists per game each season. A two-time NBA All-Star who earned one All-NBA Second-Team selection as well, Thomas also garnered serious consideration for league MVP honors in 2016–17, when he posted one of the highest single-season scoring averages in franchise history. Yet, after Thomas's exceptional play led them to a berth in the NBA Eastern Conference Finals, the Celtics chose to part ways with him at season's end, trading him to Cleveland as part of a three-way deal that brought Kyrie Irving to Boston.

Born in Tacoma, Washington, on February 7, 1989, Isaiah Jamar Thomas owes his first name to Hall of Fame guard Isiah Thomas, who his father oddly enough rooted against in the 1989 NBA Finals. Having lost a bet with a friend that his beloved Lakers would defeat the Pistons in the championship round of the postseason tournament, James Thomas found himself compelled to name his son after the Detroit guard, although he later admitted that he had already warmed to the name by the time his wife gave birth. However, Thomas' mother insisted that her son's name take the Biblical spelling.

Eventually emerging as a star in basketball at Curtis Senior High School in University Place, Washington, Thomas performed especially well as a junior, averaging 31.2 points per game. But with Thomas knowing that he needed to improve his grades to earn a college scholarship after he struggled in the classroom the following year, he traveled across the country

Isaiah Thomas earned All-Star honors twice during his time in Boston.

and repeated his senior year at South Kent High School in South Kent, Connecticut. Graduating from South Kent in 2008, Thomas subsequently enrolled at the University of Washington, where he spent the next three seasons excelling on the court, earning Pac-10 Freshman of the Year honors in 2009 and All-Pac-10 honors in each of the next two seasons. Electing to forgo his final year of college eligibility, Thomas declared for the 2011 NBA Draft, where the Sacramento Kings ultimately selected him in the second round, with the 60th and final pick.

Entering the NBA with a huge chip on his shoulder, Thomas spent his first year in the league trying to prove to the other 29 teams that they had made a big mistake by not selecting him earlier on draft day. Accomplishing his goal, Thomas earned NBA All-Rookie Second-Team honors and a seventh-place finish in the NBA Rookie of the Year voting by averaging 11.5 points and 4.1 assists in just over 25 minutes of action per contest as first man off the bench. Continuing to perform well in the role of "sixth man" in 2012–13, Thomas averaged 13.9 points and 4.0 assists per game, before becoming a regular member of the starting unit the following season, when he averaged 20.3 points and 6.3 assists per contest.

Despite the success that Thomas experienced his first three years in the league, the Kings included him in a sign-and-trade deal they completed with the Phoenix Suns on July 12, 2014, that also sent the rights to Alex Oriakhi to Sacramento.

Reprising his role of "sixth man" in Phoenix, Thomas spent the first few months of the 2014–15 campaign coming off the bench for the Suns, averaging 15.2 points, 3.7 assists, and just under 26 minutes per game before being acquired by the Celtics on February 19, 2015, in a complicated three-team trade that essentially sent Thomas from Phoenix to Boston, guard Marcus Thornton and a 2016 first-round draft pick from Boston to Phoenix, and forward Tayshaun Prince from Boston to Detroit. Although Thomas subsequently spent the rest of the season serving the Celtics exclusively as a backup, he experienced an increase in offensive production, averaging 19 points and 5.4 assists per contest.

Joining the Celtics starting unit in 2015–16, Thomas had his finest season to date, earning All-Star honors for the first of two straight times by averaging 22.2 points and 6.2 assists per game, while also shooting just under 43 percent from the field and 36 percent from three-point range. Taking his game up a notch the following season, Thomas helped lead the Celtics to the Atlantic Division title by posting averages of 28.9 points and 5.9 assists per game, shooting a career-high 46.3 percent from the field, and successfully converting 38 percent of his three-point shots and just under 91 percent of his free-throw attempts.

Generously listed at 5-feet-9 and 185 pounds, Thomas accomplished all he did despite his diminutive size, which made him a marked man anytime he drove hard to the basket. Showing no fear, Thomas often sacrificed his body, scoring many of his points by challenging much taller defenders inside. Extremely quick and elusive, Thomas also excelled at breaking down the opposing team's defense by driving toward the rim before delivering a pass to a wide-open teammate on the perimeter.

Marveling at Thomas' ability to get inside, Celtics head coach Brad Stevens stated at one point during the 2016–17 season, "It's truly amazing what he's able to accomplish in that regard, getting to the rim at his height. Here's a guy that's always had to figure out how to do it. And boy, has he figured it out. He's got that ultimate chip on his shoulder where there is no success that can make him take his foot off the pedal and no slight that he misses."

Revealing how he felt about his size, or lack thereof, Thomas told *Sports Illustrated* in 2017, "Honestly, I don't see height. I just figure out a way. I've been doing it my whole life. I've been the smallest player on every court I've ever been on in my life. But I don't feel small. I feel as big as everybody else."

Continuing his exceptional play during the 2017 postseason, Thomas led the Celtics to series wins over the Chicago Bulls and Washington Wizards by posting scoring averages of 23 and 27.4 points per game, despite losing his younger sister in a car accident just prior to the start of the playoffs and entering the series against Chicago with an injured hip. However, the pain from Thomas' injury eventually proved to be too much for him to handle, forcing him to miss most of the NBA Eastern Conference Finals, which the Celtics ended up losing to the Cleveland Cavaliers in five games.

Showing little appreciation for all Thomas had done for them, the Celtics completed a trade with the Cavaliers prior to the start of the ensuing campaign that sent him, Jae Crowder, Ante Žižić, and a first-round draft pick to Cleveland for Kyrie Irving. Unhappy over the idea of leaving Boston, Thomas expressed his dissatisfaction with Celtics general manager Danny Ainge, telling Lee Jenkins of *Sports Illustrated*: "Boston is going to be all love. I might not ever talk to Danny again. That might not happen. I'll talk to everybody else. But what he did, knowing everything I went through, you don't do that, bro. That's not right. I'm not saying f___ you. But every team in this situation comes out a year or two later and says, 'We made a mistake.' That's what they'll say, too."

Thomas, who left the Celtics having scored 4,422 points, assisted on 1,070 baskets, collected 173 steals, averaged 24.7 points and 6.0 assists per game, shot 44.3 percent from the field, and successfully converted 89 percent of his free-throw attempts as a member of the team, subsequently underwent a physical examination following his arrival in Cleveland that revealed he had been playing for several seasons with a number of secondary issues in his hip that included a loss of cartilage and some arthritis. Plagued by his physical maladies, Thomas found himself unable to appear in more than 40 games in any of the next four seasons, which he split between seven different teams. Released by the Charlotte Hornets during the latter stages of the 2021–22 campaign, Thomas failed to catch on with any other team, likely signaling the end to his playing days. If Thomas never appears in another NBA game, he will end his career with 9,715 points scored, 2,638 assists, 1,321 rebounds, and 472 steals, averages of 17.7 points and 4.8 assists per game, and shooting percentages of 43.4 percent from the field and 87.2 percent from the free-throw line.

CELTICS CAREER HIGHLIGHTS

Best Season

Thomas reached the apex of his career in 2016–17, when he earned his lone All-NBA selection and a fifth-place finish in the league MVP voting by placing third in the circuit with a scoring average of 28.9 points per game that ranks as the third-highest single-season mark in franchise history.

Memorable Moments / Greatest Performances

Thomas topped the 30-point mark for the first time as a member of the Celtics on April 8, 2015, when he scored 34 points during a 113-103 win over the Detroit Pistons.

Thomas led the Celtics to a 139-134 overtime victory over the Los Angeles Clippers on February 10, 2016, by scoring 36 points and assisting on 11 baskets.

Thomas helped lead the Celtics to a 111-103 win in Game 3 of their opening round matchup with the Atlanta Hawks in the 2016 Eastern Conference Playoffs by scoring a game-high 42 points.

Thomas helped the Celtics edge out the 76ers, 107-106, on December 3, 2016, by scoring 37 points and collecting seven assists.

Thomas starred during a 112-109 overtime victory over the Memphis Grizzlies on December 20, 2016, scoring 44 points on 10-of-16 shooting from the field, including 7-of-10 from three-point range, and 17-of-17 shooting from the free-throw line.

Thomas topped that performance 10 days later when he scored 52 points during a 117-114 win over the Miami Heat on December 30, 2016, incredibly scoring 29 points in the final period.

Thomas turned in a pair of 38-point efforts early in 2017, scoring 38 points during a 117-108 win over the New Orleans Pelicans on January 7, before matching that total just four days later during a 117-108 victory over the Washington Wizards.

Thomas starred in defeat on January 21, 2017, scoring 41 points during a 127-123 overtime loss to the Portland Trail Blazers.

Thomas again tallied 41 points during a 113-109 win over the Pistons on January 30, 2017.

Thomas led the Celtics to a 109-104 victory over the Toronto Raptors on February 1, 2017, by scoring 44 points, going 12-of-22 from the field and 15-of-16 from the free-throw line.

Although the Celtics lost Game 1 of their opening round playoff matchup with the Chicago Bulls on April 16, 2017, by a score of 106-102, Thomas turned in a memorable performance, scoring 33 points while mourning the loss of his younger sister, Chyna, who died in a single-car crash just one day earlier. Revealing his emotional state afterward, Thomas said in a statement, "I never could have imagined a day where my little sister, Chyna, wouldn't be here. She and my family are everything to me, so the pain I am feeling right now is impossible to put into words. This has been without question the hardest week of my life."

One week later, Thomas helped the Celtics even the series at two games apiece by scoring 33 points again during a 104-95 win over the Bulls. Marveling at Thomas' effort, Celtics head coach Brad Stevens said, "I can't believe it. I tried to say that earlier this week, but what he's been through and the day to day is just, it's unfathomable the way that he's performed on the court. I mean, it's been really incredible."

Thomas continued his heroics in Game 2 of the 2017 NBA Eastern Conference Semifinals, scoring a career-high 53 points during a 129-119 overtime win over the Washington Wizards.

NOTABLE ACHIEVEMENTS

- Averaged more than 20 points per game twice, averaging 19 points per contest another time.
- Averaged more than five assists per game three times.
- Shot better than 90 percent from the free-throw line once.
- Finished second in NBA with 0.909 free-throw shooting percentage in 2016–17.
- Finished third in NBA with a scoring average of 28.9 points per game in 2016–17.
- Led Celtics in scoring average three times and assists twice.
- Scored more than 50 points in one game twice.
- Holds Celtics record for most points scored in a quarter (29 versus Miami on December 20, 2016).
- Holds Celtics career record for highest scoring average (24.7 points per game).
- Ranks among Celtics career leaders in assists per game (ninth) and free-throw shooting percentage (third).
- Five-time NBA Player of the Week.
- January 2017 NBA Player of the Month.
- Finished fifth in 2016–17 NBA MVP voting.
- 2016–17 All-NBA Second-Team selection.
- Two-time NBA All-Star selection (2015–16 and 2016–17).
- 2016–17 Atlantic Division champion.

35

KYRIE IRVING

A tremendously talented player who possesses superior scoring and ball-handling ability, Kyrie Irving joined the Celtics in 2017 after spending the previous six seasons in Cleveland establishing himself as one of the NBA's premier point guards. A three-time All-Star and one-time All-NBA selection as a member of the Cavaliers, Irving continued to perform at an elite level during his relatively brief stay in Boston, earning another All-NBA nomination and two more trips to the All-Star game by averaging more than five assists and well over 20 points per game for Celtic teams that made consecutive playoff appearances. Nevertheless, Irving's immaturity and narcissistic nature made him a divisive force during his time in Beantown, making his decision to leave the Celtics via free agency after just two seasons a blessing in disguise.

Born in Melbourne, Australia, on March 23, 1992, Kyrie Andrew Irving spent his earliest years living in the Melbourne suburb of Kew, where his father, Drederick, a graduate of Boston University, played basketball semi-professionally for the Bulleen Boomers in the South East Australian Basketball League. Relocating with his parents and two sisters to the United States at the age of two, young Kyrie lost his mother to an illness just two years later, forcing his dad to rely on Irving's aunts to help raise his children.

Growing up in West Orange, New Jersey, Irving developed an affinity for basketball by attending his father's adult-league games, proclaiming as early as the fourth grade, "I will play in the NBA, I promise."

Already competing in organized leagues by the time he reached his early teens, Irving played for the Road Runners of the Amateur Athletic Union while also starring on the court for Montclair Kimberly Academy, for whom he averaged 26.5 points per game as a freshman. After leading Montclair Kimberly Academy to its first New Jersey Prep "B" state title the following year, Irving transferred to St. Patrick High School because he felt that he needed a bigger challenge. Continuing his exceptional play at St. Patrick High, Irving led the school to consecutive Union County

Kyrie Irving averaged more than 20 points and five assists per game in each of his two seasons in Boston.

Tournament championships by posting scoring averages of 17.0 and 24.0 points per game, earning in the process a spot on the US team that won gold at the FIBA Americas Under-18 Championships in June 2010.

Offered an athletic scholarship to Duke University, Irving subsequently spent just one season playing for the Blue Devils and head coach Mike Krzyzewski before announcing that he planned to forgo his final three years of college and enter the 2011 NBA Draft. Selected by the Cleveland Cavaliers with the first overall pick, the 19-year-old Irving ended up performing extremely well his first year in the league, earning NBA Rookie of the Year honors by averaging 18.5 points and 5.4 assists per game for a Cavaliers team that finished last in their division. Although Cleveland failed to advance to the playoffs in either of the next two seasons, Irving gradually developed into one of the league's top players at his position, gaining All-Star recognition both years by posting scoring averages of 22.5 and 20.8 points per game, while also averaging 5.9 and 6.1 assists per contest.

With LeBron James returning to Cleveland prior to the start of the 2014–15 campaign, the Cavaliers began an outstanding three-year run during which they advanced to the NBA Finals each season, claiming their first league championship in 2016 by defeating the Golden State Warriors in seven games. Meanwhile, Irving continued his ascension to stardom, playing perhaps the best ball of his career in 2016–17, when he averaged 25.2 points and 5.8 assists per game.

However, with Irving having grown tired of playing in the shadow of James, he requested a trade in July 2017, prompting the Cavaliers to complete a deal with the Celtics on August 30 that sent him to Boston for Isaiah Thomas, Jae Crowder, Ante Žižić, and the rights to the Brooklyn Nets' 2018 first-round draft pick.

Clearly the focal point of the Celtics' offense in 2017–18, the 6-foot-2-inch, 200-pound Irving averaged a team-high 24.4 points and 5.1 assists per game despite missing more than a month of the regular season and the entire postseason due to problems with his left knee that forced him to undergo multiple surgeries during the latter stages of the campaign. Nevertheless, the young Celtics performed extremely well in Irving's absence, advancing to the Eastern Conference Finals, where they lost to the Cleveland Cavaliers in seven games.

Fully healthy by the start of the 2018–19 season, Irving earned All-NBA Second-Team honors and his third straight All-Star selection by averaging 23.8 points and a career-high 6.9 assists per contest. However, with Irving occasionally experiencing differences with his younger teammates both on and off the court, the Celtics failed to display the same chemistry they exhibited the previous year, posting six fewer victories during the regular season, before suffering a five-game defeat at the hands of the Milwaukee Bucks in the Eastern Conference Semifinals, with Irving averaging just 20.4 points per contest and shooting only 36 percent from the field during the series.

Coming off his disappointing postseason performance, Irving, who stated earlier in the year that he intended to sign a contract extension with the Celtics at season's end if they offered him one, shocked the hometown fans when he elected to join Kevin Durant in Brooklyn and sign with the Nets as a free agent. Leaving the Celtics having scored a total of 3,062 points, assisted on 770 baskets, and amassed 562 rebounds and 168 steals as a member of the team, Irving averaged 24.1 points, 6.1 assists, 4.4 rebounds, and 1.3 steals per game during his two seasons in Boston.

Although Irving's departure seemingly doomed the Celtics to mediocrity, it ended up serving as the impetus for them to join the NBA's elite. With Irving gone, talented youngsters Jayson Tatum and Jaylen Brown, whose development had been stunted by the All-Star guard, began to flourish, allowing the team to reach new heights. Nevertheless, Celtics fans continue to hold a grudge against Irving for his two underwhelming seasons with the team, and for what they consider to be his betrayal of them.

Since leaving Boston, Irving has very much remained a lightning rod, antagonizing those in and out of basketball with his self-centered behavior, lack of commitment to his team, and distorted ideas. Seemingly disinterested in earning his paycheck, Irving sat out most of 2019–20 with a right shoulder injury, appeared in only 54 games the following season, and missed most of the 2021–22 campaign after refusing to be vaccinated against COVID-19.

Meanwhile, Irving has drawn negative attention to himself by supporting several conspiracy theories that reflect his antisocial thinking. Irving has stated that he believes the Earth is flat, adding that people "should do their own research for what they want to believe in because our educational system is flawed." Irving has also suggested that John F. Kennedy was killed because he wanted to end the banking cartel and has expressed his agreement with a conspiracy theorist on Instagram that claimed that "secret societies are administering vaccines in a plot to connect Black people to a master computer for a plan of Satan."

Irving, though, took things a bit too far in October 2022, when he tweeted a link to an Amazon listing page for *Hebrews to Negroes: Wake Up Black America*, a 2018 film based on a book of the same name that promotes Black Hebrew Israelite ideology. In addition to claiming that Black people are the real Jews and that white Jews worship Satan, the film includes quotes attributed to Adolf Hitler and noted antisemite Henry Ford, suggests that the Holocaust never occurred, and proposes that Jewish people dominated the slave trade and currently control the media. After initially refusing to distance himself from such claims by removing his tweet, Irving ultimately apologized to anyone he might have offended by promoting the film. But, with Irving's belated and insincere apology falling on deaf ears and the indifference he has shown to the success of his team the past few seasons contributing greatly to the lack of continuity the Nets have displayed on the court much of the time, it appears to be a foregone conclusion that he will need to find a new home when his current contract expires at the end of the 2022–23 season.

Best Season

Although Irving performed well in both his seasons in Boston, he posted slightly better overall numbers in 2018–19, when he earned All-NBA Second-Team honors by averaging 23.8 points, 6.9 assists, 5 rebounds, and 1.5 steals per game.

Memorable Moments / Greatest Performances

Irving led the Celtics to a 110-107 win over Atlanta on November 6, 2017, by scoring a game-high 35 points and collecting seven assists.

Irving put on a shooting clinic during a 110-102 overtime victory over the Dallas Mavericks on November 20, 2017, scoring 47 points by hitting on 16 of his 22 shots from the field and 10 of his 11 free-throw attempts.

Irving helped lead the Celtics to a 108-97 win over the 76ers on November 30, 2017, by scoring a game-high 36 points.

Irving turned in an outstanding all-around effort on November 8, 2018, scoring 39 points and collecting seven rebounds, six assists, and three steals during a 116-109 overtime win over the Phoenix Suns.

Irving led the Celtics to a 123-116 overtime victory over the Toronto Raptors on November 16, 2018, by scoring 43 points and assisting on 11 baskets.

NOTABLE ACHIEVEMENTS

- Averaged more than 20 points per game twice.
- Averaged more than five assists per game twice.
- Led Celtics in scoring average twice and assists once.
- Ranks among Celtics career leaders in scoring average (third), assists per game (eighth), and free-throw shooting percentage (sixth).
- 2018–19 All-NBA Second-Team selection.
- Two-time NBA All-Star selection (2017–18 and 2018–19).

36

CHARLIE SCOTT

I think my time spent with the Suns really helped me to appreciate what it was like to win a championship. I was more mature by the time I arrived in Boston, and I had just endured three frustrating seasons in Phoenix. I was ready to come home and help the Celtics win a championship. And that's exactly what I did.

—Charlie Scott

An extremely gifted offensive player who holds the ABA record for the highest scoring average in one season, Charlie Scott became one of the first players to jump from the fledgling league to the more established NBA when he left the Virginia Squires to play for the Phoenix Suns during the latter stages of the 1971–72 campaign. Scott continued his high-scoring ways in Phoenix, placing among the NBA's scoring leaders in each of the next three seasons, en route to earning three consecutive All-Star selections. However, in spite of his individual accomplishments, Scott derived little pleasure from his time in Phoenix, since the Suns failed to make the play-offs each season. Not until Scott joined the Boston Celtics in 1975 did he finally find himself in a winning situation, allowing the other aspects of his game to surface. Altering his style of play to fit the needs of his new team, Scott never again posted huge offensive numbers. Yet, he became more of a complete player, contributing in numerous ways to a Celtics team that captured the NBA title his first season in Boston. And, even though Scott subjugated his own game to enable the players around him to flourish, he remained a solid scorer over the course of his two and a half years with the Celtics, averaging better than 16 points per game each season.

Prior to joining the Celtics, Charlie Scott set the ABA record for highest scoring average in one season.

Born in Harlem, New York, on December 15, 1948, Charles Thomas Scott began playing organized basketball at the age of 12, after which he established himself as an elite player by the time he enrolled at New York's prestigious Stuyvesant High School. Moving with his family to the tiny town of Laurinburg, North Carolina, at the age of 15, Scott transferred to Laurinburg Academy High School, where he continued to star on the court, in much the same way that former Laurinburg graduates Sam Jones and Jimmy Walker had done some years earlier. An outstanding student as well, Scott earned the distinction of being named valedictorian of his high school senior class. Heavily recruited by several Division I colleges as graduation approached, Scott eventually decided to attend the University of North Carolina, where he became the first African-American scholarship athlete in the school's history.

Averaging 22.1 points and 7.1 rebounds per game over the course of his collegiate career, which included a stellar senior year in which he averaged 27.1 points per contest, Scott earned All-ACC honors three times and All-American honors twice while leading the Tar Heels to two consecutive Conference championships and a pair of NCAA Final Four appearances. He also helped the United States win Gold at the 1968 Summer Olympics.

Drafted by both the Celtics and the ABA's Virginia Squires following his graduation from UNC in 1970, Scott ultimately elected to sign with the Squires, who lured him to the upstart league by offering him much more money than did their NBA counterparts. The 6-foot-5, 175-pound Scott subsequently thrived in the fast-paced ABA, using his quickness, athleticism, and wide assortment of offensive moves to immediately establish himself as the league's top shooting guard. En route to earning Co-Rookie of the Year honors, a spot on the All-ABA Second Team, and the first of his five consecutive All-Star selections, Scott placed among the league leaders with averages of 27.1 points and 5.6 assists per game in 1970–71. He followed that up with an even more sensational sophomore campaign in which he averaged 34.6 points per contest, setting in the process the ABA record for highest scoring average in a season. His fabulous performance earned him All-ABA First-Team honors.

However, Scott, who briefly went by the name Shaheed Abdul-Aleem during this period, soon became dissatisfied with life in the ABA since it did not offer him an opportunity to compete against the best players in the world. As a result, with only a few games remaining in the 1971–72 season, he elected to jump to the NBA, where he joined the Phoenix Suns, who had acquired his rights from the Celtics in exchange for Paul Silas just days earlier.

Scott established himself as one of the NBA's top offensive threats after he arrived in Phoenix, placing among the league leaders in both scoring (25.3 ppg) and assists (6.1 apg) in 1972–73. Despite missing a significant amount of playing time due to injuries in each of the next two seasons, he remained one of the league's top scorers, earning his fourth and fifth straight All-Star selections by posting averages of 25.4 and 24.3 points per game. However, Phoenix's losing record each season left the highly competitive Scott feeling unfulfilled and dejected, prompting him to express to management his desire to go elsewhere.

The Boston Celtics proved to be the perfect trading partner for the Suns. With the rapidly maturing Paul Westphal likely to draw a considerable amount of attention from other teams when he became a free agent at season's end, Red Auerbach feared that he might lose the talented young guard without receiving anything in return. Therefore, Auerbach completed a trade with the Suns on May 23, 1975, that sent Westphal and a pair of draft picks to Phoenix for Scott.

Looking back at the deal that made him a member of the Celtics, Scott said, "I think my time spent with the Suns really helped me to appreciate what it was like to win a championship. I was more mature by the time I arrived in Boston, and I had just endured three frustrating seasons in Phoenix. I was ready to come home and help the Celtics win a championship. And that's exactly what I did."

Prior to Scott's arrival, though, many wondered how he would fit in on a Celtics team that stressed ball movement and the team concept. Possessing a shooter's mentality, Scott spent his first five pro seasons taking an inordinately high number of shots, placing either first, second, or third in the league in field-goal attempts in each of his first three seasons. Furthermore, writers speculated that friction might develop between the volatile Scott and his new backcourt mate, Jo Jo White, who possessed a far more laid-back personality. However, any concerns proved to be unfounded, since the two men ended up complementing each other extremely well, as Scott later revealed when he suggested, "I was a volcano and Jo Jo, a smooth stream of water. He was cool, deliberate, and he knew how to calm me."

Moreover, surrounded by other talented players for the first time in his career, Scott adapted his game to fit the needs of his team, doing a better job of playing without the ball, while also working extremely hard on improving his defense. Although Scott never again averaged as many as 20 points per game, he developed into more of a complete player, accepting in the process a somewhat reduced role on an exceptionally talented team that ended up compiling a regular-season record of 54-28 in 1975–76, en route to winning the NBA title. For his part, Scott averaged 17.6 points, 4.2 assists, 4.4 rebounds, and 1.3 steals per game, placing him third on the team in scoring, second in assists, and tying him for the team lead in steals.

Although limited by injuries to only 43 games the following season, Scott once again posted solid numbers for the Celtics, averaging 18.2 points, 4.6 assists, 4.4 rebounds, and 1.4 steals per contest. Nevertheless, with the Celtics in a period of transition by the beginning of the ensuing campaign, they elected to part ways with Scott midway through the season, dealing him to the Los Angeles Lakers for former Celtic Don

Scott spent his entire time in Boston subjugating his game for the betterment of the team. Photo courtesy of PristineAuction.com.

Chaney, forward Kermit Washington, and a 1978 first-round draft pick on December 27, 1977. Scott left Boston having amassed 2,728 points, 650 rebounds, and 680 assists as a member of the Celtics, en route to posting averages of 17.5 points, 4.2 rebounds, and 4.4 assists per game in his two and a half years with the club.

After finishing out the 1977–78 season with the Lakers, Scott moved on to Denver, where he spent his final two seasons with the Nuggets before announcing his retirement following the conclusion of the 1979–80 campaign. Scott ended his career with 14,837 points scored, 3,515 assists, 2,846 rebounds, averages of 20.7 points, 4.9 assists, and 4 rebounds per game, a field-goal shooting percentage of 44.8, and a free-throw shooting percentage of 77.3. In addition to averaging more than 24 points per game five times, he topped 5 assists per contest four times and 5 rebounds per game twice.

Following his playing days, Scott served as a marketing director for the sports apparel company Champion for several years, then as executive vice president of CTS, a telemarketing firm, before owning his own business.

Although it has now been more than 40 years since Scott played his last game for the Celtics, he still considers himself a member of the team, stating on one occasion:

> Once a Celtic, always a Celtic—Red has always said to me, and I believe it wholeheartedly. He has always made me feel that way. At that time, the coronation of being a Boston Celtic was winning a championship. That made it even more special. Even when I was traded, Red called me, talked to me, and explained the reasons behind the trade. He also tried to accommodate me and my needs. As a player, you can't ask for anything more under those circumstances. It was short—I wish it could have been longer—but fate has its reasons. My departure enabled the team to get another draft choice, which ended up helping them get Larry Bird. So all of those things have fitting rewards to them. It was short, but college was only four years and it will forever hold a special place of significance in my heart. The same can be said about my time spent with the Boston Celtics. I'll always consider myself a Celtic.

CELTICS CAREER HIGHLIGHTS

Best Season

Scott posted good numbers for the Celtics in 1976–77, averaging 18.2 points, 4.6 assists, 4.4 rebounds, and 1.4 steals per contest. However, injuries limited him to just 43 games, making the previous season easily his best in Boston. Appearing in all 82 games for the Celtics in 1975–76, Scott helped them win the NBA championship by averaging 17.6 points, 4.2 assists, and 1.3 steals per contest, finishing among the team leaders in all three categories.

Memorable Moments / Greatest Performances

Although Scott toned down his game considerably after he arrived in Boston, he still displayed his exceptional scoring ability at times, with the first such instance taking place on December 19, 1975, when he hit for a season-high 32 points during a 120–112 win over the Knicks. Scott reached the 30-point mark three other times later that season, scoring exactly 30 points during a 135–107 victory over the Buffalo Braves on January 25, 1976, a 109–108 win over the Phoenix Suns on February 13, and a 95–88 victory over the Cleveland Cavaliers on April 1.

Scott had a number of big games for the Celtics the following season as well, scoring 31 points during a 112–105 win over Buffalo on October 28, 1976. He also tallied 31 points, in leading the Celtics to a 103–101 victory over the Denver Nuggets on December 26, before hitting for another 31 points during a 105–98 loss to the Golden State Warriors on January 2, 1977.

Scott, though, turned in his two most significant performances as a member of the Celtics during the 1976 playoffs, with the first of those coming in Game 6 of the Eastern Conference Semifinals, when he scored a game-high 31 points, in leading the Celtics to a 104–100 victory over the Buffalo Braves that clinched a berth in the Conference Finals for Boston. Scott came up big for the Celtics again in Game 6 of the NBA Finals, collecting 25 points, 11 rebounds, 5 steals, and 3 assists during Boston's series-clinching 87–80 win over the Phoenix Suns.

Scott's exceptional performance against Phoenix is covered in some depth in the book, *Make It Count: The Life and Times of Basketball Great Jo Jo White*, where it is revealed that White told his backcourt partner after Boston's marathon triple-overtime win in Game 5, "Charlie, I don't have much left in the tank; we're going to need you tomorrow." Responding fully to White's challenge, Scott later commented, "I was inspired; it lifted me that a player of his caliber had that much faith in me. . . . I cemented myself as a Celtic that day. It was a proud moment and the highlight of my life."

NOTABLE ACHIEVEMENTS

- Averaged more than 17 points per game twice.
- Finished second in NBA in games played (82) in 1975–76.
- 1976 Eastern Conference champion.
- 1976 NBA champion.

37

AVERY BRADLEY

A 6-foot-3-inch, off-the-ball guard who lacked the court vision, ball-handling skills, and outside shot to effectively run an offense when he first entered the league, Avery Bradley spent his first few seasons in Boston making a name for himself with his tenacious defense. Known for hounding his man all over the court, Bradley frustrated even the league's best guards with his ability to apply constant pressure to them. Over time, though, Bradley also developed into a solid offensive player, averaging more than 14 points per game for the Celtics three times in helping them win three division titles and advance to the playoffs on six separate occasions. Having most of his finest seasons in Beantown, Bradley earned All-NBA Defensive honors twice, before being dealt to the Detroit Pistons following the conclusion of the 2016–17 campaign.

Born in Tacoma, Washington, on November 26, 1990, Avery Antonio Bradley Jr. lived a somewhat nomadic existence as a youngster since his father's military career took him all over the country. Eventually returning to Tacoma with his mother and four siblings after his parents divorced in 2001, Bradley starred in basketball at Bellarmine Preparatory School for three years before transferring to Findlay College Prep School in Henderson, Nevada, prior to his senior season. Continuing to excel on the court at Findlay Prep, Bradley earned *Parade* magazine's Player of the Year honors and an invitation to the McDonald's All-American Game, where he won the slam-dunk competition.

Offered an athletic scholarship to the University of Texas at Austin, Bradley averaged 11.6 points per game for the Longhorns as a freshman while also establishing himself as one of the top defensive guards in the nation. Named to the Big 12 All-Rookie Team, Bradley chose to forgo his final three years of college and declare himself eligible for the 2010 NBA Draft, which he entered with the following scouting report affixed to him by DraftExpress: "Bradley's physical tools will never be considered ideal, as he's undersized for an NBA shooting guard, and does not have a great frame to compensate. His wingspan is solid, and he is an above average athlete,

Avery Bradley earned All-NBA Defensive honors twice for Celtic teams that won three division titles and advanced to the playoffs six times. Courtesy of Keith Allison and All-Pro Reels Photography.

though, being extremely quick and fluid in the open floor. Offensively, Bradley is mostly a role-player for this deep and experienced Texas squad, something he appears to have no issues with. He gets most of his production spotting up on the wings, operating in transition, and creating his own shot from time to time, looking far more efficient and disciplined than your typical freshman guard."

Ultimately selected by Boston in the first round with the 19th overall pick, Bradley ended up splitting his first pro season between the Celtics and their NBA Development League affiliate, the Maine Red Claws, averaging just 5.2 minutes per game and hitting on only 34 percent of his shots from the field in his 31 contests with the parent club.

Realizing that he needed to further develop his offensive skills, Bradley worked almost exclusively on his weaknesses during the lockout in 2011, training in Las Vegas, Seattle, and Austin, before spending a month playing with Hapoel Migdal in Israel. Returning to Boston much more self-assured when play resumed in late December, Bradley said of his time in Israel, "It did a lot for my confidence. Last year, when I shot, I didn't even think it was going in. I knew it was off. Now, I really believe that everything is going in."

Appearing in all but 2 of the 66 games the Celtics played in 2011–12, Bradley started 28 contests averaging 7.6 points per game, and successfully converting just under 50 percent of his field-goal attempts. Meanwhile, Bradley began to make a name for himself as one of the league's toughest man-to-man defenders, with LeBron James saying during the latter stages of the campaign, "He's one of the best guys that we've seen. As far as [guarding his man] from baseline to baseline, he's really good. . . . He brings another dynamic to their team that they have used and works for them."

Despite missing 31 games due to injury in 2012–13, Bradley did an excellent job after he joined Rajon Rondo in the starting backcourt, averaging 9.2 points, 2.1 assists, and 1.3 steals per contest, while also earning NBA All-Defensive Second-Team honors. Still, Bradley's 40 percent shooting from the field left something to be desired. Bradley again missed a significant amount of playing time in 2013–14, appearing in only 60 games due to a sprained ankle. Nevertheless, he had his finest season to date, averaging 14.9 points, 1.4 assists, 1.1 steals, and 3.8 rebounds per contest, while hitting 43.8 percent of his shots from the field. Healthy for the entire 2014–15 campaign, Bradley averaged 13.9 points, 1.8 assists, 3.1 rebounds, and 1.1 steals per game, before posting marks of 15.2 points, 2.1 assists, 2.9 rebounds, and 1.5 steals per contest the following season, when he earned his lone NBA All-Defensive First-Team nomination.

Praising Bradley for his outstanding all-around play in 2015–16, Celtics head coach Brad Stevens said, "If you look at kind of the arc of his efficiency over the last four years, he's really risen, and he continues that rise. And that's his hard work, that's his commitment to getting better."

Denver Nuggets head coach Mike Malone commented, "Avery Bradley might be one of the most underrated players in the NBA."

Meanwhile, the 6-foot-3, 185-pound Bradley continued to draw praise for his exceptional work on defense, with Charlotte Hornets point guard Kemba Walker stating, "He's probably, if not the best, one of the best on-ball defenders in our league. He's one of those guys where, 'Damn, you got to play against him tonight?' He's like the perfect defender. When you teach defense, he's the guy that would like to learn from. . . . He knows the coverages. He knows the plays. His body position. He's just a great on-ball defender. He's hungry, and a lot of defense is about pride and wanting to do it. He's that guy. He wants to play defense. He loves to play defense. He's really good at it."

Nuggets point guard Emmanuel Mudiay added, "I think he [Bradley] is the best defender I ever played. No disrespect to anybody around the league, but he's so feisty, man."

Claiming that he developed his fondness for playing defense at an early age, Bradley said, "If you had a tape of me from the first grade, you would see a kid playing defense. It's just a gift. A lot of coaches tell you that you're not going to get on the floor if you can't play defense. I just smile and say, 'Well, I guess I'm going to play then.'"

Bradley continued, "Go ask John Wall the first time he played Avery Bradley in high school. We were 15 years old. He's going to say I was the same exact way. I picked up full court the entire game. That's just me."

Suggesting that Bradley's aggressive style of play rubbed off on his teammates, Hornets coach Steve Clifford stated, "When you take someone like Bradley that's elite at what he does, it can have a profound impact on the other players. . . . And he, in my opinion, is a lot more than a defensive specialist. I mean, he's 39 percent from three [point range]. If you go back through his career, he's had a number of absolutely enormous offensive games where they were playing to make the playoffs. I think he's one of what you have to have today to win, which is a two-way player. His defense can be good, but he's also a terrific offensive player."

Although a right Achilles injury limited Bradley to just 55 games in 2016–17, he had arguably his finest statistical season, averaging 16.3 points, 6.1 rebounds, 2.2 assists, and 1.2 steals per contest, while also shooting just over 46 percent from the field and 39 percent from three-point range. Nevertheless, with the Celtics needing to clear salary cap space to make way for signing Gordon Hayward to a max contract, they completed a trade with the Pistons on July 7, 2017, that sent Bradley to Detroit for Marcus Morris.

Expressing his appreciation to Bradley for everything he brought to the team during his seven seasons in Boston, Celtics President of Basketball Operations Danny Ainge said upon completion of the deal, "It's no secret that Avery had been one of my favorite players, and on behalf of our entire organization, I'd like to thank him and Ashley for all of their contributions on and off the court. Avery did a lot of the dirty work and often didn't get the recognition that he deserved, but our coaches, staff, his teammates, and our fans who watched him play every night appreciated what a special player and person he is."

Meanwhile, Bradley accepted his impending departure with grace and dignity, stating, "I kind of knew it could happen. There were conversations that me and Danny Ainge had, but when it does happen, it still catches you off guard a little bit destination-wise, where you end up. . . . I know it's part of the business, so I respect their decision, and I know that Danny is going to make the best decision for the Boston Celtics."

Bradley, who left Boston with career totals of 5,008 points, 1,264 rebounds, 703 assists, and 446 steals, averages of 12.1 points, 3.1 rebounds, 1.7 assists, and 1.1 steals per game, a field-goal shooting percentage of 44.2 percent, and a free-throw shooting percentage of 77.2 percent, ended up appearing in just 40 games with the Pistons, averaging 15 points per contest, before being included in a six-player trade they completed with the Los Angeles Clippers on January 29, 2018. After finishing out the year in Los Angeles, Bradley assumed a part-time role with five different teams from 2018–22, never averaging more than 30 minutes or 9.9 points per game. Released by the Los Angeles Lakers following the conclusion of the 2021–22 campaign, Bradley has yet to catch on with any other team as of this writing. If he never appears in another NBA game, Bradley will end his career with 7,279 points scored, 1,863 rebounds, 1,105 assists, 655 steals, averages of 11.0 points, 2.8 rebounds, 1.7 assists, and 1.0 steal per contest, and a field-goal shooting percentage of 43.4 percent.

Although Bradley spent much of his youth living on the West Coast and played for both Los Angeles teams during the latter stages of his career, he considers his years in Boston to be among his happiest, saying, "It's different, but I prefer my people on the East Coast. Some people might be offended by that, but I mean, especially knowing I'm from the West Coast. I don't know if it's because it's home for me or what, but I just feel like people are real good friends. That's all it is. I could go years without talking to someone in Boston but when I see them, it's a real friendship. People are honest, that's the culture. East Coast, but specifically Boston. People are just good people."

CELTICS CAREER HIGHLIGHTS

Best Season

Although limited by injuries to just 55 games in 2016–17, Bradley had his finest all-around season as a member of the Celtics, helping to lead them to their first division title in five years by posting career-best marks with 16.3 points and 6.1 rebounds per game.

Memorable Moments / Greatest Performances

Bradley helped lead the Celtics to a 111-99 win over the Cleveland Cavaliers on April 12, 2014, by scoring a game-high 25 points and grabbing eight rebounds, with five of his nine baskets coming from three-point range.

Bradley contributed to a 108-97 victory over the Knicks on February 3, 2015, by scoring 26 points on 11-of-14 shooting from the field.

In addition to scoring 23 points during a 115-110 win over the Phoenix Suns on February 23, 2015, Bradley recorded a career-high six steals.

Bradley led the Celtics to a 116-104 victory over the Charlotte Hornets on March 30, 2015, by scoring a game-high 30 points and pulling down eight rebounds.

Bradley gave the Celtics a 104-103 win over Cleveland on February 5, 2016, by hitting a three-pointer from the corner at the buzzer.

Bradley torched the Hornets again on October 29, 2016, scoring 31 points and grabbing 11 rebounds during a 104-98 Celtics win, hitting on 8 of his 11 attempts from three-point range.

Bradley came up big for the Celtics in Game 5 of the 2017 NBA Eastern Conference Semifinals, scoring a game-high 29 points and collecting six rebounds during a 123-101 win over the Washington Wizards.

Bradley came through in the clutch again in Game 3 of the 2017 NBA Eastern Conference Finals, giving the Celtics a 111-108 victory over Cleveland that marked their only win of the series by hitting a three-pointer as time expired in regulation.

NOTABLE ACHIEVEMENTS

- Averaged more than 15 points per game twice.
- 2015–16 NBA All-Defensive First-Team selection.
- 2012–13 NBA All-Defensive Second-Team selection.
- Three-time Atlantic Division champion (2010–11, 2011–12, and 2016–17).

38

DEE BROWN

People had expectations before I got hurt. Now that the injury comes, it sets me back a little with my progress as a player, but that's not going to stop me. I just have to keep plugging away. I think it's just going to take some more time for me to get to where I want to be.

—Dee Brown

Although best remembered by fans of the game for winning the 1991 NBA Slam Dunk Contest with an astonishing "no-look" slam he delivered while covering his eyes, Dee Brown also proved to be a major contributor to the Celtics during his seven and a half seasons in Boston, doing a solid job at both guard positions. Spending a significant amount of time both starting and coming off the bench during his time in Beantown, Brown averaged more than 15 points and 5 assists per game two times each for the Celtics, leading them in scoring once, while annually placing among the team leaders in assists. Yet, had it not been for a severe knee injury he suffered just prior to the start of his second year in the league, Brown likely would have accomplished considerably more during his NBA career.

Born in Jacksonville, Florida, on November 29, 1968, DeCovan Kadell Brown attended local Bolles High School before continuing his education in his home state by accepting an athletic scholarship to Jacksonville University. After earning First-Team All-Sun Belt Conference honors as a senior at Jacksonville in 1989–90, Brown found himself headed to Boston when the Celtics selected him in the first round of the 1990 NBA Draft, with the 19th overall pick, much to the dismay of Jerry West and the Lakers, who had hoped he would fall to them at number 27.

Joining an aging Boston team that featured veterans Larry Bird, Kevin McHale, and Robert Parish, Brown brought youth, speed, and athleticism to the Celtics, providing them with enthusiasm and a fresh set of legs coming off the bench each night. Appearing in all 82 games for the Celtics as a rookie, Brown averaged 8.7 points, 4.2 assists, and 23.7 minutes per contest, while serving as the primary backup for backcourt starters Reggie Lewis and Brian Shaw. Brown's solid all-around performance earned him a spot on the NBA All-Rookie First-Team. Nevertheless, the highlight of the 6-foot-1 Brown's first season took place during All-Star Weekend, when he won the NBA Slam Dunk Contest by wowing the fans in attendance by using his arm to cover his eyes as he slammed the ball through the hoop.

A willing learner who respected the veteran leadership the Celtics had in place, Brown appeared ready to take his game to the next level in his second season, before he suffered a brutal preseason injury during which he tore cartilage in his left knee. Still, Brown remained positive after undergoing arthroscopic surgery to repair the damaged cartilage, stating at the time, "People had expectations before I got hurt. Now that the injury comes, it sets me back a little with my progress as a player, but that's not going to stop me. I just have to keep plugging away. I think it's just going to take some more time for me to get to where I want to be."

After missing the first four months of the 1991–92 campaign, Brown posted solid numbers upon his return, averaging 11.7 points and 5.3 assists per game over the final 31 contests. He again played well in a backup role the following season, averaging 10.9 points, 5.8 assists, and 1.7 steals per game, before finally breaking into the Boston starting five in 1993–94. One of the few bright spots on a Celtics team that finished the regular season with a record of just 32-50, Brown averaged a team-leading 15.5 points per game in his first year as a starter, while also averaging 4.5 assists per contest. He followed that up by posting averages of 15.6 points and 3.8 assists per game for a Boston squad that won just three more games than it did the previous season.

In spite of the personal success Brown experienced during the mid-1990s, the failures of the Celtics as a team eventually began to weigh on him, as he later revealed when he said, "It was tough, because we had lost Lenny [Len Bias], and then, after Larry retired, we lost Reggie. It was tough because the two superstars who were supposed to carry the franchise for the next 20 years both passed away. And I was kind of stuck here by myself for a period of time. It was tough because we weren't winning."

Adding to Brown's frustration was the fact that the knee injury he suffered at the start of his second season ended up robbing him of much

Dee Brown became an instant celebrity when he won the 1991 NBA Slam Dunk Contest. Photo courtesy of George A. Kitrinos.

of the explosiveness he previously possessed. Although the arthroscopic surgery performed on his knee repaired the damaged cartilage, Brown never fully regained the great quickness and outstanding leaping ability he had displayed as a rookie. He also lost some of the fearlessness he had had when

A knee injury he suffered during the early stages of his career
prevented Dee Brown from ever reaching his full potential.
Photo courtesy of George A. Kitrinos.

he first entered the league, exhibiting more of a tendency to settle for jump
shots rather than taking the ball directly to the basket. As a result, even
though his teammates honored him at one point by naming him captain,
Brown never quite reached the level of excellence some predicted for him
earlier in his career.

Once again assuming the role of a backup in 1995–96, Brown had his last productive season for the Celtics, averaging 10.7 points and 2.2 assists per game, in just under 25 minutes of action per contest. After being sidelined by an injury for much of the ensuing campaign, Brown remained in Boston for the first 41 games of the 1997–98 season before being included in a seven-player trade the Celtics completed with the Toronto Raptors that also sent Chauncey Billups and two lesser players to Toronto for Kenny Anderson, Popeye Jones, and Zan Tabak. Brown left Boston with career totals of 5,512 points, 1,883 assists, 1,302 rebounds, and 675 steals, a 44.8 field-goal shooting percentage, and an 82.9 free-throw shooting percentage. He averaged 11.6 points, 4.0 assists, 2.7 rebounds, and 1.4 steals per game as a member of the Celtics.

Brown spent the next two and a half seasons coming off the bench for the Raptors, playing his best ball for them in 1998–99, when he averaged 11.2 points and 2.9 assists per game. A free agent following the conclusion of the 1999–2000 campaign, Brown signed with the Orlando Magic, for whom he appeared in a total of only 14 games over the course of the next two seasons, before announcing his retirement in 2002. He ended his career with 6,758 points scored, 2,227 assists, 1,569 rebounds, 800 steals, and averages of 11.1 points, 3.7 assists, 2.6 rebounds, and 1.3 steals per game.

Since retiring as an active player, Brown has remained close to the game, first serving as head coach of the WNBA's Orlando Miracle, before assuming the same position with that league's San Antonio Silver Stars. He also briefly served as a studio analyst for ESPN and as head coach of the Springfield Armor, a team in the NBA Developmental League. Brown later worked as an assistant coach for the Detroit Pistons, Sacramento Kings, and Los Angeles Clippers, before becoming the director of University and Athletics Relations at his alma mater, Jacksonville University.

CELTICS CAREER HIGHLIGHTS

Best Season

Brown compiled the best numbers of his career in back-to-back seasons, averaging more than 15 points per game in both 1993–94 and 1994–95. In addition to averaging 15.6 points per contest in the second of those campaigns, Brown recorded 3.8 assists, 3.2 rebounds, and 1.4 steals per game, while also shooting 44.7 percent from the field and 85.2 percent from the free-throw line. However, he posted slightly better overall numbers in

1993–94, concluding the campaign with averages of 15.5 points and 4.5 assists per contest while establishing career-high marks in rebounding (3.9 rpg), steals (2.0 spg), and field-goal shooting percentage (48%).

Memorable Moments / Greatest Performances

Brown surpassed the 20-point mark for the first time in his career on March 4, 1991, when he scored 22 points and handed out 7 assists during a 126–101 win over the Indiana Pacers.

Brown played a tremendous all-around game against Washington on November 25, 1992, contributing 22 points, 16 assists, and 4 steals during a 150–112 blowout of the Bullets.

Later that season, on February 16, 1993, Brown scored 15 points and recorded a career-high 18 assists during a 110–97 loss to the Phoenix Suns.

Brown topped 30 points for the first time in his career on December 13, 1993, when he hit for 35 points during a 112–107 win over the Philadelphia 76ers. He surpassed that mark later in the season, leading the Celtics to a 123–117 overtime victory over the Bullets on March 24, 1994, by tallying 38 points. Brown also recorded 7 rebounds and 7 assists during the contest. However, Brown turned in his most dominant performance of the season nearly one month later on April 22, when he scored 40 points during a 104–94 win over the Chicago Bulls.

Brown established a new career high in scoring on February 21, 1995, when he tallied 41 points during a 129–121 victory over Phoenix. He equaled that mark some five weeks later, on March 28, when he led the Celtics to a 126–115 win over the Bulls by again hitting for 41 points.

Nevertheless, Brown will always be remembered most for the extraordinary dunk he delivered during the 1991 NBA Slam Dunk Contest in which he covered his eyes with his forearm as he went soaring through the air toward the basket. Reflecting back on the maneuver that ended up clinching the competition for him, Brown revealed, "The first time that I did it was during the dunk contest; never practiced it. I didn't figure I was going to do that dunk until I was running toward the basket. I pretty much knew I already won the dunk contest. So I wanted to do a signature dunk. I wanted something that everyone would remember me by."

Brown continued: "As I was jumping, my hand going, my arm going, my eyes closing, and it was the first time I ever did that dunk. I was either going to make it and have people talk about me now, or I miss it and guess what and talk about it now. People would be like, 'Remember that guy that ran into the side of the backboard?' That would have been me, so never practiced it at all."

Yet, when asked to name the one thing in his career that meant the most to him, Brown responded:

People would assume it would be the dunk contest because it was an individual event. I think the really big thing that drove me and stands out was when I got drafted. To hear Red Auerbach say your name. To hear him say, "We are taking a 6-foot-2 guard from Jacksonville, Dee Brown." It is Red Auerbach . . . He has said everybody's name. Every guy that he had drafted over that 30-year time came out of his mouth. To be a part of that group, and that guy wanted you, the greatest coach of all time, to make sure that you are a part of that franchise. He wanted you to be a part of that Celtics history and Celtic pride. Just to hear him say that and be around him for so many years was such a great feeling.

NOTABLE ACHIEVEMENTS

- Averaged more than 15 points per game twice.
- Averaged more than 5 assists per game twice.
- Led NBA in games played once.
- Led Celtics in scoring average once (15.5 ppg in 1993–94).
- Ranks seventh in Celtics history in steals (675).
- 1990–91 NBA All-Rookie First-Team selection.
- 1991 NBA Slam Dunk Contest champion.

39

DINO RADJA

I was playing well. I was making a great salary in Europe. The thing about playing in the NBA was that there were so many unknowns. The NBA was more physical because the players were bigger and stronger than in Europe. I also would have had to get used to an entirely different culture.

—Dino Radja

is arrival in Boston coinciding with the beginning of arguably the darkest period in Celtics history, Dino Radja experienced very little in the way of team success during his time in Beantown. Nevertheless, after spending the previous few seasons starring in Europe, Radja demonstrated that his game translated well to the NBA, averaging more than 15 points and 8 rebounds per game three times each in his four years with the Celtics, while also shooting better than 50 percent from the field twice. During that time, Radja established himself as one of the best European players to enter the league during the 1990s, before knee problems hastened his departure from the NBA, forcing him to return to Europe, where he spent his final few seasons competing against lesser talent.

Born in Split, Croatia, on April 24, 1967, Dino Radja grew up in a war-torn territory that later experienced bombing at the hands of the Serbs. Developing his basketball skills while playing high school ball at local Technical School Ctr, Radja subsequently began his professional career with KK Split, before serving as a member of the 1988 Yugoslavian National Team that won Silver at the Olympic Games. After spending the 1988–89 campaign playing for Jugoplastika Split, who he helped lead to the Yugoslavian national championship and the European Championship

Knee problems hastened Dino Radja's departure from the NBA, forcing him to return to Europe after just four seasons.
Photo courtesy of George A. Kitrinos.

Cup Tournament title, Radja became the center of controversy when the Boston Celtics selected him in the second round of the 1989 NBA Draft, with the 40th overall pick.

Although Radja initially expressed interest in playing in the United States if he received proper compensation for his services, Jugoplastika general manager Josip Bilić refused to release him from the four-year contract he had signed with the Yugoslavian team one year earlier. With the two sides spending the next several weeks squabbling over his status, Radja finally decided to take matters into his own hands, traveling to the United States in early August 1989 and inking a one-year deal with the Celtics for a reported $500,000. However, the Split club ultimately obtained an injunction from the US District Court for the District of Massachusetts that prevented Radja from playing for Boston since he already had a valid and legally binding contract with Jugoplastika. Three months later, Jugoplastika and the Celtics agreed that Radja would return to Yugoslavia for one more season, with the understanding that his rights would be transferred to the Celtics effective June 1, 1990. Boston, in turn, paid an undisclosed sum to Jugoplastika for allowing Radja to be released from the terms of his contract two years early.

Upon returning to Split, Radja led Jugoplastika to its third consecutive Yugoslav League title and its second straight European Cup. But instead of joining the Celtics following the conclusion of the 1989–90 campaign, the 23-year-old center / power forward instead elected to sign with money-rich Virtus Roma when the Italian team offered him a five-year deal worth somewhere between $15 million and $18 million. Explaining several years later his decision to remain in Europe, even though he earlier seemed intent on playing in the NBA, Radja said, "I was playing well. I was making a great salary in Europe. The thing about playing in the NBA was that there were so many unknowns. The NBA was more physical because the players were bigger and stronger than in Europe. I also would have had to get used to an entirely different culture."

Although the Celtics did not insist on Radja honoring his contract with them, they retained his NBA rights, which proved to be crucial when he eventually decided to leave Italy after just three seasons. After helping Croatia win a silver medal at the 1992 Olympics in Barcelona, Radja spent one more year in Europe, averaging 21.5 points per game for Virtus Roma in 1992–93, before returning to the United States and signing a three-year deal with the Celtics.

After finally joining the Celtics prior to the start of the 1993–94 campaign, the 6-foot-11, 250-pound Radja made a favorable impression on his new coach and teammates in training camp. Head coach Chris Ford, who earlier suggested to the 26-year-old rookie that he relax and use his large frame to create shots for himself under the basket, said, "He's been a very pleasant surprise. He's got good moves around the basket, he's strong, his fundamentals are sound, he can shoot facing the basket, he can pass, he can rebound, and he's a big guy."

Celtics forward Ed Pinckney added, "He goes after balls. I always look for that in a player. His drive is impressive."

Meanwhile, Boston general manager Dave Gavitt contended that Radja and fellow Croatian Toni Kukoc were the two best players in Europe, stating, "If Dino was in the draft this year, he would have been a lottery pick."

Nevertheless, Radja remained somewhat concerned over the NBA's physical style of play, suggesting, "Here, in the NBA, there is no foul except when somebody kills you. If you stay on the floor with blood dripping, then they call foul. It's rougher than in Europe."

In spite of his initial reservations, Radja quickly adapted to the American game, earning a spot on the NBA All-Rookie Second Team by averaging 15.1 points and 7.2 rebounds per game, while shooting 52.1 percent from the field. After starting off the season coming off the bench, Radja eventually won a starting job, finishing second on the team in scoring, while leading the club in rebounding and blocked shots. Although limited by knee problems to 66 games the following season, Radja improved upon his overall performance, posting averages of 17.2 points, 8.7 rebounds, and 1.3 blocked shots per contest. Hampered once again by injuries in 1995–96, Radja appeared in only 53 games. Yet, he still managed to lead the Celtics with averages of 19.7 points, 9.8 rebounds, and 1.5 blocked shots per game, while hitting on 50 percent of his shots from the field.

Playing both the center and power forward positions during his time in Boston, Radja possessed good size and strength, sound fundamentals, solid rebounding skills, and an outstanding post-up game, playing equally well facing the basket or with his back to it. Perhaps his greatest assets, though, were his speed and athleticism, which frequently enabled him to beat his defender down court.

Knee problems continued to plague Radja in 1996–97, with a left knee injury sidelining him for all but 25 games. Forced to undergo arthroscopic surgery in January 1997, Radja contributed little to a Celtics team that finished with the worst record in the Eastern Conference—a mark of 15-67 that prompted management to replace M. L. Carr with Rick Pitino as head coach.

Traded to Philadelphia for Clarence Weatherspoon and Michael Cage during the subsequent off-season, Radja balked at the idea of going to the 76ers, since, according to an Associated Press story, he wanted "to be sent to a warm climate and a playoff contender." Furthermore, Radja felt betrayed by new Celtics head coach Rick Pitino, who he later said misled him. Speaking in a 2005 interview, Radja recalled:

> I went to Pitino and asked him if I fit into his plans. With a new coach, I obviously wanted to know what he thought of my game. I loved playing for Boston and just wanted to find out if there was any possibility I might be traded, because I had heard some rumors. Pitino looked me right in the eyes and said, "Dino, don't worry. You're going to be a big part of our offense. When we run a set play, the ball is going to go through you." I left the meeting feeling great. Five days later, I found out I was being traded to Philadelphia. I can't tell you how much I felt betrayed. Either Pitino lied, or something changed in a matter of a few days.

As things turned out, though, Radja never ended up playing for the 76ers, since he failed his physical after team doctors determined that he had no cartilage remaining in his left knee. With the general consensus being that Radja no longer possessed the ability to sustain the rigors of an NBA season, he reached an agreement with the Celtics in which the team bought out the three remaining years of his contract, enabling him to return to Europe. Radja left Boston with NBA career totals of 3,733 points scored, 1,883 rebounds, 356 assists, and 282 blocked shots, a field-goal shooting percentage of 49.7, and a free-throw shooting percentage of 73.5. In his four seasons with the Celtics, he averaged 16.7 points, 8.4 rebounds, 1.6 assists, and 1.3 blocked shots per game.

After returning to Europe, Radja played another six seasons, splitting his time between five different teams in two different countries—Greece and Croatia. He won two Greek championships as a member of Panathinaikos BC, before retiring following the conclusion of the 2002–03 campaign, after spending his final season with his first professional team, Croatia's KK Split. Since retiring as a player, Radja has served as president of KK Split.

CELTICS CAREER HIGHLIGHTS

Best Season

It could be argued that Radja made his greatest overall impact in Boston in his rookie campaign of 1993–94 due to the fact that he appeared in 80 of

Radja averaged more than 15 points and 8 rebounds per game in each of his first three seasons with the Celtics. Photo courtesy of George A. Kitrinos.

the Celtics' 82 games, while shooting a career-best 52.1 percent from the field and averaging 15.1 points, 7.2 rebounds, 1.4 assists, and .8 blocked shots per contest. However, even though Radja missed 16 games the following season, he compiled better overall numbers, averaging 17.2 points, 8.7

rebounds, 1.7 assists, and 1.3 blocked shots per contest. Nevertheless, the feeling here is that each of those seasons must take a backseat to 1995–96, when Radja clearly played his best ball for the Celtics. Despite missing approximately a third of the season, Radja posted career-high marks in scoring (19.7 ppg) and rebounding (9.8 rpg) while averaging 1.6 assists and 1.5 blocked shots per game and shooting 50 percent from the field. And, even though Radja appeared in only 53 of Boston's 82 contests, he started 52 of those, averaging just over 37 minutes per game, with both figures surpassing the marks he posted in each of the two previous campaigns.

Memorable Moments / Greatest Performances

Radja turned in a pair of tremendous all-around performances as a rookie, with the first of those coming on March 4, 1994, when he scored a career-high 36 points and pulled down 15 rebounds during a 109–99 win over the Lakers. Radja connected on 15 of 22 shots from the field during the contest, while also successfully converting 6 of 8 free-throw attempts. He equaled that career-high scoring total some three weeks later, on March 27, when he led the Celtics to a 124–122 overtime victory over the 76ers by scoring 36 points, collecting 11 rebounds, and assisting on 5 baskets. Radja proved to be even more accurate during that contest, shooting 12 of 15 from the field and 12 of 12 from the free-throw line.

Radja played his best all-around game the following season on November 16, 1994, when he tallied 28 points, pulled down 15 rebounds, collected 3 assists, blocked 4 shots, and recorded 4 steals during a 120–93 rout of the Seattle SuperSonics.

Radja turned in his two most dominant performances of the 1995–96 campaign a little over two weeks apart, hitting for 29 points and collecting 15 rebounds during a 100–96 win over the Detroit Pistons on November 29, 1995, before leading the Celtics to a 122–103 victory over the Toronto Raptors on December 15 by scoring 31 points and pulling down 14 rebounds.

Although Radja appeared in only 25 contests in his final NBA season, he had a pair of big games, with the first of those coming on November 15, 1996, when he scored 16 points, collected 15 rebounds, and recorded a career-high 7 blocked shots during an 82–80 loss to the Denver Nuggets. Nearly one month later, on December 11, Radja led the Celtics to a 115–113 triple-overtime victory over Toronto by scoring 13 points and pulling down a career-high 20 rebounds.

NOTABLE ACHIEVEMENTS

- Averaged more than 15 points per game three times, topping 19 points per contest once.
- Averaged more than 8 rebounds per game three times, topping 9 boards per contest once.
- Shot better than 50 percent from the field twice.
- Led Celtics in: scoring average once; blocked shots once; and rebounding three times.

40

LARRY SIEGFRIED

What we represented was not about statistics and not about money. It was about being a family. There was a sense of brotherhood on our team.

—Larry Siegfried

An outstanding role player known for his suffocating defense and mistake-free ball-handling, Larry Siegfried proved to be a key member of Celtics teams that won five NBA championships during his seven years in Boston. Capable of manning either guard position, Siegfried teamed up at different times with Sam Jones, K. C. Jones, John Havlicek, and Jo Jo White, providing instant offense off the bench before eventually earning a starting job in the Celtics backcourt. Although Siegfried assumed a starter's minutes in just two of his seven seasons in Boston, he averaged more than 12 points per game five straight times, finished second on the team in assists twice, and led the NBA in free-throw shooting percentage on two separate occasions. An extremely intelligent player, Siegfried also contributed to the Celtics with his deep understanding of the game, becoming in his last few seasons in Boston the team's de facto offensive coordinator.

Born in Shelby, Ohio, on May 22, 1939, Larry E. Siegfried attended Shelby High School, where he led the entire state of Ohio in scoring as a senior, setting in the process a state record that still stands by scoring 176 points in one month. After enrolling at Ohio State University, Siegfried continued his high-scoring ways until he adjusted his game in his junior year to compensate for the arrivals of standout sophomores Jerry Lucas, John Havlicek, and Mel Nowell. Concentrating more his final two seasons

Larry Siegfried (far right) celebrates victory over the Lakers in the 1965 NBA Finals with Celtics teammates. Photo courtesy of MearsOnlineAuctions.com.

on shutting down his man on the defensive end of the floor, Siegfried played a key role in helping the Buckeyes capture the 1960 NCAA title, serving as co-captain of the school's National Championship squad. Legendary coach Bobby Knight, who served as a backup on the team, later said of his former teammate, "I never saw a better guard in the Big Ten than Larry Siegfried. He was a great player. He was tough as hell. He was physical; he could jump . . . If I had my choice of any guard who played in the Big Ten when I coached and everything else, I'd have a hard time picking someone else."

Despite being overshadowed somewhat as a senior by his All-American teammate Jerry Lucas, Siegfried served as captain of the Ohio State team that went undefeated until losing to Cincinnati in the NCAA Final. Yet, even though Siegfried generally took a backseat to Lucas during the season, he earned All-America and All-Big Ten honors, prompting the Cincinnati Royals to select him with the third overall pick of the 1961 NBA Draft. However, still bitter over the University of Cincinnati's victory over his beloved Buckeyes in that year's national title game, Siegfried instead chose to sign with the Cleveland Pipers of the newly formed American Basketball League.

Siegfried subsequently spent his first two seasons in professional ball in Cleveland, serving as a backup to Dick Barnett and Connie Dierking on the Pipers team that won the ABL title in 1962. But, with the league folding midway through the ensuing campaign, Siegfried soon found himself without a job, forcing him to sit out the remainder of the year. After the NBA's St. Louis Hawks acquired his rights from Cincinnati, Siegfried fully expected to resume his career in St. Louis. However, the Hawks cut him in training camp due to a surplus of guards, prompting him to briefly consider leaving the game for good.

To the rescue, though, came Siegfried's former college teammate, John Havlicek, who convinced Red Auerbach to give him a tryout. Matched up against Tommy Heinsohn in his Celtics audition, Siegfried fared quite well, making an extremely favorable impression on the Boston forward, who later said that Siegfried was the only player at that time who had the ability to outplay him, one-on-one. In fact, Heinsohn eventually came to spend most of his time in practice scrimmaging against Siegfried, choosing to do so because he said, "Larry offers everything a player needs for opposition— scrap, ability, maneuverability, courage, and shooting ability." Heeding the advice of Heinsohn, who told him, "It would be a mistake to cut such a talent," Auerbach signed the 24-year-old guard to a contract, after which Siegfried spent the remainder of the 1963–64 season serving as the Celtics' 12th man.

Siegfried gradually worked his way into a far more prominent role on the team over the course of the next two seasons, establishing himself as one of Auerbach's most reliable backups by his third year in Boston. After averaging just 6.3 points, 1.7 assists, and close to 14 minutes per game in 1964–65, Siegfried posted marks of 13.7 points and 2.3 assists per contest the following season, in nearly 24 minutes of action. He also led the NBA in free-throw shooting percentage for the first of two times, hitting on just over 88 percent of his shots from the foul line.

Siegfried's solid shooting and deft ball-handling gave him the ability to play either guard position, making him extremely valuable to the Celtics coming off the bench. He also did an outstanding job of sticking to his man on defense, demonstrating his appreciation for the more subtle aspects of the game by suggesting on one occasion, "You can tell a lot about a man just by seeing him box out."

Siegfried's role on the team continued to expand after Bill Russell took over as head coach prior to the start of the 1966–67 campaign. In addition to appreciating all the things the 6-foot-3, 190-pound guard brought to the table as a player, Russell also came to depend heavily on Siegfried for his intelligence and deep understanding of the game. Blessed with, in the words of Red Auerbach, "one of the sharpest basketball minds I've ever come across," Siegfried was often sought out by Russell for his counsel and suggestions, frequently drawing up plays that the Celtics used at critical moments of contests.

Although the Celtics failed to capture the NBA title in Russell's first year as player-coach, Siegfried had one of his finest statistical seasons, concluding the 1966–67 campaign with averages of 14.1 points and 3.4 assists per game, while shooting a career-high 44.2 percent from the field. Following the retirement of K. C. Jones at season's end, Siegfried became a starter for the first time in his career—a role he maintained for the next two seasons. During that time, he helped the Celtics win back-to-back championships, posting averages of 12.2 points and 4.7 assists per game in his first year as a starter before averaging 14.2 points and 4.7 assists per contest in 1968–69. Siegfried also led the NBA in free-throw shooting percentage in the second of those campaigns, hitting on 86.4 percent of his foul shots.

Siegfried spent one more year in Boston, averaging 12.6 points and 3.8 assists per game in 1969–70, while sharing playing time at the point guard position with promising rookie Jo Jo White. Subsequently left unprotected in the 1970 expansion draft, Siegfried found himself selected by the Portland Trail Blazers, who immediately traded him to the San Diego Rockets for guard Jim Barnett. Siegfried spent one full season in San Diego, averaging 8 points and 6.5 assists per game for the Rockets in 1970–71, before joining the Atlanta Hawks early the following year after the Rockets and Hawks worked out a four-player trade on November 9, 1971. Having spent the remainder of the season serving as a reserve in Atlanta, Siegfried elected to announce his retirement following the conclusion of the campaign, ending his career with 5,960 points scored, 1,950 assists, 1,567 rebounds, a 10.8 scoring average, and averages of 3.5 assists and 2.8 rebounds per game. He also shot 40.9 percent from the field and 85.4 percent from the free-throw line over the course of his career. Siegfried's Celtic numbers include 5,420 points scored, 1,532 assists, 1,318 rebounds, and averages of 11.6 points, 3.3 assists, and 2.8 rebounds per contest.

Speaking wistfully of his time in Boston, Siegfried suggested, "What we represented was not about statistics and not about money. It was about being a family. There was a sense of brotherhood on our team."

Following his retirement, Siegfried spent most of his time giving motivational speeches, while also coaching and counseling prisoners at Mansfield Correctional Institution in Ohio. He passed away at the age of 71, on October 14, 2010, nine days after suffering a heart attack.

Looking back at the career of Siegfried, *Boston Globe* writer Bob Ryan once said, "Larry Siegfried possessed two qualities that can never be taught. He was smart, and he was tough. He was not a star, but he was something better. He was a Celtic."

CELTICS CAREER HIGHLIGHTS

Best Season

Siegfried posted the most impressive stat line of his career in 1968–69, when he averaged 14.2 points, 4.7 assists, and 3.6 rebounds per game, while leading the NBA with an 86.4 free-throw shooting percentage. However, he shot just 38 percent from the field, which represented his lowest mark since his rookie season of 1963–64. Siegfried actually performed more efficiently over the course of the 1966–67 campaign—his final season before becoming a starter. Despite averaging just under 26 minutes per contest, Siegfried posted averages of 14.1 points, 3.4 assists, and 3.1 rebounds per game, while shooting 84.7 percent from the free-throw line and a career-best 44.2 percent from the field.

Memorable Moments / Greatest Performances

Siegfried had his breakout game for the Celtics early in his second season in Boston, scoring 17 points during a 131–103 blowout of the Baltimore Bullets on October 24, 1964. He reached the 20-point mark for the first time in his career nearly three weeks later, tallying 20 points during a 110–84 win over the San Francisco Warriors on November 11.

Siegfried turned in a number of outstanding performances the following season, with his first such effort coming on December 7, 1965, when he scored 31 points, in helping the Celtics defeat St. Louis by a score of 112–96. Nearly two months later, on February 1, 1966, Siegfried hit for a career-high 39 points, in leading the Celtics to a 100–81 win over the Detroit Pistons. The following month, Siegfried put together a pair of 29-point games just six days apart, scoring 29 points during a lopsided 129–98 victory over the Baltimore Bullets on March 13, before duplicating that effort during a 126–113 win over the Knicks on March 19.

Siegfried went on the greatest scoring binge of his career during the latter stages of the 1966–67 campaign, recording at least 25 points in seven of the nine games the Celtics played between February 17 and March 3,

1967. After beginning his exceptional run by scoring a season-high 32 points during a hard-fought 120–119 victory over the Lakers on February 17, Siegfried hit for 28 points six days later, in leading the Celtics to a 122–117 win over the Knicks. He had another big game on March 2, tallying 31 points during a 114–108 victory over the Chicago Bulls before concluding his outstanding stretch of games the following evening with a 29-point performance that helped the Celtics defeat the Cincinnati Royals by a score of 111–104.

Siegfried also proved to be a significant contributor to the Celtics in postseason play, excelling against the Lakers in both the 1968 and 1969 NBA Finals. After scoring 26 points in Boston's 127–119 win over Los Angeles in Game 3 of the 1968 Finals, Siegfried tallied another 22 points in Game 6, to help the Celtics clinch the series with a 124–109 victory. The following year, Siegfried scored at least 20 points against the Lakers in three straight games in the Finals, with arguably the most important outing of his career coming in Game 3, when he helped the Celtics get back in the series by scoring 28 points during Boston's 111–105 win.

NOTABLE ACHIEVEMENTS

- Shot better than 85 percent from the free-throw line four times.
- Led NBA in free-throw shooting percentage twice.
- Ranks 10th in Celtics history in career free-throw shooting percentage (85.5%).
- Five-time Eastern Division champion (1964, 1965, 1966, 1968, and 1969).
- Five-time NBA champion (1964, 1965, 1966, 1968, and 1969).

41
JIM LOSCUTOFF

I'll tell you what type of player I was. If somebody stood in my way, I'd knock them down. Even if they didn't stand in my way, but if they were bothering another player, they'd have to deal with me. Red [Auerbach] didn't tell me to play that way. I knew that was my role.

—Jim Loscutoff

Known affectionately to his teammates and Celtic fans as "Loscy" (pronounced LAH-skee), Jim Loscutoff spent nine years in Boston serving as head coach Red Auerbach's primary enforcer for much of that time. A strong physical presence under the boards and on defense, the 6-foot-5, 225-pound Loscutoff did much of the "dirty work" for Celtics teams that won seven NBA titles between 1956 and 1964, throwing his weight around and serving as bodyguard for Bob Cousy, Bill Sharman, and several of the squad's other more talented players. By doing so, the burly forward sacrificed much of his own game, rarely allowing him to display the kind of ability that enabled him to lead the Oregon Ducks in both scoring and rebounding as a senior in college. Loscutoff's sense of self-sacrifice endeared him to everyone in Boston, prompting the Celtics to eventually honor him by adding a banner with his nickname Loscy to the retired-number banners hanging from the rafters at the Boston Garden.

Born in San Francisco, California, on February 4, 1930, James Loscutoff Jr. moved with his family some 35 miles south to the city of Palo Alto while still in high school. After earning Peninsula Athletic League Player of the Year honors as a senior at Palo Alto High in 1948, Loscutoff enrolled at Grant Technical College (now known as American River College) in Sacramento County, where he spent the next two years honing his basketball

Jim Loscutoff spent most of his nine seasons in Boston
service as the Celtics' primary "enforcer."
Photo courtesy of LegendaryAuctions.com.

skills before being offered a scholarship to attend the University of Oregon.
Drafted into the US Army after just one year at Oregon, Loscutoff subsequently spent three years playing basketball while fulfilling his military
obligation at Fort Ord, outside Monterey. Returning to Oregon for his
senior year in 1954–55, Loscutoff led the Ducks in scoring (19.6 ppg) and
rebounding (17.2 rpg), setting a single-game school record along the way
by pulling down 32 rebounds against Brigham Young University during a
1955 contest.

Taking note of Loscutoff's strong performance at Oregon, the Celtics
made the 25-year-old forward the third nonterritorial pick (fifth overall)
of the 1955 NBA Draft, selecting him right after the Rochester Royals
tabbed the ill-fated Maurice Stokes with the second pick. Yet, even though

Loscutoff displayed an ability to score at the collegiate level, coach Red Auerbach insisted that he focus on rebounding and defense after he arrived in Boston, since the team badly needed improvement in those two areas.

In discussing the significance of Loscutoff's addition to the team years later, Tommy Heinsohn stated, "Before he showed up, Cousy was our leading rebounder, and he was a point guard, so that should tell you something. He was an important component in establishing that championship team. He was a very good player until he hurt his back."

Averaging just over 22 minutes of playing time as a rookie, Loscutoff contributed 8.3 points and 8.8 rebounds off the bench for a Celtics team that finished second in the NBA's Eastern Division with a record of 39-33. The addition of Bill Russell and Tom Heinsohn the following year gave the Celtics the league's most dominant front line in terms of rebounding. For his part, Loscutoff, who spent time at both forward positions, averaged 10.4 rebounds and 10.6 points per game for the NBA champions, as he saw his playing time increase to nearly 32 minutes per contest. Unfortunately, a bad back limited Loscutoff to only five games the following season, one in which the Celtics eventually lost to the St. Louis Hawks in the NBA Finals.

Returning to the Celtics at the start of the 1958–59 season, Loscutoff found himself sharing playing time with Frank Ramsey at the small forward position. Seeing just over 25 minutes of action per contest, Loscutoff posted averages of 8.3 points and 7 rebounds per game for a Boston team that won the first of eight consecutive championships. More importantly, he assumed the role of team enforcer, dealing out retribution to anyone on the opposing squad who attempted to take liberties with highly skilled teammates such as Bob Cousy and Bill Sharman.

In discussing his role on the club years later, Loscutoff stated, "I'll tell you what type of player I was. If somebody stood in my way, I'd knock them down. Even if they didn't stand in my way, but if they were bothering another player, they'd have to deal with me. Red [Auerbach] didn't tell me to play that way. I knew that was my role."

Loscutoff added, "That's not the way I played in college, but in the pros it was different. I quickly got the reputation as a guy not to mess with."

Expounding upon his former teammate's role, Tommy Heinsohn noted, "He was one of those Phys. Ed. guys—big on push-ups, walking up the ropes, things like that. But he was the policeman on the team. In those days, coaches had a guy on the end of the bench they would send in to go after a star on the other team. There were a lot of fights. It was like hockey back then. So you needed someone to act as a policeman, and that was him."

Fully embracing his now clearly defined role, Loscutoff amassed a total of 285 personal fouls for the 1958–59 NBA champions, fouling out of 15 of the 66 games in which he appeared.

Although Loscutoff never again averaged more than 20 minutes, 5.5 points, or 4.2 rebounds per game in his five remaining seasons in Boston, his toughness and willingness to put aside his personal goals made him a key contributor to Celtics teams that won the NBA title each year. Described by one opposing player as a "hatchet-man," Loscutoff allowed his teammates to focus strictly on basketball, taking it upon himself to deal with any of the other nonsense that transpired on the court.

Reflecting back on his playing days in a June 1985 article that appeared in the *Los Angeles Times*, Loscutoff said, "Geez, it used to be a lot worse. We used to have a lot of fights; real fights. But no one ever made a big deal about it because it happened all the time."

Yet, in that same article, the man longtime Celtics announcer Johnny Most nicknamed "Jungle Jim" admitted, "But I do think the game is more physical today because the athletes are better. When we played, we just banged it out underneath. Now, they can jump so well that they can bang each other around three feet off the ground."

The 34-year-old Loscutoff elected to call it quits following the conclusion of the 1963–64 campaign, ending his career with 3,156 points scored, 2,848 rebounds, a 6.2 scoring average, and a 5.6 rebounding average. The Celtics subsequently expressed their desire to honor him by retiring his number (18). However, Loscutoff asked that his jersey number not be retired so that it might be worn by a future member of the team. Instead, the Celtics added a banner with his nickname (Loscy) to the rafters of the Boston Garden.

Following his playing career, Loscutoff accepted a position at Boston State College, where he spent the next 27 years teaching and coaching basketball. After leaving that post more than two decades ago, he spent his retirement splitting time between his homes in Florida and Massachusetts until December 1, 2015, when he passed away at the age of 85, following complications from pneumonia and Parkinson's disease.

Years after Loscutoff played his last game for the Celtics, he marveled at the impact he seemed to have made on the fans of Boston, stating, "It's unbelievable. I've been out of the game 20 years, and people still call me up and ask me about how many people I hit."

Speaking wistfully of Loscutoff, sportswriter Bob Ryan of the *Boston Globe* said, "You won't see anyone as tough as Loscy anymore. The game has changed too much."

CELTICS CAREER HIGHLIGHTS

Best Season

Loscutoff's second year in the league proved to be easily his finest. Garnering more than 30 minutes of playing time per contest for the only time in his career, Loscutoff concluded that 1956–57 campaign with averages of 10.6 points and 10.4 rebounds per game, placing in the league's top 10 in the last category. He never came close to matching either of those figures in any other season.

Memorable Moments / Greatest Performances

Although not known as a scorer after he joined the Celtics, Loscutoff turned in a number of solid offensive efforts for them, having his breakout game in his rookie campaign of 1955–56, when he scored a team-high 18 points during a 118–102 win over the Minneapolis Lakers on December 10, 1955. Just eight days later, he tallied 20 points for the first time in his career, in helping the Celtics defeat New York by a score of 95–92. Although the Celtics lost to the Philadelphia Warriors by a score of 120–104 on January 23, 1956, Loscutoff scored a season-high 25 points during the contest. Loscutoff, though, turned in his most dominant performance of the season when he established a Celtics record (since broken) by pulling down a career-high 27 rebounds in one game.

Several outstanding performances highlighted Loscutoff's fine 1956–57 season, with the first of those coming on November 17, 1956, when he scored a team-high 20 points during a 108–86 blowout of the Rochester Royals. Less than two weeks later, he scored a career-high 26 points, in leading the Celtics to a 105–93 win over the Minneapolis Lakers. Loscutoff led Boston to victory again on January 10, 1957, when he tallied a game-high 22 points during a 98–81 win over the Fort Wayne Pistons. He continued his strong play 10 days later, when he scored 21 points during a lopsided 114–78 victory over the Knicks. Loscutoff had another big game on February 21, when he helped the Celtics defeat the St. Louis Hawks, 125–112, by scoring 24 points.

In one of his more notable games, Loscutoff had the distinction of committing 5 fouls in one quarter during a 1962 contest.

Despite scoring only 3 points and committing 5 personal fouls during the contest, Loscutoff claims that he will always remember more than any other game Boston's 125–123 double-overtime win over St. Louis in Game

Loscutoff's willingness to make sacrifices for the betterment of the team made him one of the most popular players in franchise history.

7 of the 1957 NBA Finals, stating years later, "I would say that my favorite memory was winning the first world championship."

NOTABLE ACHIEVEMENTS

- Averaged more than 10 rebounds per game once (10.4 in 1956–57).
- Eight-time Eastern Division champion (1957, 1958, 1959, 1960, 1961, 1962, 1963, and 1964).
- Seven-time NBA champion (1957, 1959, 1960, 1961, 1962, 1963, and 1964).

42

GERALD HENDERSON

Henderson often gave the Celtics a spark coming off the bench, using his quickness to blanket whoever he guarded, his solid ball-handling skills to distribute the ball to his teammates, and his accurate outside shot, which he generally released from somewhere in the 16- to 19-foot range, to break down opposing defenses.

A solid but unspectacular player who spent most of his time in Boston coming off the bench, Gerald Henderson nevertheless proved to be a key contributor to two Celtics championship teams. Serving as a backup at different times to Nate Archibald, Dennis Johnson, and Chris Ford, Henderson played both guard positions during his time in Beantown, starting in only his fifth and final season with the Celtics. Still, the 6-foot-2, 175-pound Henderson's speed, quickness, defensive tenacity, and solid ball-handling skills often provided a spark to the Celtics, helping him to ignite the second unit or blend in seamlessly with the starters. Most effective after being inserted as a starter in the backcourt alongside Dennis Johnson prior to the start of the 1983–84 campaign, Henderson averaged 11.6 points and 3.8 assists per game for a Celtics team that went on to win the NBA title. However, the spindly guard likely will always be remembered most by fans of the team for one play he made in that year's NBA Finals that eventually led to the Celtics emerging victorious against their bitter rivals, the Los Angeles Lakers.

Born in Richmond, Virginia, on January 16, 1956, Jerome McKinley Henderson Sr. attended local Huguenot High School before enrolling at Virginia Commonwealth University, where he established himself as one of the finest players in that school's history, becoming the first player ever to

Gerald Henderson's quickness, deft ball-handling,
and defensive tenacity provided a spark to two NBA
championship teams during his time in Boston.

have his jersey retired by the institution. Averaging 15 points per game over
the course of his three seasons at VCU, Henderson earned All-State honors,
prompting the San Antonio Spurs to select him in the third round of the
1978 NBA Draft, with the 64th overall pick. Henderson failed to make the
Spurs roster, however, allowing the Celtics to swoop in and sign him in the
summer of 1979 after San Antonio had waived him the previous fall.

Arriving in Boston the same year as Larry Bird, Henderson gave the
Celtics meaningful minutes off the bench as a rookie, averaging 6.2 points,
1.9 assists, and 14 minutes per game as Nate Archibald's primary backup
at the point guard spot. Although Henderson never averaged more than 23
minutes per contest in any of the next three seasons, he gradually assumed
a more prominent role on the team, filling in at both guard spots while
appearing in every game for the Celtics all three years. Posting his best

numbers during that period in 1981–82, Henderson averaged 10.2 points and 3.1 assists per contest while shooting just over 50 percent from the field—one of three times he topped that mark as a member of the team.

More importantly, Henderson often gave the Celtics a spark coming off the bench, using his quickness to blanket whoever he guarded, his solid ball-handling skills to distribute the ball to his teammates, and his accurate outside shot, which he generally released from somewhere in the 16- to 19-foot range, to break down opposing defenses. An athletic and pesky defender, Henderson often proved to be a nuisance to guards several inches taller than himself. Meanwhile, even though he lacked the playmaking ability of a true point guard, Henderson did a decent job of getting the ball to his teammates in good shooting position.

Finally awarded a starting job prior to the start of the 1983–84 season, Henderson responded by averaging 11.6 points and 3.8 assists per game, while shooting a career-high 52.4 percent from the field. Furthermore, he teamed up with Dennis Johnson to give the Celtics arguably the NBA's best defensive backcourt—a fact he drove home by recording one of the most memorable steals in franchise history in the closing moments of Game 2 of the NBA Finals, when he stole a James Worthy pass and subsequently scored a game-tying layup in a contest the Celtics eventually won in overtime.

His Game 2 heroics notwithstanding, Henderson found himself being traded the following off-season to make room in the starting rotation for Danny Ainge. In exchange for Henderson, the Celtics received a future first-round draft pick from the Seattle SuperSonics, which, through the draft lottery, ended up being the second overall pick of the 1986 draft, which they used to select the ill-fated Len Bias.

Extremely unhappy over the prospect of leaving Boston after agreeing on a new contract with Celtics general manager Jan Volk only months earlier, Henderson expressed his dissatisfaction with the deal shortly thereafter by stating, "I guess they feel I'm not that important to the club. I guess they figure they'll keep one of their rookies. Maybe that way they can lighten their salary load."

Henderson continued, "You hear a lot about the Celtic mystique, loyalty, and family, all that kind of thing. As far as I'm concerned, that's all down the drain. I thought I had one of the more secure positions in the league. So that goes to show you something, doesn't it? It shows you that at any moment, any player can be traded."

He then added, "It's very disappointing. It's still very disappointing. Not just being traded to Seattle. This is a nice city and I like the team.

But it's just the fact of being traded, period. If you're a starter on a world championship team, then . . . I made concessions just to be with the team. Something I really wanted to do was be happy, so I figured I could stay here. I was optimistic about winning another championship. I wouldn't have signed if I knew they were going to trade me; I would've held out even longer."

Henderson left Boston with career totals of 3,521 points scored, 1,107 assists, 638 rebounds, and 418 steals, a 48.9 field-goal shooting percentage, and a 72.8 free-throw shooting percentage. In his five seasons with the Celtics, he averaged 8.8 points, 2.8 assists, 1.6 rebounds, and 1 steal per game.

After leaving Boston, Henderson spent eight more years in the NBA, playing his best ball for Seattle in 1984–85 and 1985–86, when he posted averages of 13.4 points and 7.1 assists per game, and 13.1 points and 5.9 assists per contest, respectively. Traded to the New York Knicks during the early stages of the 1986–87 campaign, Henderson remained a starter one more year, before assuming a backup role the rest of his career, first with the Philadelphia 76ers, and, later, with the Milwaukee Bucks, Detroit Pistons, and Houston Rockets. While serving as a backup for the Pistons in 1990, Henderson won his third NBA title.

Henderson announced his retirement following the conclusion of the 1991–92 season, ending his career with 7,773 points scored, 3,141 assists, 1,453 rebounds, 939 steals, a field-goal shooting percentage of 47.2, and a free-throw shooting percentage of 77.6. He averaged 8.9 points, 3.6 assists, 1.7 rebounds, and 1.1 steals per game over the course of 13 NBA seasons.

After leaving the game, Henderson started a real estate business with his wife in Pennsylvania, before assuming the role of president of Henderson Energy Consulting. He also remained a strong supporter of his son, Gerald Henderson Jr., who played in the NBA for eight seasons.

CELTICS CAREER HIGHLIGHTS

Best Season

Henderson played his best ball for the Celtics in the only season he started for them, averaging 11.6 points, 3.8 assists, 1.5 steals, and 1.9 rebounds per game in 1983–84. Furthermore, he shot a career-high 52.4 percent from the field, leading the team in both three-point field-goal shooting percentage (35.1) and three-pointers made (20).

Memorable Moments / Greatest Performances

Henderson got off to a fast start in his second year with the Celtics, scoring a season-high 19 points during a 130–103 rout of the Cleveland Cavaliers in the 1980–81 regular-season opener.

Henderson topped 20 points for the first time in his career on December 26, 1981, when he helped the Celtics record a 124–119 overtime victory over the Kansas City–Omaha Kings by scoring 22 points.

Henderson equaled that mark later in the season, turning in arguably his finest all-around performance of the campaign on February 19, 1982, when he scored 22 points, collected 8 assists, and pulled down 6 rebounds during a 127–117 win over the Portland Trail Blazers.

Although the Celtics lost their next game to the Seattle SuperSonics two days later by a score of 103–100, Henderson handed out 8 assists and established a new career high by scoring 24 points during the contest.

Henderson had another big game a little over two weeks later, scoring 22 points during a 111–101 victory over the Detroit Pistons on March 8, 1982.

Henderson also put forth a number of solid efforts over the course of the ensuing campaign, helping the Celtics record a 107–103 overtime win over the Atlanta Hawks on December 18, 1982, by scoring 21 points. He also scored 22 points on 10 of 11 shooting from the field, in leading the Celtics to a 124–102 victory over Cleveland on March 25, 1983, before hitting on 11 of 14 shots from the field, in tallying 22 points during a 115–113 win over the Pistons on April 10, 1983.

Playing well throughout the 1984 postseason, Henderson helped the Celtics defeat the Washington Bullets by a score of 88–85 in Game 2 of their first-round playoff matchup by tallying 21 points. He then went on to score 19 points during Boston's 115–108 Game 5 clincher against Milwaukee in the Eastern Conference Finals.

However, it was against the Lakers in the 1984 NBA Finals that Henderson cemented his Celtics legacy. In addition to collecting 9 assists during a 121–103 Boston win in Game 5 and scoring 22 points and handing out 5 assists during a 119–108 loss in Game 6, Henderson helped lead the Celtics to a thrilling overtime win in Game 2 by making one of the biggest steals in franchise history.

With the Celtics trailing the Lakers by a score of 115–113 and only 18 seconds left in regulation, former Celtics great Tom Heinsohn told CBS viewers, "Boston is going to try and make a steal . . . they have their best defensive team in there right now." As the Celtics pressed full court, James

Worthy threw a sideline inbounds pass to Magic Johnson, who, upon being double-teamed by Bird and McHale, threw the ball back to Worthy near the deep left corner. Eager to rid himself of the ball, Worthy tossed a lazy crosscourt pass in the direction of Byron Scott. However, the sphere never reached the Laker guard, as the speedy Henderson, showing excellent anticipation, cut in front of Scott, tipped the ball away, scooped it up, and, without a dribble, laid in a right-handed layup high off the glass over Worthy to tie the game with only 13 seconds remaining on the clock. The contest subsequently went into overtime, with the Celtics edging out Los Angeles by a score of 124–121, giving them their only win in the first three games of a series they eventually went on to win in seven games.

In a postgame interview, Henderson, who finished the game with 16 points, 5 assists, and 3 steals, stated, "For a minute I could hear Johnny Most going, 'Henderson steals the ball!,'" in reference to the legendary announcer's famous call of John Havlicek's steal in the 1965 Eastern Conference Finals. In actuality, Most described the play to Celtics fans thusly: "It's picked off! Goes to Henderson, he lays it up, and in! It's all tied up! What a great play by Henderson!"

NOTABLE ACHIEVEMENTS

- Shot better than 50 percent from the field three times.
- Played in every game for Celtics three straight seasons.
- Two-time Eastern Conference champion (1981 and 1984).
- Two-time NBA champion (1981 and 1984).

43

RICKY DAVIS

He's a player who has grown into the game of basketball. He's such a good player with so many skills. He's mastered a lot of skills that people don't give him credit for. He certainly makes an impact on the game.

—Tommy Heinsohn

A talented but enigmatic player who developed a bad reputation prior to joining the Celtics in 2003, Ricky Davis spent parts of just three seasons in Boston. Nevertheless, the 6-foot-6, 205-pound swingman ended up making this list due to his superb athleticism and offensive explosiveness that made him one of the NBA's best sixth men during his time in Beantown. After coming over in a trade with the Cleveland Cavaliers, Davis found his niche in Boston, excelling as the first man off the Celtics' bench for the better part of two seasons before assuming a starting role in his third year with the team. Davis provided the Celtics with an excellent third option on offense over the course of those three seasons, doing an outstanding job of complementing Paul Pierce and Antoine Walker by averaging more than 14 points per game each season. Unfortunately, Boston experienced only a moderate amount of success as a team during that period, making the playoffs twice, but failing to advance beyond the first round of the postseason tournament either time.

Born in Las Vegas, Nevada, on September 23, 1979, Tyree Ricardo Davis spent his first few years living in Chicago before moving with his family to Davenport, Iowa. Hardly a basketball prodigy as a youngster, Davis told the *Minneapolis Star Tribune* in January 2006, "I started playing ball when I was in seventh [grade], and I was terrible . . . terrible. I had nothing. I was just out there playing."

Ricky Davis used his outstanding athleticism to establish himself as a fan favorite during his relatively brief stay in Beantown. Photo courtesy of Chris Springmeyer.

Yet, in spite of his initial struggles on the court, Davis soon began to display an affinity for the game, with his natural athleticism eventually enabling him to overcome his relative lack of skills. Davis's talent first became evident to others when he dunked in a game for the first time as an eighth grader, making him the first student in the history of his school to accomplish the feat. Invited to play on Davenport North's varsity team the following year, Davis spent the next four seasons starring for his high school team, leading it to the state tournament as both a junior and a senior.

Having committed to play for the University of Iowa while still a sophomore at Davenport North High School, Davis subsequently spent just one season at Iowa, averaging 15 points and 4.8 assists per game for the Hawkeyes, before entering the NBA when the Charlotte Hornets selected him in the first round of the 1998 NBA Draft, with the 21st overall pick.

Still only 19 years old when he arrived in Charlotte, Davis spent his first two years in the league serving as a backup, averaging fewer than 5 points and 12 minutes per game each year. Dealt to the Miami Heat as part of a huge nine-player trade following the conclusion of the 1999–2000 campaign, Davis ended up appearing in only seven games with the Heat before missing the remainder of the season with a broken foot. Subsequently included in a three-team trade Miami completed with the Cleveland Cavaliers and Toronto Raptors on October 26, 2001, Davis found himself headed to Cleveland, where he garnered significant minutes for the first time in his young career. After averaging nearly 12 points per game as a backup his first year with the Cavaliers, Davis broke into the team's starting lineup in 2002–03, averaging 20.6 points, 4.9 rebounds, and 5.5 assists per game over the course of the campaign.

Even though the high-flying Davis established himself as one of the league's more exciting players in his second season with the Cavaliers, he also came to be known for his selfishness, which manifested itself during a game against Utah on March 16, 2003, when he intentionally missed a shot at his own basket in an attempt to get a rebound that he thought would give him his first career triple-double. Looking back at the incident years later, Davis acknowledged, "That was a big mistake to make when you're young and dumb. You sit back and you can laugh at that now."

Davis also clashed with Cleveland head coach Paul Silas on a number of occasions, prompting the Cavaliers to part ways with him on December 15, 2003, when they included him in a seven-player trade they completed with the Celtics. After acquiring Davis, Boston director of basketball operations Danny Ainge stated, "I think he's a fantastic talent. He's a young man that has grown up, I believe, in the last little while and has some things to prove in his career."

Although Davis spent the final 57 games of the season coming off the bench for the Celtics after earlier starting for Cleveland, he adapted well to his new role, averaging 14.1 points per game the remainder of the year. He performed even better the following season, concluding the 2004–05 campaign with a scoring average of 16 points per game, while also averaging 33 minutes per contest.

In discussing Davis's role on the team, Celtics head coach Glenn "Doc" Rivers told *USA Today* in 2005, "He's a guy you can run plays for, but he can also score just on movement. That's big in the postseason. In the playoffs, the more you zero in on a guy, you take away his options. But you can't take away movement. Having an ace on the bench, if you start off slow, you still have somewhere to go. That makes your team better and more dangerous."

Tommy Heinsohn added, "He's a player who has grown into the game of basketball. He's such a good player with so many skills. He's mastered a lot of skills that people don't give him credit for. He certainly makes an impact on the game."

After being criticized earlier in his career for being a somewhat erratic and selfish player who cared little about the success of his team, Davis became far more reliable during his time in Boston, even developing into a favorite of the hometown fans. Making an impact off the court as well, Davis, who earned the nickname "Get Buckets" for his potent scoring ability, started the Get Buckets Brigade, which awarded season tickets he purchased to underprivileged fans. He also created the Ricky Davis Foundation, which he discussed with the Associated Press, stating, "Just growing up in the neighborhoods, being unfortunate and not being able to see certain stuff, see certain people until you finally get to college, it's a great feeling to finally be able to give back to certain people, feed them, and make them happy."

Davis spent part of one more season in Boston, averaging 19.7 points and 5.3 assists per contest as a starter over the first 42 games of the 2005–06 campaign, before being traded with three other players and a pair of draft picks to the Minnesota Timberwolves for a package of four players that included Wally Szczerbiak. Davis played well in Minnesota over the course of the next season and a half, posting scoring averages of 19.1 and 17 points per game as a starter, and making an extremely favorable impression on Timberwolves teammate Kevin Garnett, who noted, "[Davis] goes to the basket hard, has attitude, yeah. I've always enjoyed somebody who plays with a lot of energy . . . Some nights you need someone to light that ignition."

Kevin McHale, Minnesota's vice president of basketball operations at the time, agreed with Garnett's assessment, stating, "Ricky's got an innate toughness about him that everybody sees every day. He's kind of a street fighter. Those are the types of guys you like having around."

Nevertheless, Davis once again found himself switching cities just prior to the start of the 2007–08 campaign, when the Miami Heat reacquired him on October 24, 2007. Appearing in all 82 games for the Heat over the course of the season, Davis averaged 13.8 points per contest as a part-time starter, before signing as a free agent with the Los Angeles Clippers at season's end. He spent the next two seasons coming off the bench for the Clippers, seeing both his playing time and offensive production gradually diminish until Los Angeles waived him on February 16, 2010. Failing to draw interest from any other NBA team, the 30-year-old Davis subsequently began a career overseas that took him from Turkey, China, France, and, finally, to Puerto Rico. His playing career officially ended on March 18, 2014, when the Erie BayHawks of the NBA D-League released him.

Davis, seen here as a member of the Miami Heat.
Photo courtesy of Keith Allison.

Over the course of 12 NBA seasons, Davis scored 9,912 points, amassed 2,550 rebounds, 2,426 assists, and 732 steals, shot 44.6 percent from the field and 78.1 percent from the free-throw line, and posted averages of 13.5 points, 3.5 rebounds, 3.3 assists, and 1 steal per game. In a total of 181 games with the Celtics, he scored 2,940 points, collected 673 rebounds, 615 assists, and 209 steals, and averaged 16.2 points, 3.7 rebounds, 3.4 assists, and 1.2 steals per contest.

CELTICS CAREER HIGHLIGHTS

Best Season

Davis compiled his best numbers as a member of the Celtics in his one year as a starter, posting averages of 19.7 points, 4.5 rebounds, and 5.3 assists per game over the course of the 2005–06 campaign, while shooting 46.4 percent from the field and 78.7 percent from the foul line. However, he appeared in only 42 games with them before being dealt to Minnesota at midseason. That being the case, Davis made more of an overall impact on the team one year earlier, when, serving as "sixth man" in Boston, he appeared in all 82 games, averaging 16 points, 3 rebounds and 3 assists, in 33 minutes of action per contest, while shooting 46.2 percent from the field and 81.5 percent from the free-throw line.

Memorable Moments / Greatest Performances

Davis had his first big game for the Celtics nearly one month after they acquired him from Cleveland, scoring 33 points during a 111–103 loss to the Milwaukee Bucks on January 13, 2004. Exactly 11 months later, on December 13, 2004, Davis helped lead the Celtics to a 134–127 double-overtime victory over the Los Angeles Clippers by hitting for 34 points and collecting 6 assists.

Davis had a big game against the Atlanta Hawks on January 14, 2005, scoring 30 points during a 106–94 Boston win; however, he turned in his most dominant performance as a member of the team on April 1, 2005, when he scored a career-high 36 points, in leading the Celtics to a 116–100 victory over the Hawks. Displaying tremendous shooting touch throughout the contest, Davis connected on 14 of 17 shots from the field and 8 of 10 shots from the free-throw line.

Davis got off to an excellent start in the ensuing campaign, turning in an exceptional all-around effort in leading the Celtics to a 114–100 overtime victory over the Knicks in the 2005–06 regular-season opener. In addition to scoring 27 points during the win, Davis recorded 5 steals, 5 assists, and 1 blocked shot.

Davis played another outstanding all-around game some two weeks later, leading the Celtics to a 100–93 win over the Toronto Raptors on November 18, 2005, by scoring 26 points, assisting on 7 baskets, and pulling down 5 rebounds.

Although the Celtics lost to the Sacramento Kings by a score of 116–112 on December 30, 2005, Davis played extremely well, tallying 33 points and recording 7 rebounds, 3 assists, and 3 steals during the contest.

Davis turned in another outstanding all-around effort in a losing cause on January 13, 2006, when he scored 33 points, assisted on 9 baskets, collected 5 rebounds, and recorded 3 steals during a 125–124 triple-overtime loss to the Philadelphia 76ers.

Davis had his final big effort for the Celtics in his next-to-last game as a member of the team, hitting for 32 points and collecting 8 assists during a 91–78 win over the New Orleans / Oklahoma City Hornets on January 23, 2006.

NOTABLE ACHIEVEMENTS

- Averaged more than 16 points per game twice, topping 19 points per contest once.
- Averaged more than 5 assists per game once.
- Finished second in NBA in games played in 2004–05.

44

CHUCK COOPER

I don't give a damn if he's striped, plaid, or polka dot! Boston takes
Chuck Cooper of Duquesne!

—WalterBrown

Chuck Cooper played in the NBA for only six seasons, the first four of
which he spent in Boston. During that time, Cooper never averaged
more than 30 minutes, 9.3 points, or 8.5 rebounds per game in any single campaign, concluding his career with modest averages of 6.7 points and
5.9 rebounds per contest. Nevertheless, the 6-foot-5, 215-pound forward
made a huge impact on the Celtics and the league as a whole by paving the
way for other men of African-American heritage to play in the NBA. The
first black player to be drafted by an NBA team, Cooper became a member
of the Celtics organization on April 25, 1950, when the team selected him
in the second round of the NBA Draft. Earl Cooper, who played for the
Washington Capitols, subsequently became the first African American to
appear in an NBA game. Meanwhile, Nat "Sweetwater" Clifton, who previously played for the Harlem Globetrotters, soon became the first African
American to sign an NBA contract when he inked a deal with the New York
Knickerbockers. But it is Cooper who will forever hold the distinction of
officially integrating the world of professional basketball.

Born in Pittsburgh, Pennsylvania, on September 29, 1926, Charles
Henry Cooper grew up at a time when segregation still remained the
law of the land virtually everywhere in the United States. Encountering a
great deal of discrimination during his formative years, Cooper nearly quit
Westinghouse High School's basketball team after he grew increasingly dis-
traught over his role on the squad, which included doing much of the "dirty
work," such as playing tight defense and creating space for his teammates

Chuck Cooper (#11) helped break the NBA's color barrier.
Photo courtesy of Boston Public Library, Leslie Jones Collection.

to score. However, persevering through those difficult times, Cooper ended up averaging over 13 points per game as a senior, en route to leading his school to Pittsburgh's city championship and earning All-City First-Team honors as a center.

Following his graduation from Westinghouse High, Cooper elected to enroll at historically black West Virginia State College, where he remained just one semester before being drafted into the US Navy during the latter stages of World War II. Serving his country until the war ended less than one year later, Cooper subsequently returned to Pittsburgh to continue his education at Duquesne University. He spent the next four years starring on the hardwood, attracting the attention of pro scouts by amassing a then school-record 990 points, leading his team to two appearances in the prestigious NIT tournament, and earning All-American honors as a senior.

Yet, even though the athletic directors at mainstream Duquesne showed their support for Cooper on numerous occasions by canceling games with Southern schools that refused to participate in integrated contests, the talented forward continued to encounter racial prejudice at times. In his book, *They Cleared the Lane*, author Ron Thomas related one particular incident that took place on the court, revealing that Cooper responded to one opposing player who had shouted "I got the nigger" with a retort of "And I got your mother in my jockstrap."

Shortly before earning his bachelor's degree in education at Duquesne, Cooper signed on with the all-black Harlem Globetrotters, with whom he earned the nickname "Tarzan" due to his agility and shot-blocking ability. Cooper, though, elected to leave the Globetrotters when the Celtics selected him with the second pick of the second round (14th overall) of the 1950 NBA Draft, making him the first player of African-American descent to be drafted by an NBA team.

Although Jackie Robinson had integrated professional sports a few years earlier when he signed with the Brooklyn Dodgers, several NBA owners expressed their concern when Celtics owner Walter Brown announced the team's selection of Cooper. According to *New York Times* reporter George Sullivan, one owner reproached Brown by saying, "Walter, don't you know he's a colored boy?" However, remaining steadfast in his decision, Brown responded, "I don't give a damn if he's striped, plaid, or polka dot! Boston takes Chuck Cooper of Duquesne!"

Reflecting back on the 1950 draft years later, Cooper stated:

> I'm convinced that no NBA team would have made the move on blacks in 1950 if the Celtics hadn't drafted me early, taking me on the second round. Seven rounds later the Washington Caps took Earl Lloyd, and a couple of months later the New York Knicks bought Sweetwater Clifton's contract from the Harlem Globetrotters. But it was a case of the Caps and Knicks following the Celtics' lead. Walter Brown was the man who put his neck on the line. It took a lot of guts to do what he did . . . I'll never forget Walter Brown. He was a gentleman with a backbone. Give all the credit to that man. He made it all possible when nobody else would.

Cooper also suggested that the concurrent arrivals of Lloyd and Clifton made his transition to the NBA a lot easier than it otherwise would have been, telling *Jet* magazine years later, "I wasn't alone. I didn't have to take all the race-baiting and heat on my shoulders like Jackie Robinson."

Shying away from comparisons made between himself and Robinson, Cooper suggested, "No, I don't see myself as basketball's Jackie Robinson. There was only one Jackie. When he broke baseball's color line three years earlier, he shouldered a terrific burden that helped all other sports. A lot of acceptance that he pioneered transferred over to all who followed in all sports."

Cooper was never given the opportunity to fully utilize his natural talent at the pro level. Photo courtesy of Boston Public Library, Leslie Jones Collection.

Cooper made his NBA debut on November 1, 1950, against the Fort Wayne Pistons in a game that also featured the Celtic debuts of Bob Cousy, Ed Macauley, and head coach Red Auerbach. Adapting well to the pro game, Cooper ended up spending most of his rookie campaign at the small forward position, posting career-high averages of 9.3 points and 8.5 rebounds per contest for a Celtics team that improved its record from 22-46 to 39-30. Looking back years later on his first year in the league, Cooper told the *Amsterdam News* in 1978: "The major thing I had to adjust to upon entering the pros was the stationary pivot. In college, with my size and agility, I liked to go down low and utilize that space, but, in the pros, a big man in the pivot would clog that area."

Despite playing well as a rookie, Cooper found himself forced to accept more and more of a reduced role over the course of the next three seasons, seeing both his playing time and numbers gradually diminish, until he averaged only 3.3 points and 4.3 rebounds per game in his final year in Boston. And, as he saw less and less of the court, Cooper grew increasingly disenchanted with the way he believed the Celtics marginalized him as a defensive, "in-the-trenches" type of player. Feeling that the NBA was not yet ready for a high-scoring black star, Cooper later expressed regret over the fact that the Celtics failed to take full advantage of his quickness and athleticism. Later in life, he also conveyed the sadness he felt over the way several NBA coaches and administrators treated him. Even though the racial prejudice Cooper encountered during his time in Boston proved to be less overt than the bigotry Jackie Robinson faced in baseball, he "had to go through hell," according to Celtics coach Red Auerbach.

After leaving the NBA at the conclusion of the 1955–56 campaign, Cooper made a complete break with the game of basketball, with his wife stating in *They Cleared the Lane*, "I think that even though he was the first trailblazer, I don't think he enjoyed that experience. I think it was painful, and nobody likes pain."

Yet, in spite of the difficulties he encountered, Cooper ended up forming close bonds with several of his teammates, including Bob Cousy, who said, "Red [Auerbach] treated Cooper like he would any new player, and we treated him the same way. He showed us that he could help on the court, and he was a great guy to be around."

The Celtics traded Cooper to the Milwaukee Hawks prior to the start of the 1954–55 campaign, after which he split his final two seasons between the Hawks and the Fort Wayne Pistons. Following his release by the Pistons at the end of the 1955–56 season, Cooper spent one year playing for the Harlem Magicians before retiring from the game after injuring his back in a car crash. Cooper went on to earn a master's degree in social work from the University of Minnesota, serve on Pittsburgh's school board, and become the city's first black department head as director of parks and recreation. He also served as the supervisor of Pittsburgh's National Bank's affirmative action program until losing his battle with liver cancer at the age of 57 on February 5, 1984.

CELTICS CAREER HIGHLIGHTS

Best Season

Cooper posted the best numbers of his career in his rookie campaign of 1950–51. Garnering more playing time than he did in any other season, the 24-year-old forward averaged 9.3 points, 8.5 rebounds, and 2.6 assists per game, while shooting nearly 35 percent from the field, which fell just short of the career-high mark of 36 percent he reached the following year.

Memorable Moments / Greatest Performances

Though not known for his scoring as a pro, Cooper put up good offensive numbers on a number of occasions for the Celtics. On November 9, 1950, in just his fifth game in the league, Cooper tallied 19 points during a 76–71 win over the Minneapolis Lakers. Less than two weeks later, on November 21, Cooper helped the Celtics defeat the New York Knicks by scoring a team-high 18 points. He played another strong game later that season, scoring 19 points during a 96–90 overtime win over the Syracuse Nationals on February 2, 1951. Although the Celtics lost to the Rochester Royals by a score of 106–91 on January 1, 1952, Cooper scored a career-high 20 points during the contest. He nearly equaled that total three weeks later when he scored 19 points during a lopsided 117–75 victory over the Baltimore Bullets.

However, Cooper unquestionably experienced the most memorable moment of his career on November 1, 1950, when he took the court for the first time as a member of the Celtics. Although Cooper ended up scoring only 7 points during the 107–84 loss to the Fort Wayne Pistons, he made history by becoming the first African-American player ever to appear in a game for the Celtics, making his NBA debut just one day after Earl Lloyd made his initial appearance for the Washington Capitols.

NOTABLE ACHIEVEMENTS

- First African-American player drafted by an NBA team.
- Second African-American player to appear in an NBA game.

45

KENDRICK PERKINS

I think he's the best teammate I've ever seen. He's not afraid to challenge. And guys know it's always about the team. He's not the same player, but he's the same worker.

—Pelicans head coach Alvin Gentry

A key member of the Celtics' 2007–08 NBA championship team, Kendrick Perkins contributed much more than mere numbers could ever reveal during his time in Boston. An imposing physical presence at center, Perkins helped Kevin Garnett anchor the middle of the Celtics' defense, providing mental and physical toughness to the team with his aggressive style of play. A true leader in every sense of the word, Perkins also served as one of the squad's emotional leaders, inspiring his teammates with his intensity, solid work ethic, and unselfishness. A pretty fair player as well, Perkins finished in double digits in scoring once, surpassed 8 rebounds per game twice, and led the Celtics in blocked shots in four of his eight seasons in Boston, in helping them advance to the NBA Finals on two separate occasions.

Born in Nederland, Texas, on November 10, 1984, Kendrick Le'Dale Perkins attended Clifton J. Ozen High School in nearby Beaumont, where he led his school to four consecutive district championships and one state championship during his high school career. Particularly dominant in his final year at Ozen, Perkins averaged 27.5 points, 16.4 rebounds, and 7.8 blocked shots per game as a senior, in leading his team to a 33-1 record and earning a selection to the McDonald's All-American Game. Considered a five-star recruit by Rivals.com, Perkins initially committed to Memphis after being listed as the number-three center and the number-six player in the nation in 2003. However, he ultimately decided to make himself eligible for the 2003 NBA Draft, in which the Memphis Grizzlies selected him in the first round with the 27th overall pick. Memphis, though, immediately traded Perkins and Marcus Banks to the Celtics for Troy Bell and Dahntay Jones, who the Celtics had selected in the same draft.

With Perkins entering the NBA right out of high school, the 19-year-old center saw very little action as a rookie, appearing in only 10 games and averaging just 3.5 minutes per contest. Although Perkins appeared in 60 games the following season, he continued to spend most of his time on the bench, averaging just 9 minutes, 2.5 points, and 2.9 rebounds per contest over the course of the 2004–05 campaign. Yet, even in his limited minutes, Perkins began to develop a reputation as one of the team's tougher players, establishing himself as the squad's "enforcer" with his physical, in-your-face style of play made more effective by his powerful 6-foot-10, 270-pound frame.

After working hard to improve his game during the subsequent off-season, Perkins received significantly more playing time in 2005–06, eventually earning the starting assignment at center following the January 26, 2006, trade of Mark Blount to the Minnesota Timberwolves. Despite averaging just 5.2 points, 5.9 rebounds, and 19.6 minutes per game over the course of the season, Perkins increased his production dramatically after becoming a regular member of the starting five, scoring as many as 17 points in one game, while pulling down 19 rebounds on another occasion.

Although Perkins continued to share playing time at center with the likes of Al Jefferson, Theo Ratliff, Michael Olowokandi, and Glen "Big Baby" Davis the next few seasons, he remained Boston's primary "man in the middle," increasing his production each year, while gradually emerging as one of the team's inspirational leaders. The Celtics' full-time starting center by 2008–09, Perkins averaged 8.5 points, a career-high 8.1 rebounds, and a team-leading 2 blocked shots per game. He followed that up by posting marks of 10.1 points, 7.6 rebounds, and 1.7 blocked shots per contest for a Boston team that lost to the Lakers in the 2010 NBA Finals. Prior to that, though, Perkins proved to be a key figure in the Celtics' successful run to the 2007–08 NBA championship, averaging 6.9 points, 6.1 rebounds, and a team-leading 1.5 blocked shots per contest during the regular season, while also doing an effective job of clogging up the middle on the defensive end of the court.

After suffering torn MCL and PCL ligaments in his right knee during Game 6 of the 2010 NBA Finals, Perkins missed the first few months of the ensuing campaign, finally making his season debut on January 25, 2011, when the Celtics fans in attendance at the TD Garden showed their

Kendrick Perkins provided toughness, exceptional leadership, and an imposing physical presence to Celtic teams that appeared in two NBA Finals.
Photo courtesy of Keith Allison.

appreciation to him for all he meant to the team by giving him a standing ovation when he entered the contest in the first quarter. However, Perkins's return to the team proved to be short-lived, since the Celtics included him in a multiplayer trade they completed with the Thunder one month later that also sent Nate Robinson to Oklahoma City, in exchange for Jeff Green, Nenad Krstic, and a 2012 first-round draft pick. Perkins left Boston with career totals of 2,917 points scored, 2,751 rebounds, and 646 blocked shots, a field-goal shooting percentage of 56.3, and a free-throw shooting percentage of just 60.3. Over parts of eight seasons with the Celtics, he averaged 6.4 points, 6.1 rebounds, and 1.4 blocked shots per game.

Perkins spent most of the next four seasons in Oklahoma City, helping the Thunder advance to the NBA Finals in 2012, when they lost to the Miami Heat in five games. Although Perkins continued to post modest numbers during his time in Oklahoma City, he furthered his reputation as one of the game's great leaders, with Kevin Durant saying to him during his tearful 2014 MVP acceptance speech, "I hated you before you got here . . . But, since the moment you arrived, you've been one of the best teammates

I've ever had. The late-night calls after games and you texting me, telling me I'm the MVP . . . That means a lot to me."

After being included in a three-team trade involving Oklahoma City, Utah, and Detroit on February 19, 2015, Perkins was waived by the Jazz two days later. However, he subsequently signed with the Cleveland Cavaliers, with whom he made his fourth NBA Finals appearance later in the year. A free agent following the conclusion of the 2014–15 campaign, Perkins signed with the New Orleans Pelicans, with whom he spent the 2015–16 season. Although injured for much of the year, Perkins continued to impress others with his ability to impact a team with his leadership, with Pelicans head coach Alvin Gentry stating, "I think he's the best teammate I've ever seen. He's not afraid to challenge. And guys know it's always about the team. He's not the same player, but he's the same worker."

Re-signing with the Cavaliers at season's end, Perkins failed to earn a roster spot, prompting him to join Cleveland's NBA G League affiliate, the Canton Charge. Returning to the Cavaliers late in the year, Perkins ended up appearing in one game, before being released and subsequently announcing his retirement. Since retiring as an active player, Perkins has served as a basketball commentator and analyst for ESPN and NBC Sports Boston, frequently appearing on sports talk shows *NBA Today*, *Get Up*, *First Take*, and *Sportscenter*.

CELTICS CAREER HIGHLIGHTS

Best Season

It could be argued that Perkins played his best ball for the Celtics in 2009–10, when, in addition to averaging a career-high 10.1 points per game, he posted marks of 7.6 rebounds and 1.7 blocked shots per contest, while hitting on just over 60 percent of his shots from the field. However, Perkins compiled slightly better overall numbers the previous season, concluding the 2008–09 campaign with averages of 8.5 points, 8.1 rebounds, 2 blocked shots, and 1.3 assists per game, with each of the last three figures representing career-high marks for him. He also shot 57.7 percent from the field, while averaging a career-high 29.6 minutes per contest.

Memorable Moments / Greatest Performances:

Perkins turned in his first truly impactful performance for the Celtics on November 30, 2005, when he scored 12 points and pulled down 19 rebounds during a 110–103 win over the Philadelphia 76ers. He had another outstanding game later in the season, on January 18, 2006, when he collected 6 rebounds and scored a season-high 17 points, in helping the Celtics defeat the Minnesota Timberwolves by a score of 103–96.

Perkins played one of his best all-around games for the Celtics on November 23, 2007, when he scored 21 points and pulled down 9 rebounds during a 107–94 victory over the Lakers. Perkins also performed extremely well against the Charlotte Bobcats on February 29, 2008, scoring 19 points, collecting 9 rebounds, and blocking 5 shots during a 108–100 Celtics victory.

Just six days later, on March 5, 2008, Perkins helped lead the Celtics to a 90–78 win over the Detroit Pistons by scoring 10 points and pulling down 20 rebounds.

Perkins, though, saved his finest all-around performance of the season for Game 5 of the 2008 Eastern Conference Finals, when he led the Celtics to a 106–102 victory over Detroit by scoring 18 points and collecting 16 rebounds.

Perkins had his two biggest offensive games for the Celtics the following season, with the first of those coming on December 19, 2008, when he scored 25 points, in helping them defeat the Chicago Bulls by a score of 126–108. He topped that effort, though, on March 15, 2009, when he tallied a career-high 26 points during an 86–77 loss to the Milwaukee Bucks.

Perkins had another big game on December 1, 2009, leading the Celtics to a 108–90 victory over the Charlotte Bobcats by scoring 21 points and pulling down 12 rebounds.

NOTABLE ACHIEVEMENTS

- Shot better than 50 percent from the field six times, topping the 60 percent mark twice.
- Finished second in NBA in field-goal shooting percentage in 2009–10 (60.2%).
- Led Celtics in rebounding once and blocked shots four times.
- Two-time Eastern Conference champion (2008 and 2010).
- 2007–08 NBA champion.

46

M. L. CARR

As a Celtics fan growing up, I was well aware of the "Celtic Mystique" and what all of those championship banners were all about.... It was so special for me, because of everything I'd been through—being cut, having to play in Israel, everything leading up to me putting on a Celtics uniform. And then to finally win that championship, there's nothing in the world like that feeling. It overcomes you.

—M. L. Carr

Remembered mostly as an agitator who antagonized opposing players and fans alike with his towel-waving from the Celtics bench, M. L. Carr nevertheless proved to be a major contributor to two NBA championship teams during his time in Boston. Taking much of the pressure off his teammates by incurring the wrath of anyone not wearing a Celtics uniform with his sometimes obnoxious behavior, Carr allowed stars such as Larry Bird, Kevin McHale, and Robert Parish to focus solely on basketball, making their jobs much easier in the process. Carr's passion and positive attitude also helped make him an excellent motivator, since he used those qualities to instill in his teammates the same sense of pride he felt in being a member of the NBA's most storied franchise. A pretty fair player as well earlier in his career, before he assumed more of a supporting role in Boston, Carr once averaged nearly 19 points per game for the Detroit Pistons, doing so in the same season that he finished third in the league in assists, en route to earning NBA All-Defensive Second-Team honors. And following the conclusion of his playing career, Carr remained a member of the Celtics family, serving the organization first as general manager, then as coach, and, finally, as director of corporate development.

M. L. Carr, seen here wearing the uniform of the Detroit Pistons, did a superb job of motivating his Celtics teammates.
Photo courtesy of NASLJerseys.com.

Born in the agricultural town of Wallace, North Carolina, on January 9, 1951, Michael Leon Carr attended Wallace Rose Hill High School in nearby Teachey, where he became one of the first black students. Although not initially fond of basketball, Carr went out for Rose Hill's team at the urging of a friend, after which he also became the first African American to represent the school on the court. After graduating from high school, Carr enrolled at tiny Guilford College in Greensboro, North Carolina, some 160 miles northwest of his hometown. Developing into a solid college player under Coach Jack Jensen at Guilford, Carr helped his team compile an overall record of 101-25 over the course of the next four seasons, earning NAIA First-Team All-American honors as a senior by averaging 18 points and 12 rebounds per game.

Subsequently drafted by both the ABA's Kentucky Colonels and the NBA's Kansas City-Omaha Kings, who selected him in the fifth round of the 1973 NBA Draft with the 76th overall pick, Carr failed to make the roster of either team, forcing him to spend the 1973–74 campaign competing in the Eastern League. He then spent the next year playing for the Israel Sabras in the European Pro Basketball League, earning league MVP honors by topping the circuit in scoring and finishing second in rebounding. In discussing his decision to play in Israel, Carr explained:

> When I first met Red [Auerbach], I'd just gotten cut from the Kansas City Kings. Red called and said he'd like to meet with me, so I go up to Boston and walk into Red's office. He tells me to sit down, and then he tells me that he doesn't have a spot for me on this team. And I'm thinking to myself that he could have told me that over the phone. Then he tells me that he thinks he'll have a spot for me next year, and that he wants to send me over to Israel for a year to play, so that he could hide me and so that I could get another year's worth of experience under my belt. And then I'm thinking, if he wanted to hide me why didn't he try to hide me somewhere in Harlem instead of Israel. But I didn't ask any questions. If Red Auerbach thought a year in Israel could get me into the NBA, then I'd pack my bags and head overseas. And that's exactly what I did.

However, the success Carr experienced while playing in Israel did not go unnoticed by other pro scouts, leading to his eventual signing with the ABA's Spirits of St. Louis, who offered him a one-year deal to return to the United States. The 6-foot-6, 210-pound Carr played well for St. Louis in 1975–76, earning a spot on the ABA's All-Rookie Team by averaging 12.2 points and 6.2 rebounds per game. But when the two leagues merged, the Spirits disbanded, making Carr a free agent under the terms of his one-year contract.

Choosing to sign with the Detroit Pistons, who offered him the best deal of any NBA team, Carr spent the next three seasons in the Motor City developing into one of the better players on a squad that had Bob Lanier and little else. Starting at small forward for the Pistons, Carr averaged 13.3 points and 7.7 rebounds per game in 1976–77, before averaging 12.4 points and 7.1 rebounds per contest the following year. Carr then had his best season as a pro in 1978–79, averaging 7.4 rebounds per game, while also posting career-high marks in scoring (18.7 ppg), assists (3.3 apg), and field-goal shooting percentage (51.4). Furthermore, Carr's rugged defense and league-leading average of 2.5 steals per contest earned him NBA All-Defensive Second-Team honors.

A free agent again following the conclusion of the 1978–79 campaign, Carr signed with the Boston Celtics after Red Auerbach came calling, as he had said he would some four years earlier. Arriving in Boston the same year as Larry Bird, Carr used his motivational skills to help rejuvenate a team that had won only 29 games the previous season. Looking back at his decision to join the Celtics, Carr said:

> For me, coming in that year was great because they were in a rebuilding mode and were coming off a lot of turmoil. Dave Cowens was making a real effort to be a part of that. Tiny Archibald was coming back from an off year. Gerald Henderson and Cedric Maxwell were also a part of that team, and we had this young kid coming to the team from French Lick that was supposed to be a pretty good player [laughs]. So Red had a good nucleus to build around, and he quickly made the decision to get rid of the players who were causing all of the problems. Red was willing to sacrifice talent but he wasn't going to sacrifice character, so, as he put the team back together, we ended up having a very good year. We didn't win it, but that put us back on the track toward being a championship caliber team.

The Celtics ended up posting a regular-season record of 61-21, before losing to the Philadelphia 76ers in the 1980 Eastern Conference Finals. For his part, Carr averaged 11.1 points, 4 rebounds, and 24 minutes per game, while serving as the first man off the Boston bench.

Although Carr saw his playing time diminish somewhat the following season, he continued to do a solid job in a reserve role, averaging 6 points, 2 rebounds, and 16 minutes per game for a team that went on to win the NBA championship. Describing how he felt after the Celtics defeated the Houston Rockets in the NBA Finals, after earlier overcoming a 3–1 deficit against Philadelphia in the Eastern Conference Finals, Carr recalled, "As a Celtics fan growing up I was well aware of the 'Celtic Mystique' and what all of those championship banners were all about. . . . It was so special for me, because of everything I'd been through—being cut, having to play in Israel, everything leading up to me putting on a Celtics uniform. And then

Carr had a knack for getting under the opponent's skin.
Photo courtesy of Jerry Wachter.

to finally win that championship, there's nothing in the world like that feeling. It overcomes you."

Carr continued: "I remember coming back from Houston and landing at the airport, and all of the people that were there to greet us. I'd never in my life experienced anything like that. People were going crazy. And I remember the parade, going through the city with all of the people there, and to me it just felt like it was more than just basketball. I guess it was because we'd just carved out our own place among all of those other great Celtic teams."

Carr then added:

> I'm a history major. You go back three years prior to us winning that championship, and it was the height of busing in Boston. There were so many negative connotations around that. I vividly remember seeing the young black men being poked with the American flag, and that was resonating with me as I traveled through the city as a hero. I remember being amazed at how I was being treated, when just three years earlier Boston had given itself such a black eye with that incident. The people were cheering us and celebrating our achievement, honoring us as champions, and I just wished we could have bottled that up and applied it to more than just the Celtics. I wished it could have been used to transform the thinking of an entire region. Obviously Boston has come around and it's one of the greatest cities in the world right now, but it went through some dark days to get here, and I think the Celtics played a part in that.

Carr again played well coming off the bench in 1981–82, averaging 8.1 points and 2.7 rebounds in 23 minutes of action per contest, before assuming a less prominent role on the court in each of the next three seasons. Yet, even though Carr averaged only 3.1 points and 9.8 minutes per game in 1983–84, he emerged as the emotional leader of a Celtics team that went on to win the NBA championship, cheering on his teammates from the bench while constantly baiting the opposition and their fans. In discussing his role on the team, which Red Auerbach delineated to him prior to the start of the season, Carr explained:

> People remember me as an antagonist because I waved that towel and got under the opposing team's skin. That was all part of the plan. If I could take some of the pressure and attention off of Larry, Robert, and Kevin, then I was doing my job because they could loosen up and focus on playing basketball. Just leave the antagonizing to me. It was a bravado that got under the skin of the fans more than the players, but it helped us as a team remember who

we were. I never let them forget that we were the Celtics and that we expect to win.

My goal was to make sure that the Celtics played as loose and as confidently as possible, and if that meant being a cheerleader and a motivator, then that was my role. And at that point in my career I wasn't on the court a lot. When I did get in the game, I tried my best to make a positive impact to help the team—a big steal, a three-point shot, a key rebound, a couple of minutes of tough defense, whatever I could contribute.

Particularly hard on the rival Lakers and their fans during the 1984 NBA Finals, Carr became the most hated man in Los Angeles following the series—something he revealed didn't bother him in the least when he suggested, "People see me as arrogant and cocky, and I don't really have any qualms with that. . . . They're probably right. I accept that image as part of the love-hate thing that is part of the Celtics. A lot of people see me as the embodiment of the Celtics because I'm into Celtic pride and Celtic mystique. I go along with it because I'd rather they yell at me on the bench than someone on the court."

Celtics teammate Cedric Maxwell added credence to Carr's statements when he told *Sport* magazine in 1985, "I went on a speaking tour last summer and everywhere I went, the first words out of people's mouths were, 'I hate M. L. Carr.' But, if you rank the most popular athletes in Boston, M. L. is number 3, behind Larry [Bird] and Doug Flutie. And if Flutie didn't throw no 60-yard touchdown pass, then M. L.'d be number 2."

Still, in spite of Carr's tremendous popularity with the fans of Boston, the Celtics elected to cut him 47 games into the 1984–85 campaign, bringing his playing career to an end. Over the course of 10 pro seasons, Carr scored 6,759 points, amassed 3,054 rebounds, 1,336 assists, and 939 steals, and compiled shooting percentages of 47.2 from the field and 73.7 from the free-throw line. In his six seasons in Boston, Carr scored 2,285 points, collected 818 rebounds, 484 assists, and 303 steals, and posted averages of 6.3 points, 2.3 rebounds, and 1.3 assists per game.

After staying away from the game for several years following the conclusion of his playing career, Carr returned to the Celtics as director of basketball operations in 1994. He also coached the team for two years, leading Boston to a dismal overall record of just 48-116 in 1995–96 and 1996–97 before transitioning into the role of Celtics' director of corporate development. After leaving the Celtics organization, Carr became president of the WNBA's Charlotte Sting before becoming a minority owner of the

Carr saw very little playing time his last few seasons in Boston, serving the team primarily as a cheerleader.

NBA's Charlotte Bobcats for a brief period of time. Currently residing in Massachusetts with his wife, Sylvia, Carr is a partner with New Technology Ventures—a tech-focused venture capital firm based in Newton.

CELTICS CAREER HIGHLIGHTS

Best Season

The 1979–80 campaign proved to be easily Carr's best in Boston. In addition to averaging 11.1 points, 4 rebounds, 1.5 steals, and 24.3 minutes per game in his first year with the Celtics, Carr shot 47.4 percent from the field, posting his highest mark in each category as a member of the team in the process.

Memorable Moments / Greatest Performances

As might be expected, Carr turned in most of his finest performances for the Celtics during that 1979–80 season, with his first such effort coming on October 13, 1979, when he scored 22 points during a 139–117 win over the Cleveland Cavaliers in just his second game as a member of the team. A little over three weeks later on November 7, Carr scored a season-high 25 points, in leading the Celtics to a 117–105 victory over the San Antonio Spurs. Coming back to haunt his former team, Carr scored 22 points during a 118–114 overtime win over the Pistons on December 4 before tallying 21 points during a 131–104 blowout of Detroit on January 23, 1980. Carr also had a big game against the Indiana Pacers on March 18, 1980, scoring 23 points during a 114–102 Celtics win, before tying his season high by hitting for 25 points during a 116–110 loss to Philadelphia in the final game of the regular season. However, Carr's most notable performance of the campaign took place in Game 4 of the 1980 Eastern Conference Finals, when he helped the Celtics complete a sweep of the Houston Rockets by scoring 23 points during a 138–121 win.

Carr got off to a fast start the following season, matching his high-point mark as a member of the Celtics by tallying 25 points during a 130–103 win over the Cavaliers in the 1980–81 regular-season opener.

Carr came up big for the Celtics in Game 1 of the 1982 Eastern Conference Semifinals, scoring 21 points during a 109–101 victory over the Washington Bullets, in a series Boston went on to win in five games.

Carr made one of the biggest plays of his career in the closing moments of Game 5 of the 1981 Eastern Conference Finals. With the Celtics on the verge of being eliminated for the second year in a row by the Philadelphia 76ers, who held a three-games-to-one lead over them in the series, Carr described the events that subsequently transpired: "I remember being in Game 5 of that series, and getting a rebound and getting fouled by Dr. J. And I'm going to the line and the Sixers call time-out to ice me, and Cedric Maxwell comes over and says, 'Don't worry about these foul shots—you make them both and we keep playing. You miss and we get to go on summer vacation.'" Carr, who sank both free throws, continued, "It was an incredible comeback, that's the reality of it, and we knew that once we beat the Sixers that it was pretty much anticlimactic. We knew we were going to beat the Houston Rockets in the NBA Finals."

Yet, Carr will always be remembered most for a play he made during the latter stages of Game 4 of the 1984 NBA Finals, when he stole a James Worthy pass and dunked the ball to secure a 129–125 road win for the Celtics that tied their series with Los Angeles at two games apiece.

Still, even though Carr played only 7 minutes and failed to score a single point in Game 7 of that series, he claims:

> More than anything, I remember the last seconds of Game 7. No one thought we could beat the Lakers. They were the thorough-breds, we were the Clydesdales. It was a very physical series, and that's exactly what we wanted because we knew that's the only way we could beat those guys. If you remember, there was Kevin McHale's hit on Kurt Rambis, and there was Larry Bird's poke of Michael Cooper out-of-bounds. The series was full of things like that. We knew that we had to physically beat them, because they had never played that kind of game. It didn't take the Lakers long to learn, but in that series it was the element of surprise that we needed. So for me, being back in the old Boston Garden for Game 7, with 12 seconds left on the clock, and knowing that we were going to be world champions when absolutely no one gave us a chance but us . . . that is the thing that I remember the most.

NOTABLE ACHIEVEMENTS

- Finished second in NBA in games played (82) in 1979–80.
- Two-time Eastern Conference champion (1981 and 1984).
- Two-time NBA champion (1981 and 1984).

47

BILL WALTON

If you were grading a player for every fundamental skill, Walton
would rank the highest of any center who ever played.

—John Wooden

Possessing a tremendous overall skill set, Bill Walton drew favorable comparisons to legendary centers Bill Russell and Wilt Chamberlain early in his career, with Dr. Jack Ramsay, his first NBA coach, once telling *Sport* magazine, "Bill Russell was a great shot-blocker. Wilt Chamberlain was a great offensive player. But Walton can do it all."

However, after capturing league MVP and NBA Finals MVP honors over the course of his first few seasons in Portland, Walton experienced a precipitous fall from grace due to a number of injuries that kept him off the court much of the time, preventing him from ever again performing at optimum proficiency. Able to appear in a majority of his team's games only three more times the rest of his career, Walton failed to reach the heights as a professional that most people predicted for him when he first entered the NBA in 1974.

Yet, even though he resembled just a shell of his former self by the time he joined the Celtics prior to the start of the 1985–86 campaign, Walton had enough left to contribute significantly to the team's successful run to the NBA championship, earning NBA Sixth Man of the Year honors in the process. Unfortunately, injuries once again riddled Walton the following year, forcing him to eventually announce his retirement and leaving us all to wonder what might have been.

Born in La Mesa, California, on November 5, 1952, William Theodore Walton III attended local Helix High School, where he starred in basketball

After beginning his career as a "franchise center," Bill Walton earned NBA Sixth Man of the Year honors in his one full season with the Celtics.

despite suffering numerous injuries that included breaks to his ankle, leg, and several bones in his feet. After enrolling at UCLA, Walton's injury woes continued, as he found himself suffering from constant back pain and tendinitis in both knees. Nevertheless, the big redheaded center went on to establish himself as one of the greatest players in school history, leading the Bruins to a record 88-game winning streak at one point, en route to earning USBWA College Player of the Year and Naismith College Player of the Year honors three straight times, as well as the distinction of being named the 1973 recipient of the James E. Sullivan Award as the top amateur athlete in the nation.

Still, in spite of the success Walton experienced on the court, he proved to be a source of constant worry to Bruins head coach John Wooden due to his outspoken nature and controversial political views. Arrested once during an anti–Vietnam War rally, the long-haired, heavily bearded Walton publicly criticized Richard Nixon and the FBI, expressing his antiestablishment feelings on one occasion by saying in a prepared statement, "Your generation has screwed up the world. My generation is trying to straighten it out. Money doesn't mean anything to me. It can't buy happiness, and I just want to be happy."

In discussing the anxiety Walton caused him to feel at times, Wooden told the *Los Angeles Times*, "I had no problem with him during the season. Off the floor, I worried. I worried when he was thrown in jail with the group that took over the administration building. I worried when he stopped traffic on Wilshire Boulevard, and when he interrupted classes giving his views on the Vietnam War."

Yet, Wooden also took time to praise the man who led his team to a pair of national titles and an overall record of 86-4, suggesting, "If you were grading a player for every fundamental skill, Walton would rank the highest of any center who ever played."

Walton's extraordinary all-around ability prompted the Portland Trail Blazers to make him the first overall pick of the 1974 NBA Draft, in spite of his controversial beliefs and history of injuries. Hailed as the NBA's next great big man upon his arrival in Portland, the 6-foot-11, 225-pound Walton got off to a fast start as a rookie, averaging 16 points, 19 rebounds, 4.4 assists, and 4 blocked shots per game in his first seven contests, causing Lakers coach Bill Sharman to tell the *Los Angeles Times*, "I was with the Boston Celtics when Russell came into the league. Walton is the same type of player. Extremely intelligent—but besides that, he has tremendous basketball instinct."

However, Walton soon found himself beset by numerous injuries that included a sprained ankle, a broken left wrist, and problems with both feet, limiting him to just 35 games and averages of only 12.8 points and 12.6 rebounds per game his first year in the league. Once again hampered by foot problems the following season, Walton appeared in only 51 games in 1975–76. Yet, he performed well whenever he felt healthy enough to take the court, averaging 16.1 points, 13.4 rebounds, 4.3 assists, and 1.6 blocks per contest.

In addition to having his play compromised by the injuries that afflicted him his first two seasons, Walton soon developed an adversarial relationship with the local media, which tended to portray him as aloof, taciturn, and unapproachable. Walton later admitted that much of his unwillingness to speak to the press stemmed from a speech impediment that he later corrected through therapy.

Walton finally began to put everything together in his third season, leading Portland to a regular-season record of 49-33 by averaging 18.6 points, 3.8 assists, and a league-leading 14.4 rebounds and 3.2 blocked shots per contest. Despite missing 17 of his team's games, Walton finished second in the league MVP voting, made the All-Star team for the first time, and earned All-NBA and NBA All-Defensive honors for the first of two straight times. He subsequently led the Trail Blazers to a six-game victory over the favored Philadelphia 76ers in the NBA Finals, averaging 18.5 points, 19 rebounds, 5.2 assists, and 3.7 blocks per contest, en route to earning Finals MVP honors.

Although Walton appeared in only 58 of Portland's 82 regular-season contests the following year, he ended up being named league MVP after leading his team to the Pacific Division title by averaging 18.9 points, 13.2 rebounds, 5 assists, and 2.5 blocked shots per game. The 'Blazers compiled a record of 50-10 with Walton in the lineup, before finishing the campaign by winning only 8 of their final 22 games when a left foot injury sidelined him for the remainder of the regular season. With Walton subsequently able to take the court just twice in the postseason, Portland lost to the Seattle SuperSonics in six games in the opening round.

Unfortunately, injuries prevented Walton from ever again reaching such heights. Suffering from a chronically broken bone in his left foot, Walton appeared in a total of only 14 games over the course of the next four seasons, which he spent with the San Diego Clippers after demanding to be traded from the Trail Blazers, whose management he accused of providing him with poor medical treatment.

After undergoing radical surgery to restructure his oft-injured foot, a beardless, shorter-haired Walton attempted to mount a comeback with the Clippers in 1982. Making an effort to mend fences with the media as well by telling *Sport* magazine, "I'm a different person now than I was when I came into the NBA," Walton started 32 games at center for the Clippers over the course of the 1982–83 campaign, averaging 14.1 points and 9.8 rebounds per contest. Playing without a significant amount of pain for the first time in years, Walton posted solid numbers for the Clippers in each of the next two seasons as well, in a part-time role. Appearing in 55 games in 1983–84, Walton averaged 12.1 points and 8.7 rebounds, in just under 27 minutes of action per contest. He followed that up by posting marks of 10.1 points and 9 rebounds per game in 1984–85, while averaging just under 25 minutes in the 67 contests in which he played.

Rapidly approaching his 33rd birthday and longing to play for a contending team once again, Walton spent the 1985 off-season attempting to engineer a trade between the Clippers and either the Boston Celtics or Los Angeles Lakers. Intrigued with the idea of having a relatively healthy Walton serving as the primary backup to Robert Parish and Kevin McHale, Celtics general manager Red Auerbach worked out a deal with the Clippers that sent forward Cedric Maxwell and a first-round draft pick to Los Angeles for the veteran center.

The move proved to be a stroke of genius, as Walton went on to appear in 80 games for Boston in 1985–86—easily the highest total of his career. Doing a superb job coming off the bench, Walton averaged 7.6 points, 6.8 rebounds, 2.1 assists, and 1.3 blocked shots per contest, in just over 19 minutes of action, en route to earning NBA Sixth Man of the Year honors. Playing with the enthusiasm of a youngster, a rejuvenated Walton reveled in playing alongside Larry Bird, McHale, and Parish on a team that finished the regular season with a league-best record of 67-15, before going on to win the NBA title. Speaking of Walton's rebirth in an article in the *Boston Herald*, McHale said, "You watch an old, old guy like that, with the most hammered body in sports, acting like a high school kid—it's both funny and inspiring at the same time. Every game was a challenge, and he didn't let any of us forget that."

The 1985–86 season ended up being Walton's last hurrah. Injured again during the early stages of the ensuing campaign, he appeared in only 10 games, although he did manage to return for the playoffs. After spending the entire 1987–88 season on the injured list, Walton chose to announce his retirement following another aborted comeback. He ended his career with 6,215 points scored, 4,923 rebounds, 1,590 assists, 1,034 blocked shots, a 52.1 field-goal shooting percentage, a free-throw shooting percentage of 66 percent, and averages of 13.3 points, 10.5 rebounds, 3.4 assists, and 2.2 blocked shots per game.

In addition to being named NBA Finals MVP and league MVP in back-to-back years, Walton earned one All-NBA First-Team selection, one Second-Team nomination, a pair of NBA All-Defensive First-Team selections, and two All-Star nominations. Despite appearing in only 468 out of a possible 1,148 games over the course of his career, Walton eventually was named to the NBA's 50th Anniversary Team. The Naismith Memorial Basketball Hall of Fame also opened its doors to him in 1993.

Summarizing Walton's playing career in a nutshell, Jack Ramsay, his first NBA coach, said, "I don't think anyone could match Bill Walton when he was at his peak. The problem is, he wasn't there long enough."

Following his retirement, Walton's ankle problems became so severe that he had both of them surgically fused. Relying heavily on pain medication

Injuries prevented Walton from going down as one of the greatest centers of all time.

for many years, Walton later admitted during a June 8, 2010, interview on *The Dan Patrick Show* that he seriously considered committing suicide for a period of time as a means of relieving himself of the constant agony he endured as a result of the injuries he sustained during his NBA career.

However, persevering through those difficult times, Walton began a lengthy career in broadcasting in 1990, serving as a color commentator on NBA games for NBC from 1990 to 2002, and for ABC/ESPN from 2002–09. Forced to relinquish his duties for one year after undergoing surgery to repair his injured back, Walton returned to the broadcast booth, first as a part-time commentator for the Sacramento Kings, and, later, as a game analyst for ESPN coverage of Pac-12 basketball—a position he continues to hold today.

CELTICS CAREER HIGHLIGHTS

Best Season

Since Walton spent just one full season in Boston, this was an absolute no-brainer. En route to earning NBA Sixth Man of the Year honors in 1985–86, Walton averaged 7.6 points, 6.8 rebounds, 2.1 assists, 1.3 blocked shots, and 19.3 minutes per game, while also shooting a career-best 56.2 percent from the field.

Memorable Moments / Greatest Performances

Walton turned in a number of outstanding performances for the Celtics over the course of that 1985–86 campaign, with his first such effort coming on November 15, 1985, when, in only 28 minutes of action, he scored 19 points, pulled down 9 rebounds, and blocked 4 shots during a 118–114 victory over the Washington Bullets.

Garnering just 25 minutes of playing time on January 26, 1986, Walton nevertheless contributed 19 points and 13 rebounds to a 105–103 win over the Philadelphia 76ers.

Walton helped lead the Celtics to a 103–88 victory over the Bullets on February 5, 1986, by scoring 13 points and collecting a season-high 17 rebounds.

A little over one week later, on February 13, Walton scored 17 points and pulled down 10 rebounds during a 107–98 win over Seattle.

Although the Celtics lost their February 17 matchup with the Phoenix Suns by a score of 108–101, Walton contributed 18 points and 10 rebounds in only 25 minutes of action. Walton continued his outstanding month of February by scoring 15 points and collecting 14 rebounds during a 91–74 win over the Knicks on February 25.

Walton had another excellent all-around game on March 28, when he tallied 20 points, pulled down 12 rebounds, and assisted on 4 baskets, in helping the Celtics defeat Washington by a score of 116–97.

Playing 28 minutes against Milwaukee on April 8, Walton recorded 12 rebounds and a season-high 22 points during a 126–114 victory over the Bucks.

Continuing his solid play in the postseason, Walton scored 10 points and pulled down 15 rebounds during Boston's 135–131 double-overtime win over the Chicago Bulls in Game 2 of their Eastern Conference First Round matchup. He had another big game against Milwaukee in Game 1 of the Eastern Conference Finals, scoring 15 points and collecting 9 rebounds, in only 19 minutes of action, in helping the Celtics record a lopsided 128–96 victory over the Bucks.

NOTABLE ACHIEVEMENTS

- Shot better than 50 percent from the field once (56.2% in 1985–86).
- 1985–86 NBA Sixth Man of the Year.
- 1985–86 Eastern Conference champion.
- 1985–86 NBA champion.
- Member of NBA's 50th Anniversary Team.
- Member of NBA's 75th Anniversary Team.
- Inducted into Naismith Memorial Basketball Hall of Fame in 1993.

48

JEFF GREEN

A versatile player who has manned all three frontcourt positions at one time or another during his lengthy NBA career, Jeff Green spent parts of four seasons in Boston, serving as a member of teams that won one division title and made two playoff appearances. Originally drafted by the Celtics in 2007, Green spent his first three and a half years in the league with the Seattle SuperSonics/Oklahoma City Thunder before being reacquired by the Celtics midway through the 2010–11 campaign. Despite sitting out the entire 2011–12 season after undergoing heart surgery to repair an aortic aneurysm, Green proved to be a significant contributor during his time in Boston, averaging more than 16 points per game twice, while seeing action at both forward positions. And since being traded away by the Celtics for a second time in January 2015, Green has performed well in a part-time role for nine other teams.

Born in Cheverly, Maryland, on August 28, 1986, Jeffrey Lynn Green grew up some five miles northwest in College Park, a city best known for being the home of the University of Maryland. Developing into a stand-out basketball player at Northwestern High School in nearby Hyattsville, Green led the Wildcats to the State Championship in 2004, earning in the process McDonald's All-America honors and an athletic scholarship to Georgetown University.

Continuing to excel on the court at Georgetown, Green shared Big East Rookie of the Year honors with Rudy Gay of the University of Connecticut in 2005, before being named to the All-Big East Second Team the following year and gaining recognition as the Big East Player of the Year in 2007. Also named Most Outstanding Player of the 2007 Big East tournament after scoring 30 points against Notre Dame in the semifinals and 21 points versus Pittsburgh in the championship game, Green led the Hoyas to their first conference championship since 1989, before helping them advance to the Final Four of the 2007 NCAA tournament.

Jeff Green made significant contributions to Celtic teams that won one division title and made two playoff appearances.

Praising Green for his exceptional play and on-court awareness, Hoyas head coach John Thompson III, stated in a *Sports Illustrated* interview, "You'll stop and think when I say this, but it's true: Jeff Green is the smartest player I've ever coached. You would know this better than most: that's a hell of a statement."

Subsequently selected by the Celtics with the fifth overall pick of the 2007 NBA Draft, Green soon became the property of the Seattle SuperSonics when the two teams completed a trade on draft day that sent Ray Allen and Glen Davis to Boston for Green, Wally Szczerbiak, Delonte West, and a second-round pick in the 2008 draft.

Performing well his first year in the league, Green earned First-Team All-Rookie honors by averaging 10.5 points and 4.7 rebounds in just over 28 minutes per game while spending most of his time at small forward. Remaining with the SuperSonics after they relocated to Oklahoma City and renamed themselves the Thunder the following year, Green manned the power forward position the next two seasons, posting scoring averages of 16.5 points and 15.1 points per game, while also averaging 6.7 and 6.0 rebounds per contest as a member of the starting unit.

After Green averaged 15.2 points and 5.6 rebounds per game for Oklahoma City over the first 49 games of the 2010–11 campaign, the Celtics completed a trade with the Thunder on February 24, 2011, that sent Green, center Nenad Krstić, and a 2012 first-round draft pick to Boston for center Kendrick Perkins and guard Nate Robinson. Serving the Celtics primarily as a bench player the rest of the season, Green averaged 23.5 minutes, 9.8 points, and 3.3 rebounds per game while backing up Paul Pierce and Kevin Garnett at both forward spots.

Following the conclusion of the NBA lockout, Green re-signed with the Celtics on December 10, 2011, only to have his contract voided eight days later after a routine physical exam detected an aortic aneurysm. The 25-year-old Green subsequently underwent open-heart surgery one month later and missed the entire 2011–12 season. However, he eventually made a full recovery, allowing him to sign with the Celtics again prior to the start of the ensuing campaign.

Excited to have Green back with the team, Celtics general manager Danny Ainge stated upon inking the forward to his new deal, "We are thrilled to have Jeff back with the Celtics. Jeff's versatility on offense and ability to guard players out on the perimeter is something that we are looking forward to having on the court this season."

Meanwhile, Green said, "I'll still be the same player, but I think my outlook on the time I have [left] in this league has changed. I think I have to be more assertive, more aggressive in different areas, not necessarily just scoring. I just have to change my outlook and my approach to the game, and that time that I had off and seeing certain spots on the floor where I can help, really helped my mindset."

Returning to the Celtics lineup in time for the regular-season opener on October 30, 2012, Green shared with reporters the personal struggles he faced during his time off, stating before the team's meeting with the Miami Heat, "It's something that's true and dear to my heart—the way I battled to get back on the court and still play at a high level. A lot of people counted me out and didn't think I'd be able to come back. So, I'm truly grateful for the work that I put in."

Appearing in all 81 games the Celtics played in 2012–13, Green proved to be an excellent weapon off the bench, averaging 27.8 minutes, 12.8 points, 3.9 rebounds, and 1.6 assists per contest, while shooting just under 47 percent from the field. Although Green posted shooting percentages of just 41 and 43 percent the next two seasons, he compiled better overall numbers after he became a regular member of the starting unit, averaging 16.9 points, 4.6 rebounds, and 1.7 assists per game in 2013–14 and 15 points, 4.2 rebounds, and 1.7 assists per contest the following year.

Capable of defending multiple positions, the 6-foot-8, 235-pound Green possessed the size and strength to guard opposing power forwards and the athleticism to stay with the league's swifter small forwards. A quality scorer as well, Green displayed good shooting range and drove the ball well to the basket. However, Green's inconsistency and inability to create off the dribble prevented him from ever reaching truly elite status. Tending to score his points in bunches, Green often hit three or four jump shots within a short timeframe and then disappeared for entire quarters. And on some nights, he failed to make his presence felt at all. Meanwhile, for someone with his size and leaping ability, Green did not rebound particularly well, never averaging more than 6.7 boards per contest in any single season.

Retaining his starting job in 2014–15, Green averaged 17.6 points, 4.3 rebounds, and 1.6 assists per game over the season's first 33 contests, before the Celtics completed a three-way trade with the Memphis Grizzlies and New Orleans Pelicans on January 12, 2015, that sent Green to Memphis for forward Tayshaun Prince, a future first-round draft pick, and guard Austin Rivers, who came to Boston from New Orleans. After finishing out the season in Memphis, Green split the ensuing campaign between the Grizzlies and the Los Angeles Clippers, assuming a part-time role for both teams. From Los Angeles, Green moved on to Orlando, Cleveland, Washington, Utah, Houston, Brooklyn, and Denver, never spending more than one full season with any one team. A member of the Denver Nuggets as of this writing, Green boasts career totals of 13,474 points, 4,569 rebounds, 1,652 assists, 728 steals, and 546 blocked shots, and averages of 12.5 points, 4.3 rebounds, 1.5 assists, and 0.7 steals per game. During his time in Boston, Green scored 3,252 points, amassed 925 rebounds, 338 assists, 153 steals, and 144 blocked shots, averaged 14.6 points, 4.2 rebounds, 1.5 assists, and 0.7 steals per game, shot 43.8 percent from the field, and converted close to 81 percent of his free-throw attempts.

CELTICS CAREER HIGHLIGHTS

Best Season

Green posted his best per-game averages as a member of the Celtics in 2014–15. However, he appeared in only 33 games before being dealt to the Memphis Grizzlies. That being the case, Green played his best ball for the Celtics in 2013–14, when he averaged 16.9 points per contest, which represented the highest mark of his career.

Memorable Moments / Greatest Performances

Green topped 30 points for the first time as a member of the Celtics when he scored 31 points during a 113-88 rout of the Phoenix Suns on February 22, 2013, also finishing the game with seven rebounds, five blocked shots, and four assists.

Although the Celtics lost to the Miami Heat, 105-103, on March 18, 2013, Green tallied a career-high 43 points, going 14-of-21 from the field, with five three-pointers, and 10-of-13 from the free-throw line.

Green led the Celtics to a 98-93 win over the Pistons on April 3, 2013, by scoring a game-high 34 points, hitting on 13 of his 19 shots from the field and five of his seven free-throw attempts.

Green gave the Celtics a 111-110 victory over Miami on November 9, 2013, when he hit a clutch three-pointer as time expired in regulation. He finished the game with 24 points on 8-of-16 shooting from the field, including 5-of-8 from three-point range.

Green turned in an outstanding all-around effort on January 22, 2014, scoring 39 points and collecting nine rebounds and three steals during a 113-111 win over the Washington Wizards.

Green helped lead the Celtics to a 114-108 win over the 76ers on February 5, 2014, by scoring 36 points on 11-of-18 shooting from the field and 9-of-12 shooting from the free-throw line.

NOTABLE ACHIEVEMENTS

- Averaged more than 16 points per game twice.
- Finished second in NBA in games played once.
- Led Celtics in scoring once.
- 2010–11 Atlantic Division champion.

49

KEVIN GAMBLE

A study in perseverance, Kevin Gamble overcame early doubts about his ability to compete in the NBA to carve out a successful professional career that lasted 10 seasons. Released by the Portland Trail Blazers after appearing in only nine games with them, Gamble spent parts of the next two seasons playing for teams in different parts of the world, before finally finding a home in Boston, where he ended up serving as a key member of teams that won two division titles and made five playoff appearances. Playing the best ball of his career during his time in Beantown, Gamble averaged more than 13 points per game three straight times for the Celtics while also shooting better than 50 percent from the field on four separate occasions. In all, Gamble spent a total of six seasons in Boston before splitting his final three years in the league between the Miami Heat and Sacramento Kings.

Born in Springfield, Illinois, on November 13, 1965, Kevin Douglas Gamble grew up in the city's John Hay public-housing projects, where he developed a fondness for basketball at an early age. Eventually emerging as a standout on the court at Lanphier High School, Gamble earned All-Conference and All-City honors his final two seasons, leading his team to the 1983 Illinois Class AA State Basketball Championship.

Enrolling at Lincoln Junior College in Illinois following his graduation from Lanphier, Gamble spent two seasons playing for head coach Alan Pickering, who had a profound impact on his life, with Gamble saying years later, "Growing up, my parents were very important to me, and I looked up to them in many ways. The thing I remember about Coach Pick was of him being the first role model of my adult life. He helped to mold me and helped to show me what I needed to do to make it at the college level. He taught me how to be a better basketball player, which I appreciate greatly, but more than that he helped me to become a man."

Transferring to the University of Iowa after his sophomore year, Gamble saw limited playing time as a junior before establishing himself as a

Kevin Gamble helped the Celtics win two division titles and advance to the playoffs five times during his six seasons in Boston.

full-time starter his senior year, when he helped lead the Hawkeyes to a 30-5 record and the NCAA tournament regional finals.

Subsequently selected by Portland in the third round of the 1987 NBA Draft, with the 63rd overall pick, Gamble earned a roster spot during training camp but played a total of just 19 minutes in nine games during the regular season before being released. Gamble then joined the Quad City Thunder of the Continental Basketball Association before heading to the Philippines, where, over the course of one month, he averaged almost 50 points per game for the Aneio Rum. Returning to Quad City prior to the start of the 1988–89 campaign, Gamble averaged more than 21 points per game for the Thunder, sparking interest from the Celtics, who signed him on December 15 after Larry Bird sustained an injury.

Commenting on his time in the Continental Basketball Association following his arrival in Boston, Gamble said, "It was good basketball there. You played hard, night in night out. They take pride in their games. When I came on the floor, guys would look at me and say, 'I'm better than he is.' Maybe some of them were. There are guys there now who could play in the NBA."

Gamble continued, "There's a lot of luck in it, being in the right place at the right time, having the right attitude. People hear different things about different players. Maybe someone says you've got a bad attitude, and someone overhears it. Maybe you DON'T have a bad attitude, but if you have that mark against you, that can hurt you. That's what happens to some of the guys there."

After joining the Celtics, Gamble spent the rest of the season coming off the bench, averaging just 8.5 minutes and 4.3 points per game before assuming a slightly greater role in 1989–90, when, serving as Larry Bird's primary backup at small forward, he averaged 14 minutes and 5.1 points per contest. With the Celtics struggling somewhat on the offensive end at the beginning of the ensuing campaign and Bird and Kevin McHale both battling injuries, new head coach Chris Ford inserted Gamble into the starting lineup, returning McHale to his earlier role of "sixth man." A perfect fit for Ford's new "up-tempo" offense, the athletic Gamble ended up averaging 15.6 points per game and finishing third in the league with a shooting percentage of 59 percent, stating at one point during the season, "He [Ford] wants us to get out and run, and pressure the ball at all times. That's my style. Basketball is a very simple game. Some people can make it difficult. If you let players play freely, you get good results. That's what Chris has done with us."

Blessed with outstanding quickness and leaping ability, the 6-foot-5, 210-pound Gamble excelled in the transition game, proving to be particularly effective on the fastbreak. Gamble's offensive arsenal also included a deadly mid-range jumper that he typically employed from somewhere between 15 and 18 feet out. Strong enough to compete under the basket, Gamble also did a decent job on the boards, although he tended to struggle somewhat on defense against some of the league's bigger and stronger small forwards.

A regular member of the starting unit in each of the next two seasons as well, Gamble posted scoring averages of 13.5 and 13.3 points per game, while also shooting slightly better than 50 percent from the field both years. Forced to share playing time with Rick Fox in 1993–94, Gamble averaged just 11.5 points and 25 minutes per contest, prompting him to sign with the Miami Heat as a free agent at season's end. Gamble, who left Boston with career totals of 4,895 points scored, 1,112 rebounds, 1,003 assists, 360 steals, and 141 blocked shots, averages of 11.2 points, 2.6 rebounds, 2.3 assists, 0.8 steals, and 0.3 blocks per game, a 0.518 field-goal shooting percentage, and a free-throw shooting percentage of 0.816, ended up spending the next three seasons serving as a backup in Miami and Sacramento before announcing his retirement after the Kings released him early in 1998. Over the course of his career, Gamble averaged 9.5 points, 2.2 rebounds, and 2.0 assists per game, shot just over 50 percent from the field, and successfully converted 81 percent of his free-throw attempts.

After retiring from the NBA, Gamble returned to his hometown of Springfield, Illinois, where he formed his own real estate development company that became heavily involved in the development of the city's east side community. In 2002, Gamble became the first head men's basketball coach at the University of Illinois, Springfield, which began play in the American Midwest Conference that season. Gamble later served as director of player development and video operations at Providence College, an assistant coach at Central Michigan, and, most recently, a scout with the Toronto Raptors.

Looking back favorably on the time he spent in Boston, Gamble said, "Playing with Bird, Parish, McHale, Dennis Johnson just makes you realize you don't know nearly as much about basketball as you thought you did. I got there and learned so much more. Those guys were winners, they just wanted to win. It was truly a team effort playing with those guys."

CELTICS CAREER HIGHLIGHTS

Best Season

After coming off the bench his first two seasons in Boston, Gamble assumed a far more prominent role in 1990–91, allowing him to establish career-high marks with 15.6 points, 3.1 assists, and 1.2 steals per game, while also shooting a career-best 59 percent from the field.

Memorable Moments / Greatest Performances

Gamble helped lead the Celtics to a 120-110 win over the Charlotte Hornets in the final game of the 1988–89 regular season by scoring 31 points on 11-of-14 shooting from the field and 9-of-12 shooting from the free-throw line.

Gamble proved to be a thorn in the side of the Hornets again on November 14, 1990, scoring 26 points and collecting nine assists during a 135-126 Celtics win.

Gamble led the Celtics to a 117-101 victory over the Knicks on February 7, 1991, by scoring a game-high 32 points, hitting on 16 of his 20 shots from the field.

Gamble scored a season-high 34 points during a 110-108 win over the Sacramento Kings on January 6, 1992, going 13-of-21 from the field and 8-of-8 from the free-throw line.

Gamble helped the Celtics end a three-game losing streak by tallying 30 points during a 98-95 win over the Philadelphia 76ers on January 17, 1992.

Gamble helped lead the Celtics to a 110-99 win over the Atlanta Hawks on February 26, 1993, by scoring a team-high 27 points, hitting on 10 of his 14 shots from the field and all five of his free throws.

Gamble led the Celtics to a 114-88 rout of the Golden State Warriors on March 16, 1993, by recording a triple-double, finishing the game with 23 points, 11 rebounds, and 10 assists.

NOTABLE ACHIEVEMENTS

- Averaged more than 15 points per game once.
- Shot better than 50 percent from the field four times.
- Led NBA in games played in 1990–91.
- Finished third in NBA with 0.587 field-goal shooting percentage in 1990–91.
- Two-time Atlantic Division champion (1990–91 and 1991–92).

50

— CHRIS FORD —

A scrappy player who spent most of his four seasons in Boston starting at shooting guard, Chris Ford overcame his somewhat limited athletic ability to establish himself as a key contributor to Celtic teams that won three division titles and one NBA championship. Although Ford, who arrived in Beantown during the early stages of the 1978–79 campaign after spending his first six years in the league in Detroit, never came close to earning All-Star honors, his intellect and selfless attitude helped the other players around him thrive, making him an important figure in the team's return to prominence. And following the conclusion of his playing career, Ford remained in Boston for another 12 years, serving the Celtics first as an assistant coach before assuming the role of head coach from 1978 to 1982.

Born in Atlantic City, New Jersey, on January 11, 1949, Christopher Joseph Ford grew up in the predominantly Italian neighborhood of Ducktown, where he got his start in basketball on the courts of Dante Hall Theater, a facility that served the community as a church hall, school gymnasium, and performing arts theatre. Developing into a standout on the hardwood while attending Holy Spirit High School in nearby Absecon, Ford set a still-standing school record by scoring 1,507 points. Particularly outstanding his senior year, Ford averaged a Cape-Atlantic League record 33 points per game, earning in the process All-America honors and an athletic scholarship to Villanova University. Continuing to perform at an elite level in college, Ford helped lead the Wildcats to three straight NCAA tournament appearances by posting scoring averages of 16.1, 13.8, and 17.9 points per game, while also setting the school record for career assists.

Subsequently selected by the Pistons in the second round of the 1972 NBA Draft, with the 17th overall pick, Ford spent his first few seasons in Detroit assuming a part-time role for mostly mediocre teams, never averaging more than 27 minutes or 8.4 points per contest. Finally becoming a regular member of the starting unit in 1976–77, Ford averaged 12.3 and

After playing for one NBA championship team in Boston, Chris Ford won another two titles as an assistant coach with the Celtics.

10.5 points per game the next two seasons, while hitting close to 48 percent of his shots from the field both years.

With the Celtics seeking to upgrade their perimeter shooting, they completed a trade with the Pistons on October 19, 1978, that sent guard Earl Tatum to Detroit for Ford and a future second-round draft pick, beginning in the process a lengthy association between the Atlantic City native and the league's most iconic team. Excelling in his first season in Boston, the 6-foot-5, 195-pound Ford averaged 15.6 points, 3.3 rebounds, and a team-high 4.7 assists and 1.5 steals per game for a Celtics squad that finished last in the Atlantic Division with a record of just 29-53.

Nicknamed "The Mad Bomber" for his willingness to launch shots from far out, Ford proved to be one of the league's more accurate outside shooters even though he employed more of a set-shot than a jumper. Ford also did a solid job on the boards and on defense, where his intelligence and excellent instincts helped compensate for his lack of superior speed, strength, and jumping ability.

Although Ford posted a less-impressive stat-line in 1979–80, concluding the campaign with averages of 11.2 points, 2.5 rebounds, 2.9 assists, and 1.5 steals per contest, the arrival of Larry Bird helped the Celtics compile a record of 61-21 that enabled them to capture the division title. With Kevin McHale and Robert Parish joining the Celtics prior to the start of the 1980–81 season, Ford assumed a somewhat diminished role on offense, averaging only 8.9 points and 3.6 assists per game. Nevertheless, his steady play and veteran leadership made him one of the most respected figures on a team that ended up winning the NBA championship after finishing the regular season with a record of 62-20.

Sharing playing time with M. L. Carr and Danny Ainge in 1981–82, Ford averaged just 5.7 points, 1.9 assists, and 1.4 rebounds per game for a Celtics squad that won its third straight division title, before losing to the Philadelphia 76ers in the Eastern Conference Finals. Choosing to announce his retirement following the conclusion of the campaign, Ford ended his 10-year pro career with 7,314 points scored, 2,394 rebounds, 2,719 assists, and 1,152 steals, averages of 9.2 points, 3.0 rebounds, 3.4 assists, and 1.6 steals per game, and a field-goal shooting percentage of 46 percent. In his four years with the Celtics, Ford scored 3,194 points, amassed 708 rebounds, 1,021 assists, and 367 steals, averaged 10.3 points, 2.3 rebounds, 3.3 assists, and 1.2 steals per contest, shot just over 45 percent from the field, and hit on close to 75 percent of his free-throw attempts.

Remaining in Boston following his retirement as an active player, Ford spent seven seasons serving as an assistant under head coaches K. C. Jones and Jimmy Rodgers, winning another two NBA titles before taking over for Rodgers after the Celtics suffered a surprising five-game defeat at the hands of the New York Knicks in the opening round of the 1990 NBA Eastern Conference Playoffs. Ford coached the Celtics for the next five seasons, leading them to two division titles, four playoff appearances, and an overall record of 222-188, before being replaced at the helm by former teammate M. L. Carr following the conclusion of the 1994–95 campaign.

After leaving Boston, Ford continued to coach at various levels for most of the next eight seasons, serving as head man in Milwaukee from 1996 to 1998, Los Angeles (Clippers) from 1999 to 2000, and at Brandeis University from 2001 to 2003, before ending his coaching career as an assistant with the Philadelphia 76ers in 2004. Ford subsequently scouted for the 76ers and briefly served the Knicks as a coaching consultant. Retiring to Ocean City, New Jersey, following his many years in basketball, Ford spent nearly two decades serving as a member of the Board of Directors at Ocean City Home Bank before dying of a heart attack at the age of 74 on January 18, 2023.

Upon learning of his passing, the Celtics released a statement that read: "As a player and coach, Chris Ford's career spanned over a decade of Celtics basketball, and he made his mark every step of the way. 'Doc,' as he was affectionately known by his teammates, was a fundamentally versatile all-around guard. . . . The Boston Celtics sends their deepest sympathies to the Ford family and their many friends."

Meanwhile, Ford's family said in a statement released by the Celtics: "Chris was beloved by his family, friends, and teammates. He had a great love for his family, the city of Boston, the fans, and the entire Celtics family. He always showed humility and respect for all those that were fortunate enough to be a part of his life."

CELTICS CAREER HIGHLIGHTS

Best Season

Although the Celtics finished a dismal 29-53 in 1978–79, Ford had his finest season as a member of the team, posting career-high marks with 15.6 points and 4.7 assists per game, while also shooting just over 47 percent from the field.

Memorable Moments / Greatest Performances

Ford topped the 20-point mark for the first time as a member of the Celtics when he scored 22 points during a 120-118 victory over the Denver Nuggets on November 17, 1978.

Ford helped lead the Celtics to a 121-105 win over the Indiana Pacers on December 20, 1978, by tallying 32 points, hitting on 14 of his 19 shots from the field and four of his six free-throw attempts.

Although the Celtics lost to the Golden State Warriors, 113-98, on January 5, 1979, Ford scored a game-high 30 points and assisted on 11 baskets.

Ford scored a career-high 34 points during a 103-102 victory over the Warriors on January 28, 1979, hitting on 17 of his 24 shots from the field.

Ford nearly matched that total on February 7, 1979, tallying 31 points during a 107-100 win over the Seattle Supersonics.

Ford starred in defeat on March 7, 1979, scoring 33 points, assisting on eight baskets, and stealing the ball four times during a 114-107 loss to the Philadelphia 76ers.

Ford made history on October 12, 1979, when, with 3:48 left in the first quarter of a matchup between the Celtics and Houston Rockets at Boston Garden, he became the first NBA player to sink a three-point field goal. The Celtics went on to win the contest by a score of 114-106, with Ford tallying 17 points.

NOTABLE ACHIEVEMENTS

- Averaged more than 15 points per game once.
- Led Celtics in assists and steals once each.
- Three-time Atlantic Division champion (1979–80, 1980–81, and 1981–82).
- 1980–81 Eastern Conference champion.
- 1980–81 NBA champion.

SUMMARY

aving identified the 50 greatest players in Boston Celtics history, the time has come to select the best of the best. Based solely on the rankings contained in this book, I have listed below my all-time Celtics team, which includes the top center, power forward, small forward, point guard, shooting guard, and "sixth man" in franchise history. I have selected a second team as well.

All-Time Celtics First Team:

PLAYER	POSITION
Bill Russell	Center
Kevin McHale	Power Forward
Larry Bird	Small Forward
Bob Cousy	Point Guard
Bill Sharman	Shooting Guard
John Havlicek	Sixth Man

All-Time Celtics Second Team:

PLAYER	POSITION
Dave Cowens	Center
Kevin Garnett	Power Forward
Paul Pierce	Small Forward
Jo Jo White	Point Guard
Sam Jones	Shooting Guard
Frank Ramsey	Sixth Man

GLOSSARY

ABBREVIATIONS AND STATISTICAL TERMS

apg: Assists per game.

BLKS: Blocked shots.

BPG: Blocked shots per game.

FG%: Field-goal percentage. The number of successful field-goal attempts divided by the total number of shots attempted.

ppg: Points per game.

REBS: Rebounds.

rpg: Rebounds per game.

spg: Steals per game.

STLS: Steals.

SELECTED BIBLIOGRAPHY

BOOKS

Bjarkman, Peter C. *The Biographical History of Basketball.* Chicago: Masters Press (Division of NTC Contemporary Publishing Group, Inc.), 2000.

Hareas, John, foreword by John Havlicek. *NBA's Greatest: The NBA's Best Players, Teams, and Games.* New York: DK Publishing, Inc., 2003.

Koppett, Leonard. *24 Seconds To Shoot: The Birth and Improbable Rise of the NBA.* Kingston, NY: Total/Sports Illustrated, 1968.

Salzberg, Charles. *From Set Shot to Slam Dunk.* New York: E. P. Dutton, 1987.

Shouler, Ken, Bob Ryan, Sam Smith, Leonard Koppett, and Bob Bellotti. *Total Basketball: The Ultimate Basketball Encyclopedia.* Toronto, Ontario: Sport Media Publishing, Inc., 2003.

Sugar, Bert Randolph. *The 100 Greatest Athletes of All Time.* New York: Citadel Press (Division of Carol Publishing Group), 1995.

VIDEOS

Champions: The NBA's Greatest Teams. CBS/FOX Company, 1992.

Sports Century: Fifty Greatest Athletes—Bill Russell. ESPN, 1999.

WEBSITES

Biographies, online at HickokSports.com
(hickoksports.com/hickoksports/biograph)

Celtics Stats, online at NBA.com
(nba.com/history/celtics/history/stats)

Hall of Famers, online at HoopHall.com
(hoophall.com/hoophall/hall_of_famers)

The Players, online at Basketball-Almanac.com
(basketball-almanac.com/players)

The Players, online at Basketball-Reference.com
(basketball-reference.com/basketballreference/players)

The Players, online at NBA.com
(nba.com/history/players)

The Teams, online at Basketball-Reference.com
(basketball-reference.com/teams/BOS)